Music and the Silent Film

Music and the Silent Film

Contexts and Case Studies, 1895–1924

Martin Miller Marks

New York • Oxford • Oxford University Press • 1997

Oxford University Press

Oxford New York
Athens Auckland Bangkok Bogota Bombay
Buenos Aires Calcutta Cape Town Dar es Salaam
Delhi Florence Hong Kong Istanbul Karachi
Kuala Lumpur Madras Madrid Melbourne
Mexico City Nairobi Paris Singapore
Taipei Tokyo Toronto

and associated companies in
Berlin Ibadan

Published by Oxford University Press, Inc.
198 Madison Avenue, New York, New York 10016

Library of Congress Cataloging-in-Publication Data
Marks, Martin Miller.
Music and the silent film : contexts and case studies, 1895–1924 /
Martin Miller Marks.
p. cm.
Revision of thesis (doctoral)—Harvard University, 1990.
Includes bibliographical references and index.
ISBN 0-19-506891-2
1. Silent film music—History and criticism. I. Title.
ML2075.M242 1997
781.5'42—dc20 93-25082

1 3 5 7 9 8 6 4 2

Printed in the United States of America
on acid-free paper

For my parents and sister,

Marks of love, wisdom, and faith

Preface and Acknowledgments

The twentieth century is *on film*.
It's the filmed century.

—Don DeLillo[1]

Reflecting the manner in which film touches all aspects of twentieth-century life, a pioneering bibliography was published in three separate volumes: *The Film as Art*, *The Film as Industry*, and *The Film in Society*.[2] The titles suggest that those who would investigate film music do well to venture into domains of aesthetics, economics, general history, and sociology, looking for ideas and data about particular motion pictures and their scores; and though the bibliography is now somewhat out of date, it makes one point very clear: the field offers scholars enough challenging material for a lifetime.

This book took a significant portion of my lifetime to complete: after a lengthy gestation period it first appeared as my doctoral dissertation, "Film Music of the Silent Period, 1895–1924" (Harvard University, 1990), and that work has now been extensively revised. A selective approach has been followed: the focus is on five innovative scores created between 1895 and 1924, analyzed in relationship to their films and placed within historical context. I hope these studies will be taken as a useful prelude to further research, especially because most of the material found herein—and the methods used to organize and analyze it—cannot be found in earlier scholarly work within the field.

There are five chapters. The first presents an introduction to the material, the problems it poses for research, and the literature of film music written over the past eight decades. In the second, attention is given to two examples of early scores for silent films, created in Germany (for Sklandanowsky's Bioskop exhibitions in 1895 and 1896, by persons unknown) and in France (for *L'Assassinat du Duc de Guise* in 1908, by Camille Saint-Saëns). Attention then shifts, in the third and fourth chapters, to scores that appeared in America during the silent film's middle years (*An Arabian Tragedy*, 1912, by Walter Cleveland Simon, and *The Birth of a Nation*, 1915, by Joseph Carl Breil); in the last, attention shifts again, to a French score from late in the period (*Entr'acte*, 1924, by Erik Satie), the first film score of consequence by an avant-garde composer.

All of these scores may be seen to offer unique solutions to the problems confronting musicians when they seek to craft accompaniments for particular silent films, and as the films contrast with one another, so, too, do their scores. Yet despite obvious differences of style the scores display common methods, and throughout the book the reader will find that connections have been made. For example, a main theme of the second chapter is that the two principal methods of film scoring, *compilation* and *original composition*, were each based on nineteenth-century traditions and thus came readily to hand during the earliest years of silent film. This theme is newly developed in Chapter Three through consideration of ways in which opera inspired the creation of film scores in America, and through study of Simon's original music and Rothapfel's orchestral compilations. In the last two chapters the theme is developed most fully, through detailed examination of relationships between film and music in the compiled score for *The Birth of a Nation* and in the original score for *Entr'acte*. Both Breil and Satie employed techniques found in earlier scores, with impressive results.

From the first chapter to the last I have sought narrative continuity; but I make no claim here to have written a comprehensive history of music for silent films. For one thing, many important scores which appeared after 1924 await case studies, including the joint compilation by William Axt and David Mendoza for *The Big Parade* and Edmund Meisel's modernist music for Eisenstein's *Potemkin* (both 1925); the elaborate leitmotivic construction by Gottfried Huppertz for Fritz Lang's *Metropolis* (1926); and Shostakovich's bitter, humorous, heroic music for *The New Babylon* (1929), a very late entry into the field that may well be the greatest of all scores for silent films. Also, the vast repertoire of pre-existent music and newly composed pieces in incidental collections needs to be catalogued and analyzed with regard to type (e.g., "love theme," "misterioso," "agitato," and "neutral"—a peculiar category: what features of musical style are inherently neutral?). Wagner's relationship to film music is another important theme waiting to be sung: his was the name most often invoked by those in the profession (as will be seen in the case of Breil, below), but the degree to which his methods were understood is not clear. A major study could perhaps be written on the idea of the leitmotif and the actuality of its usage in film scores of the teens, twenties, and after.

Of course, film music did not stop in 1929; on the contrary, music for silent films became a prelude to a new genre, and studies could profitably be undertaken of the transition period, and of the conventions that emerged with the transformation of music's functions. We might compare Breil's score for *The Birth of a Nation*, say, to Steiner's for *Gone With the Wind*, since the latter film was in some respects modeled on the former; likewise, we might compare the avant-garde music of *Entr'acte* to the soundtracks of thirties documentaries such as *Night Mail*, with music by Britten, or to the so-called "minimalist" essays of Philip Glass for Godfrey Reggio (*Koyaanisqatsi* and its sequel). And one challenge offered by scores for other sound films that do not seem comparable to their predecessors is to explain how and why the new styles came about.

In short, there are many histories of film music to be written. The field is a source of moving, enduring, energizing fusions, it has developed through interaction with many other types of dramatic music, and its future is wide open. (There are signs today that presentations of silent films with live musical accompaniment will again become regular events all around the world. From Pordenone to Telluride, at restored theaters and in new venues, we now hear a fascinating variety of musical styles. Informed, musically sophisticated reconstructions of period scores now co-exist with exemplary new works by modern ensembles. Thus we are reminded that music for silent films was ever-changing, because live, and that to be true to the spirit of the period, it must continue to change.) The excitement that I feel in the contemplation of film music's past and future is the starting point of this volume, and I hope it is shared by the reader as he or she ventures on.

While writing, I have received support from a great many individuals; I extend heartfelt thanks to some of them here. First of all to John Ward, who guided me throughout the journey; also to many other members of the Harvard Music Department, among them Luise Vosgerchian and Reinhold Brinkmann, for their advice, financial support, and congeniality; to Lowell Lindgren, whose superlative scholarship, devoted teaching, and astonishing wit have made him a star; to Vlada Petric and others at the Harvard Film Archive, who gave me my first opportunities to perform scores and to study films, aided by their expertise; to the courteous and ever-generous librarians at Harvard (with a wink to Larry Mowers), USC, UCLA, the University of Minnesota, the Motion Picture Academy, the Museum of Modern Art, the Library of Congress, the British Film Archive and British Library, the Bibliothèque Nationale, and the Deutsche Kinemathek; to Gillian Anderson, Gero Gändert, Fred Steiner, Clifford McCarty, Win Sharples, Jr., Clyde Allen, William Camfield, Alan Gillmor, Jonas Mekas, Anne Dhu McLucas, Claudia Gorbman, Jane Gaines, and Ron Magliozzi—scholars who have done much for the field, as well as for me; to John Green (in memoriam), who made *Entr'acte* come alive; to Alex Rigopoulos, the master of musical technology; to Jon Harris, Patrick Loughney, Lee Zamir, and Alice Donaldson for their fine, fleet photography; to David Grayson, Peter Hoffenberg, Fred Rackmil, Carla Rosen, Peter Engel, Ken Getz, Peter Mason, and Jon Lewis, each a crucially helpful friend; and lastly, to my colleagues at MIT (with the warmest of hugs for Nancy Cavanagh and Alan Brody) who helped me tremendously through the many stages of book-making. I would also like to express my gratitude to all the talented and kindly people at Oxford University Press who have helped me in so many productive ways, especially to Sheldon Meyer, Andrew Albanese, and Stephanie Sakson, for their editorial wisdom.

You and many others have enabled me to complete this book. May it prove useful to all who are as fascinated as I am by our filmed and "musicked" century, so rich in mysterious pleasures for both eye and ear.

M.M.M.

Somerville, Mass.
August 1996

Contents

Appendix Contents

Figures

Music and the Silent Film

ONE

Film and Music

An Introduction to Research

The Material[1]

From the time of the first public demonstration of a Lumière *cinématographe*, for which a pianist is said to have improvised an accompaniment, until today's wide-screen features with their multi-channeled, digitally recorded scores, there has always been music for motion pictures.[2] The pictures have fostered an abundant and rich variety of music-making, which for more than eight decades has affected us in ways both simple and subtle. Yet most of us have a very poor knowledge of what film music is all about. Why should there be this discrepancy? Why are the facts of film music not widely understood? Why should Peter Odegard, in a review of two mid-seventies reference works devoted to music of the twentieth century, have to take both to task for all but ignoring film music, "the most widely dispersed repertoire being performed today, and hence in its peculiar way the most influential"?[3]

The answer, first of all, derives from the nature of the medium. Because film operates (at least potentially) through a conjunction of visual and auditory signals, research into film music requires an understanding of not one but two non-verbal systems of communication, as well as the problematical jargons with which we attempt to describe each of them in speech. In this age of specialized studies, few scholars have been able to master more than half of the subject. Those in film have been preoccupied with the broad essentials of its history and theory, with the result that music has been granted mostly cursory consideration.[4] The subject also stands on the periphery of musicology. That discipline, little older than film itself, has emphasized the historical study of Western fine-art and folk idioms, along with the ethnological study of music in other cultures; relatively little attention has been given to recent music in the professional and popular idioms—the idioms through which film music usually communicates.[5] Textbooks of music history provide examples of neglect: though they occasionally mention a respected composer's venture into film music, this peculiar hybrid idiom is mostly ignored.[6]

Film music is a neglected subject not only because it straddles two disciplines, but also because its material poses many problems for the researcher. This is a point that even Odegard apparently overlooks. Through his choice of words he associates film music with concert music, comprising a "repertoire" from which (presumably) selections are "performed." Between these two kinds of music, however, a fundamental distinction must be made: unlike concert music, film music does not usually come out of, or go into, a repertoire; it exists only as an accompaniment to a film. (One may, however, speak of a repertoire of *arrangements* of film music for concert use; and there are also repertoires of sheet music and, in a looser sense, soundtrack recordings.) Furthermore, since the invention of synchronized sound, film music has been heard not in continuous live performance, but through mechanical reproductions of many fragmentary performances assembled by recording "engineers." In other words, strictly speaking there is no repertoire of "pieces of film music" at all—only pieces of film, with music photographically or electromagnetically inscribed on a band alongside the image. The primary material of film music, both for the audience and the researcher, is not a recording or a score but the film itself.

It would appear that for scholarly inquiry into film music to advance, film ought to be studied with music at the center of observation rather than on the periphery; but this is far from an easy thing to do, especially when inside a theater. As we view a film, our minds must contend with the ever-changing content of the moving image and the soundtrack. The individual elements (not just music, but also lighting, camera work, editing, and so forth) are submerged into the flow of images on the screen. Hence the engrossed audience rarely perceives these elements consciously; it is simply carried along by the stream of sights and sounds.

The film-viewing experience is in some fundamental sense a passive one; yet film study, like the study of any subject, requires an active state of mind. This problem has been formulated in many ways, but perhaps never more eloquently than by Walter Benjamin in his profound study, "The Work of Art in the Age of Mechanical Reproduction." That essay, while primarily concerned with the political implications of twentieth-century art, contains an illuminating passage on the psychology of film perception:

> Let us compare the screen on which a film unfolds with the canvas of a painting. The painting invites the spectator to contemplation; before it the spectator can abandon himself to his associations. Before the movie frame he cannot do so. No sooner has his eye grasped a scene than it is already changed. It cannot be arrested. Duhamel, who detests the film and knows nothing of its significance, though something of its structure, notes this circumstance as follows: "I can no longer think what I want to think. My thoughts have been replaced by moving images." The spectator's process of association in view of these images is indeed interrupted by their constant, sudden change. This constitutes the shock effect of the film, which, like all shocks, should be cushioned by heightened presence of mind.[7]

Film's ability to "arrest" our contemplative faculties, advises Benjamin, should be countered by a "heightened presence of mind." For the purposes of film study, however, mere mental preparation may not suffice. Even the most attentive viewer (in the analytical sense) has great difficulty in comprehending all there is in a film, likewise in remembering just what has been seen and heard after leaving a theater. Of course, it helps both to see a film many times over and to see many films; such repeated viewing mitigates the medium's "shock effect." One should also seek out other ways of taking the film in: for example, special viewing machines such as movieolas or videotape and laser disc players, which facilitate repetitive viewing and frame-by-frame analysis.

These machines can convert a film into a succession of short segments or photographic stills that "invite the spectator to contemplation," but they will always be inadequate substitutes for the film experience. An essential part of that experience depends upon watching films on large screens in dark theaters, as a member of the audience. Cable television and video have made an enormous quantity of films available for home viewing with great economy and convenience, but (like plays and operas) they are fundamentally altered and diminished in terms of depth and texture, as well as color and image size. Thus, lacking the power of spectacle and communally shared fantasy, much of their excitement is lost. (Benjamin's description of film's "shock effect" may seem incomprehensible to a generation for whom television is the primary medium; music videos demonstrate how meaningless such shocks can become, when given to the viewer indiscriminately, around the clock.) To be sure, some films have less to lose than others in their translation to a television screen. As Pauline Kael has noted, old Hollywood black and white movies "with good, fast energetic talk seem better than ever on television"; indeed, "movies like Joseph L. Mankiewicz's *A Letter to Three Wives* and *All About Eve* look practically the same on television as in theatres, because they have almost no visual dimension to lose."[8] Nevertheless, as a general rule one needs to see a film *as* a film before truly coming to terms with it.

"Films cannot be studied in any other way than by seeing them," Raymond Spottiswoode cautions students; and he further warns that "nothing effective in film corresponds to the text of a play or a musical score."[9] His points are well taken. No written language can adequately transcribe what the camera sees and the microphone hears. The film text is in fact, as another writer has put it, an "unquotable text."[10] Still, there are many useful supplements: in particular, scripts, cue sheets, scores, and recordings. Inevitably these non-celluloid materials remove us even further than video tapes from the original film, by singling out individual components of the audio-visual whole; yet for the purposes of film study, they have unique values.

Scripts are of two kinds.[11] The *preproduction* or *shooting script* guides the making of the film. Like a musical score or the text of a play, it provides a set of directions for a performance, but with an important difference. Scores and play texts are always required to determine each performance anew, but shooting scripts are no longer functional after films have been completed. If, for the moment, one discounts the circumstances of exhibition, it might be said that a film always is given an identical "performance"; and as a result, the script becomes a valuable historical document. Like an architect's blueprints or a composer's sketchbook, it reveals one or more stages in the making of a work, and could help to clarify the writer's contribution to this, the most collaborative of arts.[12]

The *postproduction* script, usually assembled by someone other than the filmmaker or writer, aids in the close analysis of a film's structure. Publications of this kind have been criticized for falling far short of what is desirable. For example, when Vlada Petric reviewed all the texts in the Simon & Schuster series of *Classic* and *Modern Film Scripts*, he found that "no less than 90 percent of their breakdown of visual and auditory structure is inaccurate, and therefore useless for serious film study."[13] Petric is right to push for more accurate publications, but "useless" is too strong a word. Most scripts can correct or sharpen our memories of particular films; they are inadequate but necessary transcriptions of what we have seen and heard.

The *cue sheets* that composers use are much less widely known than scripts. In principle they are little different, being a kind of setting-down of sequences from a film in shorthand. Their function, however, is quite special: to link the music to the rest of the film. In the silent period cue sheets provided a series of suggestions for music to be used in accompaniment, "cued" to the titles and action on the screen. (These will be discussed further below, as part of the literature of film music.) Sound film cue sheets, normally prepared by a film's "music editor," describe the action, dialogue, and (some) sound effects of scenes for which the composer is to write music. Since the composer often works from these cue sheets after viewing the film, they become important clues to the compositional process, telling us what details were thought by the composer to deserve musical emphasis.[14]

Many details from cue sheets are copied into *scores* of film music, as an aid to the conductor during recording sessions. This combination of cue sheet and score may actually provide a more detailed transcription of (segments from) a film than does a script. By themselves, however, scores pose certain problems for research. As Charles Berg has noted, in the silent period the very concept of an "original score" was ambiguous. Many a score said to be "original" was actually a mixture of new and old music "composed by" (read "arranged by") a compiler.[15] These scores could be used in quite varied fashion from theater to theater, with fidelity to the text dependent upon such matters as the number of musicians available and the taste of the music director. In short, music for the silent film was an independent, ever-changing accompaniment.

Music for sound films is an integral part of an unchanging soundtrack, attached unambiguously to the film; but the value of the score as a tool for study is diminished somewhat by the film's integral character. With the exception of the cue-sheet transfers mentioned above, scores tell us only about a film's music, without indications of simultaneous dialogue and sound effects. As of yet no satisfactory method of transcribing a whole soundtrack has been found, any more than a method of transcribing film images.[16]

Only *recordings* can provide us with integral soundtracks. Unfortunately, most commercial recordings are as inaccurate in their own way as script publications. The problems with such recordings are: (1) the music has often been newly arranged or recorded (in which case the recording may be dubbed—again ambiguously—an "original" motion picture score; (2) even genuine "motion picture soundtracks" are often greatly abridged and restructured, as well as limited to music alone; and (3) they go rapidly out of print and into a highly expensive collector's market.[17] It should be noted that film composers often prefer recordings such as these (and frequently produce them themselves), simply because they allow the most important (or commercial) music to be clearly heard. For scholarly purposes, however, the most desirable recordings are the studio originals, comprising both the separate components of a soundtrack and the final mixed version.

The accessibility of all these supplementary materials is at present a serious problem. Only scripts and soundtracks have been issued in any great number (with the drawbacks already noted).[18] For the most part, scripts, cue sheets, scores, and recordings are scattered in private collections, libraries, and film studios, often uncatalogued. To track down any of these items for a particular film requires inordinate amounts of money and time. The studios, moreover, have allowed a great deal of the material to be lost or destroyed. They are still the first place one should inquire, but there is every possibility that the door will be closed to the researcher or that the shelf will be empty.

The picture is dark, to be sure, but in recent years the light has begun to increase. The Warner Brothers scores, for example, are now on deposit at the University of Southern California and can be consulted by the serious scholar. Moreover, many archives and libraries have shown themselves increasingly sensitive to the matter of film music. Two leading institutions in this regard are the Museum of Modern Art in New York (henceforth MOMA) and the Library of Congress (LC). Both contain sizable collections of silent film scores, and these have now been preserved on microfilm, along with hundreds of silent film cue sheets—all catalogued in Gillian Anderson's valuable guide.[19] Moreover, LC also houses one of the country's largest collections of sound film scores, and eventually hopes to preserve these on microfilm as well. Other significant collections can be found at the Free Library in Philadelphia, at the library of the Academy of Motion Picture Arts and Sciences (AMPAS) in Los Angeles, and at many university libraries: among them, California at Los Angeles (UCLA), California State at Long Beach, Southern California (USC), Brigham Young, Oregon, Wisconsin, and Wyoming.[20] USC should also be singled out for having taken a significant step forward in 1976, with the creation of the Alfred Newman Memorial Library—an archive where scores and other materials pertinent to that composer's career have been stored.[21]

What is still greatly needed is a large-scale film music archive.[22] Although there are now more than ninety film archives around the world, most of them are not capable of fulfilling this need.[23] Their limited budgets are marked for the preservation and study of films, not film music, and inevitably, their holdings reflect this bias. (England's National Film Archive, for example, though among the world's largest and oldest, contains scores for only a handful of films. MOMA's unusually large collection of silent film scores was acquired over many years, as a result of its longstanding tradition of screening silent films with live music; it contains no sound film scores. LC's holdings are another special case: the result of its unique access to deposits in the Copyright Office, one of the great archives of twentieth-century music.) Given the costs of acquiring, cataloguing, and maintaining such collections, for many years to come the only feasible approach may be to strive for a "web" archive: a cooperative network of studios and institutions like those named above. The idea may seem far-fetched, but it is not inconceivable, given the loose bonds which already link the American Film Institute to the Library of Congress, and the world's archives into an International Federation. In this country, an important step forward was taken in 1984, with the founding of the Society for the Preservation of Film Music in Los Angeles. One of its stated purposes is "to coordinate the donation and dissemination of film music collections to institutional libraries for preservation and access"; and toward that end, the Society is currently preparing a *Guide to Film Music Collections in the United States*, to be followed by a comprehensive *Union Catalog of Film Music*.[24]

This project is but one indication of the ever-strengthening tendency to take films seriously in all their aspects: as historical documents, sociological phenomena, and works of art. Scholars wrote in the early seventies of an "explosion" in film study.[25] The boom still continues, and its larger context is the explosive growth and change within the medium itself. What was at the turn of century a crude, lower-class entertainment has become an all-encompassing medium, a connoisseur's fine art, and a conglomerate industry. Likewise, film music has been transformed from the anonymous accompaniments of invisible pit musicians to the Dolby digital symphonic scores of celebrity composers, who are apt to make equal use of popular songs, concert works, jazz or folk idioms, synthesizer or sitar. Films and their music are *both* peculiar hybrids, quick to change and thus ever-fresh; yet no matter how much popular excitement or scholarly interest they arouse, they will remain far from easy to work with. As we look into them, we find ourselves confronted by materials that seem to withhold as much information as they give. If we push further, it is because they can stir us so deeply, and because, like Benjamin, we feel the urge to come to grips with the work of art in the age of mechanical reproduction. In order to smooth the course of inquiry, I now propose to examine how others have wrestled with film music's recalcitrant materials—to see what they have written.

The Literature: A Survey to 1990

Is there a literature? The tendency has been to suppose not. In 1977 a survey of film music was published under the title *A Neglected Art*, and at the outset author Roy Prendergast put forward a case for his choice of title:

> This book is the first attempt at a comprehensive look at the history, esthetics, and techniques of film music. Seldom in the annals of music history has a new form of musical expression gone so unnoticed. While the use of music to accompany film is a relatively new phenomenon, beginning in the last decade of the nineteenth century, its relatively new appearance should not have precluded a body of intelligent and perceptive writing on the subject.
>
> The fact remains, however, that there is no such body of critical literature on film music, with the notable exception of a few penetrating articles by critic Lawrence Morton.[26]

Certainly film music is a neglected art, but Prendergast's assertion that the subject had gone "unnoticed" in print was misleading. By 1977, there was already an extensive literature on the subject, and it continues to grow apace; moreover, after a bit of sifting it remains an "intelligent and perceptive" literature. However, it is far from easy to come by, and this is one reason for its own neglect. Books on film music pass speedily out of print, while articles lie scattered and buried in ephemeral or out-of-reach journals; until recently, the bibliographies that sought to resurrect them were often obscure, error-prone, and far from comprehensive.[27] Also, the literature has been neglected in the sense that no one has written much about it. There are only two principal surveys, and each is so brief that it can only point at some sources in passing.[28] The following survey does its share of rude pointing at selected items, but it is written with a different end in view: to chronicle some of the most important methods and tendencies of film music research. (It has been limited to sources in English, French, German, and Italian; discographies and film musicals have not been considered.) The resultant "montage" of long shots and close-ups should clarify the principal patterns of thought that have been inspired by this "new form of musical expression."

The process of recording sound photo-electrically alongside an image on a single strip of film was not adopted for commercial use until the late twenties. Before this time, despite various attempts to synchronize sound and film mechanically, the movies were mostly silent, accompanied by live music.[29] As has already been noted, this music was not all of a piece; it consisted of improvisations, compilations, and original scores, mixed in many ways. The tens of thousands of theaters across Europe and America varied enormously in size and decor, and in the number and types of musicians employed.[30] There were amateurs and professionals, pianists, organists, small ensembles, and orchestras. Rather like musicians of the Baroque period, these silent film players enjoyed a great deal of freedom to realize their music according to talent and circumstance; for though "playing to pictures" owed much to nineteenth-century traditions of theater music from opera to pantomime, it was fundamentally as new an art as playing from a figured bass had been three centuries earlier. And just as in the Baroque period there accumulated a large number of books written to guide players in the choices they had to make, in the silent period a literature developed that was designed to aid in the preparation of an accompaniment. This was the first literature of film music: a mass of materials fulfilling a variety of practical functions.

One early function was to guide musicians in the selection of music for individual films. Beginning in 1909 the Edison Company, a leading film producer, printed brief "Suggestions for Music" for its weekly film rentals in the *Edison Kinetogram*. The suggestions were welcomed, other companies followed suit, and "cue sheets," as they came to be called, remained in use until the demise of the silent film.[31] In general, rather than name specific pieces of music, which musicians might not have owned or been able to play, early cue sheets specified only a tempo, or mood, or kind of music appropriate to the situation on screen. The forewarned player could then either improvise something appropriate, or, if time permitted, select a suitable piece to fit the cue.

As publishers sensed the growing need for such "suitable"—and readily handy—music, they began to bring out anthologies containing assorted popular favorites, classical selections (often newly "arranged"), and original "incidental" pieces of cinema music. They also brought out indexes of their music for use by the cinema player. These anthologies and indexes classified music along the same lines as the cue sheets: that is, by mood, dramatic situation, tempo, and meter. Thus, they constitute the first typologies of film music.[32]

Cue sheets, anthologies and indexes all helped in the preparation of accompaniments, but they tell us nothing directly about how the accompaniments were to be played. Some information of this kind might be included in an introduction, however, as in Erno Rapée's *Encyclopedia of Music for Pictures* (New York, 1925). In fifteen highly compressed chapters, the author (then known as both a pianist and a composer, as a compiler of scores, and as a conductor at several leading motion-picture theaters)[33] gave detailed advice on such matters as the kind of music appropriate to various film genres, the uses of the organ, and ways to organize and rehearse theater orchestras. The Rapée introduction was an offshoot of a second branch of silent film literature, of which the principal function was to advise players on both "What and How to Play for Pictures." This was the title of an early little manual written by Eugene Ahern in 1913. Published far from New York (in Twin Falls, Idaho), it was quite different in tone from Rapée's work. Ahern offered advice to the small-town pianist, for whose benefit he stressed a few basic points: not to call attention to the music by playing too loudly, not to change the music too often in the course of the picture, and to be sure to vary the repertoire from week to week lest audiences get bored.

Manuals such as Ahern's were the first *books* on film music. They multiplied rapidly, and were addressed variously to pianists, organists, and conductors.[34] Often they provided instruction in music theory, on all levels from the rudiments of reading music to advanced harmony—one indication of the great disparity of musical practice from theater to theater. For this reason they are of value to us, since they convey all kinds of information about performance practices throughout the period (and, more broadly, about the nation's musical culture).

Similar information is found in one of the fledgling industry's most important trade weeklies, *Moving Picture World* (henceforth *MPW*). Early volumes of this magazine, founded in 1907, contained advertisements for mechanical instruments, anthologies of music, and specially compiled and composed scores. For 1909 there appeared editorials, letters, and articles calling for the improvement of music;[35] and in the next year, a column of advice on "Music for the Picture." This column, which ran for more than eight years, published cue sheets and addressed itself to many problems: the types of music appropriate for various film genres; whether a piano, organ, or orchestra was preferable; the place of sound effects in an accompaniment; and the value of special scores. Often the editors printed letters on these matters from across the country. In this way the column—and others like it—became national forums on film music, drawing together thousands of isolated musicians (like Eugene Ahern), who welcomed the chance to communicate with others of their profession.[36]

Cue sheets, anthologies, columns, and handbooks all first appeared at very nearly the same time, around 1910, and this sudden development of a literature seeking to improve music in the theater, by example and advice, is a phenomenon partly to be explained in economic terms—as in these words from the editorial introduction to the first column of "Music for the Picture": "The demand for good music is such that it is now as much of a rivalry between exhibitors to brag of their good orchestras as it is of bragging of the quality of their pictures."[37] The sentence, despite the grammatical lapse, makes sense. At the time, theaters were beginning to grow rapidly in number and size, while pictures were becoming both more popular and more respectable. "The growth of picture houses in America in the period 1910–20 was phenomenal," writes Dennis Sharp; "'Movie Madness' pervaded society, and by the middle of the decade it has been estimated that 25,000 picture theaters were in use and the average daily attendance was in the region of six million people."[38] To compete for the widening audience, producers created film spectacles, while theater managers installed spectacular organs, expanded their orchestras and musical shows, and hired better musicians. As a result, film music and its literature thrived.[39]

Practical literature continued to thrive until the end of the silent period. Cue sheets and manuals became more detailed and sophisticated, anthologies more encyclopedic (like Rapée's). At the same time, musicians within the trade and critical observers from outside never ceased to ponder how to "reform" film music. Various kinds of reform were envisaged: the introduction of more "classical" music into the theater (with better playing), more original scores, and better systems of compilation, whereby the music would produce greater dramatic effect.[40]

Better compilations were the object of the period's most sophisticated and wide-ranging book: Hans Erdmann and Giuseppe Becce's *Allgemeines Handbuch der Filmmusik*, edited by Ludwig Brav, in 2 volumes (1927). Erdmann, Becce, and Brav had all composed for silent films, and campaigned for improvement of musical practice; the *Handbuch* was the culminating synthesis of their efforts.[41] Its first volume was given over to an essay, unique in the literature of the period, surveying the theory, history, and techniques of film music "Vom Atelier bis Theater." The second volume contains a "Thematisches Skalenregister," or index, which follows the most elaborate system for categorizing musical moods ever attempted in this kind of literature. Music of several publishers is included, with abundant cross-references from one category to another. In its attempt to be so systematic and comprehensive, the *Handbuch* surpassed all earlier indexes and manuals. It opened a door to altogether new kinds of research—a door, however, which no one at the time passed through. It was an unusually complex book, and published too late in the day to have much impact.

The year 1927 marked the phenomenal success of *The Jazz Singer*. The silent film then entered its twilight phase, and synchronized sound began its triumphal rise. Within a few years, silent films, along with their musicians, had slipped into obsolescence. No longer functional, the music and literature of the period were mostly forgotten.[42]

The transformation was more in the nature of a slow "dissolve" than a quick "wipe." For a time silent and sound films shared the screen, and also music, since many of the early "talkies" were given continuous accompaniments little different from those which had been heard in silent theaters. (For example, except for its sung portions, Louis Silvers's score for *The Jazz Singer* is very much in the tradition of silent film compilations.[43]) The quality of recorded sound, however, was initially much inferior to live music, at least as it had been performed by the better theater orchestras. Hence, some deplored the "symphonic hurly-burly" created by the sound film; as late as 1929 film critic Harry Alan Potamkin could still assert that the best way to combine "Music and the Movies" was to use live chamber ensembles rather than synchronized orchestras.[44]

Potamkin was one of the writers who remained loyal to the silent film. Indeed, many theorists had based their reasoning on the premise that the medium was inherently, or "purely," a visual one, and sound seemed to them a blemish. Others welcomed the transformed medium with enthusiasm. Sound triggered "an avalanche of manifestos," full of prophecies, speculations, and attempts to establish governing principles.[45] A trio of Russian filmmakers—Eisenstein, Pudovkin, and Alexandrov—set the tone with their brief manifesto-like "Statement on the Sound Film" of 1928: "The first experimental work with sound must be directed along the line of its distinct non-synchronization with the visual image."[46] They were disturbed by the prospect of an excessively literal use of sound—its use, in other words, merely to confirm things already visible on the screen—because such mechanistic synchronization threatened the theory and practice of montage as it had been developed during the twenties. Though more progressive than Potamkin, these writers, too, felt their loyalties divided.

In the films Eisenstein and Pudovkin made in the thirties, they decisively left the esthetic of silence behind, and revised and amplified their ideas in many books and articles.[47] Elsewhere Rudolf Arnheim (not a filmmaker) published his theory of *Film als Kunst*, a complex work with a complex section on sound. He incorporated some of the same terminology as the Russians, using such words as "contrapuntal" and "asynchronous," but also wrote in favor of more "naturalistic" soundtracks.[48] Béla Balázs likewise stressed film's naturalistic character when combined with sound, in his treatise *Der Geist des Films*; and he foresaw the day when musical accompaniments would become a "program music" made from abstract and natural sounds into "symphonies of noise."[49]

All four of these writers, as well as others whose manifestos have been forgotten, kept their discussions of music abstract. They were not musical professionals, like the writers of silent film manuals and the compilers of anthologies; and although two of them worked with leading composers, their knowledge of music appears not to have been very deep.[50] It is interesting to observe how many European writers who *were* musically educated adopted a similar style—especially in the periodicals *Die Musik* and *Melos*. From 1928 to 1933, these two periodicals brought out a large amount of film music literature by musicians; and much of it floats on the same abstract plane as the literature cited above.[51]

In 1928 and 1929, most of the articles in *Die Musik* appeared under the general heading of "Mechanische Musik."[52] One recurrent theme within such literature was that the new media of phonograph, radio, and film could become powerful sources of patronage and stimulation for the musical avant-garde.[53] (Elsewhere at this time, Paul Valéry wrote of the exciting prospects created by the "new intimacy of music and physics."[54]) Soon, however, disappointment set in, as music's place within commercial films dwindled. The public's attention was directed toward talkies full of talk but not much music, and toward musicals full of song and dance. (In fact, the two categories overlapped, since songs were apt to be inserted into any kind of film, no matter how awkward the context.) By 1931, moreover, the public's appetite for musicals was temporarily exhausted; and the decline of the genre's popularity coincided with a general abandonment of continuous accompanimental music.[55] (One rationale for the spreading silence was that in the "naturalistic" context of the sound film, music seemed out of place, much like the pantomimic gestures and facial expressions of some silent film actors.) Owing partly to these new trends, when musicians wrote about music they dwelt mostly on the exciting, exceptional examples of creative uses of sound, and on the theoretical future rather than on the immediate present. Of the movies as they were, they had formed a pretty low opinion.[56]

In the mid-thirties opinions and opportunities began to improve. From Hollywood, in 1933, came *42nd Street* and *King Kong*—two movies less important in themselves, perhaps, than as signals of renewal for both musicals and dramatic scores. (The songs of the former were by Al Dubin and Harry Warren; the music of the latter was by Max Steiner.) In each film a fresh set of techniques was quickly established as Hollywood conventions.[57] Commercial film music was back on its feet, and in the following year Hollywood granted it official recognition with the institution of Academy Awards for outstanding scores.[58]

Recognition of a more inquiring kind was granted at the first International Congress of Music (ICM) in Florence in 1933, where sessions were held on "Radio, film, grammofono," and "La musica e il film."[59] This marked the beginning of a new outpouring of literature across all of Western Europe. A special issue of *La Revue Musicale* was devoted to "Le Film sonore."[60] New periodicals were established: *Cinema Quarterly* and *Sight and Sound* in Great Britain, *Bianco e nero* in Italy; and each of them published many articles by composers, critics, and theorists.[61] From the city of London, moreover, came the first two books on music in the sound film.

Leonid Sabaneev's *Music for the Film: A Handbook for Composers and Conductors* (1935) and Kurt London's *Film Music: A Summary of the Characteristic Features of Its History, Aesthetics, Technique and Possible Developments* (1936) were as different as their subtitles suggest. Each had its own antecedents. Sabaneev's handbook revived the style of silent film manuals, avoiding abstractions (except, to some degree, in a chapter on the "Aesthetics of the Sound Film"), and describing in practical terms each stage of the film-scoring process. London's "summary" followed Erdmann and Becce in trying to survey the whole subject systematically.[62] Yet in one respect the two books were very much alike: Sabaneev and London shared a fascination with the idea of "Music for the Microphone"—a popular term in the literature of the time, like that of "Mechanical Music," to which it was closely related[63]—and both authors gave the idea considerable play. They explained in detail how the acoustics of the recording studio altered the sounds (for better and worse) made by instruments alone and in groups; and from these observations, they sought to generate idiomatic principles of film composition and orchestration. As it turned out, neither their observations nor their principles endured for long. Recording technology was changing so rapidly that large portions of each book soon became obsolete.[64]

London had anticipated this "possible development." Near the conclusion of his book (pp. 249–61), he called for the creation of a "Microphone Academy" for the scientific study of the microphone's properties and for the training of a new generation of composers. No such academy was created, however, nor did any books come to join these two until after World War II. Sabaneev and London rode a wave of interest in film music at its crest, but by the end of the decade that wave had broken on the shoals of politics and war. Literature continued to issue from Europe, but slowed to a trickle. The main achievements of those years were probably the second ICM at Florence (1938), which sponsored three sessions on film music,[65] and three dissertations from Germany—including a valuable, if obscure, study of music for silent films.[66]

At the same time a much stronger "new wave" of literature began to pour from the United States, swelled by the great number of refugee filmmakers, composers, and critics. In the thirties, American literature had followed its own course. It was, in general, less concerned with theoretical problems than with descriptions of techniques and trends written for a lay audience.[67] This practical, popularizing tendency set it apart from much European writing. A comparison of two articles from 1937 is instructive: French composer Maurice Jaubert was preoccupied by the aesthetic principles of "Music on the Screen," while Max Steiner (Viennese-born, but in matters of film music Hollywood-bred) described the processes and history of "Scoring the Film."[68] It was not that Steiner lacked ideas about what film music should do, but that he displayed them as the fruits of his working experience rather than as theoretical precepts in the manner of Jaubert. One magazine that combined both approaches was *Modern Music*. Since the late twenties, it had functioned, like *Melos*, as a promoter of the avant-garde's ideas about film music.[69] Then in 1936 it took the innovative step of hiring one of the avant-garde's members to be its film music reporter and critic of news "On the Hollywood Front." For four years George Antheil held the job, writing in a lively, thoughtful fashion of his experiences both as an observer and as a participant.[70]

Hollywood in those years was a lively place for music, so there was a great deal of news to report. Lengthy symphonic scores had become normal accessories to feature films, and in addition to Hollywood's regulars, the musical community was swelled by visitors from the East Coast and refugees from Europe. However, because late-romantic styles were prevalent, when some of these "modern" composers tried their hand at films, despite occasional promising announcements and tantalizing speculation, they were often disappointed. Antheil's columns noted upturns and downturns with rollercoaster speed. In the spring of 1937, for example, he wrote enthusiastically of Boris Morros, the "musical man of the hour" and "Russian generalissimo of Paramount's musical destinies," for bringing Stowkowski and Werner Janssen into films; and he noted the rumors of impending film scores to be composed by Schoenberg, Stravinsky, and Honegger. But in the column which appeared the following autumn, Antheil complained that "Hollywood, after a grand splurge with new composers and new ideas, has settled back into its old grind of producing easy and sure-fire scores."[71]

Antheil's subsequent experiences, measured against those of Hollywood professionals, made him even less sanguine. In 1940, Alfred Newman was appointed music director at Fox, and composed or supervised music for fifteen films; Steiner was a leading composer at Warner Brothers, for whom he scored seven films; by contrast, Antheil wrote one film score in that year, and then gave up on Hollywood until after the war.[72] Describing the system's hostility to modern music, he called Hollywood a "closed proposition," echoing Oscar Levant, who had previously termed the studio music departments "pretty much a closed shop for specialists."[73] The best openings for progressive composers tended to come (with luck) from independently minded producers: for example, Ben Hecht, who wrote, produced, and directed *Angels over Broadway* (1940) and *Spectre of the Rose* (1946), two films that were scored by Antheil.[74] In the early forties, Aaron Copland and Hanns Eisler both scored films produced by United Artists, a company known for its willingess to sponsor high-quality independent productions.[75] Documentaries were another fruitful path, and in 1940 (according to McCarty) the following composers wrote scores for films of this kind: Marc Blitzstein, Paul Bowles, David Diamond, Eisler, Louis Gruenberg, Roy Harris, Werner Janssen, Gail Kubik, and David Raksin. Of these, only Raksin had much Hollywood experience, and most of that came late.[76]

As composers wrote more and more film music, they also wrote more and more *about* film music; and in America what they wrote depended on whether they stood inside the Hollywood circle or out. In the article by Max Steiner discussed above, for example, his point of view is that of the insider looking out. He's a professional interested in communicating what he does and how he does it, with larger issues left out of the picture. On the other hand, Antheil, Copland, and Eisler tended to see film music in much broader contexts, sometimes with humor, sometimes seriously. Antheil writes with the vivacity of a "bad boy" ever on the move, from continent to continent and coast to coast; his tales often read like black comedy. Copland's approach is more philosophical, his style is more refined and measured, and his feelings about Hollywood more amiably ambivalent.[77] (As one of America's most successful composers, perhaps he could afford to be.)

The most extended work of this period to reflect on the Hollywood milieu was Eisler's *Composing for the Films* (1947), which has little ambivalence and few light touches.[78] Indeed, it is as severe a critique of Hollywood music as has ever been published. The book began as a seemingly scientific collaboration between Eisler and Theodor Adorno in the early forties; both were at the New School in New York, Adorno investigating radio music, and Eisler heading a "Film Music Project" funded by the Rockefeller Foundation.[79] Eisler once described this project in terms of a laboratory experiment, with theoretical determination of special problems, experiments, and public tests of the results.[80] Yet *Composing for the Films* contains passages of Marxist rhetoric so high-pitched that they defy all notions of dispassionate research:

> . . . it is preposterous to use words such as "history" with reference to an apocryphal branch of art like motion picture music. The person who around 1910 first conceived the repulsive idea of using the Bridal March from *Lohengrin* as an accompaniment is no more of a historical figure than any other second-hand

> dealer. Similarly, the prominent composer of today, who, under the pretext of motion-picture requirements, willingly or unwillingly debases his music, earns money, but not a place in history. The historical processes that can be perceived in cinema music are only reflections of the decay of middle-class cultural goods into commodities for the amusement market. . . . It would be ludicrous to claim that motion picture music has really evolved either in itself or in its relation to other motion picture media [p. 49].

The ideological tone has turned more than one American reader away. Prendergast goes so far as to term the book "testy and relatively valueless" (*Film Music*, p. 3), but much of what Eisler writes is of great value. The book contains revealing general comments on film music "function and dramaturgy," as exemplified by segments from several of Eisler's own scores.[81] It concludes with a fascinating "Report on the Film Music Project" (pp. 135–57), which contains detailed analysis of a sequence from *Fourteen Ways of Describing Rain* (Op. 70), a chamber score composed for the Joris Ivens film *Rain*. Eisler then moves to a "counter-example": the sequence known as the "Battle on the Ice" from *Alexander Nevsky*. As was noted above, Eisler subjects Eisenstein's comments on this score to careful scrutiny (and offers criticisms on which Prendergast himself relies).[82] This portion of the book does much to raise the level of film music discourse, and some may wish that Eisler had placed the critique at the heart of the book, rather than relegating it to an appendix. Moreover, for all its defects the book is conceptually on firmer ground than most others about film music, because it so intelligently and unyieldingly affirms its main point. In Eisler's opinion, the point was that modern music, particularly twelve-tone music, was an ideal style for the film medium; but the industry, with its barriers of "prejudices and bad habits" (described in the book's first chapter), made it impossible for such music to be heard.[83]

As for the composers who got along very well in the industry, they wrote about it far more brightly. Two examples in book form are English composer Louis Levy's memoir of a life spent making "music for the movies," and Hollywood composer Frank Skinner's step-by-step case history of his experiences composing music for *The Fighting O'Flynn*.[84] Skinner approaches the assignment uncritically, in the pragmatic manner of the Hollywood professional; but he was far from being the most Pollyanna-like of writers. That credit may well belong to Nathaniel Finston, Music Director at Metro-Goldwyn-Mayer, for claiming that "every film today contains in its making the painstaking efforts of the best minds in the musical world."[85]

Finston and Eisler stood face to face, across an apparently unbridgeable gap, with public-relations puffery on one side, and an attack on the whole socioeconomic structure of the "cultural industry" on the other. Yet in one fundamental sense they wrote for the same reason: to bring their art to light, from the realm of "background scores," barely noticed, into the foreground of public acclaim or critical scrutiny (depending upon one's point of view). Moreover, even though Eisler himself seemed pessimistic as to the chances for any improvement of film music (his own book notwithstanding), others with negative views put far more faith in the power of criticism to effect positive change. "If the music critics, especially those of New York, Boston, and Philadelphia, would band together," Antheil

wrote, "and turn a searchlight upon Hollywood, Hollywood would soon see to it that these background scores did not continue to be the unmitigated tripe they now are."[86] A similar opinion was expressed a decade later, without the East Coast bias, by London music critic Hans Keller, in several articles and, most pertinent, in a lively pamphlet entitled *The Need for Competent Film Music Criticism*. He wanted critics equally knowledgeable in film and music to "thrust" film music from the "unselective preconscious into open consciousness, in fact into an aural close-up," so that "film music will be heard for what it isn't worth."[87]

At the time Keller took up the pen, it appeared as if the above-named need might well be met. The profession of film music criticism attracted many practitioners during the war years and after, in both the United States and England.[88] They were all very much interested in seeing film music improve, but their common goal did not prevent them from sparring just as much as composers over such issues as the relative merits of American and European film music, and the state of the art in Hollywood. The critic who described that state with perhaps the nicest blend of wit, sympathy, and insight was Lawrence Morton.[89] Though he engaged in his share of debate, especially with English critics,[90] his writing is distinguished from everyone else's by its pointed precision. Morton expressed precisely what he thought, without the hyperbole that seemed to come naturally to a writer like Keller. Rather than summarily condemn or approve, he gave reasons for his opinions and rested them on solid factual ground.

He also broke new ground with a pioneering study, "The Music of *Objective: Burma*," published in *Hollywood Quarterly* 1 (1946), 378–95. In this article, for the first time, a score is analyzed cue by cue. After listing the six main themes, Morton describes every one of the twenty-four "separate compositions," with several score excerpts provided. Then he concludes with this assessment of the composer and his milieu:

> "Musicality" is an inclusive term, and it is not axiomatically applicable to everyone who writes music. A wit once remarked that "the only difference between Alban Berg and other Viennese atonalists is that Berg was musical." Franz Waxman is one of no more than a dozen composers for whom the same can be said in Hollywood.

It was a polemical age, and sweeping evaluations were common. But Morton's analysis makes every attempt to define the Waxman score's "musicality" (harmony, theme, and structure) in terms of the relationship of music and drama. Few other critics were able to justify their opinions with such carefully marshaled evidence, although Frederick Sternfeld followed Morton's lead with four comparable studies.[91] Earlier in his own article, Morton called himself "counsel for the defense" (p. 394, where he acknowledged Tovey's *Essays in Musical Analysis* as the source of the phrase). Film music was considered to be on trial; so was Waxman, for becoming a part of that world; and so was the idea that film music could be deserving of serious analysis. Very little could be taken for granted by writers seeking to end public and professional neglect.

Was the neglect passing? It had already seemed so to Kurt London several years earlier. After emigrating to America, he was hired by the short-lived but

prestigious periodical *Films* (1939–40) as a critic of film music. In his last column he optimistically wrote of a change in attitudes:

> Slowly but surely, motion picture professionals and laymen are coming to recognize that music for the movies is not a mere by-product of film-making, but an important part of the cinematic art. We have had various signs of this awakening during the past year [No. 4, p. 25].

The "signs" to which London pointed were the Film Music Project under Eisler and the formation of a Federation of Film Music Clubs across this country: developments which might indeed have appealed to "professionals" on the one hand and "laymen" on the other. And in fact, one sees similar signs before, during, and after the war years. An "awakening" could be said to have begun with Antheil's criticism in *Modern Music*, which pointed the way to a flourishing profession. The formation of film music clubs led in 1941 to the establishment of *Film Music Notes*, the first and longest-lived of American periodicals devoted to the subject.[92] Beginning in the same year, a number of sophisticated studies of the aesthetics of film music were published, as innovative in their own way as the analytical essays already cited.[93] Above all, composers wrote about their craft. Books and articles by many—e.g., Antheil, Copland, Eisler, Hopkins, Jaubert, Levant, Levy, Skinner, Steiner, and Stothart—have already been noted and discussed. In addition, Bernard Herrmann and Adolph Deutsch contributed valuable articles on individual scores.[94] Moreover, in keeping with the spirit of the war years, there came a series of collective publications representing common locales and views: at one end of the decade, a symposium of mostly East Coast composers; across the decade, four anthologies focused on music in Hollywood; and at decade's end, a volume of papers, mostly by Italian composers and scholars, published under the joint auspices of the Venice Film Festival and the seventh International Congress of Music in Florence.[95]

From the "Hollywood Front" to the Florence Congress, the literature expanded impressively. What had come awake with full force was the urge to explain film music, through description of its functions, methods, quality, and possibilities for improvement. Yet though in a general sense the range of the literature was always broadening, taken piece by piece its narrowness is undeniable. Most writers were caught up by ideas and music of the moment and did not attempt to catch the overall drift. Retrospective views and scholarly works were few in number.[96] So it is not surprising to read this description of the literature by Morton, written in 1953:

> If the truth be told, it is not very distinguished. Some of it is pertinent but uninteresting, or interesting but fanciful; much of it is mere reportage, spot news; little of it has any permanent value. As opinion, as judgement, it represents a varied assortment of ant's-eye views of film-music events in isolation, a great deal of special pleading, and a still larger amount of prejudiced derogation. Its shortcomings have not prevented it, however, from being made the basis of broad generalizations. These exist, for the most part as catch-words, epithets and imprecations. They do not reflect, in any true sense, a general view with either critical or historical perspective.[97]

Morton's "general view" of the literature covers a lot of ground, including his own. As a critic, he too was obliged to view "film-music events in isolation." Indeed, what is his study of the music of *Objective: Burma*, if not "special pleading" (by a self-professed "counsel for the defense") on behalf of Franz Waxman's virtues as a film composer? Still, his words contain a good deal of truth, and apply just as well to much of the literature written since. There have never ceased to be "ant's-eye views" of contemporary events, pleas and prophecies for the improvement of film music, dependent upon the latest technical and stylistic trends. Thus (to cite one set of examples out of a number too large and too scattered to be contained in this survey), *Films in Review* has published a column from 1952 to the present called "The Sound Track," little different from its predecessors as a repository of capsule reviews, brief essays, and summary judgments. Until 1993 it was being written by Page Cook, whose colorful and emotional prose made him one of film music's most passionately opinionated critics.[98]

Yet in the literature of the fifties, one begins to perceive signs of a second, more scholarly "awakening." *Films in Review* itself went beyond spot criticism with a series of articles calling attention to silent film music, as well as studies of important Hollywood composers.[99] Also during the fifties, various film and music reference works began to include surveys and bibliographies.[100] A still brighter sign was the 1953 book for which Morton wrote his description of the literature (from which he quite rightly excepted the new work): Clifford McCarty's checklist of *Film Composers in America*. This was the first book to tackle the formidable problem of gathering accurate music credits for thousands of films; and because of McCarty's slow and careful research, it is still the most successful reference work of its kind.[101]

A work as important as McCarty's, but for different reasons, is Roger Manvell and John Huntley's *The Technique of Film Music* (1957). It is important as the first example of the kind of book that has predominated in recent years, the "general view" of the subject, presented within a variety of perspectives: history, theory, and criticism either mix or take turns. *The Technique of Film Music* is of the turn-taking sort, since each of its five chapters has little to do with the others. The first two cover the history of music, first in silent, then in early sound films (to 1939). The next chapter attempts to categorize the functions of music in the sound film, with discussion of numerous excerpts to exemplify each. In the fourth chapter the authors turn to studio matters: the role of the music director, and recording techniques. The final chapter shifts to a presentation of "The Composer's View": fourteen composers are cited on such matters as their feelings about being a member of a "team," their freedom to experiment, and the problem of writing music to accompany dialogue. The book concludes with three appendixes: a chronology of film music's history (told through yearly lists of "principal events and film music compositions"), reprints of a few examples of film music criticism, and a bibliography.[102]

It is clear that *The Technique of Film Music* is not just about film music's "technique," but it is difficult, if not impossible, to put its contents into focus. (The misleading title was chosen because the book is part of "The Focal Press Library of Communication Techniques," and all the titles in this series begin with the same three words.) Full as the book is of useful information and ideas, little of the information is accounted for, and few of the ideas are taken beyond a page or two. At the heart of Chapter Three, for example, four of the excerpts selected to illustrate the functions of film music are given very special treatment: the music is laid out in short score, with photographic stills and descriptions of dialogue, sound effects, and action all in vertical alignment. The authors have thus made an original and lavish attempt to quote these "unquotable" texts; but since they say nothing more about the excerpts in their own text, the significance of this group of "analyses" derives mainly from the method of transcription.[103] There are other gaps, too. One isn't given any explanation, for example, why the authors consider the films listed in the "chronological outline" to be *the* "principal film music compositions." Nor is there any way to correlate them with the rest of the text, for they are not included in the index. In short, the book has much to offer, but the contents must be examined bit by bit, rather like an untrustworthy potpourri.

Until 1957, when *The Technique of Film Music* first appeared, the number of general views of film music was small: Erdmann and Becce's *Handbuch* (1927), London's *Film Music* (1936), and to some extent Eisler's *Composing for the Films* and Huntley's solo *British Film Music* (both 1947). Compared with this rate of one or two books per decade, during the next quarter-century the pace of such publications greatly quickened, and no fewer than fifteen books followed Manvell and Huntley's *Technique*:

Georges Hacquard, *La Musique et le cinéma* (1959)
Hans Alex Thomas, *Die deutsche Tonfilmusik* (1962)
Henri Colpi, *Défense et illustration de la musique dans le film* (1963)
Zofia Lissa, *Aesthetik der Filmmusik* (1965)
François Porcile, *Présence de la musique à l'écran* (1969)
Tony Thomas, *Music for the Movies* (1973)
Irwin Bazelon, *Knowing the Score* (1975)
Mark Evans, *Soundtrack* (1975)
Roy Prendergast, *A Neglected Art* [*Film Music*] (1977)
Alain Lacombe and Claude Rocle, *La Musique du film* (1979)
Ermanno Comuzio, *Colonna sonora* (1980)
Helga de la Motte-Haber and Hans Emons, *Filmmusik* (1980)
Wolfgang Thiel, *Filmmusik in Geschichte und Gegenwart* (1981)
Sergio Miceli, *La musica nel film* (1982)
Hans-Christian Schmidt, *Filmmusik* (1982)

Like *The Technique of Film Music*, many of these books are compromised by their diffuseness. In the French group, for example, Colpi, Porcile, and Lacombe and Rocle all mix history, theory, and criticism in uneasy combinations, while at the same time offering biographical dictionaries with information on many European composers.[104] Bazelon's *Knowing the Score* is another awkward mix: one may tend to skim the first half—an often abrasive compendium of analysis and polemics, which leaps confusingly from film to film—and linger over the second, in which are printed a series of interviews with fifteen versatile and varied composers, followed by fifty pages of score excerpts, many of them reproduced from composers' manuscripts.[105] The three other American books, by Tony Thomas,

Evans, and Prendergast, are primarily historical surveys of sound film music, with descriptions of the lives and/or works of several prominent Hollywood composers.[106] Thomas abounds in factual details and entertaining anecdotes, but the two types of information are combined indiscriminately, with no attempt to account for sources; nor does he have much to say about the music itself. Evans shows more interest in both general styles and individual scores, but his ideas are often underdeveloped. The following excerpt from his description of Newman's style may be taken as typical:

> Often countermelodies, in a lyrical mode appropriate for an operatic aria, would be offset against the main theme. Newman's melodies were characterized by wide leaps, often harmonized in thirds or sixths. Like Strauss, he knew how to manipulate the colors of the harmonic palette. His scores are always tonal, his uncanny ability to use deceptive cadences, to alternate between major and minor, and to infuse his music with a breathless, surging quality of emotionalism accounts for much of its unique quality [p. 52].

One may wish to ask, among other things, whose arias (with "counter-melodies") the author has in mind; and what is "unique" about a composer whose style seems to rely on devices used by a host of composers including Strauss (and perhaps Schubert)?

Given the choice of Evans or Prendergast, readers will understandably prefer the latter, because *Film Music* contains more detailed and sophisticated analysis than any earlier book published in America. However, its spotlight is turned too unblinkingly upon Hollywood music, and only a small portion of it at that, for the book to achieve its stated goal: "to illumine the subject as a whole."[107] Moreover, it borrows heavily from other sources, many of them not cited. These sources tend to belie the author's contention that film music is "a neglected art," and because Prendergast often strings together quotation and paraphrase without comment, the book's value as "a critical study" is seriously undermined.[108]

Writing of greater strength and density is to be found in the remaining works from the list above, all but one in German, beginning with Hans Alex Thomas's carefully documented survey of music in early German sound films, and Lissa's expansive study of film music aesthetics.[109] These books do not adhere to the normal motley pattern, and have been designed with a careful balance of general concept and specific detail. Within their respective spheres of history and theory, they stand as sturdy foundations for further research; and one can note with pleasure that the last four "general views"—three in German, one in Italian—are equally substantive, with special features sharply in focus. La Motte-Haber and Emons offer a concise and "systematic description" of film music in functional terms.[110] Thiel's large-scale work includes a lengthy chapter on film genres as a formative principle of musical style, and while it is somewhat weak on Hollywood, it contains much data on film composers from the Soviet Union and Eastern Europe.[111] Miceli's work goes into more detail than most on the history of the silent period, and pays extended attention to two of Italy's most important film composers, Nino Rota and Ennio Morricone.[112] Finally, one should not overlook Schmidt's *Filmmusik*, despite its self-professed intention of serving the secondary school student.

Within a lucid chronological framework, dozens of films are discussed in detail, with accurate plot synopses, many score excerpts, and two discs of recorded examples.[113] Translated into English this book could make a useful text for a film music survey, by no means out of place at college level.

However significant such surveys may be, their accumulation from the fifties to the eighties was by no means an isolated phenomenon: other types of books also showed rapid increase—especially reference works, manuals, biographies, and anthologies[114]—and even quite specialized tomes multiplied, thanks to pioneers whose methods and monographs broke new ground. One such individual is Robert Faulkner: a sociologist, as well as an experienced jazz musician, he has written *Hollywood Studio Musicians* (1971), an examination of their careers, and *Music on Demand* (1983), about Hollywood composers and the pressures they face.[115] Others, principally Germans, have done much to facilitate the study of music for silent films: most useful are Herbert Birett's *Stummfilm-Musik* (1970), a compendium of primary source materials; the articles by Lothar Prox and others in *Stummfilmmusik Gestern und Heute* (1979), an anthology published on the occasion of a symposium on the subject held in Berlin; Hanjörg Pauli's survey, *Filmmusik: Stummfilm* (1981), which draws upon much recent scholarship; and Ulrich Rügner's *Filmmusik in Deutschland zwischen 1924 und 1934*, valuable for its scrutiny of scores for nearly a dozen key films, from *Caligari* to *Kuhle Wampe*.[116] In the United States, the main pioneering achievements in this field have been Charles Berg's *Investigation* (1976)—a book made from the first American dissertation on the subject[117]—and Gillian B. Anderson's *Music for Silent Films* (1988), which contains the first published inventory of scores, parts, and cue sheets in five major American repositories, together with a fine introductory essay on performance practice by this peripatetic conductor/librarian.[118]

As can be judged from the topics, methods, and titles of these books, they have been written *by scholars for the use of scholars*—quite a change from the literature of the silent period, which was mostly written by musicians and for musicians; clearly the "explosion" in film studies has had a powerful impact on this peripheral area of research. Such a conclusion seems all the more inescapable when one takes into account these developments: the reprinting of several forgotten early works that are now of value primarily to the scholar;[119] the accumulation of dissertations, those in English numbering at least a dozen since 1975;[120] and, as was observed in the first part of this chapter, the active interest in film music taken by libraries and other research institutions, which has led, at the American Film Institute and the Library of Congress, to publications based on materials in their collections.[121] Should still more evidence be needed, one may consider Steven D. Westcott's *Comprehensive Bibliography* (1985). The book marshalls a huge range of sources—more than 6300 numbered bibliographic entries—accurately and ingeniously, and owing to the author's thoughtful arrangement, systematic cross-indexing, and careful annotations, it goes far toward meeting its titular goal of being "comprehensive." Thus it has become an indispensable new "general handbook," reminiscent of Erdmann and Becce's, except that it is designed not for performers so much as for those engaged in research.

Even Westcott, or any other lone bibliographer, must now find it difficult to keep track of recent periodical literature, because it, too, has seen explosive growth, especially since the mid-1970s. Prior to that time, articles were of three principal types, of which the first two have already been mentioned: (1) topical journalism, such as is found in *Film Music Notes* and *Films in Review*; (2) views in retrospect, designed to reawaken interest in some part of film music's past, as in the examples cited from the latter periodical; and (3) essays probing the subject in theoretical terms.[122] These essays, generally more complex than other articles, and often more cognizant of earlier literature, can be said to have planted the seeds for recent work of a new and flourishing type, case studies of individual composers and films. In themselves such studies may not seem all that original, since examples were cited above that date back four decades. But the essays by Morton and Sternfeld were contemporary views of scores at hand—models for the film music criticism of the day—rather than retrospective scholarship. Present-day essays mostly concern films of the past, currently held in high esteem, and the writers move around freely in an exploratory fashion, from theory to analysis and from history to theory, with sound scholarship as their guide. As a result, these case studies tend to have broad implications for future work, far beyond the range of the particular topic.[123]

Among those who have made pioneering contributions to this new, scholarly literature stand three influential American writers, namely, Douglas Gallez, Frederick Steiner, and Claudia Gorbman: all have written dissertations on film music (cited in n. 120), as well as several essays apiece, mostly focused on analyses of music within specific films.[124] They also have shown a common concern for establishing a theoretical and/or historical context for their work. For example: in his study of Satie's music for *Entr'acte*, Gallez presents what may be termed the first "source study" in the literature, by interpreting one of Satie's puzzling sketches for the score.[125] Steiner combines his study of Leith Stevens's music for *The Wild One* with a valuable overview of the development of jazz idioms in film scoring. In Gorbman's case studies of music in films by Fellini, Clair, and Vigo, she raises fundamental questions of methodology (as in her comments on transcription in "Vigo/Jaubert"), while the analyses offer convincing demonstrations of the power of new modes of criticism, derived from recent film theory. The culmination of her work to date—and surely one of the most significant English monographs on film music ever published—is *Unheard Melodies* (1987), which presents theoretical approaches to narrative film music in five chapters, followed by three case studies.[126]

Alongside Gorbman's book, another publication which ranks among the most challenging recent additions to the literature is the special issue of *Yale French Studies* (1980), entirely devoted to "Cinema/Sound." The purpose of the issue, as explained at the outset by its editor, Rick Altman, is to counter the longstanding "hegemony of the visual" within the domain of film criticism and theory, and to "suggest new directions and possibilities for a more integrated approach to the entire film experience." The essays in the collection indeed look in many new directions, though they are grouped under four headings in the table of contents: "Theory" (5 essays), "History" (3), "Music" (4, including one by Gorbman, which she revised as the first chapter of her book), and "Case Studies" (3).[127] In all of these groups the authors speak the sophisticated language of contemporary theory—as in Gorbman's essay, which formulates principles governing the relationship between music and cinematic narrative. To uninitiated readers this language, now common currency in academia, may seem either frustratingly opaque or unnecessarily complex for the material at hand; yet for all its difficulties it is worth the trouble. It compels us to rethink assumptions and contexts, leading us to a point where films can be seen, and their music heard, anew. In all likelihood, as these and other recent writings demonstrate, this type of critical discourse will be a major influence upon film music research for many years to come.[128]

In recent years the literature has found new ways to proceed while also following the old ways at an accelerating pace. The same can be said of film music itself. In theaters today one encounters multi-cultural variety and a wide spectrum of styles, from popular songs of the hour to the latest avant-garde techniques.[129] Yet there are also many recent scores that resonate with allusive meanings, in parody and homage to the past.[130] All kinds of scores have worked well, in films both artful and profitable. Moreover, even as film's "golden age" disappears from view (and for different people this can be any time from the twenties to the fifties), videos and soundtracks resurface, and film music societies do their best to bring the age back.[131] Research is thus being pushed forward by waves of both scholarship and nostalgia, as we seek to keep abreast of the present and to recapture the past.

The literature of film music has outlived several generations of filmmakers, composers, and researchers. It has been shown to be both heterogeneous and abundant, and though Prendergast complained of a lack of "intelligent and perceptive writing," we have seen instances of such writing in every phase of the literature's history. What continually changes is the direction in which the intelligence and perception are applied.

Within this survey, five principal currents of literature have been charted, with these points of origin and tendencies:

(1) The Edison Company's "Suggestions for Music," 1909: aids for the preparation of accompaniments;
(2) the "Statement" by Eisenstein, Pudovkin, and Alexandrov, 1928: theoretical speculation on the principles and potentialities of the sound film;
(3) Antheil's column, "On the Hollywood Front," 1936: explanations and critical debates focused on music in contemporary films;
(4) Manvell and Huntley's *Technique of Film Music*, 1957: general views of film's music theory and history, amplified by criticism; and
(5) Gallez's "Theories of Film Music," 1970: scholarly case studies with broad implications for further research.

Morton's eloquent assessment of the literature needs reconsideration. In 1953, when he described the literature as mostly "mere reportage" with no "permanent value," he had in mind the third current of writing, which had predominated in America for nearly twenty years. The primary example of the kind of literature he wished to see—the "general view"—was London's *Film Music* (1936), a book then much out of date. Such books are now more plentiful, and since the publication of *A Neglected Art* in 1977, much progress has been made toward Prendergast's stated goal: the development of a "critical literature." By this he presumably meant the careful, critical studies of particular examples of film music within a historical context, and certainly such studies have come to the fore.[132]

Such is the backdrop for this book, which puts a spotlight on film music's beginnings and intends to display both innovative analysis and substantive historiography. All the same, the work owes much to the pioneering scholars mentioned above, from Morton in the forties to Gorbman in the eighties: each pointed the way for the analyses to come. Furthermore, the impermanence of the older literature—its very topicality—has made it an indispensable foundation for present research. (As demonstrated in Chapter Three, for example, the "mere reportage" of *Moving Picture World* provides crucial information about early American film scores.) The fact is, no matter the period we choose to explore, every bit of the material and literature of film music, however celebrated or obscure, challenges us both to understand its unique features and to place it in context. With our introductory survey concluded, a response to the double challenge can now begin.

TWO

First Stages, Dimly Lit

Sources and Scores Prior to 1910

The Origins of Film Music

Little has been written about the music of early cinema, and it is easy to understand why. First, let us be clear about the period in question: altogether it comprises about a decade and a half, from the mid-1890s, when motion pictures made their public debuts, until circa 1910, when the film industry began to emerge. As demonstrated in Chapter One, most of our information about music and silent cinema dates from after 1910; earlier than that, documents are lacking and extant scores are few. Moreover, such materials as do exist have generally been disregarded, because the attention of most film historians has been absorbed by other pressing projects, which relate only indirectly to music. Much work has been done, for example, tracing the origins of cinema's technological apparatus (what is sometimes called its "prehistory"[1]), including the various methods of synchronizing sound which came to fruition in the 1920s.[2] More important, during recent years, while research into early cinema has flourished as never before, leading scholars have had more than enough to do bringing long-neglected films to light. Thus, musical matters remained largely unexplored.[3]

Even the most probing historians of film music have tended to pass quickly over the early years, in the course of introductory discussion. Consider, for example, the opening sections of Manvell and Huntley's influential book. At the outset the authors make a point of music's longstanding association with drama (from Greek tragedy through Elizabethan theater to nineteenth-century stage plays), and they cite a few valuable sources, including an illuminating turn-of-the-century essay by theater composer Norman O'Neill, and also an intriguing passage from the memoirs of Cecil Hepworth (to which we shall return below). All this is contained in an initial section of five pages, followed by two pages devoted to music between 1895 and 1910.[4]

A somewhat different approach can be seen in the detailed surveys of silent film music by Berg and Pauli. Both authors draw upon Manvell and Huntley's work and attempt to go beyond it; but both also admit frustration at the lack of available source materials and turn attention elsewhere—to what Berg calls the "motives" for film music, with emphasis given to its aesthetic and psychological underpinnings.[5] In taking this approach, the two have adopted a mode of inquiry previously used by Erdmann and Becce, London, Eisler (aided by his silent partner, Adorno), Kracauer, and Lissa.[6] All of them have sought to explain the origins of film music primarily in functional terms, by considering its ability to satisfy certain fundamental needs, both practical and psychological: for example, the need to drown out distracting noises (such as those made by the projector), or to compensate for the ghostly silence of the film itself, or to provide some sort of continuity to the choppy images. While these authors differ on the hierarchy and formulation of such needs, they mostly agree in regarding them as inherent in the experience of viewing silent films. The result of their work has been an imposing legacy of received ideas (which Gorbman has eloquently summarized in her own probing discussion of the question "Why music?"[7]); but as history it is problematic.

One widely shared idea that proves particularly troublesome is the assertion that the *content* of early film music was irrelevant, since it was intended only to satisfy certain basic needs. Berg, echoing London and other predecessors (though not Manvell and Huntley) states the matter as follows: "In the early days of the commercial motion picture the music bore little or no relationship to the content of the film. An accompaniment of any kind was acceptable."[8] The point needs to be challenged, because it runs counter to much available evidence—indeed, counter to some of the best insights offered by these very authors. For example, in his own book London also suggests an altogether different way of thinking about early film music in the following passage:

> The reason which is aesthetically and psychologically most essential to explain the need for music as an accompaniment of the silent film, is without doubt *the rhythm of the film as an art of movement.* We are not accustomed to apprehend movement as an artistic form without accompanying sounds, or at least audible rhythms. . . . It was the task of musical accompaniment to give [films] accentuation and profundity.[9]

Implicitly at issue here is the kinship between silent film and stage pantomime or ballet, since all three theatrical genres can be said to be dependent upon "movement as an artistic form"; and historians may well assume that both ballet and pantomime, with their reliance on "accompanying sounds," did much to create musical traditions useful for cinema. But surely these traditions were not based on the idea of "an accompaniment of any kind," so much as on music of specific types, intended to give "accentuation" at once rhythmic and psychological to what was presented on stage.

Turning upon London in this way brings us back to the historical partnership between music and drama, Manvell and Huntley's initial point, which ought to be broadened. For centuries before the advent of cinema, a wide range of Western theatrical genres featured music, including opera, operetta, ballet, pantomime, plays with "incidental" music, melodrama, the variety show, and other intermixed types; and one of the principal tasks before us is to show how all of them helped to pave the way for film music, by offering well-tried methods of composition and compilation (as well as improvisation) to musicians working in the new field.

Recently a few scholars have taken up the task, with fruitful results. In particular, the detailed musicological studies by David Mayer and Anne Dhu Shapiro enable us to see how very similar are the functions of music for nineteenth-century melodrama and for silent film—though perhaps less so for very early films than for those made later, once the narrative conventions of the older genre had been thoroughly absorbed into the newer one.[10] Mayer has also co-edited a collection of such melodrama music, the first of its kind to be published in recent times, containing dozens of "melos"—a common nineteenth-century term for such functional bits and pieces—composed by Alfred Edgar Coopér and a few other anonymous musicians of the late nineteenth century. Detailed study of such music has yet to be undertaken, but one need only glance at these pieces to see how similar they are to those in anthologies for picture players (for example, "agitatos," "furiosos," "misteriosos," "hurries," etc.), such as were published in abundance during the second half of the silent period.[11] There is equal potential in the work of David Robinson, who gathered thirty or so items illustrating connections between film music and its theatrical forerunners for an exhibition mounted in conjunction with the 1990 festival at Pordenone. His achievement lives on in the exhibition catalogue, which ought to stimulate further illuminating research into the origins of film music.[12]

Despite these advances we still know relatively little about links between film music and its theatrical forerunners, particularly music for many types of *optical entertainments*. The term, apparently coined by Robinson, encompasses shows focused on pictorial representations rather than on live performers, including shadow plays, painting shows (e.g., the diorama), and magic lantern exhibitions, as well as other presentations making use of photographic devices.[13] Such shows flourished during the hundred-year period leading up to the invention of motion pictures, and in their evolving technology and use of musical accompaniment they helped to prepare the way. Of course, not of all of these entertainments relied upon music—lantern slide exhibitions of scientific material, for example, seem normally to have been conducted by lecturers alone[14]—but for other sorts of shows, especially spectacles of fantasy and the supernatural, we find considerable iconographic evidence that lanternists either played music themselves or else depended upon others to provide an accompaniment, usually on keyboard or mechanical instruments.[15]

For the most part we can only surmise what this music was like; but in the following passage (originally cited by Manvell and Huntley), one pioneering film director, Hepworth, provided a revealing description of music which accompanied a segment of his traveling show during the mid-1890s. It was a transitional sort of show, featuring both lantern slides and film, as was then common:

> I remember one little series which always went down very well indeed. It was called *The Storm* and consisted of half a dozen slides and one forty-foot film. My sister Effie was a very good pianist and she travelled with me on most of these jaunts. The sequence opened with a calm and peaceful picture of the sea and sky. Soft and gentle music (Schumann, I think). That changed to another seascape, though the clouds looked a little more interesting, and the music quickened a bit.

> At each change the inevitability of a coming gale became more insistent and the music more threatening; until the storm broke with an exciting film of dashing waves bursting into the entrance of a cave, with wild music (by Jensen, I think).[16]

In miniature, what Hepworth describes is a type of accompaniment used throughout the silent period: the compilation of pre-existent music, matched in mood and in the style of performance to the images it accompanies; in this case, matched as well to a change from photographic slides to film footage. Hepworth also names two composers, Schumann and Jensen, whose music became staples of the silent film pianist's repertoire.[17]

Another pre-cinematic optical entertainment of the 1890s employed a different type of accompaniment: an original score, which apparently fit its subject at least as carefully as the improvisatory compilation described by Hepworth. Beginning in November 1892, at the Musée Grevin in Paris, Emile Reynaud presented his first program of hand-drawn animated films, projected by means of his "Praxinoscope." Three short films were shown, entitled *Pauvre Pierrot* ("pantomime"), *Clown et ses chiens* ("intermède") and *Un bon Bock* ("scène comique"); original piano music for all three was composed by Gaston Paulin, and published under the title *Pantomimes lumineuses*. Facsimiles of the cover of the score, a page of music from *Pauvre Pierrot*, and one from *Un bon Bock*, are reproduced by Deslandes, who notes in a caption "how closely the composer has followed the 'cutting' of Reynaud's pantomime."[18] That is, there are descriptive cues set above the music, which tie it closely to the visual narrative. Much the same sort of cueing can be found in many subsequent film scores, and also in some elaborate original scores which were composed for stage pantomimes of the period.[19]

Might it have been the case, as these examples suggest, that from the outset many pictures were accompanied by suitable scores either compiled or composed? Of course the answer to this question depends partly upon the nature of the films, and partly upon the circumstances of their presentations; but there is strong evidence to support an affirmative answer, in two of the earliest scores known to be extant. One is a compilation, created for Max Skladanowsky's presentations of his Bioskop films, beginning in 1895; the other is an original score composed by Saint-Saëns for *L'Assassinat du Duc de Guise*, in 1908. While their existence has been acknowledged for some time, no one has yet made them the object of comparative study, in relationship to the films they accompanied; in this chapter they are placed under the spotlight, center stage.

Certainly it is illuminating to think about film music in more speculative terms and to recognize, as earlier writers have done, that any music used to accompany a film will fulfill *some* needs; or, as Gorbman asserts, that any film music will be perceived by the viewer/listener to "*do something*."[20] But the historian probably does better to begin with the following two premises: first, that all film music, no matter its origin, can be perceived to do *many* things; second, that what it does can only be fully explained by considerations of context and content. The scores for Skladanowsky and for *L'Assassinat* have very different characteristics, exactly as one would expect, given the striking differences between the films for which they were created and the venues where they were performed. As a pair, they demonstrate that even within the period now commonly dubbed "early cinema," there was no lack of attention to ways of adjusting music in the pit to images on the screen. To put the point another way, they show us that musical content mattered very much indeed.

Compilation and Composition: First Cases

During the late 1890s and early 1900s, audiences often saw moving pictures as one portion of variety entertainments that were presented in music halls and vaudeville theaters within major European and American cities. For example, the Vitascope was first presented as part of the show at Koster and Bial's Music Hall in New York for seventeen weeks during the spring and summer of 1896.[21] Subsequently, as Musser tells us, it was featured at B. F. Keith's vaudeville houses in Boston (twelve weeks) and Philadelphia (nine weeks), at Hopkins' South Side Theater in Chicago (twenty weeks), and for shorter periods at Orpheum houses in San Francisco and Los Angeles.[22] Another example is provided by the initial itinerary of a rival American machine, the Biograph. As one of the acts in a touring vaudeville show, it made debuts in several cities during September and October, 1896: first at the Alvin Theatre in Pittsburgh, ultimately at the Grand Opera House in Manhattan. Shortly afterward, the Biograph was seen in two other New York theaters, Hammerstein's Olympia and Koster and Bial's. It settled in Keith's Union Square on 18 January 1897 and remained there, with only a four-month hiatus, until July 1905.[23]

Many of the film programs that made up such exhibitions were themselves variety shows in microcosm. That is, they contained a succession of contrasting films, anywhere from five to fifteen in number, whose subject matter ranged from documentary footage of current interest to skits and/or performances by stage artists.[24] Although most of the individual films were very short—durations of thirty seconds or less were not uncommon—they were often spliced one by one into loops and screened several times in a row for periods lasting several minutes, so that audiences had time to savor these unfamiliar novelties. In this way, each short film became comparable in length to other "numbers" on the bill.[25]

For such presentations of motion pictures the musicians of the variety theaters may well have played in much the same manner as they did for the rest of the show. For as Berg states, the vaudeville milieu provided "a tradition of musical accompaniment," and so "it seems reasonable, despite scant evidence, to assume that [in these arenas] appropriate music and sound effects were provided for films from the outset."[26] Actually the evidence in support of this reasonable assumption is not as scant as Berg supposed, but most of it is vague at best. Consider, for example, the following three items concerning early Vitascope exhibitions. (1) A review of the Vitascope debut at Koster and Bial's does indicate the presence of music:

> On the stage . . . a big drop curtain was lowered. It had a huge picture frame painted in the center with its enclosed space white. The band struck up a lively air and from overhead could be heard a whirring noise that lasted for a few moments; then there flashed upon the screen the life-size figures of two dancing girls who tripped and pirouetted and whirled an umbrella before them.[27]

The "lively air" mentioned here was probably part of a complete program of appropriate music, but except for this passing reference there appears to be no record of what was played that night. Still, we are lucky to have even this comment, since many other reviews of the premiere—as is typical of theatrical reportage, then and now—make no mention of music at all.[28] (2) Theater programs published during the spring and summer months of 1896, when the Vitascope was featured at Koster and Bial's, tells us that an orchestra was always on hand to provide overtures, intermission music, and concluding concerts; but these programs never indicate whether the musicians actually played during the films.[29] (3) In a promotional brochure dating from 1896, one finds an artist's rendering of an exhibition in a packed theater with both a lecturer on stage and an orchestra in the pit; but the musicians are shown facing the screen even as they play, their backs to the conductor. Thus the illustration seems to be fanciful, not based on an actual event.[30]

For the most part the sources for early exhibitions in London and Paris are as vague as those for the Vitascope in America; however, according to Manvell and Huntley, a piano accompanied the screening of Lumière's *cinématographe* at the Grand Café (28 December 1895), and "by April 1896 orchestras were accompanying the films exhibited at the Empire and the Alhambra music halls."[31] In support of the latter statement is a playbill for the London debut of the *cinématographe* at the Empire Theatre, on 9 March 1896 (reproduced by Deslandes): beneath the list of ten picture titles is the announcement that "A Selection of Music will be performed under the direction of Mr. GEORGE BYNG."[32] Also noteworthy is a review cited by Barnes, concerning the debut of Paul's Theatrograph at the Egyptian Hall, April 1896: we are told that for the first picture, showing a band practice, "the music of the march that one may imagine is being played is given on the pianoforte by Mr. F. Cramer."[33]

What is wanting in all these instances is specific information about actual music—something that will shine in front of the dim backdrop; and that is why the Skladanowsky case takes on so much importance, despite its relatively obscure position in film history, and also despite the many questions it leaves unanswered. Beginning on the first of November 1895 (and thus pre-dating by almost two months the first Lumière exhibitions in Paris), as part of the variety show at the Wintergarten theater in Berlin, Max Skladanowsky projected a group of motion pictures he had filmed the previous summer using his own invention, the "Bioskop." The machine eventually proved to be, as Musser puts it, "the most eccentric and commercially unimportant of European inventions";[34] but Skladanowsky enjoyed enough momentary success to exhibit his films at the Wintergarten for a month, then to go on tour during the spring and summer of 1896, bringing his Bioskop to theaters in four capitols across Northern Europe (Oslo, Amsterdam, Copenhagen, Stockholm).[35]

A sizable portion of the music used to accompany these presentations survives. I examined the music in 1978 at the Deutsche Film- und Fernsehakademie, which had preserved a set of folders containing parts for an incomplete orchestral ensemble, including violins, eight woodwinds and eight brass instruments; now the folders are kept at the Stiftung Deutsche Kinemathek, and at least one additional part, for string bass, has also come to light.[36] The parts are of different types, both manuscript and printed, and in varying condition. Most are hand-copied on separate sheets, though some of these sheets have been pasted back to back and some have been gathered into folios. All of the parts show signs of use, including titles and numbers that have been penciled in, music crossed out and/or inserted, and handwritten remarks of varying legibility, such as the signatures of a few players in cities visited during Skladanowsky's tour. It has been claimed that the numbers and other annotations were the director's own.[37]

No folder is without gaps; however, by correlating their contents—with particular attention to those for violin and flute, which are the most comprehensive—one can chart extant music or indications of music for fifteen numbered pieces, one unnumbered piece, and an Introduction and a Finale which frame the compilation. These pieces are listed in Appendix part 1 (along with an inventory of surviving parts for each); and there it will be seen that about half of them use pre-existent material: the unnumbered waltz following no. 2, and nos. 4, 6, 12, 13, and 15—the last three consisting of printed parts, previously published. The rest of the pieces, all in manuscript, appear to have been composed specifically for Skladanowsky's show; but just who composed the original music and assembled the compilation is not certain. Though it has been claimed to be the work of Hermann Krüger, a man identified as a friend of Skladanowsky,[38] no composers are named on any of the manuscript parts. Several of them do bear the stamp of one "F. Hoffmann, Kapellmeister," with the address of Manteuffelstrasse 112a, Berlin (see Fig. 1). So it is possible that Krüger and Hoffmann worked on the compilation together in Berlin, and also that other persons helped them, or revised the music during the tour.

Authorship of the compilation is just one matter of uncertainty; others concern how it was used and when it took its current form. For despite the numbering of pieces, suggestive of careful planning, various factors cast doubt on the idea that all of the pieces were ever meant to be performed consecutively during a single exhibition. Instead, the compilation probably evolved to its present condition while serving to accompany a continually changing program of films, both in Berlin and on the road. Nevertheless, one principle apparently guided the compiler(s) throughout: each film in the program should be accompanied by a separate and generally suitable piece of music.

The case for this view is strongest in connection to the debut program at the Wintergarten, where information is most complete. To be sure, various authoritative scholars list different numbers of films for this program, and in different order; but the most recent and reliable account seems to be that of Lichtenstein, who describes the following nine subjects seen at the premiere: (1) an Italian peasant dance executed by two children; (2) a comic acrobatic scene with the Milton brothers, who perform on parallel bars; (3) a "Serpentine Dance" by Mlle. Ançion; (4) a juggler, Paul Petras; (5) an acrobatic potpourri featuring the Grunato family, eight in number; (6) a boxing kangaroo, featuring "Mr. Delaware"; (7) *Kamarinskaja*—that is, a Russian dance by the three Tscherpanoff brothers; (8) a boxing match between Greiner and Sandow; and (9) an "Apotheosis" featuring the Skladanowsky brothers, taking bows.[39]

FIGURE 1. Music for Skladanowsky's Bioskop exhibitions (1895–1896): Flute part for the *Introduction.* (Figs. 1–4: Kranichphoto, courtesy of the Stiftung Deutsche Kinemathek.)

Based on various kinds of evidence, we can match some pieces of music to films in this program with a fair degree of certainty. The most obvious case is that of Glinka's *Kamarinskaja*, which must have accompanied the film of the Russian dance. For the rest, the indications are more indirect. For example, as indicated in Appendix part 1, the titles for two of these films have been written above pieces in a few parts: "Jongleur" (Juggler) above the violin music for two different galops (numbers 3 and 5), and "Ringkampf" (Boxing Match) above the bassoon music for number 7, an appropriately brisk march. The duplicate ascription of music for the film of the juggler suggests that at some point early on this picture was shifted from one spot to the other on the program and its galop recomposed, a hypothesis supported by the fact that numbers 3 and 5 are both in A major and similar in style. Whether it was moved forward or backward is not clear, but shifting it from the fifth to the third position would have opened a space for the film of the acrobatic potpourri in the position claimed for it by Lichtenstein. Moreover, the first part of the program also had to accommodate the insertion of a very different kind of music, evidently as an accompaniment to Mlle. Ançion's Serpentine Dance. Pasted to the back of the violin part for number 2 is the melody of Gillet's *Loin du bal*, a popular piano waltz which had already become associated with such dances in other circumstances;[40] and in most remaining parts the words "Serpentintanz tacet" (or "tazet") appear ahead of the music for number 3. (See, for example, the horn part given in Fig. 2.) Evidently, either because the film was inserted late into the program and time was pressing, or because it was more intimate than the others, or simply for the sake of variety, the waltz was scored for a reduced ensemble, possibly just violin and piano.[41] But whatever the explanation, both this film and that of the juggler seem later to have been removed, because the violin waltz is crossed out, as are most of the "Serpentintanz tacet" inscriptions in the other parts, together with the music for number 3.

Without more information, not all of the changes in the compilation can be satisfactorily accounted for; nevertheless, it does seem clear that the Wintergarten program was accompanied entirely by numbers in what is now the first half of the compilation, together with the Introduction and Finale. Here is Lichtenstein's list of films, together with the musical numbers in their present order.

Film Subject		*Surviving Music*
		Introduction
Peasant Dance	(1)	Polka
Acrobatic Duo	(2)	Galop
Serpentine Dance		Waltz (*Loin du bal*)
Juggler	(3)	Galop
Boxing Kangaroo	(4)	Spanish March
Acrobatic Potpourri	(5)	Galop (?)
Russian Dance	(6)	*Kamarinskaja*
Boxing Match	(7)	March
"Apotheosis"		Finale

By the time the compilation took its present form, it included music for several additional films of different types. Deslandes mentions that Skladanowsky made a "scenario" picture, longer than his previous films, and Magliozzi catalogues two films shot in Stockholm and Copenhagen, where the Bioskop was subsequently exhibited.[42] Most important, Lichtenstein describes an entire "Second Program" of five films shot in Berlin in August 1896.[43] Taken together these would account for seven or eight new films, and in some fashion they were apparently accompanied by the remaining musical numbers (8–15).

Even though we know little about this half of the program, it is intriguing to

FIGURE 2. Skladanowsky music: Horn part in F for the *Galopp* [no. 3].

note some points which set the music apart from the original material. First, there is the problematic fact that no music survives for numbers 8–11. Possibly these films were excised, along with the music; alternatively, it is possible that the music for one or more of these films was improvised, since a few parts have well-known song titles and keys penciled in, either directly after number 7 or before number 12. (See, for example, Fig. 3, containing the violin part for number 7: at the bottom of the page is written "Lang, lang ist her, C Dur"—a reference to the well-known tune, *Lang, lang ist's her*, in C major.[44]) By contrast, numbers 12–15 include printed

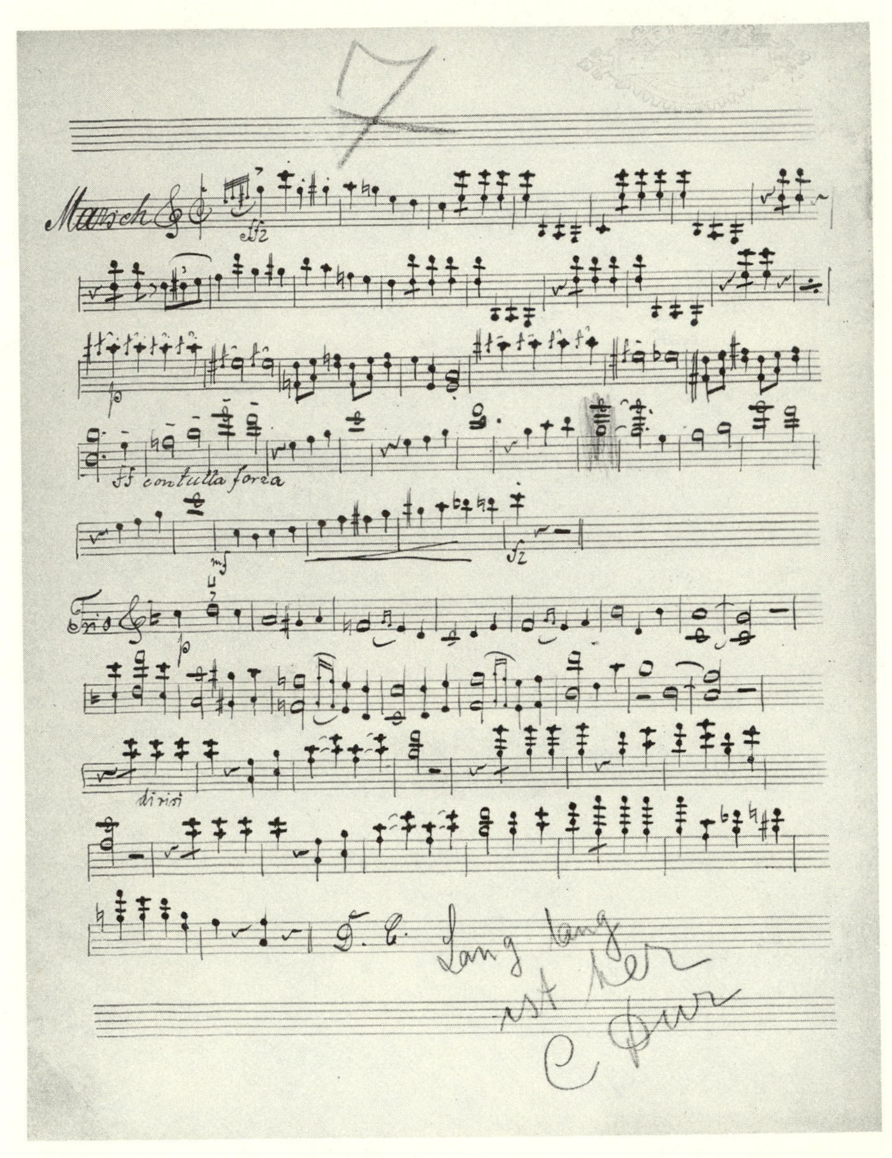

FIGURE 3. Skladanowsky music: Violin part for the *Marsch* [no. 7].

music (two galops and a march) punctuated by a percussion solo. All three of the printed pieces are exuberant, the noisiest of all being number 15, appropriately titled *Mit Bomben und Granaten*: as can be seen in Appendix part 1, section B, its brass contingent is considerably larger than that of previous numbers.[45] In short, the new pieces seem to have been intended to provide various types of contrast, moving from a sentimental interlude to a bombastic climax, capped by the original Finale.

There are clear differences between various segments of the program, yet overall

TABLE 2.1

<table>
<tr><td>INTRO</td><td></td><td>A</td><td></td><td></td><td></td><td></td><td></td><td></td><td>B</td><td></td><td>(Trio)</td><td></td><td></td><td></td><td>A (Da Capo)</td></tr>
<tr><td></td><td></td><td>a</td><td>a'</td><td>b</td><td>b'</td><td>a</td><td>a''</td><td></td><td></td><td></td><td>c</td><td></td><td>d</td><td></td><td></td></tr>
<tr><td>4</td><td>||</td><td>8</td><td>8</td><td>8</td><td>8</td><td>8</td><td>8</td><td>||</td><td>2</td><td>||</td><td>:8:</td><td>||</td><td>:8:</td><td>||</td><td></td></tr>
<tr><td></td><td></td><td>4 + 4</td><td></td><td>4 + 4</td><td></td><td></td><td></td><td></td><td></td><td></td><td>4 + 4</td><td></td><td>4 + 4</td><td></td><td></td></tr>
</table>

the compilation shows a fundamental consistency of style, very much in keeping with the variety-show milieu. Like live stage acts, these films were full of *movement*—that was one basic cause for the excitement produced by early moving pictures—and the music matched (or interpreted) this movement by means of pieces in popular idioms, characterized by catchy rhythms and clear-cut structural patterns. Included in the extant music are seven slightly old-fashioned social dances (a polka, five galops, and a waltz), two marches, and one dance song (*Kamarinskaja*); and all but the last of these pieces has a conventional A-B-A ternary structure, with symmetrical repeats and subdivisions. The A sections are preceded by introductions, usually of four or eight measures, and are divided into two or more strains, often themselves in a-b-a form. The B sections, which in several numbers are labeled "Trio," are similarly constructed; and following the B sections, there are instructions to repeat the A sections "Dal Segno" or "Da Capo," sometimes extended by a brief coda. These forms were traditional enough to be instantly clear to audiences and players; they could also easily be abridged or cut short, to match the lengths of individual films.

Despite their conventionality, these pieces are well crafted and possess distinctive traits, as the first number will illustrate. It is a polka (see the transcription given in Ex. 1), with square-cut phrases in the form shown in Table 2.1.

The individuality of the piece stems principally from details of harmony and texture: for example, the suave shift from A major to F major for the middle strains of the A section, and the contrapuntal combination of melodies in high and low registers (flute and violin, horn and bassoon) within the Trio. These features impart to the piece a certain charm; yet we may wonder if its style has much to do with the film it probably accompanied. In no way does it seem especially Italian, or childlike, or suggestive of a peasant dance (unless a polka per se can be so construed). Moreover, the polka was one of several numbers which accompanied films of stage performances, and without viewing these films we have no way of knowing whether they were intended to match the performers' movements phrase by phrase, in choreographic fashion. Even if they were, for other films, such as the boxing match, details of musical style probably had little to do with image content, no matter how appropriate the music in a general sense.

Further discussion of specific functional relationships between music and individual films must be deferred until those that do survive have been closely examined. However, it is worth noting that the two framing pieces, the Introduction (marked Andante mosso) and the Finale (marked Maestoso), seem to have been composed with details of the show specifically in mind. Both of them are more continuous than the other pieces, without any internal repeat signs or contrasting B sections, and these "free" structures probably originated in the special

EX.1. Skladanowsky music: *Polka* (no. 1)

EX.1. *(continued)*

EX.1. (*continued*)

EX.1. (*continued*)

EX.1. (*continued*)

EX.1. *(continued)*

EX.I. (*continued*)

EX.I. (continued)

EX.1. *(continued)*

EX.I. (*continued*)

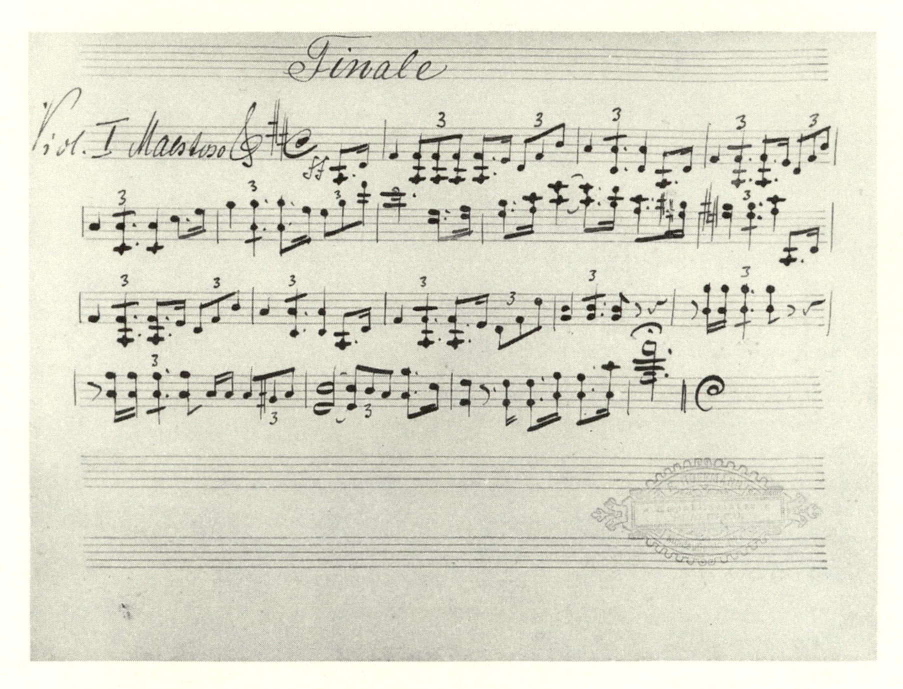

FIGURE 4. Skladanowsky music: Violin part for the *Finale.*

functions of the music. The Introduction gives prolonged emphasis to the tonic key, sustained by swirling arpeggios, scales, and repeated notes (cf. Fig. 1): its style is that of an exciting overture in miniature, meant to launch the program as a whole rather than to accompany a particular film. As for the Finale, it has a simple type of parallel structure: two similar phrases (8 + 9 measures), each filled with conventional fanfares (Fig. 4). The music was conceived for the final film, the show's "Apotheosis," wherein the Skladanowsky brothers took their bows; we may presume they did so to generous applause from the audience, encouraged by the orchestra's bright chords.

With the Skladanowsky music one confronts basic questions faced by all compilers: How many pieces should be used? What types of pieces should they be? How long should each be played? Each film program of the 1890s may have forced musicians to rethink their answers to these questions. Such at least is the inference to be drawn from a brief comparative examination of a second compilation, dating from 1897.

In this second case the music is not known to survive, but a detailed program does: it was printed on silk for a "command" performance of the *cinématographe* before Queen Victoria at Windsor Castle.[46] The program lists fifteen picture titles side by side with musical numbers, which were played by the Empire orchestra under Leopold Wenzel, as follows:

Cinématographe picture	*Music (and composer)*
PART I	
1. The Bois de Boulogne	PAS DE CINQ from *Monte Cristo* Ballet (L. Wenzel)
2. The Czar of Russia in Paris	MARCHE DE COURONNEMENT (Preisgekrönt)
3. Spanish Dancers in Castille	DANSE ESPAGNOLE from *Dolly* Ballet (L. Wenzel)
4. A Charge of French Cavalry	INFANTERIE CAVALERIE CHARGE (C. Millôker)
5. Blacksmiths at Work 6. Hussars Passing through Dublin	LES VOLONTAIRES MARCHE (O. Métra)
7. Carnival at Nice	LE PETIT BLEU VALSE (L. Wenzel)
PART II	
8. A Scene in Parliament Street 9. The Disputed Fare	LOIN DU BAL (E. Gillet)
10. A Soudanese Swimming Bath 11. A Joke on the Gardener	VALSE from *By the Sea* Ballet (L. Wenzel)
12. Serpentine and Butterfly Dances	VALSE from *Versailles* Ballet (L. Wenzel)
13. The Naval Review	A LIFE ON THE OCEAN, NAUTICAL SELECTIONS (E. Binding)
PART III	
14. The Diamond Jubilee Procession	a. A WEDDING MARCH (ON THE OCCASION OF THE DUKE OF YORK'S WEDDING) b. VERCINGETORIX MARCH c. JUBILEE MARCH from *Under One Flag* Ballet (L. Wenzel)
15. Scene Taken from a Moving Train near Clapham Junction	MÉTROPOLITAIN GALOP (Ch. Hubans)

This program, intended to be an evening's entertainment for a royal audience, was more elaborate and more varied than Skladanowsky's. Apparently, some skits (or story films) were included at the start of the second part of the program (nos. 9 and 11, possibly nos. 8 and 10 as well), followed by a dance film like the one in Skladanowsky's program, and a bit of documentary footage. Moreover, the program included three additional items (not shown in the list above), which were used to introduce each part: an Overture taken from Massenet's *Le Cid*, an entr'acte taken from the Overture to Gounod's *Philémon et Baucis*, and a live act featuring performing dogs, accompanied by a waltz, *La Nuit*, by O. Métra.

The music, too, differs from the compilation prepared for Skladanowsky. Wenzel, unlike Krüger, is named as the composer for more than half of the numbers, mostly consisting of excerpts from his ballet scores; and in all three parts there are places where he did not adhere to the method of accompanying each film with a separate piece of music. Perhaps the most striking example involves *Loin du bal*, which accompanied the Serpentine Dance in Skladanowsky's program; here it seems to have been matched—for no self-evident reason—to two dissimilar films at the start of Part II. Possibly some of the films were so short that Wenzel thought it best to use one piece of music to cover two films at a time, thereby allowing the music's lyric and rhythmic patterns to be heard more fully. In Part III, by contrast, a single film, "The Diamond Jubilee Procession," is accompanied by three marches in a row. We cannot know Wenzel's reasons with certainty; but in comparing the Skladanowsky and Windsor programs, we can see different ways of reflecting individual film content—or not reflecting it—in musical terms.

Compilation was a pragmatic method of providing music for variety programs, both live and on film, and it insured that some sort of appropriate music would be heard number by number; but by the end of this century's first decade, filmed "varieties" had given way to programs containing fewer and longer films. These were mostly narratives, and with their ascendance arose new problems for musicians: in particular, how to match music to specific details of the narrative, while at the same time creating a sense of continuity and coherence. We shall see, in subsequent chapters, how some American pioneers dealt with these matters in scores they compiled for films produced between 1910 and 1915; but for the moment we turn from examples of compilation to the music composed by Saint-Saëns in 1908 for *L'Assassinat du Duc de Guise*. While perhaps not the earliest example of an original film score, it was certainly the first by a composer of his stature, and he met the challenge well: the music integrates small-scale dramatic details within a large-scale musical form to a degree rarely equaled during the rest of the silent period.

L'Assassinat was among the first and most successful films to be made by the Société Film d'Art, a company founded in 1907 and known during the next several years for its innovative productions.[47] As the term implies, "Films d'Art" were meant to earn the respect of the cultural elite as well as the patronage of large audiences, and one way of achieving these goals was by means of elaborate historical dramas, concerned with noble characters—for example, *L'Assassinat*. Lasting longer than was then usual (about eighteen minutes), the picture more or less accurately depicts the events of the day in 1588 when King Henri III summoned his powerful rival, Duke Henri de Guise, to his chambers at the Château de Blois, and had him brutally murdered.[48] As in other motion pictures of the period, this one has its share of lurid thrills, and the pacing is quick throughout; but it was better acted than most, and carefully staged in a realistic, albeit theatrical manner. Events transpire on sets with painted backdrops, and the camera records each scene from a single stationary position, equivalent to a seat on the main floor of a theater, not far from the "stage"; and it was precisely these theatrical qualities which audiences found impressive, as they did the credentials of its production team. Co-directors André Calmettes and Charles Le Bargy were both eminent actors, and Le Bargy, a member of the Comédie française, appeared in the film as Henri III; other cast members were drawn from the Maison de Molière; sets and costumes were the work of Émile Bertin, well known in Paris for his stagecraft; and the creator of the script, Henri Lavedan, was a successful playwright and member of L'Académie française.

Saint-Saëns was a logical choice for such a prestigious venture, because, at age seventy-three, he was probably France's most celebrated composer, and he had acquired extensive experience in elevated genres of theater music;[49] but information about how he approached the project is scarce and somewhat ambiguous. Bonnerot, his friend and biographer, tells us first that he worked out the music "scene by scene before the screen"; second, that owing to the approach of winter he left Paris before the film's premiere, leaving to Fernand LeBorne the task of conducting the orchestra—and presumably of making sure the music fit the film.[50] Thus, the premiere was held in the composer's absence, at the Salle Charras on 17 November 1908.[51] Yet Saint-Saëns thought highly enough of the music to see that a piano reduction of the score, dedicated to LeBorne, was published by Durand that year; and in 1909 there appeared a set of parts for what was perhaps the original ensemble: a chamber orchestra, consisting of four woodwinds, piano, harmonium, and strings.[52]

In its own way, the occasion for *L'Assassinat*'s premiere was as much a variety show as Skladanowsky's had been thirteen years earlier, though in this case the show was a high-toned one throughout, befitting such an "art film." Sponsored and advertised by the Société under the title "Visions d'Art," the various entertainments mostly combined mute imagery and live music. According to notices in *Le Temps*, which included a thoughtful review by Adolphe Brisson,[53] there were two other films beside *L'Assassinat*, each with an original score of its own. The first, *Le Secret de Myrto*, termed "a musical legend," depicted ballerina Regina Badet dancing to music of Gaston Berardi. The second, *L'Empreinte*, a "mimodrame" with music by LeBorne, contained a series of "picturesque tableaux" using silhouettes of Pierrot and other pantomime figures; and it was said to be mimed "with extraordinary fantasy" by Mistinguette and Max Dearly. (The scores for *Myrto* and *L'Empreinte* were published at about the same time as the one for *L'Assassinat*.[54]) The program also included color photographs of the Orient, described as "fairy-tale views" taken by Gervais-Courtellemont; and Le Bargy recited Rostand's poem *Le Bois sacrée*, which was said to be "illustrated by a ballet—or rather, a choreographic vision."[55]

Brisson was intrigued but not entirely convinced by the attempts to place artistic styles of dance and pantomime on film; and in the case of *L'Assassinat* he wondered whether film should really attempt to reproduce historical drama in the manner of live theater. But though some aspects of the affair he considered "imperfect," he noted with approval the innovative, experimental nature of the program as a whole; and at the conclusion of his review, he commented most favorably on the score by Saint-Saëns, which he termed "a masterpiece of symphonic music."[56]

To praise a score in such terms is to imply that it can be appreciated like concert music, apart from its film—a dangerous claim for any film score, and one that often suggests the critic has missed the point. But for once the claim has some validity. *L'Assassinat* has sufficient intricacy, coherence, and expressive power to be compared, for example, with the tone poems composed by Saint-Saëns thirty years before. However, although the tone poems might be considered as ancestors to the film score, since both genres "translate" narratives into music, even the longest of the earlier works (*La Jeunesse d'Hercule*, 1877) is shorter than *L'Assassinat*; and, having been written for the concert stage, they were shaped according to different principles. A closer relation to *L'Assassinat* is to be found in the functional music of *Javotte*, a "ballet in one act and three tableaux," for which Saint-Saëns composed the score in 1896. The published score contains music of two distinct kinds: (1) pantomimic segments in which the music changes frequently and is carefully cued; and (2) autonomous dances constructed in regular metric units, with very few cues or none at all. For example, in the first Tableau, the music accompanying a scene in which the dancers mimic a conversation has cuing so precise that seven times the word "Non!" is aligned with the second or third beat of a measure. (One can see a resemblance to Paulin's score for Reynaud's *Pantomimes lumineuses*, discussed above.) A counter-example is supplied a few pages later by the beginning of the Bourrée, which lacks any indication of stage action. Thus, in a manner typical of its genre, *Javotte* combines fluid pantomime with patterned ballet.[57] In the case of *L'Assassinat*, owing to the intense subject matter, one finds abundant music of the first type, but none of the second. Though the printed score contains only nine terse cues (for example, "Entrée du page," "Entrée du Duc," "Départ du Duc," etc.), study of the music in relationship to the film makes clear that it follows much of the action just as closely—with and without cues—as in portions of *Javotte*.[58]

What is remarkable is how successfully Saint-Saëns achieved this result, within a well-wrought musical form that is almost entirely dictated by the structure of the film. Both story and score are laid out in a series of "Tableaux," each introduced by one or more title cards which set the scene and/or explain the gist of the action. Paraphrased translations of those titles are given in italics below, supplemented by bracketed sentences which appear in published versions of the scenario, though apparently not in extant copies of the film.

I. [At the Château de Blois, in the apartment of the Marquise de Noirmoutiers. Friday, 23 December 1588, 5 a.m.] *The Duke de Guise is warned of the King's sinister intentions.*

II. [The bedchamber of the King at the Château de Blois. Same day, same time.] *King Henri III plans the assassination of the Duke de Guise.*

III. *The council room. The King has the Duke de Guise summoned.*

IV. [The Murder.] *The King's guards (the "Forty-Five") stab Henri de Guise.*
   [1. The King's bedchamber.]
   [2. The antechamber of the "Cabinet Vieux."]
   [3. The Cabinet Vieux.]
   [4. The antechamber of the Cabinet Vieux.]

V. [5. The King's bedchamber.]
Henri III makes sure that the Duke is actually dead.
VI. [The Corpse.] *The guard room.*[59]

As can be seen in this outline, Tableaux I–III and VI were all filmed in one setting apiece (and in a single shot); but in Tableaux IV and V, which depict the murder, there is a different, innovative sort of mise-en-scène: through five consecutive shots, symmetrically arranged, the camera records the struggles and death throes of the Duke as he moves from the King's bedchamber into the "Cabinet Vieux," and back again.[60] Accordingly, Saint-Saëns treats these tableaux as a unit, and divides his score into five such segments rather than six, preceded by an Introduction. Analogous to the film's use of titles, each musical tableau is set apart from the others by a pause; and each begins with a clearly defined meter, tempo, theme, and key that contrast with those that precede and/or follow.

The structure is one of classical clarity, as was customary for Saint-Saëns; moreover, it enabled him to achieve powerful dramatic effects by means of two favorite techniques. (1) *Thematic transformation*: four main themes are introduced early on, then brought back at several points in both varied and original forms.[61] (2) *An arching harmonic design, rich in modulation*: overall the key of the score is F♯ minor, but after the Introduction this key is mostly avoided until the close of the fifth tableau. These elements are summarized in Appendix part 2, which outlines the structure of the score, and serves as the basis for the analysis that follows. (Henceforth, Arabic rather than Roman numerals shall be used to designate the score's Tableaux.)

All four of the recurring themes (three introduced in the course of the Introduction, one within Tableau 1), are distinctive, open-ended fragments capable of flexible treatment; and as presented and manipulated by Saint-Saëns, they are charged with dramatic significance. For example, the first two themes, juxtaposed at the beginning of the Introduction, make a sharply contrasted pair, suggestive of the conflict between the film's two principal characters (Exs. 2a and 2b). The first possesses a chromatic, serpentine motion that seems to reflect the cunning and menace of Henri III; the second, with its initial upward leaps of a fourth, fifth, and fourth, followed by a descending sequence, perhaps symbolizes the ambition and arrogance of the Duke, as well as his eventual death.[62]

The tension created by this pair of themes is largely a result of their harmonic and rhythmic instability. The first theme, in F♯ minor, begins on the dominant degree of the scale, descends to circle chromatically around the tonic, and returns to its starting point by way of the sharped fourth degree. As if in reply, the second theme begins with a cadential figure that leaps from dominant to tonic, and ends by moving chromatically to the relative major (D), again by way of the sharped fourth degree. Thus, neither theme finds a stable resting point; and the feeling of restlessness is accentuated by the continuous accompaniment, consisting of arpeggiated sixth chords deep in the bass. This texture is maintained, and tension increased, through the sequencing of the whole passage in the relative major key, until the music dovetails into a new theme: a two-measure fragment with a tremolo accompaniment more agitated than before (Ex. 3, mm. 21 and 22).

EX. 2A. Saint Saëns, *L'Assassinat du Duc de Guise*, Introduction, mm. 1–5

EX. 2B. *L'Assassinat*, Introduction, mm. 6–12

With the new theme the Introduction comes to an ominous climax, matched to the film's beginning. As can be seen in the example below, Theme 3 is headed by the score's first cue, "l'annonce," which indicates the appearance of the title of the picture on screen. Presumably Saint-Saëns meant for the previous music to be heard before the picture began (while the audience sat expectantly in the dark); now he explicitly associates the third theme with the story's main action, and the first word of the title, "L'Assassinat." (As confirmation of this point, it may be noted that once introduced, the theme does not return until the middle of Tableau 4, when the assassination actually takes place.) The third theme has a particularly strong impact, because like both previous ones it begins on the dominant (C♯), which is now reinterpreted as a dissonant appogiatura above a diminished triad; and also because, as the credits continue, it is extended with sequential chains of suspensions, moving upward to its highest and loudest point above a dominant pedal, approached in the bass once more from the sharped fourth degree. From here the music moves downward to an inconclusive cadence on the tonic. It lacks a sense of closure, because the melody hangs on the fifth of the chord while the harmonies underneath continually shift, and even the fleeting appearance of F♯ major is unsettling: the raised third of the chord falls back down, and the key shifts from the minor tonic to its relative major, for the start of the first tableau (Ex. 4).

The beginning portion of Tableau 1 serves to demonstrate how Saint-Saëns uses both new and old themes to follow the action closely.[63] The story begins with a brief morning scene for the solitary Marquise de Noirmoutiers, the Duke's mistress. As she is seen to emerge from her bedchamber, a lively theme in minuet style

EX. 3. *L'Assassinat*, Introduction, mm. 21–26

EX. 4. *L'Assassinat*, Tableau 1, mm. 1–5

appears—the score's only Javottian moment—and lifts the dark spell cast by the Introduction. But the sense of relief is short-lived. When the Marquise learns of a threat to the Duke's life (by means of a warning note brought by her page), Saint-Saëns depicts her distress by returning to the opening pair of themes and their darker harmonies (Ex. 5, mm. 21–31). Following Theme 1 in B minor, Theme 2 returns to F♯ minor for an emphatic cadence (mm. 31–33); however, after a leap to C♯ in the highest octave yet heard, the music modulates immediately to the remote key of C major (m. 37). The cue for this sudden shift is the Duke's entrance, after which the Marquise, knowing that he will react impetuously, tries to hide the warning note, and to distract him with affectionate caresses. In accompanient to her actions comes the fourth main theme, marked "*espressivo*" (mm. 38 and 39, etc.).

This theme and its development have much to tell, for like Theme 3, it is a two-measure fragment that is extended and worked to a climax. Its lyrical elements, especially the upward appoggiatura and major sixth (m. 39), communicate the Marquise's tender feelings for the Duke; at the same time, there is subdued tension in the unyielding dominant pedal point and the lack of a root harmony in the bass, suggestive of her suppressed fears. At first it seems as if those fears have been vanquished, when the throbbing bass line drops out and the melody broadens in approach to a cadence (Ex. 6, mm. 46–49); but at this point the Duke discovers the warning note, and the cadence is thwarted. A new version of Theme 1 is sequenced up over two agitated chords (mm. 50–54), and the temporary tonic (C) is pushed aside—just as the Duke repulses the Marquise, despite her pleas.

As such analysis demonstrates, the music of Tableau 1 is full of twists of harmony and transformations of theme, inspired by the fluid, emotional narrative; and so, too, is the unsettling manner in which the tableau closes, by means of two contrasting cadences in C major. The first is broad and emphatic, to match the Duke's defiant departure, and it seems to announce the end of Tableau 1; but, in a gesture appropriate for a coda, the cadence is dovetailed with a shift to the subdominant harmony (F major) and a return to Theme 4, as the Marquise is seen to gaze smilingly at her lover through an open window. Then, as she closes the window and turns back into the room in evident distress, there is a final agitated statement of Theme 1, now in C minor. (At this moment it is more than ever appropriate to think of Theme 1 as the King's theme, because it is heard while the

EX. 5. *L'Assassinat*, Tableau 1, mm. 21–40

Marquise crosses the room to make her exit and passes his portrait; she acknowledges it with a defiant toss of her head.) The theme subsides as quickly as it arose, and gives way to a second cadence on C; but it is approached unconventionally (from a diminished seventh chord rather than from a dominant), and seems tentative at best. Moreover, in the larger context, C major cannot be construed as a restful resolution, because it is as far away from the true tonic (on the circle of fifths) as one can get; and it is immediately undercut by the beginning of Tableau 2, in C♯ minor.

EX. 6. *L'Assassinat,* Tableau 1, mm. 46–53

Saint-Saëns follows similar strategies throughout the rest of the score, so that tension remains high until the story comes to its tragic denouement in the final tableau; yet in some respects Tableaux 2 and 3 seem more classically balanced than the others, because each has a clear, essentially tripartite, rounded form. That is, the composer begins each of them with a new theme that is extensively developed (*c* and *f* in the structural outline given in Appendix part 2); and later he returns to each after introducing contrasting themes. Even so, at least two of them (*e* and *g*), bear some resemblance to earlier material; and the reappearance of Theme 2 in the course of the second Tableau, and of Theme 4 at the end of the third, disrupt the symmetries. Moreover, like Tableau 1, the second and third both remain unresolved within the larger harmonic context, owing to emphasis on keys in dominant regions: Tableau 2 begins and ends in C♯ minor, Tableau 3 begins in F minor and ends in F major, with a sudden surprising shift to D♭ major in the final bars.

Notwithstanding these points, Tableau 2, and especially Tableau 3, accompany segments of the film which are shorter than the others and more limited in action, and this accounts for the music's relative simplicity; it is in Tableau 4 that Saint-Saëns achieves his richest formal and dramatic effects, inspired by the film's most cinematically exciting moments. The music begins with a wrenching gesture, matched to the opening title and the entrance of the Duke: after the soft close of Tableau 3 in D♭ major—the disguised dominant of the home key—Saint-Saëns abruptly tears off the disguise and sounds a forceful statement of the first part of Theme 2 in F♯ minor (Ex. 7, mm. 1 and 2). What follows is new material (Theme *h*, shown in Ex. 7, mm. 3–8), heard as the Duke is seen being led into the King's inner chambers, where assassins are poised. This music is in the style of a conventional *misterioso*, except that the chromatic profile of the melody and the unpredictable direction of its modulations lift it above convention. The measure-long chromatic phrase seems like a slowed-down version of Theme 1—probably meant to suggest the presence of Henry III, waiting for his victim—and in irregular fashion the music sequences through F♯ minor, A minor, E♭ minor

EX. 7. *L'Assassinat*, Tableau 4, mm. 1–7

and F minor, finally settling upon C minor, when there comes a measure's expectant pause (Ex. 8, mm. 14–17).

When the assassins spring, the music explodes into a *presto* development of Theme 2, the Duke's, now subjected to an intense transformation and agitated development, filled with tritones and diminished seventh chords (Ex. 8).[64] By placing this passage in C minor, Saint-Saëns has further developed one key aspect of the score's harmonic design, the tritonal opposition between F♯ and C that was established in Tableau 1. In the present scene the music modulates furiously while the Duke struggles and drags his assailants from one room to another; but for his collapse and death, the music returns to C minor, first in a quiet passage on a dominant pedal, then in two new versions of the Duke's theme, the second giving solid confirmation to the key (Ex. 9, mm. 54–57 and 58–61).

From this point to the end of Tableau 4 there are additional musical surprises which match developments in the narrative. First and most intriguing is a seriocomic episode based on Theme *j* (Ex. 10), heard when the king, displaying caution and cunning, makes sure that the Duke is actually dead. Anthologists later in the silent period would be apt to label music of this type as "suitable for spooky or grotesque comedy scenes"; and as such, it borrows a page from Gounod's *Funeral March of a Marionette* (subsequently made familiar as the theme of the Alfred Hitchcock television series). The allusion to Gounod's piece seems appropriate, because here, as throughout the film, the king's movements are decidedly jerky and puppet-like. Still, in the present scene the king enjoys himself—the puppet becomes master, lording it over his victim—and Theme *j* plays itself out at length, firmly in F minor. Then come further surprises. First the body is removed and Henri, left alone, begins to pray; likewise the music turns to F major for a solemn religious codetta. But the close is undercut immediately by a shift back to F minor

EX. 8. *L'Assassinat*, Tableau 4, mm. 14–21

for the gruesome scene that follows. Soldiers are seen to carry the corpse down a winding stairway, and the music returns to the passage in *misterioso* style with which Tableau 4 began—that is, Theme *h*, now transposed down a semitone (Ex. 11).

A subtle connection can be drawn between the music of these two passages: both in Theme *j* and in the return of Theme *h* there are fragments that descend

EX. 9. *L'Assassinat*, Tableau 4, mm. 50–61

EX. 10. *L'Assassinat,* Tableau 4, mm. 86–90

and ascend chromatically, from F down to D♭ and back up to F. (Compare Exs. 10, mm. 89 and 90, and 11, m. 139.) This unifying device leads to another, covering a still broader span, in the Tableau's final moments; for after sinking chromatically measure by measure, the melody's D♭ is reinterpreted as C♯ (beginning in m. 142), the same pivotal enharmonic shift that was heard in the move from the end of Tableau 3 to the beginning of Tableau 4. In this way the music eventually comes to an inconclusive pause on the dominant of F♯ minor—an unexpected key in its immediate context, but one that serves to round the structure of Tableau 4 as a whole and point toward resolution.[65]

Within Tableau 5 the resolution comes, but only after still another harmonic surprise: in a sudden reversal of the previous passage, the key shifts back to F minor for restatement of Themes 1 and 2 in the same forms they had at the beginning of the Introduction. With these gestures, Saint-Saëns simultaneously points the music toward closure of its dramatic arc and delays it. True closure is achieved only in the second half of the Tableau, through restatements of all four themes in the score's home key, followed by many emphatic repetitions of the tonic chord.

This culminating music begins in accompaniment to another grotesque scene: soldiers have placed the Duke's body in a large hearth and set it on fire, at which point the Marquise finds it. Appropriately, as a comment on her mounting hysteria, Saint-Saëns brings back Theme 4 (her love theme) in extremely agitated forms, first in E♭ minor, ultimately in F♯ minor (Exx. 12a and 12b).

EX. 11. *L'Assassinat,* Tableau 4, mm. 139–142

EX. 12A. *L'Assassinat,* Tableau 5, mm. 45–47

EX. 12B. *L'Assassinat,* Tableau 5, mm. 61–63

At the end, while the Duke's theme and F♯ minor chords are hammered out, the Marquise is seen to be "so crazed with grief [that] she throws herself toward the king, who, as if to defend himself, abruptly removes his mask. The young woman recognizes him, falls backward and faints in the arms of two soldiers."[66]

Of course, this denouement partakes at least as much of melodrama as of "film d'art"; and to a great extent the music invokes melodramatic styles as well. Nevertheless, when the final chords sound, they bring a sense of resolution that is fully earned; for the composer has built the score to its climactic pages by means of complex thematic and harmonic techniques rarely encountered in most melodramas. We may not agree with Brisson's assessment of the music as a "masterpiece," but we can surely appreciate its virtues as theater music: neatly divided into six distinct segments, it follows the film closely, all the while displaying a rich variety of material, as well as convincing unity and dramatic power.

The foregoing analysis makes clear that the music for Skladanowsky's Bioskop shows and the score by Saint-Saëns are fundamentally different. Invoking current theoretical categories for two main types of early cinema, we may describe the former as an example of the "music of attractions," the latter as "music of narrative integration."[67] Additionally, we may note that each score invokes its own distinctive forerunners: Skladanowsky recalls the kaleidoscopic compilations of (mostly popular) music frequently encountered in music halls; *L'Assassinat,* some of the nineteenth century's most complex styles of dramatic music, as well as various styles of pantomime and melodrama. Still, in one respect these scores stand together, to share applause upon a single stage. As pioneering efforts, pointing the way ahead, they demonstrate that film music of the earliest years encompassed the same broad range of possibilities encountered in dramatic music before and after. Furthermore, though both scores have now been pretty much forgotten, the problems they confronted, and the solutions they proposed, remain constant. In various ways all film music—at least of the silent period, perhaps in every period—can remind us of one or the other, or both.

THREE

Film Scores in America, 1910–14

Overview

This chapter examines a transitional period within the history of music for silent films in America—a period that saw the emergence of feature films and special scores to go with them. Within this period the term "special score" took on a particular meaning, divorced from musical content: it came to designate scores that were created for *and distributed with* particular films, as opposed to accompaniments that were improvised or prepared by musicians within individual theaters. Special scores were reproduced—and in some cases published—in multiple copies, to be performed in as many theaters as possible. Before sound film, and within the structure of an industry that encouraged exhibitions of the same film across the country simultaneously, they represented the most elaborate efforts to control the music for such exhibitions in a systematic fashion.

A significant number of special scores appeared in America between 1910 and 1914. Sixteen are known to be extant for films made during 1912 (mostly by Walter Cleveland Simon); five scores survive from 1913 (two anonymous, three by Giuseppe Becce—the latter were originally published in Germany); and ten from 1914 (by three American composers—George Colburn, Manuel Klein, and Noble Kreider). These 31 scores, many of which were registered for copyright and survive in LC, will be found listed in Appendix part 3. In that list they are not alone. For although they are the only *extant* scores from these years, there is indirect evidence pointing toward the distribution of special scores for dozens of other films. With these titles added to the list, the number exceeds one hundred.

The greatest single source of indirect evidence—indeed, "the most valuable research tool of the period"—is *Moving Picture World* (henceforth abbreviated as *MPW*).[1] Some of this trade weekly's early literature on silent film music was described in Chapter One; in the present chapter scrutiny is given primarily to many miscellaneous items—in particular, to its weekly film advertisements, reviews, and "Manufacturer's Advance Notes"—because in these can be found many brief comments concerning music for individual films. Of course, information from this type of literature is often inaccurate and at best incomplete. Nevertheless, *MPW* provides glimpses of many films and film scores that might otherwise be forgotten.

Referring to the important early features recovered during the 1970s, Everson suggested that "1913/1914 may be one of the great lost frontiers of film scholarship, likely to reveal more examples of modernity and sophistication in film-making than historians have ever suspected."[2] Leaving aside the question of modernity—to confront it would be premature—historians of film music are faced with a similar "lost frontier," from which much remains to be recovered. For example, while there are several extant scores by Simon dating from 1912, the films they accompany have not been found; conversely, the 1912 film *Queen Elizabeth* survives without its score, even though the latter was evidently registered for copyright (Appendix part 3, no. 29). Still, despite the gaps we can draw at least one important conclusion by looking carefully at *MPW*'s reportage during this period and at those special scores which remain. Generally speaking, they were of two distinct types: early on, most were composed or compiled for piano; the years 1912–14 saw the advent of orchestral compilations, fewer in number but ultimately of greater consequence.

Both types of scores will be investigated below, in three stages. First there comes an account of preliminary developments, together with a brief discussion of some of the earliest scores listed in Appendix part 3; second, a study of the Kalem series, focused on Simon's score for *An Arabian Tragedy* (no. 19); and third, a summary of what is known about the careers and works of two key figures in the history of film music, S. L. Rothapfel and Joseph Carl Breil, between 1912 and 1914.

Until now the special scores of this period have not been made the object of detailed inquiry. One reason is that during the later years of the silent film most of them were already forgotten. A trade book published in 1927 illustrates this point: it states that "*The Birth of a Nation* [released in 1915] marked the initial attempt at a fully synchronized score for a photoplay."[3] Similarly, in a manual published in 1921 George Beynon states that before Griffith's film special scores were almost non-existent:

> During the slow growth of the cue-sheet, musical scores crept into existence. The Essanay company of Chicago produced a feature of five reels accompanied by a piano score which could be played on the organ. These scores were rented to the exhibitor at fifty cents a day and proved very helpful, but not a financial gain to the company. This was in 1912, and there were no further experiments in musical scores until the run of *The Birth of a Nation* in New York during the year of 1915.[4]

Beynon was an arranger and conductor of scores, not an historian;[5] perhaps for this reason, in his manual he devoted only a short chapter to an overview of "the evolution of picture music" before moving on to more practical matters of musical presentation. Even so, his memory is remarkably fuzzy. The paragraph quoted above ignores many scores that appeared only five to eight years before the date of his book's publication.

Perhaps because *The Birth of a Nation* was successful enough to remain in circulation many years, and because the score for the film made a very strong impression, Beynon and other first-hand observers over-emphasized the music's historical significance. None of the films and film scores listed in the Appendix endured in a manner comparable to *The Birth of a Nation*; but when many of them first appeared, they were heralded, in *MPW* and elsewhere, as important steps forward. There is a need to return to the perspectives of that pre-*Birth* era to give them their due.

The following study places some of these scores in context, and thereby helps to chronicle a little-known period in the history of American film music. Its point of departure is the ideal of suitable and repeatable accompaniments, an ideal that *MPW* did much to promote. Today it may seem that *The Birth of a Nation* was the first film to make the ideal a reality; but en route to Griffith's film, a hundred or more special scores marked the way.

Preliminary Steps and Early Scores

The premiere of *L'Assassinat du Duc de Guise* in Paris was a well-publicized theatrical and musical event. When the picture traveled to the United States, it was treated very differently. There is no trace of any special premiere for the film like the "Visions d'Art" program described above. In *MPW* Pathé Frères simply announced the picture as one of its current "dramatic" releases in February 1909, at a length of 853 feet—considerably shorter than the version for which Saint-Saëns had composed his score; and the company dropped the film from its listings five weeks later.[6]

L'Assassinat was a special film with a special score, and neither was suited to the nickelodeon-centered American film industry of 1909. *MPW* ignored the music altogether (and we can infer from its silence that the score probably was not heard in America at that time); toward the film, *MPW*'s attitude was ambivalent. For example, in late February an anonymous reviewer made clear that he admired the production, but he doubted the film's success with American audiences, who were ignorant of the story's historical basis.[7] A few weeks later, his reservations were echoed in a letter with the pointed title, "Simpler Subjects Needed." The correspondent criticized the current crop of films on "historical subjects," claiming that they appealed to the "cultured classes" but not to the "public of today"; in a postcript the editors concurred, offering the opinion that many recent films ran "'above the heads' of the popular audiences."[8]

Elsewhere in the same issue one of *MPW*'s editors, Thomas Bedding, wrote about the film in quite a different manner. His inaugural article for a series entitled "The Modern Way in Moving Picture Making" singled out *L'Assassinat* as a promising model for the future, with this strong endorsement:

> *The Assassination of the Duke of Guise* . . . is comparable to the finest productions of Sir Henry Irving. . . . I have no hesitation in pronouncing the film in question as an ideal piece of stage craft in the way of silent drama.[9]

Today the wooden "stage craft" of films such as *L'Assassinat* make them seem archaic, just as any attempt to define moving pictures solely in theatrical terms seems inadequate. But as Bedding saw them, Film d'Art productions stood at film-making's cutting edge, and in this opinion he was not alone. One finds equal praise in an essay by Walter Eaton that appeared in *American Magazine* (a progressive journal) later in the same year. Bedding had focused his remarks upon *L'Assassinat*; Eaton's observations took a more extensive view. He compared this country's "canned" (i.e., filmed) dramas with those put out by the French and found the latter to be "far ahead" on many fronts. They had better photography, better acting, and, most important, better dramatic construction; Eaton further characterized the Pathé "films d'art" as "real dramas, with real actors portraying real emotions." His hope was that such productions would elevate the tastes of American moviegoers and induce "a better understanding of theatric art."[10]

These commentaries signaled the beginning of major shifts in both the content of films and the economic system for their production and distribution. Regarding *content*, one can see gradual expansion of the length and narrative complexity of films only a few years after the appearance of *L'Assassinat*. In 1911 and 1912 the "art film" genre established by Pathé began to find large American audiences; they welcomed the import of many European spectacles, along with the indigenous "Famous Plays with Famous Players" of Frohman and Zukor. It was at this time, too, that films came to be called "photoplays," a term that remained current during the remainder of the silent period (and one that reflected film's imitation of theater in a far more appealing way than Eaton's "canned drama"). With such photoplays in the lead, the industry moved toward production of feature-length pictures which gradually became the norm.[11]

Within this same period one finds equally important changes in the *economic system* of film production and distribution. Early on much of the impetus for change came from public outcries against the supposed immorality of films. Partly in response to these pressures, and partly to increase efficiency, American film producers formed the Motion Picture Patents Company through the imposition of a license agreement that took effect beginning on 1 January 1909. This oligarchy has recently been credited with "ending the foreign domination of American screens" (by companies such as Pathé), "increasing film quality through internal competition, and standardizing film distribution and exhibition practices."[12] Owing to these developments, middle-class audiences were drawn to the movies in increasing numbers.[13]

One element of film exhibition that between 1909 and 1911 became a matter of increasing concern was music, and attention now turns to three ways in which attempts were made to promote its improvement and standardization: first, the reform-minded criticisms of film music in *MPW*; second, the publication of early cue sheets and anthologies; and third, the distribution of special scores. With each of these developments the range of possibilities for film music broadened; and one of the most interesting aspects of the period is the way various reformers looked toward opera for inspiration.

During *MPW*'s earliest years (between 1907 and 1910) music was not altogether neglected; but at first most of the writing concerned peripheral matters, such as "illustrated songs." These were live performances of popular numbers, matched line by line or verse by verse with colorful lantern slides. Such numbers had been common in vaudeville theaters for years, and from there they spread to the nickelodeons—a continuation of film music's ties to the "variety" show.[14] Most early issues of *MPW* during this period contained lists of current songs for which lantern slides were available and also detailed descriptions of the slides for a few songs.[15] *MPW* also gave considerable attention—in both articles and advertisements—to phonographic synchronizing devices, special types of mechanical instruments, and lectures for individual films, which contained brief suggestions for music.[16]

At first the only hints of a *critical* literature appeared in general reports on economic trends and theatrical management;[17] but after mid-1909, impelled by the reformist current, *MPW* began to subject musical practices to sustained criticism, placed in prominent parts of the magazine. Judging from this literature, we can conclude that there was much to criticize—that, indeed, dramatically appropriate accompaniments were the exception rather than the rule. To illustrate the point, four pioneering examples of *MPW*'s criticism are summarized below.

1. "Editorial: The Musical End." *MPW* 3 July 1909, 7–8. In this, the first article on the subject of music to appear in *MPW*, prominently placed at the head of the issue, the music heard in "nearly every moving picture theater in New York City" is termed "lamentably deficient":

> The piano and some sound effects are usually considered sufficient: and oh, and oh, the piano and the players we sometimes hear and sometimes see! The former is more often than not out of tune, and the latter, though he can strike the keys with something like accuracy and precision, if not violence, cannot play music, or, if he can, he does not. In other words, speaking generally, the musical end of the moving picture house programme is, as a rule, so unsatisfactory that we think it our duty specially in this article to call attention to it.

Following this overview some ameliorative advice is offered: "to engage a small orchestra of strings" in addition to the pianist and the sound effects (drummer) normally heard, and to consider automatic instruments for the purpose of variety. The conclusion of the editorial is also constructive—and specifically informative: it applauds the music heard in New York's Keith and Proctor houses, where "it is a pleasure to sit and listen to the piano music."

2. Lux Graphicus [pseud.]. "On the Screen." *MPW* 4 September 1909, 312. Following the same constructive approach that appeared at the conclusion of the editorial cited above, the writer tries to stimulate musical improvement by drawing attention to a praiseworthy example—the pianist and the drummer at the Bijou Dream on Fourteenth Street, New York City:

> Never, at a moving picture theater have I heard, or seen, a girl enter so completely into the spirit of the pictures shown. She absolutely adapts her music to them. Every emotion, every sentiment, every movement, every mood illustrated on the screen, is duplicated by the tones of the piano. It is a perfect concordance of sound, movement and thought. . . . So with the drummer. He is absolutely master of the necessary effects. No animal is shown which does not find his peculiarities of articulation illustrated by some one of the drummer's battery of weird and

> startling instruments. He almost makes men and women talk, almost; they groan, they laugh, kiss, whisper, under his magic touch.

The writer concludes with a climactic litany of the two musicians' virtues: they work well together, subordinate themselves so as to play to the picture, please audiences, and "succeed because they are artists." The "moral of the song": music and effects "are of supreme importance in the proper presentation to the public of the moving picture play."

3. "Weekly Comments on the Shows: Among the Chicago Theatres." *MPW* 25 September 1909, 412. The crusade shifts to a new locale. The anonymous critic reports on three modest theaters, and in the last of them—the Pastime, on Madison Street—he observes "an exceptionally fine pianist who entertains the audience during intermission with well rendered selections." During the films, however, the entertainment ceases:

> . . . at no one of these three houses did the pianist apparently pay the slightest attention to the action in the film. In one house she played a religious selection while an S. & A. [Essanay] rip-roaring farce was being enacted, and (this is fact) in another picture, while the father and son were parting in tears she set forth the strains of "Don't Take Me Home." Such work is bad—very bad. In my judgement, managers who do not make their pianist follow the film closely with their music commit a very serious error.

4. F. H. Richardson. "Plain Talks to Theatre Managers and Operators, Chapter XXII: Seating/Music." *MPW* 30 October 1909, 599–600. As in the previous item, some "very bad" conditions are described, intermixed with advice:

> Get a good piano player, who can read any music at sight and make him or her attend strictly to business. Pay a salary which will justify you in demanding the best work and then see to it that your player makes good. A piano player who cannot read music at sight has no rightful place in a moving picture theater, especially if illustrated songs are run. But the song is a comparatively small matter. Always and invariably the piano player can help out a film wonderfully if he or she wants to and knows how. Often and often have I entered a theater while the film was running and seen the piano player industriously engaged in talking to a friend, dividing her attention impartially between the friend and a wad of gum. . . . The piano player should have a wide range of "know it by heart" music; [and] should watch the picture closely and play suitable music.

In larger houses (that is, theaters seating 300) drummers are also recommended—good ones—despite the cost: for the author "cannot impress too strongly on managers the advisability" of getting all they can out of the music.

The world of American film music, it seems, was filled by pianists (and drummers) of widely varied abilities and widely differing interest in the films for which they played. *MPW* addressed its remarks less to these musicians than to the exhibitors, and urged them to hire capable performers, and to make sure that the musicians "watch the picture closely." One thing *MPW* did *not* propose as a means of standardizing film music was the distribution of prepared scores. The musicians might improvise, "read at sight," or know the music "by heart": the mix was left to them to determine as they observed each picture.

Two types of published material—cue sheets and anthologies—facilitated the improvement of film music while allowing for varied use; and the earliest known examples of these aids to film music appeared within a few months of the literature cited above, in prototypical forms. The bimonthly *Edison Kinetogram* published its first lists of suggestions for music in mid-September, 1909, under the heading "Incidental Music for Edison Pictures"—a phrase which, as Berg has noted, tied them to earlier kinds of theater music.[18] It seems likely that pianists with theatrical experience would have found these suggestions easier to use than would newcomers to the field, because the suggestions refer mostly to categories of incidental music. For example, under the title of the first film, *How the Landlord Collected His Rent*, nine scenes are briefly described, with these musical recommendations: "1. March, brisk; 2. Irish jig; 3. Begin with Andante, finish with Allegro; 4. Popular air; 5. Ditto; 6. Andante with Lively at finish; 7. March (same as No. 1); 8. Plaintive; 9. Andante (use March of No. 1)."[19]

Such a list of cues was but a bare outline for the creation of a compiled score. Anthologies supplied pianists with specific pieces that could turn such outlines into actual compilations. The earliest known anthology, prepared by Gregg A. Frelinger, was entitled *Motion Picture Piano Music: Descriptive Music to Fit the Action, Character or Scene of Moving Pictures*.[20] It contained fifty-one pieces, all short and simple, and all headed with functional titles similar to those that appear in later, more elaborate anthologies. For easy reference these titles were indexed alphabetically at the front of the volume: "Aged Colored Man, Aged Persons, Ancient Dance, Andante, Antique Dance, Apparitions, Artistic Dance, Assembly Bugle Call, Bag Pipe Imitation," and so on. Some titles refer to tempos and moods; others to types of characters or incidents or plot.

MPW did much to promote both of these generically conceived aids to accompaniment. An editorial published in the fall of 1909 (between the third and fourth critical items summarized above) mentioned the Edison company's new policy of publishing suggestions for music, and noted that plans were being made for publication of an unnamed anthology.[21] Frelinger's collection was advertised for the first time at the year's end (under the heading "Descriptive Music"), and *MPW* called attention to the collection in a brief item the following week.[22] Two more piano collections were announced in 1910 (though neither appears to survive): the *Emerson Moving Picture Music Folio*, advertised for one week only, and the *Orpheum Collection of Moving Picture Music*, for eleven weeks.[23] (For advertisements of all three collections, see the reproductions in Figures 5, 6, and 7. In Figure 5, Frelinger's advertisement rests above four others [not shown], including one for song slides and one for lectures—signs of the varied exhibition practices of the period. In Figure 7, music has become the subject of an entire page of advertisements, with many musical instruments offered.) As for cue sheets: another film producer, Vitagraph, was praised by *MPW* for picking up Edison's idea and offering suggestions for its own films.[24] And at the end of 1910 *MPW* established a weekly column on "Music for the Picture," with cue sheets frequently included.[25]

Even as *MPW* tracked these developments, its editors began to look beyond cue sheets (and implicitly, beyond the anthologies to which they were connected) toward accompaniments of a different sort. In the spring of 1910 a lead editorial

Descriptive Music to Fit the Pictures
"Motion Picture Piano Music" is a Piano-Folio of Descriptive Music, (arranged for both hands, Treble and Bass Clefs) to fit the Action, Character or Scene of Moving Pictures. Price, One Dollar, postage free. Circular, fully describing this book will be sent free to any one upon request.
GREGG A. FRELINGER, Publisher
1069 FERRY STREET - - - LAFAYETTE, IND.

FIGURE 5. Advertisement for "Descriptive Music to Fit the Pictures." *MPW* 11 Dec. 1909, 845. (The photographs seen in Figures 5–10 were taken by Jon Harris, using the complete set of *MPW* in the Department of Film at MOMA, courtesy of Mary Lea Bandy and Ron Magliozzi. I am grateful for their assistance.)

termed the efforts of the Edison Company and others "a preliminary step," and the author(s) now evisaged a more "scientific" approach:

> Just as Wagner fitted his music to the emotions, expressed by the words in his operas, so in course of time, no doubt, the same thing will be done with regard to the moving picture.[26]

This analogy pointed the way toward special scores, though it seems that *MPW* did not truly anticipate scores in Wagner's style, despite the reference. Directly below the editorial, a second article praised a "special musical program" that had been prepared by William E. King, music director of Chicago's "exemplary" Orpheum theater, to accompany a Gaumont film, *A Penitent of Florence*. The description of King's music is vague and suggests a compilation (of unspecified music) rather than a continuous leitmotivic score. What excited *MPW*'s editors in this case was not the style of the music, but the care with which it had been prepared; and they promised to print the "musical program" for the film the following week.[27]

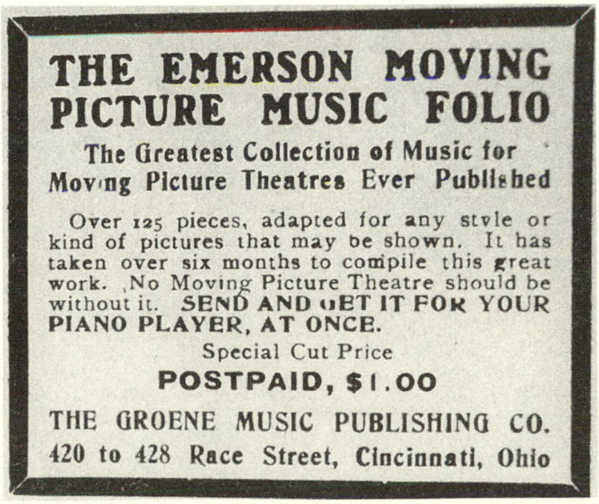

THE EMERSON MOVING PICTURE MUSIC FOLIO
The Greatest Collection of Music for Moving Picture Theatres Ever Published
Over 125 pieces, adapted for any style or kind of pictures that may be shown. It has taken over six months to compile this great work. No Moving Picture Theatre should be without it. SEND AND GET IT FOR YOUR PIANO PLAYER, AT ONCE.
Special Cut Price
POSTPAID, $1.00
THE GROENE MUSIC PUBLISHING CO.
420 to 428 Race Street, Cincinnati, Ohio

FIGURE 6. Advertisement for "The Emerson Moving Picture Music Folio." *MPW* 2 July 1910, 36.

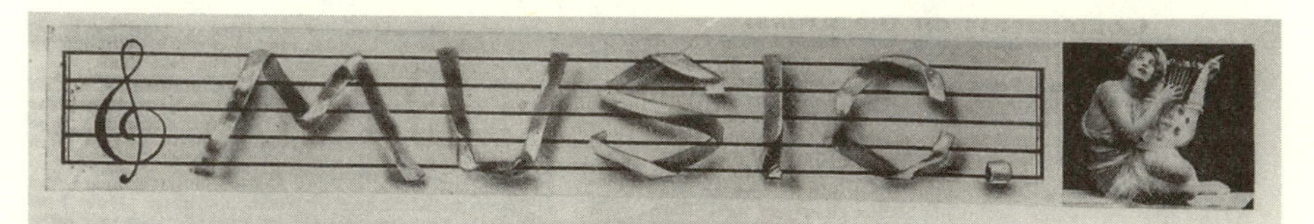

Real Music That Really Fits the Picture

"MOTION PICTURE PIANO MUSIC"

FIFTY CENTS A COPY.

A Piano Book that contains descriptive Music to fit all probable Scenes, Actions, Characters, etc., shown in Moving Pictures. Composed and compiled by a Professional Pianist of twenty years' experience in Theatrical lines. Brimfull of practical suggestions for the inexperienced Pianist in a M. P. Theater. Descriptive Circular sent free upon request. Book will be sent promptly upon receipt of fifty cents. Address,

FRELINGER MUSIC COMPANY
LAFAYETTE, IND.

Drums, Traps, and all Moving Picture Show Effects

Our New Beautifully Illustrated Catalogue now ready and will be sent free to any address upon request.

LOUIS B. MALECKI & CO.
272 WABASH AVENUE, CHICAGO.

The Pedal of the Hour

This latest invention eliminates all pedal worries. Produces natural arm struck tone. Ease of action phenomenal. Constructed entirely of metal. Strong and durable. Folds in space 9½ x 3½. Weight only 35 oz. Just the thing for vaudeville. Keep in touch with progress. Write for complete description and testimonials. We have everything you need for your line. We supply Chicago's leading picture houses with drums and effects.

LUDWIG & LUDWIG
134 E. Van Buren St., Room 610, Chicago, Ill.

Xylophones, Orchestra Bells, Chimes, Forks, etc. Send for free illustrated catalogue.

J. C. DEAGAN
3800-3810 N. Clark St., Chicago, Ill.

WURLIZER

Automatic Musical Instruments

They do the work of expert musicians and reduce operating expense.

Wurlitzer is the world's largest manufacturer. We supply the U. S. Government musical instruments. Write for big 84-page catalogue showing the only complete line of self-players, from a small electric piano to automatic orchestra representing 35 musicians. Easy payments.

Concert Piano Orchestra.

RUDOLPH WURLITZER & CO.

CINCINNATI—117 to 121 E. 4th; NEW YORK—25 & 27 W. 32d (bet. B'way & 5th Ave.); CHICAGO—266 & 268 Wabash Ave.; PHILADELPHIA—1835 Chestnut; ST. LOUIS—912 Pine; CLEVELAND—206 Prospect Ave., S. E.; COLUMBUS, O.—57 E. Main.

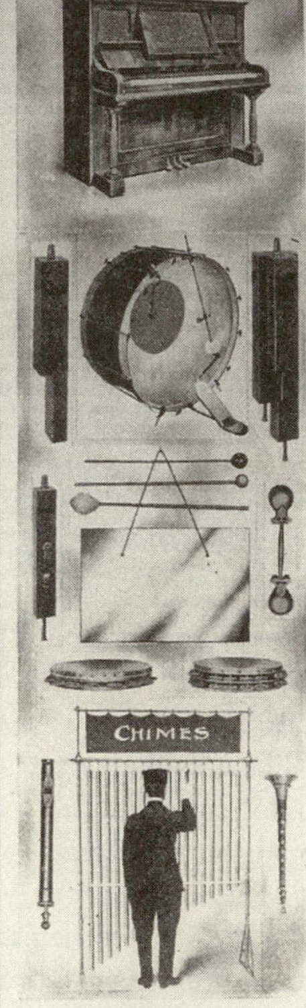

WURLITZER

OUR PATENT ELECTRIC BELLS create great enthusiasm in Moving Picture Houses, play from a keyboard as a solo instrument, or as an accompaniment to songs. Twenty-five Bells, two octaves chromatic, including resonators, magnets and keyboard, $75.00.

J. C. DEAGAN
3800-3810 N. Clark St., Chicago, Ill.

Moving Picture Pianists

Are you "working up" your pictures? If not, why not? If so, you want some good melodramatic music. Send for free sample page of "Orpheum Collection of Moving Picture Music." Now being used and praised by many of the best houses in the country.

PRICE.................................75 CENTS

Also latest cue music (series 1910) for 10 parts and piano...................................$1.00

¼ discount on both numbers.

Clarence E. Sinn
1501 Sedgwick St., CHICAGO, ILL.

Sound Effects

In Picture Machine Theaters it is very essential that the imitations and sound effects are of the kind that can be depended upon. We make only practical and serviceable imitations that will give the exact reproduction of the original. We also manufacture Chimes, Tympani, Bells, Xylophones, Drums and accessories.

LEEDY MANUFACTURING COMPANY
1055 E. Palmer St., INDIANAPOLIS, IND.

TO TRAP DRUMMERS

A Limited Time Offer

Special Offer } Size Shell 8 x 14
$10.00 } Size Shell 3 x 15

Solid Maple, Rosewood or Walnut, 10 fine plated thumb screw rods, Kangaroo, Angora or Slunk Calf Drum Heads.

We ship with privilege of 6 days trial

E. P. ZEIDLER DRUM CO.
Dept. F. Cleveland, Ohio

Send for my large free catalogue of Folding and Parlor Organs, suitable for use in Moving Picture Theaters.

Address

J. C. KAY
4036 Ellis Ave., Chicago.

FIGURE 7. Advertisements for "Music." *MPW* 1 Oct. 1910, 815.

As it turned out, the musical program was not printed.[28] If it had been, it probably would have been similar to a cue sheet, though one with more specific descriptions of content than are found in the suggestions for music published by the Edison Company. In 1910 anthologies and cue sheets were novelties, not yet settled into standardized forms, and *MPW*'s discussion of *A Penitent of Florence* demonstrates that its ideas concerning film music were in flux. What had been created for the film *was* a score; its apparent reduction to a cue sheet came after the music had been tried out. A few weeks later, the film now forgotten, *MPW* envisaged a further step: distributing such music in printed form. With the formulation of this idea, special scores moved distinctly above cue-sheet compilations to film music's highest ground.

Two complementary essays concerned special scores, the first in idealistic and the second in practical terms. In the first, opera was once again invoked: indeed, the author was Pilar Morin, the star of an Edison film based on Bizet's *Carmen*. In terms that call to mind *L'Assassinat* and other *films d'art*, she stressed the affinity of film with both opera and pantomime: all three arts, she stated, depend upon music to "illuminate the emotions of acting." She regretted the poor quality of film music, compared with the two other genres; and after mentioning Wagner (in a rather fanciful context) she concluded with this hopeful vision:

> The day will yet come when musicians will write for picture plays, manufacturers will print the music for such films, managers will gladly pay for same, pianists will be engaged to enchant the public, who are so willing to go and hear as well as see that which it craves for, good music in connection with silent picture plays, music that speaks for itself—the music of silent drama.[29]

Thus was articulated, perhaps for the first time, the idea of commissioned film scores, widely distributed and performed.

A subsequent *MPW* editorial on the subject endorsed Morin's "very interesting ideas," and made them more immediate. The editors looked forward to examples of cooperation between film manufacturers, music publishers, and performers in the theaters:

> There will be issued, let us say, a fine Essanay comedy, while, at the same time, suitable music for either the piano or other instruments will be especially made for it, and purchasable by the exhibitor.[30]

This idea, the editorial continues, had already been proposed to *MPW* by a music publisher (unfortunately not named). What the editors had in mind was to pass it on to "those most interested," for they believed it to be an idea of immediate potential. It was not just Essanay whose films could stimulate musical composition; Biograph, Pathé, Vitagraph, Selig, and Kalem all now offered subjects "ready made for the composer who will gain fame and riches" in moving pictures.

The editorial quoted above preceded actual examples of special scores by about half a year. When the first examples appeared, they were not for comedies by Essanay, but for films of the operas *Il Trovatore* and *Faust* by Pathé; moreover, several other opera-related films were given special scores within the next few years. (See Appendix part 3, nos. 1, 2, 5, 20, 33 (?), 64, 86, and 94.)

A silent film of an opera seems an oxymoron. The mute medium robs such a work of its dramatic essence; and even if the accompanying score were to include vocal as well as instrumental parts (which does not often seem to have been the case), the original theatrical balance has been lost. In the minds of film producers and audiences, however, these problems of adaptation probably counted for less than the fact that operas were popular works possessing glamor and prestige—qualities that most silent films of the period lacked.

Many films based on operas had been produced before Pathé's, and to compensate for their silence, attempts were sometimes made to give them synchronized music using either phonograph recordings or live performers.[31] Sadoul states that Méliès had scores prepared for his 1904 films of both *Faust* and *The Barber of Seville*, "reproducing the most famous arias."[32] In 1907, Kalem pirated a ten-minute film of *The Merry Widow* (falsely advertised as being by the original Viennese cast), and promised what may have been the first special score to be prepared in America: the music of the operetta "condensed into a version which can be put on by any house using a pianist and a singer."[33] When Edison released a version of *Faust* in 1909, the company provided suggestions for music in its *Kinetogram* and claimed to have "gone to considerable length to specify the exact music from the opera."[34] The following spring Edison offered a film version of *Carmen*, for which *MPW* pointedly urged musicians to use the music of Bizet.[35]

Pathé's films of *Trovatore* and *Faust* were *films d'art*, of the series *L'Assassinat* had inaugurated two years before. We can speculate that this connection, together with the growing awareness of film music's importance (as expressed in *MPW*), prompted Pathé to have scores for the two opera films prepared for distribution. But the company's exact reasons for taking such a step at this time remain unknown, as does the identity of the arranger(s) of these scores, and the scores themselves are not known to survive. Information on both comes mostly from Sinn, who enthusiastically promoted them in his "Music for the Picture" column. He first announced the music for *Trovatore* in this brief manner:

> Pathé, of New York, have taken a step in furthering the association of suitable music with the moving picture which we desire to applaud. . . . Pathé engaged the services of a competent man to prepare the music of the opera for use when the film is projected. So it comes about that for something like fifty cents, the exhibitor can procure the music of *Trovatore*, especially arranged for simultaneous use with the film.[36]

A few weeks later Sinn communicated his pleasure in having seen the film (scheduled for release on 27 January 1911): "In dramatic structure it adheres closely to the libretto," he wrote, "and any one familiar with that opera should be able to give a fair melodic setting to the picture after looking at it once." But then he reminded readers that Pathé itself had provided such an accompaniment, that their "enterprise" deserved encouragement, and that the score would be a useful "piece of property to have in your library."[37]

Sinn returned to this subject a third time, one month later, and made three points. He advised readers how to play from the score (thereby indicating how unfamiliar such accompaniments were); he once again encouraged pianists to invest in this musical "stock"; and he described the score, demonstrating that the music was not just a medley of opera highlights—it was a careful adaptation serving this particular film:

> There are twenty-seven pages of music full piano size, clean print on good paper, and the titles (which are the "music cues") are in large type easy to read at a glance. The music is all selected from Verdi's opera and the compiler knows how to adapt it to a moving picture.[38]

Half a year later Sinn described the score for *Faust* in much the same terms:

> A splendid musical setting has been arranged for this picture by a musician who certainly understands his business. There are 38 (thirty-eight) pages of music, which covers the two reels of film. It sells for 75 cents—a trifle less than two cents a page, and all selected from Gounod's immortal masterpiece. I feel that I cannot urge too strongly the advisability of ordering this music.[39]

How extensively readers responded to Sinn's exhortations and availed themselves of these scores is not known. One film musician, Buel Rissinger, recalled both of them five years later as the earliest examples of film scores he had seen; and he described how the score for *Faust* was used:

> I also remember a production of *Il Trovatore* in 1910 put out with the music from the Verdi score, but very much "cut up"; also one of *Faust*, along the same lines, both produced by Pathé. This score was for the piano only, but the writer was leading a house in Memphis at the time, using ten men, and had the score arranged for orchestra from the piano solo, also using pipe organ with orchestra.[40]

Rissinger's comments suggest that *Faust* was regarded as an unusual film, exhibited with care. He implies that his theater's manager(s) hoped the film would draw audiences large enough to justify the time and expense needed to have the piano score arranged; and it is possible that this "house in Memphis" was a vaudeville or legitimate theater, because the size of its ensemble was unusual for film theaters of that period.

In short, opera films were high-toned novelties, and for both filmmakers and musicians they posed special problems: how to condense them into "cut-up" films lasting ten or twenty minutes; how to turn their lengthy orchestral and vocal scores into coherent piano accompaniments; and (in the example of *Faust*) how to turn such a piano score back into orchestral music. Yet these abridged scores—they might be termed "mono-compilations," each being drawn from a single source—may well have helped to promote the use of operatic music for other compiled scores as well. So suggested Sinn, at least, when he urged his readers to buy the Pathé scores, arguing that that way they would be sure to have the music "in stock." Moreover, not long after *Faust* some important non-operatic films were provided with special scores using operatic music—the earliest being the third film listed in Appendix part 3, *Dante's Inferno*.

This film was a five-reel Italian import, first introduced to the country by touring companies on a road-show basis. Sinn called attention to the score in mid-1911, and cited the Milano Film Company's announcement that the music had been arranged by "'Signor Caravaglios, composer of some note' (in Naples, Italy)."[41] Half a year later the film was still in release, and described by one commentator as requiring "the most capable sound effect artist that could be secured."[42] Later in the decade a musician still remembered the impression made by both the film and its accompaniment:

> Four years ago a most wonderful production was brought to our town in seven reels [*sic*]. It was *Dante's Inferno*, and was the most spectacular picture witnessed here. Special music was set for it from *Mefistofele*, a wonderfully descriptive set of cues. The man who travelled with the picture said he had shown it in a great many states, and he found only one pianist who would use them.[43]

The adaptation of *Mefistofele* to *Dante's Inferno* is an example of arranging a pre-existent operatic work for attachment to a new narrative, sometimes with only a tenuous connection; in most compiled scores that followed, excerpts from *several* dramatic works were normally collected into an accompaniment for a single film, and the connections loosened still further. Such a compilation had in fact been proposed for *Dante's Inferno*, in an *MPW* article by W. Stephen Bush, then one of *MPW*'s most thoughtful writers on the roles of music and the human voice in silent film exhibitions. For the *Inferno* he offered both a lecture and detailed musical suggestions. (He does not mention the Caravaglios score, and his silence tends to confirm the statement quoted above, to the effect that the special score was rarely used.) Bush's recommendations for music include three excerpts from the operatic repertoire: the overture to *William Tell*, the "strains of the 'Evening Star' from *Tannhäuser*," and the "well-known air from Mascagni's *Cavalleria Rusticana*." French grand opera, Wagner, and post-Verdi verismo are all represented in one compilation, along with such diverse items as the "Garibaldi Hymn" and a series of "Gregorian" melodies, including the *Dies Irae*.[44] According to Bush, *Dante's Inferno* was a great film, deserving only the best of compositions: "After you have witnessed a performance of that great production with either 'faked' or shockingly unsuitable music," he wrote, "you fell as if it were a solemn duty to prevent any further desecration." Although some observers now might consider his compilation to be the real desecration, in 1912 what he proposed was generally taken as both a practical and an aesthetically pleasing solution to the problem of inappropriate accompaniments. In this way operatic excerpts found ever-wider distribution and utility.

Special scores for film adaptations of operas were never all that common: during 1912 *MPW* refers to only two more of them, *Mignon* and *Fra Diavolo* (Appendix part 3, nos. 5 and 20), and information about each is quite limited. (Neither score was mentioned by Sinn.) A review of *Mignon* concluded by noting that "special music, adapted from the score of the opera . . . will be distributed by the exchanges."[45] More interesting is the manner in which Solax announced its three-reel production of *Fra Diavolo*, "The Great Photo-Opera, from Auber's Masterpiece": a full-page advertisement twice heralded a "musical accompaniment," the second time as part of the film's "advertising matter," together with lobby posters and the like.[46] The approach was a novel one, and it was also being followed in advertisements for various non-operatic films, beginning with the three-reel Monopol production of *Homer's Odyssey* (a film whose model, at least in title and

Homer's "ODYSSEY"

SPECIAL ADVERTISING MATTER

In Any Quantity

Paper—Full line litho and block paper made by *Morgan Litho & Courier Co., of Buffalo.* 24 sheets, 8 sheets, 3 sheets, 1 sheets, ½ sheets, in litho, 4 colors, and black. Dates, snipes, throw-aways, hand bills, programs, and type sheets.

Music—Grecian music, overture and scene music, written by *Mr. Edgar Selden,* general manager Shapiro Music Co., of New York City, who spent three months in the musical libraries of Greece.

Effects—Lighting and novelty effects by *Kliegl Bros.,* of New York City.

Statues—Plaster of Paris busts of Homer made by *Luccesh1, Italy,* imported by us. Six inches to seven feet high. Prices, 50c to $100 each.

Costumes—Grecian costumes for lecturers made by *Rovilo & Co., of Turin, Italy.*

Souvenir Booklets—10½ x 14½ inches, 24 pages. Fifty half-tone illustrations; bound in royal blue ribbon. Finest deckle-edge paper. Printed by *S. L. Parsons & Co., of New York.* To sell for 25 cents each.

Cuts—One hundred and fifty varieties of half-tones, in copper and zinc, and line cuts made by *Standard Engraving Co., of New York.*

Photos—One hundred and fifty varieties made in Italy.

Lobby Displays—Glass-front folding frames. *Cloth Banners,* in all sizes.

Heralds—The biggest, best, and flashiest herald ever printed. Four colors, lithographed front and back. Size of a one-sheet, folded once. *Positively* the greatest piece of advertising matter ever seen. Absolutely original in design and execution.

Booklets—For your patrons, 10 x 12 inches; good quality paper. Complete story of "Odyssey." Program of film profusely illustrated with cuts.

Books—Complete book of Homer's "Odyssey," the greatest epic poem in all literature; paper covered, cloth or leather. Either in Greek or English; in quantities of 1,000 to 100,000.

Post Cards—Bound in covers with perforated edge, announcing the playing date of "THE ODYSSEY" (to be filled in). Beautiful half-tone illustration on reverse side. Distribute among your audience; they address these cards, leave them at the box office, you put on the one-cent stamp and mail the cards. This is a rather new publicity stunt and is finding *great favor in New York.* Nearly all the theaters, prominent hotels and cafes have adopted it. The cards are cheap, but very attractive, and will result in good press work for your theatre.

Press Matter—Fifty different stories, all kinds and sizes, written to fit every occasion; written by practical newspaper men under the personal direction of *Frank Winch,* late *General Press Representative* for *Buffalo Bill's Wild West Shows.* Stories either in separate sheets or neatly bound in booklets, each leaf detachable.

Lecture—Written by *Stephen Bush.* Comprehensive, elegant and in simple language.

Literature—*Any or all of it* supplied in any language (special low prices). Translations by Prof. Hallen.

Programs—Printed on one side only, giving description of each scene in the film.

Lobby Display—Decoration, grottoes, caves, stucco effect, very elaborate. Directions for grotto-effect making without cost.

Photos for Lobby Displays—Life size for lobby. These are made by *Apedo Studio,* New York, and at the following prices: 30 x 40 inches, $8.00; 40 x 60 inches, $12.00.

In all—We have ordered twenty million pieces of printed matter for the exploitation of "THE ODYSSEY." There is no limit to the advertising possibilities that you may take advantage of. Everything at cost price.

Write Now or Wire Prepaid. ***State Rights are Open***

MONOPOL FILM COMPANY

145 West 45th Street
NEW YORK, N. Y.

FIGURE 8. Advertisement for *Homer's Odyssey. MPW* 24 Feb. 1912, 706.

in literary subject, was evidently *Dante's Inferno*). Moreover, the *Odyssey* advertisement (given in Fig. 8) commands attention because it makes no clear distinction between display items, subsidiary merchandise (for example, posters and postcards), and aspects of the presentation, including the special score and a separate lecture for the film by W. Stephen Bush. In short, the page offers a confusing jumble (perhaps to make it seem more impressive), yet its message is clear: all these things can be used to sell the film. Thus, special scores, uneasy mixtures in and of themselves, came to be prized for their promotional as well as musical values. In serving such a mix of functions, they are symbolic of the way nearly all movies combine elements of business, entertainment, and art—just as do many operas; in this way, too, the new medium carried on venerable traditions.

By 1912 special scores had begun to blossom, garnering much attention and yielding some intriguing hybrids—notably a series of piano scores crafted by Simon. It will be seen that in his hands film music could be as far removed from the polyglot operatic adaptation as from the coherent symphonic style of Saint-Saëns.

The Kalem Series and Walter Cleveland Simon's Music for *An Arabian Tragedy*

During the early teens the Kalem Company emerged as one of America's most innovative producers of films. One innovation was to send film-making crews abroad under the direction of Sidney Olcott, who led excursions first to Ireland and Germany in 1910, then again to Ireland in late 1911, and to the Middle East in 1912. He brought back films of distinction, including a three-reel adaptation of *Arrah-Na-Pogue* in 1911, and a five-reel film of the life of Christ, *From the Manger to the Cross* in 1912.[47] A second innovation concerned music: between November 1911 and May 1913 the Kalem Company—the same company that had advertised a score for its version of *The Merry Widow* in 1907—commissioned piano scores for as many as two dozen of its releases.

In Appendix part 4 will be found a list of these film scores, derived from three sources: references in *MPW*, the U.S. *Catalogue of Copyright Entries*, and copies of scores in the Library of Congress. The films include three adaptations of Boucicault plays filmed by Olcott in Ireland; twelve war stories filmed in this country, mostly dealing with the American Civil War; seven exotic stories, filmed by Olcott in the Middle East; and two Westerns. The list contains inconsistencies. For example, some scores were advertised by Kalem in *MPW* but not registered for copyright (nos. 1, 2, 5, 9, 21–24); others were registered for copyright but not advertised in *MPW* (nos. 16, 17, 20). Also, there are some uncertainties concerning the first two films. (1) *The Colleen Bawn*, released in October 1911, is included at the head of the list, because Sinn referred to a score for the film, though not until the spring of 1912.[48] When *Colleen* first appeared, Sinn offered his own musical suggestions for the film, without any reference to a special score.[49] It is possible that a score was issued later but except for this one reference, there are no specific *MPW* announcements or advertisements of a *Colleen* score, such as appeared for subsequent Kalem films. (2) *Arrah-Na-Pogue* was released in November 1911, a month after *The Colleen Bawn*, and in *MPW*'s review there appeared the following announcement of a special score:

> Walter C. Simons [*sic*] has been engaged by the Kalem Company to write a complete piano score for *Arrah-Na-Pogue*. He will also prepare a four-piece orchestration for the same subject. The arrangement for piano and orchestra will be published by the Kalem Company and sold to exhibitors at a nominal price to

FIGURE 9. Advertisement for *Arrah-Na-Pogue. MPW* 25 Nov. 1911, 813.

> cover the bare cost of production. The music will be ready for distribution Nov. 21. Mr. Simons has had long experience as a pianist and composer and has been playing the pictures for several years.[50]

The week after the review appeared, Kalem included a similar announcement of "Special Music" in its *MPW* advertisement of the film. (See Figure 9.[51]) Then, about a month later, similar announcements appeared for the first time in the

Kalem Kalendar, the company's house organ, from which additional details can be gleaned. It is explained that "the recommendation of old Irish airs to be played in connection with *The Colleen Bawn* met with such success" that the Kalem company had special music prepared for *Arrah-Na-Pogue*; and that the score consisted of an introduction (a "melodious" original composition), followed by "an arrangement of old Irish airs, particularly adapted for the action."[52] In other words, at the end of 1911 no actual score for *Colleen* existed; what had been offered was a "recommendation," probably some sort of cue sheet. *Arrah* was another matter: a score was published and available for purchase. All the same, this music—the only score for which Kalem offered both solo piano and four-piece arrangements—was not registered for copyright, and no copy is known to exist.

The third film listed in Appendix part 4 is *A Spartan Mother*, released in March 1912. Its piano score was advertised in *MPW* and registered for copyright, and a copy exists in the Library of Congress. It is thus the oldest piano score for an American film score known to be extant; and fifteen other Kalem piano scores from 1912 also survive—the first *series* of film scores to be published in America.

There are many reasons for considering all the published scores beginning with *A Spartan Mother* to be part of a unified series. One reason is that several Kalem advertisements mentioned the scores in groups. For example, the advertisement for *Missionaries in Darkest Africa* and *The Drummer Girl of Vicksburg* (reproduced as Fig. 10) also listed five films previously released, for which scores were still available; and in mid-June, the company went so far as to claim that "special piano music" was available for *all* Kalem features.[53] A second reason is that the published scores show considerable uniformity of design. Though some minor changes can be observed in the layout of the title pages and music of the earliest surviving scores (*A Spartan Mother*, *The Spanish Revolt of 1836*, and *Fighting Dan McCool*), the score for No. 7 (*Under a Flag of Truce*) established a standard format. Title pages took this form:

Special Piano Music for
[Film title, within a rectangular border]
[Kalem Trademark]

Kalem Company
225-239 West 23d Street
New-York, N.Y.

Copyrighted 1912 By Kalem Company

With regard to layout, *Under a Flag of Truce* and all remaining scores had the following features in common: the composer's name given at the top right-hand corner of the first page, the title of the film written (above a page number) at the top of each subsequent page, and cues (in the same hand) preceding and following every musical segment.

Perhaps the most important reason for regarding these scores as a series is that the great majority of them were composed by the same man, Walter Cleveland Simon. His name appears on all but one of the sixteen published scores in LC.[54] He was also mentioned in Kalem advertisements for two others—*Arrah-Na-Pogue*

KALEM

Special Piano Music, 25 cents, postage prepaid

Missionaries In Darkest Africa

This extraordinary production was made in a small settlement on the River Nile, Egypt, and in the African jungle. With the exception of three Kalem artists, all of the characters are native tribesmen of the African jungle.

Special one, three and six sheet, four color lithograph posters for this feature.

Released Monday, June 3rd

The Drummer Girl of Vicksburg

Another Thrilling Feature War Story. Special one, three and six sheet litho's. Special Piano Music, 25 cents.

RELEASED WEDNESDAY, JUNE 5th

The Pugilist and the Girl

A novel farce portrayed by a company of *real* comedians. Write your exchange to book you for this feature.

RELEASED FRIDAY, JUNE 7th

MR. EXHIBITOR: We have issued special piano music at 25 cents per copy for "A SPARTAN MOTHER," "THE SPANISH REVOLT OF 1836," "WAR'S HAVOC," "FIGHTING DAN McCOOL," "THE FIGHTING DERVISHES OF THE DESERT." Order from your exchange or Kalem Company direct.

KALEM COMPANY
INCORPORATED
NEW YORK, 235-239 W. 23rd St.
86 Wardour St., LONDON, W.
BERLIN, 35 Friedrich Str.
PARIS, 13 Rue du Faubourg Montmartre

FIGURE 10. Advertisement for Kalem Films. *MPW* 25 May 1912, 702.

and *The Tragedy of Big Eagle Mine*—standing at the beginning and end of the list in Appendix part 4 (nos. 2 and 24).

When he began to compose these scores, Simon was apparently about twenty-six, and already an experienced theater musician.[55] The *MPW* announcement of the score for *Arrah-Na-Pogue* (cited above) tells us that in 1911 Simon had been "playing the pictures for several years." Also, a month before the score for

Arrah-Na-Pogue was announced, a small advertisement offered pianists a *Progress Course of Music* to help them play for "Moving Pictures, Vaudeville and Dramatic Shows properly." The advertisement named no author, but in the same issue Sinn announced the publication of the *Progress Course* as Simon's work. In doing so he supplied a portrait of the composer:

> Mr. Simons [*sic*] is qualified to give instruction as to the proper method of playing picture and vaudeville accompaniments. He has filled the position of pianist in various theaters of the West and was pianist for Lyman Howe for one year; he also has a number of song successes to his credit which places him in the composer class. Wherever Mr. Simons has appeared, either in pianologue or as accompanist, his work has been characterized as a feature of the entertainment by the critics. He is a young man of pleasing address and speaks with authority upon his chosen subject.[56]

Simon was next described by *MPW* in reports of two exhibitors' previews sponsored by Kalem during the spring of 1912. According to both reports, a Kalem official (William Wright) called attention to the special music that exhibitors could purchase for the films being screened, and also to the composer's presence at the piano. The following excerpt comes from the report on the first preview, held at New York's Auditorium Theater on 27 February 1912:

> The music arranged for this subject [*A Spartan Mother*] by Mr. Simon consists of a careful blending of a number of patriotic airs with other appropriate music composed by him for the picture. It greatly strengthens and punctuates the dramatic periods of the picture and adds to its charm and effectiveness. Many expressions of approval were voiced by the critical audience.[57]

At the second preview (held on 16 May), several of Kalem's "Oriental" features were screened, and the music was described by *MPW* in these words:

> One of the features of the exhibition was the rendition of special music which Kalem has had prepared for these productions. The composer, Mr. W. C. Simon, presided at the piano, and the weird strains that accompanied the incidents on the Sahara Desert and the trials of the missionaries in the African jungle were very impressive. . . . Mr. William Wright . . . announced that the special music which they had enjoyed during the exhibition . . . could be secured for 25 cents—a complete piano score.[58]

Within these reports the descriptions of Simon's music differ significantly. Just as *Arrah-Na-Pogue* was said to contain "an arrangement of old Irish airs, particularly adapted for the action," so the score for *A Spartan Mother* is characterized as "a careful blending of patriotic airs with other appropriate music"; but at the later screening, it is Simon's "weird strains" that make an impression. In short, whether the film is set in rural Ireland, in the South during the Civil War, or in a mysteriously exotic locale, Simon adapts himself to the narrative in a convincing manner. With this general point established, the next step is to undertake examination of one particular score in detail: the music that has been chosen was composed for an "exotic" film and illustrates some of the most intriguing peculiarities of Simon's self-subordinating style.

For *An Arabian Tragedy*, a one-reel feature, Simon composed a complete original score, divided into fourteen discrete pieces. As shown in the three pages from the score given in Figures 11–13, each piece is cued by a title and/or description of the action on screen. It happens that most of these titles and action cues appear almost verbatim in a synopsis of the film printed in *MPW*; so even

FIGURE 11. Walter C. Simon's score for *An Arabian Tragedy* (New York: Kalem Co. [1912]), p. 1. (I am grateful to Patrick Loughney of the Motion Picture, Broadcasting, and Recorded Sound Division at LC for providing me with the photographs of score pages from *An Arabian Tragedy* seen in Figs. 11–13.)

without seeing the film, which is not known to survive, one can infer some important points concerning the music's relationship to the story on screen.[59]

MPW's synopsis is given below, with bracketed numbers inserted to reflect the playing of successive pieces from Simon's score. The synopsis begins with the score's third number, because Simon instructs the performer to play the first number "the moment you see [the] announcement *An Arabian Tragedy* appear on screen," and to segue directly into the second number. The latter may be meant to accompany a prefatory title not given in the synopsis, as well as an introductory scene: so we can infer from the fact that the performer is told to repeat the second number "until [the] 2nd title appears, then finish strain and segue." The remainder of the score corresponds to portions of the synopsis as follows:

> [3] Ayub Kashif becomes embittered toward his wife Fatima, because their union has been childless. [4] He eventually determines to divorce Fatima and free her slave, whom he then will wed. [5] Fatima, who still loves her husband, lives a life of sorrow, praying that her husband's love will return to her. [6] A year later, Allah grants Ayub an heir. [7] Fatima, hearing of the event, writes Ayub, requesting that she be allowed to attend his wife as a slave. This request Ayub denies.
>
> [8] Four years later, Ayub, with a number of other merchants, departs to take rich merchandise across the desert. While on the journey he is attacked by a dread disease and, according to Turkish custom, is left to die.
>
> [9] Fatima, in her dreams, sees that her husband is about to perish. [10] Haunted by the vision, she seeks the wife and begs her to send aid to the suffering Ayub. The former slave, caring only for her personal comfort, laughs at the discarded wife, [11(=8)] and Fatima, accompanied by two slaves, starts out in quest of Ayub. [12(=1)] The fast-failing merchant is digging his own grave, [13(=8)] when Fatima arrives after an exhausting journey across the burning sands of the desert, [14] and with a prayer that he be forgiven, Ayub dies in her arms.

Like many other thousand-feet films made between the years 1908 and 1912, this one crowds a large amount of action into a short narrative; and for most new developments in the narrative—usually represented by a jump ahead in time and/or a change of scene—Simon moves to a new piece of music, as illustrated by the numbers above.

Simon's numbers change with successive scenes; within scenes the numbers seem mostly independent of the action, owing to their structure. Each number contains a series of short segments, usually repeated, and often lasting two or four measures, though there are less regular phrase lengths, too. The opening number, for example, contains a two-measure unit which is repeated, followed by a five-measure unit (which itself contains a repeated measure); that is, its form is aab, or 2 + 2 + 5. The second number begins with an ostinato vamp for two measures, followed by an eight-measure phrase aab (2 + 2 + 4). This phrase is repeated with a varied cadence (the first time open, the second time closed and extended by one measure), and then the performer is instructed to repeat the whole number "dal segno," which in this case leads back to the beginning. (See Fig. 11 for the score's first page, containing both of these numbers.)

All the numbers contain short segments that are repeated one or more times in succession, and all take different shapes. Some are essentially a single strain (nos. 1, 7), some have two similar halves (nos. 2, 5, 6, 10, 14), and some contain two or more strains (nos. 3, 5, 8); and even those numbers with similar shapes proceed from segment to segment in dissimilar ways. These two points—the use of repeating segments and the individuality of each piece's structure—are demonstrated in Appendix part 5, which contains an outline of the score's contents.

The outline helps to illustrate an additional point: the principles of musical structure in Simon's score are quite different from those employed by Saint-Saëns in the music for *L'Assassinat.* In Simon's score, each number contains its own distinctive—and for the most part tuneless—fragments; each piece is written to come to a full close, although Simon indicates that some repetitions may break off before cadences; and the score ends in a key that is different from the one in which it began. By contrast, within the Saint-Saëns score there are many prominent themes (especially those for the Duke and the Marquise); almost all segments are smoothly elided, and many are interrelated; the tableaux are self-contained, but the endings of all but the last one are charged with harmonic tension; each tableau must be played complete, without repetition; and the music is rounded so as to end climactically in the same key in which it began.

In short, whereas two essential goals of the Saint-Saëns score are forward motion and fluid continuity, the Simon score often seems to stand still, or to move in discontinuous blocks. Indeed, some of Simon's numbers (especially 5, 6, and 10) are so unvaried in rhythm and minimal in melody that they evoke the stasis of Satie's *Gnossiennes* of 1890, which in their own way are also full of exotically "weird strains." This quote from the *MPW* review reminds us that in 1912 Simon was no avant-garde iconoclast. His music was perceived to be appropriate for this film, perhaps in large part *because* of its discontinuity. Some of the ways in which various individual numbers of the score serve the film are elucidated below.

MPW's synopsis of *An Arabian Tragedy* presents a story without the kind of action that would call for overtly dramatic segments: for example, misteriosos, agitatos, or hurries. The tragedy is often sentimental and—within its compressed framework—slow. In keeping with these qualities, there is considerable clichéd sentiment in Simon's music for scenes depicting Fatima's enduring love. For example: the barbershop-style close harmonies of number 7 ("the request that was denied"); the waltz-like rising melody—a rare one in the score—combined with ethereal tremolos in number 9 (Fatima's dream); and the final "affetuoso" number, with its chromatic turns of harmony and pulsing chords (like slowed-down tremolos), which Simon instructs can be played "two octaves higher ad lib." (See Exs. 13–15.)

Other numbers are not so sentimental, and relate to the film somewhat differently. In number 3, for example, there are four changes of style in eighteen measures: a decisive opening (perhaps reminiscent of the music of number 1); an adagio phrase descending an octave in C minor; a sequence of three tremolos; and a pair of phrases that—like others in the score—oscillate without a sense of forward movement. (See Fig. 12.) With all these changes the music seems pantomimic; however, there are no descriptive cues to confirm the point; and Simon's instruction to repeat the number "dal segno" would seem to be independent of action on screen. In number 8 (see Fig. 13), the music follows the action closely in another manner: the steady, dissonant ostinato, combined with the pseudo-

EX. 13 Simon, *An Arabian Tragedy*, no.7, mm. 8–10

Arabian phrases of melody (each lasting four measures), are probably meant to evoke the scenes of travel through the desert (by camel). The music is imagistic, and might be termed a distant cousin of Tchaikovsky's "Danse Arabe" from *The Nutcracker*.[60] But number 8 has its dramatic qualities, too. It is the score's longest piece (and one of the loudest), and it is repeated three times for desert scenes, as the story approaches its climax.

In between the second and third appearances of number 8, Simon builds up to a climax with a sharp musical contrast for a change of scene: he returns to the score's opening number, as Ayub is shown preparing to dig his own grave. Unlike number 8, the solemn, rather jagged melody of number 1 is not particularly "Arabian," but its reappearance near the end of the film offers a semblance of musical rounding. Moreover, though numbers 1 and 8 are contrasted in style, together they provide an emphatic prolongation of the score's opening key, C minor, before the turn to A♭ major at the end. Thus numbers 1 and 8 demonstrate in a simple way the dramatic efficacy of two basic structural devices, repetition and return.

Of course, these devices were commonly used in compiled scores of the period: nearly all of them contain repeats of large blocks of (pre-existent) music, without (notated) variation; and Simon's score also resembles a compilation in its unyielding discontinuity. Yet, although it could never be mistaken for a unified score like the one by Saint-Saëns, Simon's music *is* original; and one of its most striking achievements is to speak eloquently for the film in several ways, despite halting syntax and limited vocabulary. In his years of playing motion picture and vaudeville accompaniments, Simon must have learned very well the various techniques of playing "suitable music." For *An Arabian Tragedy* he drew upon some of them, assembling sentimental and "weird" strains, tuneless fragments and lengthy ostinatos into a score that is perhaps simple to play, but one whose effects are not so simply explained.

EX. 14 *An Arabian Tragedy*, no. 9, mm. 1–8

EX. 15 *An Arabian Tragedy*, no. 14, mm. 1–2 and 16–18

An explanation of the history of the Kalem series is also not simple. As shown in Appendix part 4, the score for *An Arabian Tragedy* appeared in June 1912, in the midst of the Kalem series. Nineteen scores for Kalem films were issued by the end of July 1912, most of them within a three-month period; then the pace slackened, with only five additional scores appearing during the next ten months, until May 1913, when the series ceased. The last scores on the list were never registered for copyright (and thus do not survive in LC); apparently Kalem did not find the scores issued in 1913, at the reduced price of fifteen cents, worth the trouble and expense of registering them.

In May 1912, at an early stage of the series, Sinn urged his readers to acquire the Simon scores:

> The Kalem Co. promises us an Egyptian picture with music May 27th [i.e., *The Fighting Dervishes of the Desert*]. As they have not disappointed us in the past we may safely expect a welcome addition to our list of Oriental music, for it is a safe bet that a great deal, if not all, of it can be used later for other pictures of like nature. I know of some who are still using numbers from *Colleen Bawn*, *Arrah-Na-Pogue*, *Spartan Mother*, *Il Trovatore*, and *Faust*, whenever the opportunity offers. And why not? It pays to get this special music when issued by these enterprising producers, and it likewise pays to keep it. So you see you profit doubly.[61]

Sinn makes no distinction between Simon's original music and the operatic adaptations he had previously promoted: both could be used "for other films of like nature." Possibly so, but one problem he does not seem to anticipate is the difficulty of cataloging and retrieving such music: it would require much effort on a pianist's (or music director's) part to store and pull individual segments from Simon's scores. Anthologies accomplished the same thing in a less roundabout manner.

Sinn never again promoted special scores in his column with the enthusiasm

FIGURE 12. *An Arabian Tragedy*, p. 2.

displayed in the passage cited above. Instead he focused increasingly on cue sheets, with occasional passing remarks concerning special scores. Indeed, during July 1912, he offered a set of suggestions for music to *An Arabian Tragedy*, with no mention of Simon's music for the film;[62] and in autumn of the same year he published a letter from a music director containing these comments on the Kalem series:

> . . . I have been unable to find it practical, as, should it be universally used, it would mean the outlay of a great deal of money per week—and lengthy rehearsals necessary for proper rendition. This brings us to the fact that we dare not interfere with the musician's repertoire (with which he is familiar), as this gives him a free hand to watch for cues.[63]

Similar opinions were expressed in a letter published by Sinn the following spring. Once again a cue sheet was expressly preferred to one of Kalem's complete scores:

FIGURE 13. *An Arabian Tragedy*, p. 5.

> From the "Crown Theater," Hartford, Conn.: "I am enclosing my musical program to Kalem's *The Cheyenne Massacre* [Appendix part 4, no. 22]. Though they had a special piano score for this picture, I did not use it, as I would have had to make an orchestration. My orchestra consists of five men in the winter months and four in the summer."[64]

In the face of such preference for cue sheets over special scores, the Kalem series ended, though there were at least two successors. From March to November 1913 the Vitagraph company advertised "special music" (piano scores) for thirty of its "special releases." (In Appendix part 3, the first Vitagraph film score appears as no. 42, the last as no. 80.) Unlike Kalem, however, Vitagraph never registered its scores for copyright, and no copies of any of the advertised scores have been located.[65] Similarly, at the year's end Thanhouser offered free orchestrations of special music for three of its "Big Productions." (See Appendix part 3, nos. 82–84.) Though the music was said to be the work of "E. A. Price of the Tams Music Library, a composer of regular show productions," no scores were copyrighted, and Thanhouser ceased its efforts in early 1914.[66]

A last reference to these series appeared in Sinn's column in March 1914. Sinn had passed a letter from one of his readers to Kalem and Vitagraph asking whether the two companies were still issuing music. (The writer was perhaps ignorant of the Thanhouser scores.) Each company replied to Sinn, and he published their answers. Vitagraph stated tersely that its special scores had been discontinued, and that cue sheets could be found in its monthly bulletin. Kalem answered the inquiry at greater length:

> We have abandoned the issue of special music for our photoplays. We find that the average exhibitor is not sufficiently interested to return to us the first cost of the music, and from experience you know it is rather an expensive luxury to get out a special arrangement, and sell only a limited quantity.

Sinn appended this comment:

> And there you have it. . . . A number of producers have at different times given their attention to special music with no thought of profit thereby . . . but when the exhibitors do not take enough interest to pay the initial cost, it becomes an "expensive luxury."[67]

Despite these comments, special piano scores did not disappear; however, the number of them diminished. In 1914 only one film company, All-Star, announced a series of eight piano scores, and Witmark published seven of them, all composed by Manuel Klein, the musical director of the New York Hippodrome. (See Appendix part 3, nos. 87, 89, 90, 92, 96, 97, 99, and 100.) Compared with Kalem's scores, these are problematic: the All-Star films were longer than Kalem's—each running five reels or more, whereas Kalem's films ran one to three reels—yet all but one of Klein's published scores were about the same length as Simon's. Indeed, most of Klein's scores seem more like collections of themes for the films than complete accompaniments, but they were not described in this way by the company.[68]

The disparity between the lengths of the All-Star films and their scores points toward a problem which confronted film musicians with increasing frequency in 1913 and 1914: how to accompany features that were steadily growing longer. For companies that considered distributing scores with their films there was an additional problem to consider: in many new and large theaters, organs and orchestral ensembles were employed in addition to pianists.

In connection with these developments, film music can be seen to have followed three trends during 1913 and 1914. (1) Cue sheets (some distributed by studios, others by special services such as *MPW*'s column) became the dominant method—practical and inexpensive—for preparing suitable accompaniments for most features. (2) When special scores *were* prepared, many of them were arranged for orchestra rather than (or in addition to) piano. In the Thanhouser series, for example, free "orchestrations" were offered; and for *The Patchwork Girl of Oz* (Appendix part 3, no. 101), Gottschalk's music was offered "with a complete Orchestra, Piano and Organ Score." (3) Beginning in 1914, the evidence suggests that original scores (like Simon's and Gottschalk's) were rarities; most special scores were compilations—written out cue-sheets, as it were. Some important examples of these compilations will be discussed below.

Though Kalem's films and Simon's piano scores may have been eclipsed by these new developments, Simon's film work continued. In 1915 he published an anthology of music for *Society Dramas [in] One Reel* (a rather curious title for a practical collection);[69] in 1916, he copyrighted a score for Kalem's 1916 five-reel adaptation of a hoary melodrama, *The Black Crook*;[70] and at the end of the decade he was still going strong, with a score for another five-reel picture, *The Echo of Youth*. *MPW* praised the latter:

> The music fitted the picture admirably. . . . One of the points noticeable in Mr. Simons' [*sic*] cinema opera was the anticipation of the reappearance of certain characters of the picture. . . .
>
> Walter C. Simons is not new at fitting music to the picture, and has to his credit some twenty-seven musical arrangements for photodrama.[71]

According to *MPW*'s description, the score for *The Echo of Youth* may have been quite different from Simon's music for *An Arabian Tragedy*. One would not be tempted to call the earlier film score a "cinema opera"; nor does it contain "anticipation of the reappearance of certain characters." The phrase suggests the use of symbolic themes, such as might be found in the music of Saint-Saëns or Wagner (or Breil, as we shall see). Simon may have employed such themes in *The Echo of Youth*, or even in some of the other Kalem scores he composed in 1912; in the score for *An Arabian Tragedy* he did not. There he followed procedures quite distinct from those of nineteenth-century opera. In this respect he stands well apart from other important figures; but like them he was a pioneer, whose place in the history of music for silent films is secure.

Postscript: The Special Case of From the Manger to the Cross

Within the Kalem series mentioned above, there were many "Egyptian pictures"—that is, pictures made in the Middle East, like *An Arabian Tragedy*—and between April and July of 1912 most of these were issued with scores. Later in the year, Kalem announced one more film that had been produced "in authentic locations in Palestine and Egypt": ultimately titled *From the Manger to the Cross*, it was an elaborate five-reel version of the life of Christ. This was one of perhaps no more than half a dozen five-reel American films made during all of 1912.[72] It took longer to shoot than the other Kalem pictures and, because of its subject, had to be handled differently. Its release was delayed until early 1913, and musically, too, it was kept distinct.

There were many films of the life of Christ made before Kalem's, and they were often treated specially. Perhaps the screen's earliest, *Passion Play*—as Ramsaye described it, one of film's "first steps toward conscious art"—had been a 2100-foot version passed off as being from Oberammergau, but actually filmed in New York. Though the fraud was exposed, the picture was successfully exhibited at the Eden Musée with a lecturer, and "musical numbers were given in the two intermissions between the three reels to add to the effect."[73] Between 1905 and 1907 Pathé began to issue various versions of *La Vie de Jésus*, and apparently continued to do so until 1914.[74] A piano score was composed for some version of this film by Charles Quef, and published in France, possibly as early as 1907.[75] Zukor imported the Pathé film to America during the early days of the nickelodeon (probably in 1908), and presented it under the title *Passion Play* as a three-reel, hand-colored film.[76] For this version a special lecture was prepared, along with suggestions for music by W. Stephen Bush.[77]

Bush's purpose in offering these materials was partly to demonstrate that the film could be presented in a dignified manner; in this way he hoped to encourage exhibitors to show the film, despite the belief, shared by many, that the life of Christ was unsuitable film fare (especially for disreputable nickelodeons). In 1912, this belief still had to be countered, and *MPW* attempted to do so by including lengthy discussions of Kalem's new film in three successive October issues. First there appeared a special review, with several attractive stills, by the Reverend W. H. Jackson. It concluded in this way:

> As [the Passion Play] is the world's greatest theme, it follows that this is the greatest picture, and the Kalem Company must receive due commendation for placing before the world this wonderful film which places the highest and best uses of the moving picture in its most exalted place.[78]

In the next issue, one of *MPW*'s regulars, Epes Winthrop Sargent, offered suggestions for "Handling the Kalem Release." He argued that any clergyman hostile to the film could be won over to its support, once he had seen the film, whose reverent tone and absence of theatrical effect would surely prove persuasive. Sargent also outlined a "dignified and simple" promotional campaign for the film, and then turned to the film's presentation, with these comments:

> If it is possible to get a minister to lecture the film do so, but be certain that he will not preach a sermon instead of lecturing the subject. The leaders [i.e., titles] are full and explanatory and the remarks supplementing these should be brief and to the point. An organ and quartette will be better than an orchestra, the orchestra [an error: Sargent means the organ] playing the picture, but the quartette to be used only during the changing of the reels except, perhaps, that some selections may be very softly sung during the last reel, though it should be seriously impressed upon the singers that they are accompanying the film and are not rendering a number.[79]

Sargent's suggestions may have influenced Kalem (or vice versa), since the approach he recommended was followed by the company during that same week. On 14 October (two days after Jackson's review appeared), Kalem gave a preview of the film in the auditorium of Wanamaker Stores, New York, "arranged especially for the clergy." According to *MPW*'s report, there were several members of the film's cast on hand and the Reverend Jackson himself provided "a brief word of introduction." Music, too, was an important adjunct to the occasion:

> There had been considerable preparation by the Kalem Company in order to give the production a proper presentation before so distinguished an audience. The Schubert [vocal] Quartette was engaged, and with Mr. Alexander Russell, organist at the Auditorium, held several rehearsals of vocal and instrumental selections of appropriate character. . . . Suitable vocal and instrumental music was rendered as the various parts and scenes were unfolded, producing a most profound effect upon the audience. Before the second part had been shown, there was scarcely a dry eye to be found in the entire assemblage.[80]

Directly above this anonymous report, *MPW* gave prominence to W. Stephen Bush's review of the same event. His praise for the film was as strong as Jackson's, but he had some temperate criticism of the music he had heard at Wanamaker's, with suggestions for ways in which it could be bettered:

> A musical program has been compiled which has some merit. It is, however, by no means the last word in musical accompaniment. A little Gregorian chant and music interspersed with classic music of a religious tinge would seem to be at least as fully effective as the singing of a number of hymns. The works of Gounod, Haendel and Bach will be found full of good popular suitable music.[81]

Although Bush mentions "a musical program" compiled for the film, it seems that neither a cue sheet nor a score was distributed. When *From the Manger to the Cross* went into wide release in February 1913, Kalem's advertisements in *MPW* contained no references to the music, though the first one did offer a "lecture, couriers, photographs, etc."[82] Exhibitors were thus left to choose their own approach, but two types of accompaniment had at least been suggested. As envisaged by Sargent and carried out by Kalem, the presentation featured an unusual performing ensemble and an unusual repertoire. Bush left the question of ensemble open and called for a compilation comprised mostly of classical excerpts: music of more variety and complexity, apparently, than was heard at the preview. (His suggestions echo those which he made for *Dante's Inferno*, cited above.) Both types of accompaniment were far removed from the piano scores of Simon and the cue-sheet compilations of Sinn and others; both were meant to "exalt" the film beyond the reach of criticism.

Exotic in origin, atypical in subject and style, sanctified by a poetic title and rarefied music—in the Kalem annals *From the Manger to the Cross* was very much a special case. However, it had good company further afield: in 1912 and after, an increasing number of American and foreign features were given special "handling," particularly with regard to their musical accompaniment. Of these, perhaps the most consequential were produced by the two men to whom we now direct our attention.

Pioneers of Orchestral Scores, 1912–14

The history of film music in America owes much to Samuel Lionel Rothapfel, an exhibitor and theater manager, and Joseph Carl Breil, a composer and conductor. Each is now remembered primarily for later achievements (beginning in 1915), and none of their early scores is known to survive. However, important information concerning the initial stages of their careers has been discovered, and it is summarized below, with attention to two principal questions: (1) What is known about their earliest scores? and (2) In what ways did each man influence the field of film music during this period?

Samuel Lionel Rothapfel's Art of Exhibition

In 1911, less than three years after he began his career as an exhibitor, Rothapfel was dubbed "the Belasco of motion picture presentation." The phrase was the title of an article by McQuade published in *MPW* in 1911, in which the author surveyed Rothapfel's origins and rise in the motion picture field as follows. He was born in 1882, in Stillwater, Minnesota, to a German immigrant shoemaker; his family moved to Brooklyn twelve years later; at age eighteen he joined the Marines for six years, then drifted through a number of jobs, landing in Forest City, Pennsylvania, where in 1908 he married a saloon-keeper's daughter; and there, in January 1909, he opened a motion-picture theater in an abandoned dance hall next to the bar. His life's work had begun in earnest:

> In three months after opening [his "Forest City Family Theater"], he had a splendid business and no competition. . . . Ambitious to enter a larger field, he went to Philadelphia, where he installed his new idea of projection in Keith's Bijou Theater, being the first to project well-defined pictures in a lighted house. This success resulted in a contract with the United Booking Offices, by which he made a tour of the country, improving projection. . . . Later he conducted several picture enterprises for the U.B.O. people. He next entered the picture field in Milwaukee, where he opened Shubert's large house, the Alhambra, and offered its now celebrated pictures de luxe and broke all records for that house. He amazed the picture world as well as people in the dramatic business by his performances and success. Afterwards he came to Minneapolis, where he has far eclipsed his Milwaukee record.[83]

To extend McQuade's metaphor, it seems that every new stage in Rothapfel's career eclipsed the one before. In his move from the Alhambra in Milwaukee to the 1700-seat Lyric in Minneapolis (1911), the pattern was set. He moved in 1912 to the Lyric Theater in Chicago and was appointed general manager of the Shubert Circuit. Next he went to New York to preside over the opening and management of ever-grander theaters: the 2000-seat Regent, the first deluxe motion-picture theater in New York City (1913); the 3000-seat Strand, the first motion-picture theater to open on Broadway (1914); the Rialto in Times Square, dubbed "The Temple of the Motion Picture," with a forty-piece orchestra (1916); the Rivoli, with a façade modeled on the Parthenon, again on Broadway (1917); the 5300-seat Capitol (which opened in 1919, but was refurbished under Rothapfel's guidance and reopened in 1920); and finally his own "Cathedral of the Motion Picture," the 6200-seat Roxy (1927).[84]

Though Rothapfel's presentations in New York's "picture palaces" of the twenties are what he is best remembered for today, from the beginning of his career as an exhibitor his innovative practices were considered news. Twenty-eight articles concerning Rothapfel have been found in issues of *MPW* published between mid-1910 and early 1915. (They are listed in Appendix part 6.) The publications begin with Rothapfel's pioneering essay on film music, the first written by an exhibitor on the subject for *MPW*; they conclude with a six-part profile of Rothapfel by W. Stephen Bush, given the title "The Art of Exhibition" (nos. 20–22, 24, 26, and 28). In between there are a number of reports of Rothapfel's work in particular theaters: for example, Sinn's description of Rothapfel at the Alhambra and McQuade's of Rothapfel at the Lyric (nos. 2 and 3—the latter being the article containing the biographical information cited above). These and other items in Appendix part 6 contain information concerning three topics discussed below: Rothapfel's credits, the theatricality of his presentations, and his ideas about compiled scores.

ROTHAPFEL'S CREDITS. Throughout the silent period Rothapfel was credited with very few special scores. From the period in question, references have been found to only two: the first for the Cines film *Josephine*, described in cue-sheet fashion in one of Sinn's columns during the spring of 1912; the second for the Selig production of *The Coming of Columbus*, mentioned in a review of the film by McQuade, during the same period. (See Appendix part 6, nos. 5 and 6.[85]) In addition, Rothapfel may also have helped to prepare an arrangement of "sixty standard classics" announced by Selig for *The Spoilers* in February 1915.[86] (He had supervised the film's presentation with an elaborate acompaniment at the Strand ten months earlier: see Appendix part 6, no. 18.) Two compiled scores were published under Rothapfel's name in November 1915: one for the Vitagraph production of *The Battle Cry of Peace*, and one for Paramount's *Carmen*.[87]

Except for the *Josephine* cue sheet and these three or four scores, it seems that Rothapfel's compiled accompaniments were normally *not* prepared for distribution. Instead they were presented solely in theaters under his management. Yet these presentations were distinctive enough to earn considerable attention from *MPW*—more, indeed, than was given to most special scores.

Rothapfel's presentation of *Quo Vadis* provides an example: the film was shown with two types of accompaniment before Rothapfel's, but his received the most attention. In America, *Quo Vadis* was first exhibited at the Astor Theatre in New York during the spring and summer of 1913. According to the *New York Times*, "special incidental music was provided on a mechanical orchestral player."[88] In June of 1913 *MPW* announced that the film's distributor, George Kleine, planned to have fifteen companies touring the United States and Canada by September 1, with a presentation divided into three acts—"and special music has been arranged and composed for the performance."[89] In February 1914 Rothapfel offered his own presentation of the film at the Regent in New York, with a different orchestral accompaniment; and *MPW*'s reporters described this presentation in detail, with enthusiasm. (See Appendix part 6, nos. 14 and 15.)

In creating a compiled score for *Quo Vadis*, Rothapfel was observed working closely with the theater's music director, Carl Edouarde.[90] Such collaboration with professional musicians seems to have been a necessity for Rothapfel throughout his career. "The very first thing for the careful manager to do," Rothapfel stated in his 1910 essay (Appendix part 6, no. 1), "is to get a good musician; it will turn out to be the best investment you ever made." Once he found such musicians, Rothapfel apparently liked to tell them what to play and how to play it. In McQuade's review of a rehearsal for the presentation of *Cinderella* at the Lyric Theatre in Minneapolis (Appendix part 6, no. 3), there appears this description of Rothapfel at work:

> At a signal the operator began projecting the first picture. As it was being run off and watched by all, Mr. Rothapfel announced the score, and details for sound effects. He mentally seizes on the musical selections, on the spur of the moment, as if inspired. If an afterthought flashes the intelligence that a better selection than the one announced would be more appropriate, he signals the operator to stop and run several scenes over again. . . . It is strange that Mr. Rothapfel should state that he does not know a note of music, except by ear, yet he has the scores of every light opera and musical comedy at his command, and can draw on grand opera and on the symphonies to assist him in playing the pictures. In addition, he is familiar with the popular lyrics of many countries. When dissatisfied with the manner in which a musical selection is being conducted, he has been known to jump in and wield the baton himself. He gets at the very soul of a score, and brings out its beauty, or its weirdness, with the skill of a master.

A good manager, Rothapfel later stated (in item no. 21), "must control and inspire the leader"; and Bush, the author of this profile, described Rothapfel's inspiring conducting in terms as laudatory as those of McQuade:

> Watching him at such moments from the wings it is easy to get the right perspective of his passionate love and study of music. In his hands the baton indeed becomes a magic wand. His orchestra realizes the intimate touch between himself and them and this is a great advantage. It infuses into them a spirit of cooperation and responsibility.

Rothapfel may have had no formal musical training, but these two quoted passages suggest that he possessed strong musical instincts plus wide knowledge of repertoire. His talents enabled him to take control of the music to a degree that seems to have been rare among exhibitors. In two *MPW* items (nos. 15 and 16) Rothapfel was dubbed the "Napoleon" of motion-picture presentations, not a flattering term, perhaps, but one that communicates his wide-ranging ambition. His goal was to control and coordinate all the theatrical elements of film presentation himself; and it was his ability to do so, combined with the financial success that he brought to each theater he managed, that (in McQuade's phrase, taken from no. 3) "amazed the picture world." Though he helped to prepare few scores for distribution, his unique presentations of many films caught the attention of the public and those in the field.

THEATRICALITY. According to a playbill dating from the period when Rothapfel first began to manage the Family Theater in Forest City, the films were preceded by a different solo musical number every evening of the week: "a musical treat you won't forget."[91] This mixture of entertainment reflected the tradition of the variety show, and was nothing new; but for longer films Rothapfel came to seek more unified presentations, in which elements of live theater supported the films. For example, as manager of the Alhambra, he stated (in no. 2 of Appendix part 6) that "we are presenting pictures in this theater in an advanced form, using an orchestra on the stage with special stage settings, a staff of soloists, and effects to make the performance as realistic as possible." Similarly, as manager of the Lyric in Minneapolis, Rothapfel was praised (by McQuade, in no. 3) for the way he "staged" the pictures, using music and theatrical scenes to introduce them.

An elaborate example of such a staging is given in *MPW*'s description of *Quo Vadis* at the Regent, as put on by Rothapfel in February 1914. (See Appendix part 6, no. 14.) For this spectacle there were four presentations daily: two accompanied by pipe organ at 1 and 5 p.m., and two "deluxe" shows with orchestra at 3:15 and 8:15. According to the *MPW* report, the deluxe shows began as follows:

> Mr. Rothapfel had a competent dramatic speaker, William Calhoun, enter a box on the left side of the auditorium, and, with the answering of a question as to the meaning of *Quo Vadis?* from a young man sitting in the same box the speaker started to give a succinct little talk on how the author of the book, Henry Sienkiewicz, obtained his idea for the story. After Mr. Calhoun had given a brief story of the film the heavy asbestos curtain was raised to singing and displayed the orchestra garlanded in flowers. The singers' romantic recesses on each side of the stage were also festooned in greenery.
>
> Three resounding blasts from trumpets accompanied by the rest of the orchestra started the entertainment proper on its way.

A second example of Rothapfel's staging of a film is described in *MPW*'s account of a "Notable Showing of *The Eternal City*," at New York City's Lyceum Theater in December 1914 (Appendix part 6, no. 25):

> Although Mr. Rothapfel had but a few days in which to prepare the premiere, he succeeded materially in enhancing the pleasure of the performance and in increasing the atmosphere of the big Roman production. Two large stage sets had been prepared, one being shown just before the performance, and the second just following the intermission. The first showed the Tiber, with the light shining across the water from buildings on the shore. The second preceded the showing of the stormy scenes in the Coliseum.
>
> Cheering men massed behind the curtain lent verisimilitude to the views of

> the throngs applauding David Rossi in the jubilee procession and later in the Coliseum. A bell tolled at the indicated times added to the effectiveness. The music, given by a concealed orchestra, was well chosen.

These reviews illustrate how carefully Rothapfel "set the stage" for his film presentations; and by calling attention to live performers before the films began, he invested each presentation with theatrical legitimacy. His primary purpose, however, was to use theatrical effects to focus audience attention on the films. Sound effects and crowd noises, for example, made the films seem more realistic (in theatrical terms) than they would have seemed with musical accompaniment alone. As for music, Rothapfel once stated (in Appendix part 6, no. 21) that its "main object is to interpret the story on the screen. . . . When a musician begins to think that the people come mainly to hear the music and that the pictures are but an incident, he has outlived his usefulness with me." To achieve such musical interpretation Rothapfel devised elaborate compiled scores.

ROTHAPFEL'S IDEAS CONCERNING COMPILATION. The earliest known description of the contents of a Rothapfel score are his musical suggestions for the Cines film *Josephine*, which he contributed to Sinn's column. (See Appendix part 6, no. 5.) These suggestions resemble those of a cue sheet, but Rothapfel's comments indicate that he was describing a score that had been performed under his supervision (probably at the Lyric, in Minneapolis). He offered detailed performance instructions and specified the most effective ensemble for the music (though he left the task of creating an arrangement for the recommended ensemble to others):

> At the opening of picture play *Sunshine and Shadow* waltz, with spirit, until Josephine's husband and children are arrested; then break into *Marseillaise*. Play pianissimo until mob breaks into room, then crescendo. Continue until mob leaves room; gradually diminish as Josephine [has] vision of her husband's death.
>
> Crescendo again at the sub-title "After the Death of Robespierre, Josephine and Her Two Children Are Liberated." Play with spirit. . . . Play *Pomp and Circumstance* march, Elgar, very slow tempo, first movement. By repeating this movement it will just about bring you to the [wedding] ceremony. Swing into second movement, play with very slow tempo until sub-title "Napoleon Announces. . . ."
>
> As she reads [letter] mute all strings and play with great feeling *Simple Aveu*; this is to be continued throughout the balance of the picture and can be used with crescendo where Napoleon shows the new-born baby to the populace, but must diminish again as Josephine reads the letter which advises her that a new heir is born.
>
> This arrangement is made after a practical demonstration and will be found very efficient and simple, only four numbers being used in the entire picture; [it] can be played effectively with piano, organ or orchestra of any number of pieces. The best effect will be obtained by a pipe organ, piano, two violins, 'cello, flute, clarinet, trombone, cornet and tympani. If lecturer is used, mute all instruments.

Rothapfel's accompaniments were not limited to one type of repertoire. The *Josephine* score contained four pieces, including light concert fare (*Pomp and Circumstance*), salon music (*Simple Aveu*) and an anthem (the *Marseillaise*). When *Quo Vadis* was presented at the Regent (in early 1914), the music was apparently very different. The reviewer mentioned (but did not identify) selections from *Faust*,

Tannhäuser, *Tosca*, and *Parsifal* in the score; and the film's "awe-inspiring prelude" was described as follows:

> Delicately interwoven were selections from noted composers, symbols of parts of the picture, such as the march of the gladiators, the chariot race, the burning of Rome, etc. This [prelude] . . . as well as the rest of the accompaniment, held one spellbound. . . . The music alone was well worth the admission price. It is difficult to estimate the value of such appropriate accompaniments [Appendix part 6, no. 14].

The use of music by "noted composers" was a way for Rothapfel (and the conductor, Carl Edouarde) to match the grandeur of this particular eight-reel film.[92]

For Rothapfel the goal was not to present one type of music, but to use the repertoire to illustrate the film, and in selecting pieces, to avoid the clichés of melodrama. He commented on these goals to Bush (in item no. 21) making two key points. First, he discounted the "hackneyed stuff" which usually comes into "playing the pictures": "little 'hurries' for galloping horses, a little pathos for a touching scene, etc." Second, he discussed the basic requirements for a good accompaniment:

> . . . each big picture—the feature of the program, if you will—must be interpreted musically by a general theme which characterizes the nature of the film play. To select this theme it is, of course, necessary to study the entire picture. Let me give an example. In the play of *Such a Little Queen*, in which Mary Pickford takes the leading part, a little waltz from *Sari* [a Broadway musical of early 1914] appealed to me. It had a note of pathos alternating with brilliancy and I thought it typical of the character of the queen. . . . I had the original waltz played as the little queen was coming down the stairs, and it interpreted in a flash the characteristics of the leading character. . . .
>
> I can give no hard and fast rules for the selection of such a theme. A little knowledge of musical repertoire is needed, of course, and one really cannot have too much of this. A musical memory, too, is essential. . . . After having chosen a general theme for my big feature, I feel at liberty to introduce incidental music which has no relation to the general theme. Such incidental music may be a march, a few bars of a popular or patriotic song, etc. This incidental music must fit episodes and situations that are not directly and intimately connected with the main character or the strict dramatic action of the photoplay.

From the description of the *Quo Vadis* score quoted above, and from this general passage, we can infer that Rothapfel's ideas about accompaniment had evolved beyond his thinking at the time of *Josephine*. In certain respects the score for *Josephine* was similar to Simon's for *An Arabian Tragedy* (which appeared in the same year, 1912). Each of these scores contained a series of separate numbers, performed in succession; each score repeated or varied certain numbers for dramatic effect; and neither of them contained a "general theme" for the film. They were both in a sense compilations of incidental music, one of new pieces, one of borrowed material, in which all segments weighed more or less equally.

By 1914 Rothapfel had come to feel the need for a theme to accompany each new "big picture," probably so as to give unity to his compiled scores as the length of features grew; and in his distinction between theme music and incidental music he anticipated the kind of compilation Breil created for *The Birth of a Nation* the following year. (However, the Breil score contained several themes rather than one and most of them were composed by Breil rather than selected from pre-existent repertoire.) At this stage of his career Rothapfel did not call for *composition* of a score, or even themes for a score. "There are a wealth of excerpts from operas and overtures that have never been used," he stated, in continuation of the last passage cited above, "and they will be found suitable for all kinds of occasions." His art of exhibition was focused on compilation, a method that enabled him to supervise the music along with the rest of the presentation; and he demonstrated to others that one does not need to be a composer (though one does need professional musicians) to create a dramatically effective score for a film. It remained for Breil to demonstrate how effective a compilation using original music could be.

Joseph Carl Breil's Earliest Film Scores

Breil (b. Pittsburgh, 1870 – d. Los Angeles, 1926) spent much of his career composing for the theater. Of particular importance to his career was the incidental music for Edward Locke's stage play *The Climax* in 1909; music for D. W. Griffith's films *The Birth of a Nation* in 1915 and *Intolerance* in 1916; and a one-act opera, *The Legend*, which was performed three times at the Metropolitan in New York in 1919.[93] These dramatic compositions gained Breil much attention in print; and owing to *The Legend*, his name appeared in a number of reference works not normally open to film composers of the silent period.[94] Before and after *The Legend*, moreover, Breil penned many essays and gave lengthy interviews. He also left behind a collection of materials pertinent to his career: clippings, manuscripts, and scrapbooks containing personal documents.[95] As a result, sources on Breil are numerous (far more so than on Simon, for example); and many of them provide evidence of his significance as a pioneer in the field of film music.

Yet Breil's earliest achievements as a pioneer are at present difficult to assess, since none of the film scores he composed, arranged, or conducted before *The Birth of a Nation* is known to survive. However, the sources which have been discovered shed light on the circumstances of his entry into the field and include Breil's descriptions of two of his earliest scores, *Queen Elizabeth* and *Cabiria*. Though the material is sketchy, it suggests that Breil's ideas about film music differed from those of Simon and Rothapfel, and that he did much to expand the possibilities for film music in America at this time.

Three sources from the teens give detailed information concerning Breil's youth and the early stages of his career: a 1914 theatrical *Who's Who*, a musical *Who's Who* published four years later, and a 1919 interview given by Breil in advance of the first performance of *The Legend*. In the interview Breil spoke of his childhood, stating that his mother started him on violin lessons at age eleven. Early on he developed a passionate interest in the theater; but his father, a prosperous lawyer, disapproved of such a career and "regarded the law as the one suitable profession for his only son." Nevertheless, Breil composed an opera at age seventeen, and continued to pursue private musical studies while attending colleges in Pennsylvania and the University of Liepzig, where he was sent to learn law. When he returned to Pittsburgh, his father gave him some very simple cases to handle; but he "blew" them all and was told that henceforth he would have to get along "by his own purse and perspiration."[96]

Much of what Breil recounts here is also found in the 1914 and 1918 biographical dictionaries, though more concisely and in dry, impersonal terms. Where the dictionaries are most helpful is in the information they supply about the various stages of Breil's career, from the 1890s into the early teens. (For a summary of this data see Appendix part 7, which also incorporates pertinent facts gathered from materials in the Breil collection at UCLA.) For nearly two decades, the record suggests a slow but steady increase in recognition, gained through continuous experience as a singer, conductor, arranger, and composer.[97] The turning point came in 1909, when he wrote the incidental music for the Broadway production of *The Climax*.[98] Various reviews pointed out the importance of the music in this play and praised Breil's compositions.[99] In particular, the *Song of the Soul* found a large audience; it became one of Breil's most popular songs and was published in several arrangements, including some dating from more than two decades later.[100]

After *The Climax*, Breil seems to have devoted himself mostly to dramatic composition. He composed songs and incidental music for five comedies between 1910 and 1913, and five stage works of varied types (including the opera *The Legend*) between 1914 and 1926.[101] In addition, during the early teens Breil turned to film music, and about a decade later one source credited him with "many hundreds of film scores."[102] The figure is very likely inflated: today Breil is known with certainty to have composed, arranged, and/or conducted music for about two dozen specific films. Yet those titles do include several important features of the early teens, principally *Queen Elizabeth* in 1912 and *Cabiria* in 1914. Owing to his work on these and other features, Breil was later dubbed "The Father of Motion Picture Music," a misleading phrase, but one that attests to his pre-eminent position in the field.[103]

On Breil's earliest film scores, the biographical dictionaries cited in Appendix part 7 are not in agreement. The 1914 *Who's Who* makes no mention of films, perhaps because at that time they weren't considered to be worthy of notice in a theatrical reference work. By 1918, with scores for *Birth of a Nation* and *Intolerance* to his credit, Breil's achievements as a film composer were not to be ignored; and the entry in the second *Who's Who* lists six films of 1912 and 1913: *Queen Elizabeth*, *Camille*, *Mme. Sans-Gêne*, *The Prisoner of Zenda*, *Tess of the D'Urbervilles* and *In the Bishop's Carriage*.

In the literature by and about Breil this list of film scores is unusual, because four of them are not mentioned elsewhere. The composer often recalled his score for *Queen Elizabeth*, and sometimes *The Prisoner of Zenda*, but he ignored (or forgot) the others. Indeed, Breil regarded the score for *Queen Elizabeth* as his most innovative work before *The Birth of a Nation*. In an essay written for *Metronome* in 1916 he claimed that it was "the first original score ever composed (in the world) for a 'movie.'"[104] At other times he dropped the word "original" from his claim, as in the 1918 *Who's Who*, which simply termed the music for *Queen Elizabeth* the "first score ever written for a moving picture"; the latter version was repeated in many subsequent reports on Breil.[105] Both statements are incorrect, as we have seen, since Breil's scores were preceded by those of Saint-Saëns and Simon (though Breil may have been unaware of them); moreover, Breil might have written scores for *Camille* and *Mme. Sans-Gêne* before *Queen Elizabeth*.

Camille and *Mme. Sans-Gêne* were star vehicles for Bernhardt and Réjane, produced by the Film d'Art company in 1911, and released in America in February 1912 as two halves of a double bill.[106] To date, only one article in *MPW* has been found to contain any information about music for the two films:

> The reels will be offered together to state rights men with a stipulation that they shall form an evening's entertainment and shall be used only in first-class houses. With the possible exception of the well-known Dante pictures [i.e., *Dante's Inferno*] this program will form the most pleasing evening's entertainment that has yet been offered in this or any other country. Appropriate music has been prepared for these subjects and a fine line of advertising will accompany the pictures. Their appearance will set a new standard in the motion picture exhibition business and give a wonderful impetus to the feature picture in America.[107]

Perhaps the "appropriate music" mentioned in this article was the same as the pair of scores for these films credited to Breil in the 1918 *Who's Who*, but there is no evidence to connect the two. Indeed, none of the many advertisements for these films mentioned music at all; nor did subsequent reviews of the films in either *MPW* or the *New York Dramatic Mirror*.[108]

The film of *Queen Elizabeth* was also a vehicle for Bernhardt (based upon a play she performed in Paris in April 1912).[109] In America it was distributed with great financial success by the Famous Players Film Company, formed by Adolph Zukor (who had bought the American rights to the film and helped to finance its production), in partnership with theatrical producer Daniel Frohman.[110] Their promotion of the film was planned in several stages. First a private screening was arranged in New York, in July 1912, for exhibitors and the press, at Frohman's theater, the Lyceum.[111] Second, innovative advertisements for the film began to appear in *MPW* in July.[112] Third, on 12 August the film made its public debut at Powers', a legitimate Chicago theater, on a reserve-seat basis, two shows a day.[113] Moreover, the premiere at Powers' seems to have been planned to coincide with a national convention of motion-picture exhibitors then being held in the city—an efficient way to promote the film nationwide.[114]

In announcing *Queen Elizabeth*'s Chicago premiere, *MPW* noted that the exhibition would be "billed like a high-class legitimate road attraction . . . presented with special music and lecture."[115] As had been the case with the Film d'Art double bill, the composer of this "special music" was not identified. However, Breil's score for the film was registered for copyright by Famous Players, and in the copyright entry its date of publication was stated to be 15 August 1912, three days after the date of the Chicago premiere.[116] Three days later—that is, on 18 August—an advertisement for the film appeared in the *Chicago Tribune* mentioning "incidental music by Carl Joseph Breil" (*sic*).[117]

From these sources one can infer the Breil's score was heard during the film's engagement in Chicago, and the inference has now become a virtual certainty, thanks to a pair of clippings discovered in one of the Breil scrapbooks. They contain identical versions of the same article, cut from two different trade papers, one without any publication data, the other headed *The Music News* but lacking a page number or date. (It is not known which of these items was published first; evidently one was a reprint of the other, or both were reprints of an earlier article.) Titled "Moving Pictures Extraordinary," the first half of the article lauds the film, the second half the music. The most pertinent passages follow:

> At Powers' Theatre there is being presented *Elizabeth* in moving pictures, these having been made in Paris where the great play is now current. . . . The production is one of superb finish and wonderful sweep, . . . and an evening spent watching this presentation is well worth while. . . .
>
> Mr. Joseph Carl Breil, composer of *The Climax*, has written an especial score for it, and this is of great elaborateness as well as being accurately descriptive to the most minute detail. At Powers it is given with piano only, but even in this attenuated shape it shows marvelous care on the part of the composer, and the movement of the play is followed very accurately.
>
> There is considerable "leit motif" used, and the stress and accent of the music follows the line of the story in surprising degree. . . . Between the parts of the play a young woman, wearing a Chicago Musical College medal, sings some old English songs very prettily.

The last sentence reminds us that Rothapfel was by no means the only showman who sought ingenious concoctions of play and photoplay, of spotlight solos and subordinate accompaniments: in theaters everywhere, audiences encountered delightful blends of attractions. Unusually for the time, though, in the present case it was the special score that prompted considerable comment—if only for a moment. For despite the favorable notice, the strong possibility exists that Breil's score for *Queen Elizabeth* was not heard at very many presentations in Chicago, due to an ongoing dispute between the musicians' union and several theater owners, led by none other than Powers. The strife may explain why only a piano version of the score—played by Breil himself?—was heard; but whether or not labor grievances were a factor, no other mention of Breil's music for *Queen Elizabeth* dating from 1912 has been found.[118] Only later, as Breil worked on *Cabiria*, *The Birth of a Nation*, and *Intolerance*, were additional descriptions of his music for *Queen Elizabeth* published; intriguingly, each stressed the innovative qualities of the score, in a manner consistent with the review cited above.

The earliest of these descriptions was published when Breil was conducting the music for *Cabiria* in San Francisco, during July 1914. The latter film and its music received much attention from the *San Francisco Chronicle*, and the newspaper made Breil the subject of two profiles. (What they tell us about *Cabiria* will be discussed below.) In one of these profiles the music for *Queen Elizabeth* was described, with what seem to be Breil's words, as follows:

> Briel [*sic*] was the first composer of quality to be attracted to the motion picture as an inspiration to composition. For Frohman's "Famous Players," he wrote the synchronizing score to *Queen Elizabeth*, which attracted the attention of musicians generally by the modern spirit in which it was penned. Each of the principals in the cast was given a "motive," such as Wagner identified his mythological characters with, and these themes, characteristic of the personages in the

> drama of the Stuart Queen, the Duke of Essex, the Duchess of Nottingham, Earl of Nottingham and the rest of the persons [in] the play, including the masculine Queen herself, were woven ingeniously in the texture of Briel's orchestral score.[119]

Two further descriptions of the score were published in *Metronome* in the second half of 1916, both in response to an article by Victor Herbert, who had recently composed a score for a Griffith-influenced (but inferior) epic, *The Fall of a Nation*. Herbert took pains to stress that his score's "every note was original," and he criticized the "patchwork" scores then common, with pointed allusions to the music of *The Birth of a Nation*.[120] The first rebuttal came in a lengthy letter from a conductor for films, Buel Rissinger. He sought to set the record straight by recalling some early scores "overlooked" by Herbert. First he remembered the operatic adaptations for *Il Trovatore* and *Faust*. (His remarks about them were cited above, in the discussion of the earliest special scores.) His most detailed comments—and strongest praise—were reserved for *Queen Elizabeth*:

> In 1911 [*sic*] Carl Breil wrote an original score for the production of *Queen Elizabeth*, with Sarah Bernhardt in the title role. The writer personally conducted the score in several houses of the Valentine Circuit, carrying six men and using the house men. I particularly remember our arrival in Toledo. The house leader was greatly surprised that a rehearsal should be called for a moving picture, and even more so when he learned that the picture was carrying a few men and a leader. . . . This score was complete and perfect in every detail, covering the action of the entire six reels [*sic*], and, aside from the fact that the British national air was used during the scenes depicting the return of the victorious British fleet over the Spanish Armada, the score was original. The writer conducted this score over the circuit above mentioned and also in several of the larger picture houses in that territory, using from ten to fifteen men, six of whom we carried.[121]

Rissinger makes clear that the score was distributed with the film after all, in a manner far removed from conventional practice (and from the peculiar circumstances of the Chicago premiere). He also confirms that the score was "original," although he says nothing about its use of leitmotifs.

It took Breil to hammer the point (as he had done before) in his own response to Herbert, an essay published by *Metronome* in November 1916. He began by looking back on conditions within the industry as they had struck him before his entry into the field:

> The dramatization portrayed on the screen in those days were of the same lurid type as the melodramas of some thirty years ago. Among legitimate actors the movie field was derided. . . . The "pianist" of those days too was execrable. . . . I rarely attended screen productions and then only at the urgent solicitations of some friend who happened to be interested in it.

Breil painted a picture too dark for a period of great flux; his purpose was to stress the impact made by *Queen Elizabeth* upon his musical imagination. As in his description of the score published in the *Chronicle* in 1914, in his *Metronome* essay he compared his own method to Wagner's:

> . . . when Daniel Frohman entered the movie field and called upon me to write a score for Sarah Bernhardt's *Queen Elizabeth*, I suddenly awoke to the possibilities of the "Moving Picture." Here was a real drama played by the greatest of artists. I realized at once that trivial music would not do, and set to work to write a score that would portray human emotions from a truly diginified point of view. With the limited means of a small orchestra put at my disposal then, I set to work and wrote a dramatic score built very much upon the motif lines set down by Richard Wagner. That was about six years ago [*sic*], and the score to *Queen Elizabeth* was the first original score ever composed (in the world) for a "movie."[122]

Rissinger and Breil described the score for *Queen Elizabeth* four years after it had appeared, seeking to diminish the significance of Herbert's contribution to the history of film music, and to magnify Breil's. Perhaps for these reasons, both men placed the date of the film too early—Rissinger in 1911, Breil in 1910—thereby making the score seem a more impressive achievement. Both may also have described the style of the music incorrectly, or overestimated its importance. We have no way of knowing whether the entire score was actually original. (All of the scores by Breil which *do* survive contain borrowed material.) There is also this discrepancy to bear in mind: despite Breil's attention to *Queen Elizabeth* in later years, at the time of the film's original release, he seems to have been barely noticed. For example, Breil's name never appeared in *MPW* when *Queen Elizabeth* was in circulation; he emerged in that periodical for the first time as the composer of the score for *The Prisoner of Zenda*, the next Famous Players film.[123]

The earliest *MPW* reference to Breil in connection to *Zenda* is found in a report on the completion of the film in February 1913; thereafter, Famous Players promoted the score, and identified Breil as its composer, in all *Zenda* advertisements during March and April of the same year.[124] Yet he apparently never spoke or wrote of this score as he did of *Queen Elizabeth*. He also kept silent about his scores for two other Famous Players films of 1913, *Tess of the D'Urbervilles* and *In the Bishop's Carriage*, though both are listed in the 1918 *Who's Who*; likewise, the *MPW* advertisements for these films make no mention of music.[125] As these points illustrate, many unanswered questions surround Breil's earliest film scores; nevertheless, the extant sources suggest that by 1913 the composer had taken a leading role in the field, a role he continued to play the following year, through the presentations of *Cabiria*.

Between 1911 and 1914, as Pratt has stated, Italian films, which were "long familiar in one-reel comedies and dramas, . . . blossomed into spectacles."[126] Two of these films, *Dante's Inferno* of 1911 and *Homer's Odyssey* of 1912, were discussed above, in the survey of the earliest special scores. They were among the first feature films to be distributed across the United States by means of touring companies, and to be presented in legitimate theaters. In 1913 and 1914 several more films were presented in a similar manner: among them, *Quo Vadis*, *The Last Days of Pompeii*, *Antony and Cleopatra*, *Spartacus*, and what Pratt terms "the climax of Italian importation," *Cabiria*. These films were elaborate productions lasting six reels or more; and all were provided with special scores. (See Appendix part 3, Nos. 58, 79, 85, 95, and 98.)

Cabiria was indeed the climactic film in this series of Italian epics. It was the only one to be reissued in the early sound period, and to be revived in recent times with the accompaniment of its original score.[127] It was also the only one to be credited to a leading author: in the literature of the period the film was often advertised as [Gabriele] "D'Annunzio's Photoplay." Press releases made extravagant claims for the film (a cast numbered at 5000, a budget said to be $250,000), and drew attention to the film's unprecedented length (12 reels), and popularity. Its unusual success was the subject of many *MPW* advertisements, including one published on 9 January 1915, more than seven months after the film's American premiere at the Knickerbocker Theater in New York:

CABIRIA
Master Film of the Age
Now Playing to Record Breaking
Receipts Everywhere Shown

7 Months on Broadway, New York City
at Knickerbocker, Globe and Weber's Theaters
to nearly 1,000,000 admissions
5 MONTHS IN CHICAGO
10 WEEKS IN SAN FRANCISCO
12 WEEKS IN BOSTON
10 WEEKS IN PHILADELPHIA
. . . at prices ranging from 25 cents to $2.00.[128]

Cabiria's success was such that abundant documentary material survives: for example, in *MPW* alone there are reports on the film virtually every week from May 1914 until the end of the year.[129] Moreover, the publicity surrounding the film and its music includes Breil's earliest known detailed comments about the nature of film music, comments that appeared in the daily press. This was the first time film music came to be so honored.

The importance of the music for *Cabiria*, and the grand theatrical manner of the film's presentation, were points stressed in *MPW* by the anonymous reviewer who attended the film's New York premiere:

> The staging of *Cabiria* was in a manner befitting the dignity of the subject. The specially written music was interpreted by an orchestra or fifty or more pieces. A large chorus concealed on the stage gave several numbers during the course of the evening. . . . To say that never before had such a presentation of a motion picture been given in this country seems well within the bounds of conservative statement. The magnitude and the manner of the presentation of the production, as well as its musical accompaniment, both instrumental and vocal, justify the remark.[130]

Who composed the music which was found to be so effective? Therein lies a tricky question. One composer often given credit for the *Cabiria* score is Ildebrando Pizzetti, but as Cherchi Usai has explained, Pizzetti, though paid 20,000 lire to write music for the film, became "daunted" by the magnitude of the task, and "decided to confine his efforts to the *Sinfonia del Fuoco*, leaving the rest of the music for a film some three and a half hours in length to be written by his pupil Manlio Mazza."[131] Sure enough, when the film traveled across the United States, various sources did identify Mazza (and, variously, Marza and Mazzo) as the score's creator, without mentioning Pizzetti; but they also implied that the music was more compiled than composed. Furthermore, Breil (or "Briel") is sometimes credited as the conductor, and, as in the case of *Queen Elizabeth*, it remains difficult to determine the full extent of his role.[132]

We know that Breil conducted the score in at least three major cities (Chicago, San Francisco, and Los Angeles); we can assume that he also helped to adapt the score for the film's American tour, but to an undetermined degree. In the *Metronome* essay written in 1916, two years after the film had appeared, he himself stated that "when *Cabiria* was in the making, the American managers called upon me to provide it with a musical setting."[133] In this context "to provide" is an ambiguous infinitive which could mean to compose, adapt, or arrange, and the ambiguity may have been intentional—Breil's way of stretching the language to expand his own role. He was more forthright about these matters, but not consistent, in the summer of 1914, while engaged with the score in San Francisco—a time and place when it would have been easier to catch him in misstatements. Here is what he wrote about his role in a letter to the *Pacific Coast Musical Review*, trying, as was his wont, to set the record straight:

> Thank you for your kindly mention of my work with *Cabiria* in your latest issue. But the choruses are not operatic selections. The Baal Baal [*sic*] is from Mendelssohn's *Elijah*. The "Men of Carthage" (trip over the Alps) and the "Fire Chorus," during the burning of the fleet, are both my compositions, the latter composed especially for this scene, while I was aboard the Twentieth Century from New York to Chicago to produce the show there. The last chorus is from "Cowen's Rose Maiden." With kindest regards. . . .[134]

Nowhere else does Breil paint so vivid a picture of his hectic preparation for *Cabiria*, and this is the only time he seemed eager to claim particular segments of the score as his own. (The implication of his remarks is that Pizzetti's contribution to *Cabiria*, for whatever reason, was replaced by Breil's.) Before and after the letter quoted above, when his views were printed at length in the *San Francisco Chronicle*, he adopted a more magisterial tone, placing the burden of the music squarely on Mazza's shoulders. The first article, a profile of the composer given the impressive title "Music and 'Movies' Offer New Art Form," begins by recalling Breil's music for *The Climax*. There follows a paragraph concerning his "modern" score for *Queen Elizabeth* (quoted above), which shows the composer's eagerness to put himself in the vanguard and to equate himself with the "future Wagners" of film music. (The latter phrase appears in the article's subtitle.) In the next paragraph Breil praises the "manifest merit" of Colburn's original score for *Antony and Cleopatra*.[135] Only then are his views of the score for *Cabiria* quoted, with explicit reference to its compiler:

> The musical score to *Cabiria* was arranged by an Italian composer, Manlio Mazzo [*sic*], whose convictions in favor of the old school of music are discovered in the

> selections he has chosen as interpretative of the scenes. Musicians will be entertained in locating from their memory the various complete selections and themes he has taken. Mendelssohn's *Fingal's Cave* music, a Spontini march, another march from Donizetti's *Lucia de Lammermoor*, a Mozart Gavotte, and a selection from Gluck's *Alceste* are some of the classic compositions employed by Mazzo, who has attempted no other work than conjoining the music of the classic related composers by the simplest of modulations.[136]

In a second *Chronicle* article, Breil's attitude toward the score seems quite different, even though the title, "New Form of Music Born of the 'Movies,'" is almost indistinguishable from that of the first:

> "No easy task confronts the composer who attempts to fit his music to a motion picture," says Briel [*sic*], who, as the first American composer of prominence to undertake this work, is entitled to respectful attention. "Frequently a composer will find already at hand some orchestral work that will meet exactly the requirements, as for instance the introduction in *Cabiria* of the beautiful melody by Gluck from *Alceste*, which could not be bettered in so far as it expresses the sweetness and tenderness of the little Sicilian girl. At other times the composer or arranger for motion picture music must find within himself the music which will at once be inspired by the episode it accompanies and represent it as well.
>
> "The nicest difficulty is encountered in rendering the music synchronous with the picture, as for instance the little flute motive taken from Mozart which is heard when the pan pipes are played in the picture. The music here must be coterminous with the action, for it would be absurd were the melody to continue after the pipes had been removed from the lips of the figure in the picture."[137]

In the first article, Breil speaks somewhat patronizingly of Mazza's fondness for repertoire of the "old school"—that is, pre-Wagnerian, non-leitmotivic music. He also makes Mazza's task seem easy: merely the "conjoining" of compositions "by the simplest of modulations." In the second article, Breil seems more favorably inclined to recognize both the virtues of compiled scores and the difficulties to be faced when assembling them. Together, the two reports suggest more than a little ambivalence on his part concerning the enterprise in which he was involved; acknowledging the impressive aspects of the score for *Cabiria*, Breil nevertheless seems to think that the "novel field" of film music offers a wider range of styles than were drawn upon by Mazza.

When the film opened in Los Angeles in the fall, two articles in the *Los Angeles Times* also focused on the impact of the music, but without much attention to Breil, hence, with other perspectives on its contents. The first one noted the score's operatic qualities:

> . . . This wonderful story of the Punic Wars is an epic brought down from the Mediterranean mythology, and has been transfigured into poetry demanding a musical surrounding, and so Manlio Marza [*sic*], Italy's composer, sharing honors with Mascagni and Leoncavallo, composed the music for this great photoplay. The music demands a large orchestra and a big chorus of mixed voices, and the libretto requires special attention. It has been taken from the works of Ovid and D'Annunzio, and its arrangement was effected by Belli Simonson, while the presentation at Trinity Auditorium will be under the direction of Josef Carl Breil.[138]

The writer of the second article in the *Los Angeles Times* was even more enthusiastic. The large role given to the chorus, one of this score's most unusual features, was described, and some of its contents identified:

> Vivid and wonderful as the pictures of D'Annunzio's *Cabiria* are, the all-pervading music—it cannot be called Incidental—of Manlio Marza [*sic*], is hardly less so. Together these two, the haunting music and the beautiful moving-picture drama, give us a new departure in the realm of the rapid film, and one which will undoubtedly place this art among the classics. *Cabiria* marks the beginning—what wonders will follow? . . .
>
> The large audiences in attendance at Trinity Auditorium heard a chorus selected from the various choirs of our city—a chorus that had been at work in rehearsal for many days under the baton of Joseph Dupuy, and a good symphonic body of players uniting under the master hand of Conductor Briel [*sic*]. These interpret the music of Marza.
>
> The composer, however, has felt free to draw upon his own opera of *Orfeo* for much of the music of *Cabiria*, graceful melodies that lend their color to the quieter scenes. There are operatic settings for Hannibal crossing the Alps, there is stirring war music before the walls of Carthage, selections from *Elijah* in the scenes in the Temple of Moloch, and the *Marche Héroique* presents stirring magnetic and triumphant color to the noise of battle. Plaintive airs of the Orient are introduced in the desert scenes, while there are quick, stirring rhythmic measures in the court scenes of the palace.[139]

The six commentaries cited above do little more than hint at the contents of the score for *Cabiria*, but they make one very clear point about this elaborate compilation: here was film music of unprecedented impact. The same point was stressed, forcefully yet reflectively, in another description of the score published late in 1914 that commands our attention. Originally an editorial in the *Bridgeport Morning Telegram*, subsequently reprinted by Sinn in his *MPW* column, it was headed "The Music Drama of the Future"; but despite the Wagnerian title, the writer began by asserting that neither opera nor melodrama (that is, spoken drama with music) could contain the ideal "wedding of musical art to dramatic art." The first genre was too full of absurdities, the second too unbalanced a mixture. Having seen *Cabiria* (at Poli's theater, in Bridgeport), he was now convinced that moving pictures solved all such problems—or promised to:

> The acting is perfect, the staging is incomparable, the whole is in pantomime, and a production once fixed in the films, is absolutely standardized and can be set to music once and for all, as perfectly as a glove fits the hand. The producers of *Cabiria* have attempted to realize, in part at lest, this ideal, and hence the big orchestra that accompanies the play, and the hidden chorus have a score that follows every turn of the great drama that is presented. Perhaps one of the world's great future musicians will see the possibilities thus presented and such a combination of music and drama will be established as a permanent form of art.[140]

Sinn followed these words with a reminder that he had prophesied in much the same vein four years before, and he affirmed his belief that there was no "perhaps" about it, such a wedding "must come." In the meantime, readers were advised to go see *Cabiria*, as an example of an art "now well on its way."

The Bridgeport editorial brings this survey of early special scores in America back to its starting point: the idea, expressed in *MPW* from 1910 onward, that film music should look to the dramatic music of the past for inspiration. As has been seen above, well before *The Birth of a Nation* film music in America *did* look to the past in many different ways. Newly composed film scores, such as Simon's for *An Arabian Tragedy*, assembled bits and pieces of music full of clichés, but in a novel manner. Compiled scores, such as the ones created by Rothapfel for *Quo Vadis* and by Mazza (and Breil) for *Cabiria*, borrowed from established repertoires; and if compilers pasted music together out of expediency, some also sought to elevate the quality of the film experience by insuring, in Breil's words, that the selections would "meet exactly the requirements" of the film. However, the "conjoining" of borrowed music is in fact no easy thing when the repertoire ranges from *Alceste* to *Elijah*, from Mozart to Mazza, from a Donizetti march ("D'immenso giubilo"?) to a song of rosy maidens and a symphony of fire. So Breil, at times uncomfortable with the task, also looked back to the past for another method, the use of leitmotifs—an approach he professed to find both "dignified" and "modern," and therefore more suitable to the innovative films with which he was associated.

At present, there are still too many uncertainties about Breil's early scores to know much about how these methods were actually applied, and there are a lot of uncertainties about most of the other special scores created in America before 1915 as well. Attention now turns to *The Birth of a Nation*, in part because of its historical significance, and in part because it is the first score composed for an elaborate feature which can be studied in full, in relationship to the images it accompanies. The music, with its mixture of borrowed material and newly composed themes (which Breil termed "leitmotifs"), brings questions about the nature of compiled scores into sharper focus.

Sinn, in his comments on *Cabiria*, looked ahead to the true "wedding" of film and music. In a conventional novel (and many a twentieth-century film), once the wedding has come, the story happily ends. For the analyst, such a wedding marks the beginning of the story, one to be watched, listened to, and written about. One of the first writers who attempted to analyze the contribution to *The Birth of a Nation* made by Breil's score termed the fusion "a marriage of music and spectacle."[141] He did so about half a year after the marriage had begun; four score years later, we are still trying to understand its workings.

FOUR

Breil's Score for The Birth of a Nation

Significance

This and the next chapter contain studies of contrasting scores for two enduring silent films. The first, *The Birth of a Nation* (1915), is a three-hour epic with a compiled score by a minor American composer. The second, *Entr'acte* (1924), is a twenty-minute non-narrative comedy with an original score by an influential figure in the French avant-garde. Each composer worked in collaboration with the director of the film, an unusual arrangement during the silent period; each sought to compose music uniquely suited to a particular film, yet each employed techniques found in various scores considered above.

The Birth of a Nation is more difficult to discuss than *Entr'acte* (or *L'Assassinat*, or *An Arabian Tragedy*) because it evokes more ambivalent responses. Many critical observers feel compelled both to honor and to condemn it, even in a single sentence. For Jean Mitry, one of the film medium's eminent theorists and historians, "it is with *The Birth of a Nation*, Griffith's first perfected film, cinema's first authentic masterpiece, primitive though it was, that cinema as an art was born."[1]

Mitry's use of the word "primitive" carries a double meaning. Most directly it reminds us that the film was made early in the history of cinema and that its style and production methods now seem somewhat crude, though compared with other films of the period—and especially with those that had come before—*The Birth of a Nation* offered an unprecedented demonstration of the power of cinematic language; for that reason, Mitry and others have recognized the film as "cinema's first authentic masterpiece," and made it the object of extensive study.[2] But the word "primitive" has another connotation that is not so easily deflected, because it points to the film's treatment of black characters. In this film they are played mostly by whites in blackface and limited to roles of faithful slave servants and lustful, ambitious schemers. From the film's point of view, all blacks are seen as simple or savage, needing to be ruled by whites for everyone's good; and these stereotypes and grotesque distortions are essential to the film's plot.

Griffith based most of his story on Thomas Dixon's *The Clansman*, a successful novel which the author had also adapted for the stage,[3] and in all of these versions, the history of the Civil War and Reconstruction are seen mainly from a Southern point of view. The director followed Dixon by focusing the narrative on the interaction of two families, the Stoneman household in the North and the Camerons in the South, and by setting the story principally in the fictional town of Piedmont, South Carolina. There, in early scenes that take place before the war begins, the Camerons are shown to enjoy an idyllic way of life, and they receive the visiting Stoneman sons with gracious hospitality. During the war, opposing sons die side by side on the battlefield. After the war, the love between various members of the two families is impeded by "bitter memories" and by the turmoil of Reconstruction. When a black "renegade" attempts to rape Flora, the youngest Cameron daughter, she leaps to her death; and from this point in the story, the action becomes more and more hectic and violent. Members of both families are besieged by blacks, until, according to a title late in the film, "the former enemies of North and South are united again in common defence of their Aryan birthright."[4] Leading the defense is the Ku Klux Klan, depicted as a noble order of knights, which avenges Flora's death and rescues the besieged whites. At the end of the story, the Klan disarms the blacks, white supremacy is restored, and a double honeymoon ensues. Griffith's conclusion, meant to tie together various themes, is calm and grandiose: a shot of the lovers gives way to a vision of the Heavenly City, to which Griffith adds a plea that war be perpetually vanquished, followed by a title with Webster's words: "*Liberty and Union*, now and forever, one and inseparable."[5]

From the time of its first exhibitions this film's power to move audiences was widely recognized, and there was great controversy: protests from progressive leaders and the NAACP, repeated calls for censorship, and court suits to have the film banned.[6] (In these controversies Griffith became passionately involved; and he inserted several titles into the film to justify his views.[7]) At the same time the film was promoted and received with extravagant praise, and it drew record-breaking audiences (and profits) during a nationwide "first run" that lasted more than a year.[8]

The Birth of a Nation was successful for many reasons: among them, the narrative's combination of melodrama with visual spectacle, the naturalism and intimacy of much of the acting, and the richness of the film's photography and editing techniques. Moreover, unlike earlier spectacle films such as *Quo Vadis* and *Cabiria*, the film was, as a reviewer wrote, "American in story, in scene and in production"; and in 1915 most audience members either accepted the film's version of American history as fact, or were willing to overlook the distortions for the sake of Griffith's moving imagery.[9] Within the first half of the film Griffith depicted the heroism and suffering of the South during the Civil War, stressing the theme, in one of the film's titles, of "war's bitter, useless sacrifice."[10] These words probably meant a great deal to the film's early audiences, posed as they were at the edge of World War I; and viewers were also probably impressed by the manner in which "the most dramatic events in our United States history," as one advertisement proclaimed, were "reproduced with striking realism."[11] In particular, the battle of Petersburg was enacted on a lavish scale, and other memorable incidents (including Lee's surrender to Grant and Lincoln's assassination) were filmed with fidelity to the historical record.[12]

One of the most eloquent descriptions of the greatness of *The Birth of a Nation*, as it impressed audiences throughout the silent period, is found in an essay by James Agee written in 1948, on the occasion of Griffith's death. Cognizant of those who found the film offensive, Agee nevertheless insisted that *The Birth of a Nation* remained unique in the power with which it realized its "majestic theme": how, through the pain caused by the war and its aftermath, a united nation was born. He went so far as to call *The Birth of a Nation* "the one great, epic, tragic film," and he also drew attention to the special qualities of Griffith's visual style:

> . . . he was a great primitive poet, a man capable, as only great and primitive artists can be, of intuitively perceiving and perfecting the tremendous magical images that underlie the memory and imagination of entire peoples. . . . [Such images as] the homecoming of the defeated hero; the ride of the Clansmen; the rapist and his victim among the dark leaves . . . have a dreamlike absoluteness which, indeed, cradles and suffuses the whole film.[13]

For all his praise, Agee's paragraph contains one negative word in common with Mitry's sentence—"primitive." Though Agee applies the word to the director more than to the film, his essay provides another example of the ambivalence with which even the most sympathetic observers respond to *The Birth of a Nation*. And today, more than four score years after the film was first released, its "primitive" qualities are the ones most easily noticed. To us the film's facts and characters, whether historically based or imaginary, are now apt to seem unconvincingly black or white, in the tradition of melodrama. We would have them more subtly mixed in hue—no further apart, one might say, than muted tones of blue and gray.

The power of *The Birth of a Nation* to move us has considerably diminished, so the film survives primarily as an object of study, to be watched from a critical distance. Perhaps this shift in perspective is for the best, but we may nevertheless regret the changed circumstances of *Birth*'s exhibitions. In deteriorated copies, it is usually seen on college campuses, in archives and museums, or on videotape at home. These arenas are conducive to analysis, but they do not allow us to see or understand the film as audiences did in 1915. At that time it was usually presented in legitimate theaters with the accompaniment of Breil's orchestral score; and as was stated above, earlier film scores were quickly forgotten, but this one was not. To arrive at a full understanding of the problematic artistry of *The Birth of a Nation*, we need to examine the score, a pivotal one in the history of motion picture music: in particular, to study how it was created, and how it reflects or perhaps alters the film's meanings.

Sources

The Breil Score

Copies of the Breil score have been located at MOMA, LC, the University of Minnesota, UCLA, USC, and George Eastman House. MOMA's copies, which are the oldest and most numerous, are now on deposit at LC, the latter institution having no copies of its own;[14] likewise, the copies at Minnesota are part of a collection that once belonged to silent-film pianist Arthur Kleiner, who had served as MOMA's music director from 1939 to 1967.[15] Among all these collections, no manuscript copy of the Breil score has been discovered; all we have are offset reproductions of professionally copied manuscripts. Also, no orchestral scores have been found—only piano scores and sets of orchestral parts, as described in the following inventory.

PIANO SCORES: These are of two types, here designated the MOMA score and the Tams Copying Bureau score.

1. The *MOMA score* contains 151 pages of music; in addition to the hand responsible for the music, four or five different hands added tempo and dynamic markings, cues, numbers, and verbal instructions. At least nine copies of this score are extant.

   a. Five copies are at LC (in the MOMA collection). One of these appears to date from the time of the film's initial release: it has the words "Small Orchestra" printed on its cover, and was originally included with the third set of orchestral parts described below. Four other copies have spiral bindings, new covers, and title pages on which MOMA's name appears. They are stamped "The Museum of Modern Art Film Library" at the bottom of the first page of music. These copies are reprints of an unidentified original, with some handwritten annotations.

   b. One copy given to me by MOMA, like those described directly above. Reproductions of select pages from this score can be seen in Figs. 14–27, to be discussed in detail later in this chapter.

   c. Two copies are at Minnesota (both from the library of Arthur Kleiner). One is identical to the copies now at LC, except that it has Kleiner's annotations, which he inserted as aids to his performances. The other is a photostat copy of the same, reduced and bound.

   d. One copy at Eastman.[16]

2. The *Tams Copying Bureau score* (Scribe B) is labeled "Small Orchestration" on its cover. The bottom of the first page of music has the printed notice "Tams Copying Bureau." It contains 157 pages of music and differs from the MOMA score in the way cues and other verbal instructions are positioned on the page, as well as in other details. One offset copy is known to exist, among the materials in the Breil collection at the Theater Arts Library, UCLA. In addition, three bound photocopies, taken from an unidentified original, are at USC.[17]

ORCHESTRAL PARTS: Four sets are known; the first three described below are at LC, the fourth is at Eastman.

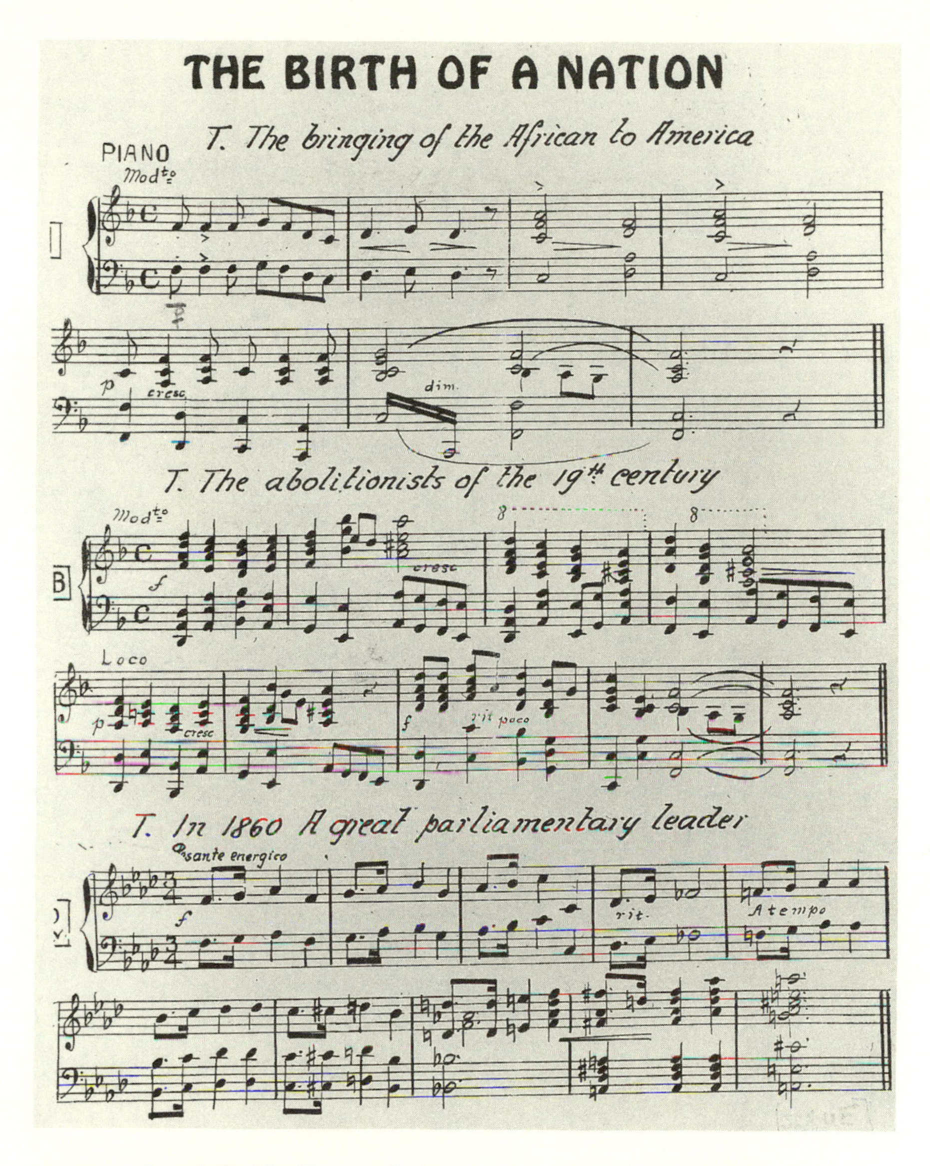

FIGURE 14. Joseph Carl Breil's score for *The Birth of a Nation* (1915), MOMA reprint, p. 1: Act I, nos. 1, 1B, and 2. (Figures 14–27 reproduced courtesy of MOMA.)

FIGURE 15. *The Birth of a Nation*, p. 5: Act I, no. 4, end, and no. 4 1/2, beginning.

FIGURE 16. *The Birth of a Nation*, p. 6: Act I, no. 4 1/2, end.

FIGURE 17. *The Birth of a Nation*, p. 8: Act I, no. 5 1/2, and no. 6, beginning.

FIGURE 18. *The Birth of a Nation*, p. 9: Act I, no. 6, middle.

FIGURE 19. *The Birth of a Nation*, p. 10: Act I, no. 6, end, and no. 7, beginning.

FIGURE 20. *The Birth of a Nation*, p. 12: Act I, no. 10.

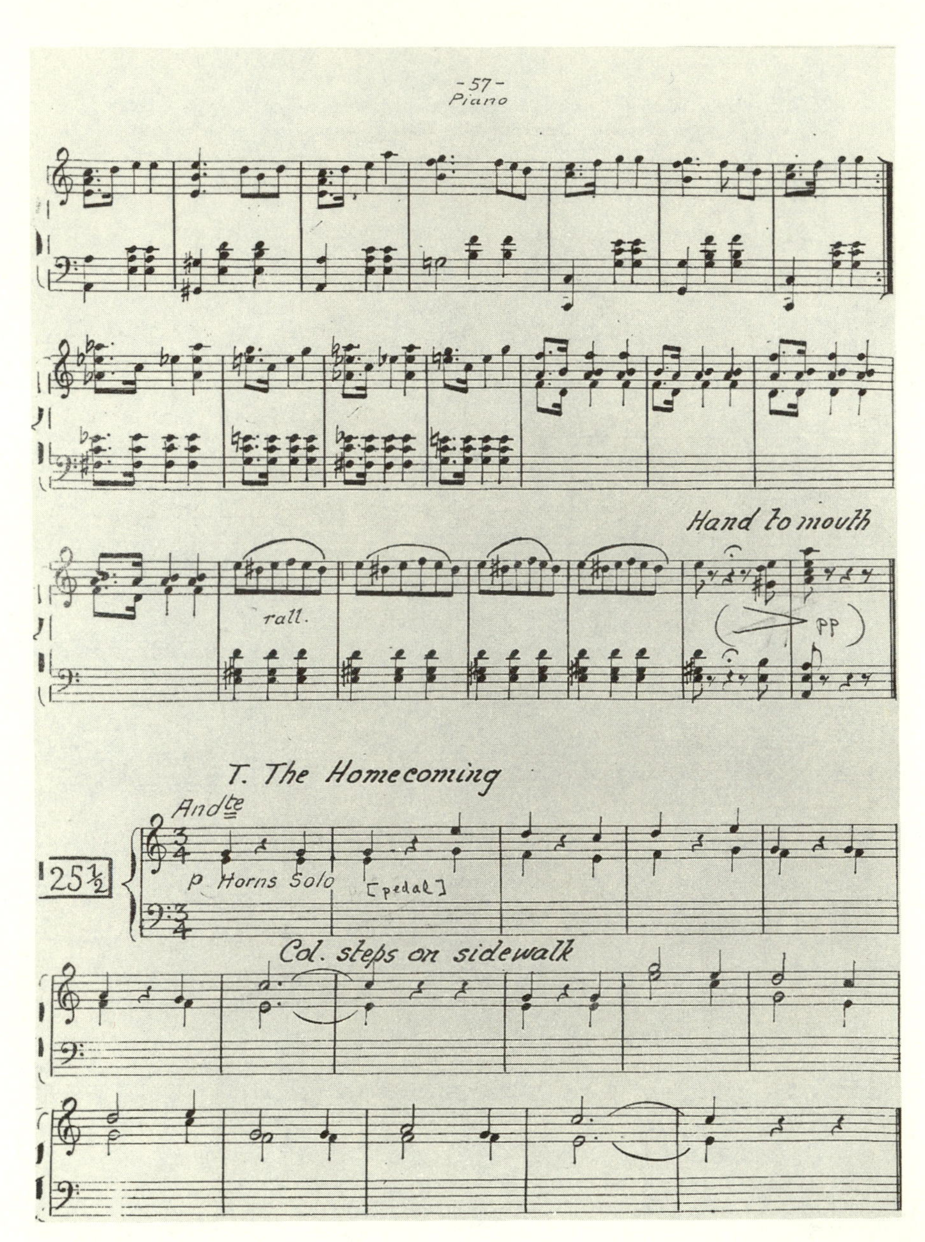

FIGURE 21. *The Birth of a Nation*, p. 57: Act I, no. 25, end, and no. 25 1/2, beginning.

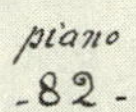

FIGURE 22. *The Birth of a Nation*, p. 82: Act II, no. 5.

FIGURE 23. *The Birth of a Nation*, p. 83: Act II, no. 5A.

FIGURE 24. *The Birth of a Nation*, p. 84: Act II, no. 5B.

FIGURE 25. *The Birth of a Nation*, p. 102: Act II, no. 14, end.

FIGURE 26. *The Birth of a Nation*, p. 125: Act II, no. 25.

FIGURE 27. *The Birth of a Nation*, p. 143: Act II, no. 26 1/2, near end.

1. *Large Orchestra Set* (also containing one part from a *Medium Orchestra Set*). All parts are 35 x 26 cm., bound, with the words "D. W. Griffith / presents / *The Birth of a Nation*" printed on their covers; and all except the first violin parts are stamped "Office" on the upper right-hand corner. (Also, in each part, at the top of the first page of music, is the heading: "*The Birth of a Nation*.") This is the only LC set containing indications of use: pencil-markings, changes of numbers, verbal instructions, and so on. Some parts contain inserted slips of music; some the names of musicians; there are even a few caricatures of the conductor (bearded), with humorous comments. The set comprises twelve parts: oboe (30 pp.; cover stamped "Large Orchestra Set F"), 2 clarinets (one part, 59 pp.; cover stamped "Large Orchestra Set A"), bassoon (31 pp.), two horns (one part, 46 pp.), 2 cornets (one part, 38 pp.), 2 trombones (one part, 20 pp.), tuba (18 pp.), drums (18 pp.), harp (11 pp.; contains a hand-written itinerary of the orchestra's touring schedule through New Jersey, New York, and Pennsylvania, between August 1915 and April 1916), 2 first violin parts (54 pp. each; one marked "II Desk" in pencil), second violin (44 pp.), and viola (13 pp.; cover stamped "Medium Orchestra Set No. 1").[18]

This set of parts appears to belong to an earlier version of the score than LC's other two sets. It contains twenty-seven numbers in Act II, the other sets thirty, and the concluding music in the "Large" set is less complete. In several of the individual parts, "No. 28" is penciled in, with a reference to Herrmann's *Cocoanut Dance*, which is inserted on separate sheets. This dance was added to the score early in 1915, to accompany a sequence added by Griffith.[19] In the other sets of parts, and in all of the offset copies of the MOMA piano score, number 28 is an integral segment.

2. *Epoch Producing Corporation Set.* Set 2 comprises ten parts, each 31 x 24 cm., bound in beige and labeled "D. W. Griffith / presents / *The Birth of a Nation* / Property of / Epoch Producing Corporation / New York, N.Y.," the company established in February 1915 to oversee the distribution of the film.[20] At the top of the first page of music, all parts are headed: "Music Score / of / *The Birth of a Nation*." The set contains: flute (32 pp.), clarinet (40 pp.), cornet (31 pp.), trombone (23 pp.), drums (19 pp.), first violin (52 pp.), second violin (45 pp.), viola (39 pp.), cello (43 pp.), and bass (31 pp.).

3. *Small Orchestra Set.* Set 3, bound in lighter beige covers than set 2, comprises eight parts, each labeled on its cover: "Small Orchestra / D. W. Griffith / Presents / *The Birth of a Nation*." The eight parts include: flute (31 pp.), clarinet (40 pp.), cornet (31 p.), trombone (23 pp.), percussion (timpani and other drums, 19 pp.), first violin (58 pp.; part labeled in red pencil "Leader"; contains a great many printed music cues designating others instruments, perhaps because the first violinist sometimes acted as conductor, or covered for instruments not available), cello (43 pp.), and bass (30 pp.). When this set belonged to MOMA, it included the copy of the piano score described above (No. 1a).

4. *The Eastman Set* contains nine parts: flute, clarinet, cornets, trombone, first violin (3 copies), cello, and bass.

In sum, many different performing editions of the score for *The Birth of a Nation* were prepared, intended for use under changing circumstances; perhaps because the scores *were* performing editions, and not intended for sale to the public, they lack attributions to any composer. (Similarly, attributions were lacking in the Skladanowsky music described above.) However, the Tams score at UCLA does have Breil's full name handwritten at the top of the first page, as do the photocopies at USC, in what might be his signature; and on the covers of the MOMA reproductions of the piano score are printed these words: "Music written, selected, and arranged from various sources by Joseph Carl Breil and David Wark Griffith," a joint attribution unlike any that appeared in 1915.

Apart from these appearances of Breil's name, abundant evidence for his authorship of the music, as well as further information concerning the distribution of the scores in 1915, is to be found in other sources, especially newspaper announcements and reviews (many of them clipped and pasted into Breil's scrapbooks). The earliest group concern the film's New York opening at the Liberty Theatre, on 3 March 1915: in these items his name is almost always given as "Briel," just as it is in the Liberty playbill for the opening.[21] Breil is also mentioned, his name correctly spelled, in what appears to be the first article which surveys the contents of the score in detail, by Harlow Hare, written in the summer of 1915, while the film was being shown in Boston. Hare was the man who called the *Birth* "a marriage of music and spectacle" (the phrase cited at the conclusion of Chapter Three), and from his description we can be certain that the music he heard was very similar to the Breil score as it survives in the copies described above.[22] Furthermore, Breil is named as the composer in two souvenir programs, one published by Epoch in New York some time after the premiere,[23] the other in conjunction with the film's opening at the Scala Theatre in London, in December 1915.[24]

Of great importance are a series of publications of Breil's music, issued by Chappell in London and New York between 1915 and 1917, each drawing on material contained in the *Birth* score. First came the principal love theme, under the title *The Perfect Song*. It was published in five versions between February and August 1915: in arrangements for band and for orchestra, and in sheet music for piano, for violin and piano, and, with lyrics added by Clarence Lucas, for voice and piano.[25] These constituted one of the first (if not the very first) examples of the marketing of a "theme song" from a film, and copies of royalty statements kept by Breil from the years 1915–18 confirm that Chappell's venture made for good business.[26] Further evidence of the song's success is to be seen in its issue on a piano roll in November 1915.[27] Moreover, in 1929, four years after Breil's death, it became the "Musical Theme of the Pepsodent Hour," a popular, long-lived radio program later known as the *Amos 'n' Andy* show; and Chappell continued to publish new editions and arrangements of the song at least until 1953.[28]

In 1916 Chappell issued a *Selection of Joseph Carl Breil's Themes from the Incidental Music to "The Birth of a Nation."*[29] Again, this was an unprecedented type of publication, attesting to the film's as well as the music's impact. Included are six piano pieces, the last being the same as the sheet-music arrangement of *The Perfect Song* for piano which had been published separately. Numbers one through five are arrangements of other segments from the score, made to sound more pianistic in texture, with octave doublings, richer chordal figurations, and so on. What is most instructive about the collection are the name tags attached to several of the themes, as follows:

1. "*The Motif of Barbarism*" corresponds to Act I, no. 1.
2. "*The Elsie Stoneman Motif*" corresponds to Act I, no. 2 1/2.
3. "*Stoneman and Lydia Brown, the Mulatto*" corresponds to Act I, nos. 5-1/2[B] and 6, with these labels given to the second through seventh segments of no. 6: "Lust and Passion," "The Pride of Ignorance," "Anger," "Violent Anger," "Fury," and "Fury Allayed."
4. "*The Ku Klux Clansmens' [sic] Call*" corresponds to the beginning of Act II, no. 11.
5. "*Flora's Death*" corresponds to the end of Act II, no. 15.

These pieces cover a wide variety of moods; and perhaps with this in mind, Breil incorporated several other excerpts from the *Birth* score in a subsequent Chappell publication, his *Original Collection of Dramatic Music for Motion Picture Plays*. This was a typical compendium of general purpose music for moving-picture accompaniments, issued in 1917 in two versions: one for piano or organ solo, another in a set of loose-leaf parts for orchestra, with piano accompaniment.[30] There are twelve numbers in the collection, each divided into three or more sections in such a way that, as Breil writes in his Foreword, "it is possible to pass from one section of one number into almost any section of another." Four of the numbers contain excerpts from the *Birth* score, although most have been changed considerably, and Breil gives them functional labels rather than name tags associated with the film, as can be seen in the following list. (Segments based on music from *The Birth of a Nation* are marked with an asterisk.)

1. *Molto Agitato.*
   - A) For Storms, Battles, Fires, Explosions
   - *B) Consequent Mob Excitement [corresponds to Act I, no. 15]
   - C) Victory or Rescue
3. *Agitato Misterioso and Grandioso col Morendo.*
   - *A) For Scenes of Fear, Inner Dread, Hopelessness, Premonition of Doom, etc. [corresponds to a segement of Act II, no. 24]
   - *B) An Outcry of Despair or Indignation, a Desperate Appeal [corresponds to a later segment in the same number]
   - C) An Utter Sense of Hopelessness, or a Calm and Soothing Aftermath
4. *Misterioso e Lamentoso.*
   - *A) Fear, Doubt, Trepidation, Haunting Scenes or Memories [corresponds to music in Act II, no. 7, which reappears in nos. 22 and 24]
   - *B) Despair, Sadness, or Grief [corresponds to a theme introduced in Act II, no. 10]
   - C) Resignation or Consolation
12. *Marcia Funebre.* For Death Scenes, Executions, etc.
   - *A) [There are no labels for the segments of this number. The music of
   - B) sections A and D is the same, and corresponds to a funeral march
   - C) heard in Act I, nos. 16 and 21.]
   - *D)

Some of these labels are well suited to the type of scene the music accompanies in the film. For example, 3B ("An Outcry of Despair or Indignation," etc.) accompanies Elsie's shocked, scornful reaction to Silas Lynch's proposal of marriage; 4B ("Despair," etc.) is a melancholy theme associated primarily with the "agony" of Ben Cameron and Elsie Stoneman; and segments 12A and 12D (the "*Marcia Funebre*") are based on music for scenes in which the deaths of the Cameron and Stoneman sons are reported to each family. Other labels are tied more loosely to scenes from the film. No. 1B ("Mob Excitement") accompanies a war scene, culminating in the deaths of the youngest Cameron and Stoneman sons on the battlefield; and 4A ("Fear, doubt, trepidation," etc.) occurs with scenes of violent action.

In addition to providing some indications of Breil's ideas about the functions of the music in his score, Chappell's publications help us to identify which portions of the score are his. However, there is a great deal more original music in the score than appears in these publications, and we have no way of knowing for certain how much of it was composed by Breil. This uncertainty, together with the task of identifying borrowed material, leaves the origin of some material in the score open to question. For example, a few segments in Act II (in nos. 1, 6, and 8) may be based on minstrel songs or nineteenth-century dances which have not been identified.

At LC, indexes are attached to some copies of the MOMA piano score. These are carbon copies of a three-page typescript that lists music number by number. A distinction is made between music composed by Breil and heard more than once and "original" music which appears only once in the score. Here, for example, is the beginning of the list:

Number 1	Negro theme (Breil)
1b	original
2	Stoneman theme (Breil)
2 1/2	Elsie Stoneman theme (Breil)
3	Swanee River and development by Breil
3 1/2	same as number 2
4	Where Did You Get That Hat and original
4 1/2	original introducing In the Gloaming and the Love Strain (Breil)
5	Turkey in the Straw
5 1/2	Freischutz Overture
	⋮

The list is by and large accurate. Though anonymous, and without indication of what purpose it was meant to serve, it has proved a valuable starting point for the analysis of the score's contents and the indexes presented below.

Also valuable is the recording of excerpts from the score of *The Birth of a Nation* conducted by Clyde Allen and released in 1985. The liner notes, by Allen and others, contain hitherto unpublished documents and analytical comments; and Allen, using copies of the "Large Orchestra Set" of parts, recorded about half of the music composed by Breil as well as the concluding arrangements of *The*

Ride of the Valkyries and *Dixie*. However, the recording was conceived more as a concert performance than as an accompaniment to the film: indeed, the tempos are often too fast or too slow to fit film segments, and the numbers are sometimes played as closed or rounded forms (e.g., A B A, with repeats of each part), even though they must be abridged or extended ad lib in performance.[31]

The surviving performance materials appear to have been put together ad hoc and in haste, amid changes of mind and circumstance; they contain wrong notes (as Allen discovered) and errors in the cues. They also present problems to performers in two other ways. (1) The numbering of the sections is inconsistent: some numbers are plain, some are coupled with letters of the alphabet or the fraction "1/2," still others have both a letter and a fraction. The purposes these suffixes were meant to serve are difficult to explain, since they do not always indicate relationships based on musical or narrative content. In Part I, for example, the music of number 3 is unrelated to the music of number 3 1/2, and each of these numbers accompanies a separate scene; the same is true of numbers 4 and 4 1/2, 11C and 11D, and so on. (2) There is no music for the long series of titles that begins each half of the film. Griffith probably changed them many times, from one early presentation of the film to the next; yet it is most unlikely that they were screened without music; and in the "Large Orchestra Set" in LC, there are instructions for playing material from elsewhere in the score at the beginning of each act. In Kleiner's copy of the piano score at Minnesota, he, too, penciled in such instructions, but the music he played was not the same as what was called for in the orchestra set, and was probably his choice.[32]

These materials, of course, tell us little about how the Breil score was created. Before we take up that subject it will be necessary to consider what is known about a separate score for *The Birth* and its relationship to Breil's.

The Clune's Score

Two different orchestral scores were created for Griffith's film in 1915. The first was, at least in part, the work of Carli D. Elinor and was introduced together with the film at Clune's Auditorium in Los Angeles, on 8 February 1915 (the film bearing its original title, *The Clansman*); with a few interruptions it played there for twenty-two weeks, accompanied throughout by the Elinor score.[33] The second score was Breil's, introduced at the Liberty Theatre in New York, where the film, now titled *The Birth of a Nation* and given a well-publicized premiere on 3 March 1915, played for forty-four weeks; throughout the engagement the film was accompanied by Breil's score.

We know that Breil's score (or perhaps more precisely, Breil and Griffith's score) was the principal one for the film—the one which Griffith helped to create, and which he approved for printing and distribution. What we do not know for certain is why the score at Clune's preceded it, nor the exact nature of the relationship between them. No one connected with the making of the film or its music discussed these matters in any known published or unpublished sources. Many copies of the Breil score survive, but no copy of the one presented with *The Clansman* at Clune's has been discovered. Knowledge of its contents rests on sketchy descriptions, such as are found in the weekly theater programs distributed at Clune's Auditorium during the film's engagement there.

The first scholar to consider these matters was Seymour Stern, in an elaborate and influential essay published in 1965. In it he discussed the history, contents, and influence of the music for *The Birth of a Nation*, with special attention to many previously unexamined sources, including the Clune's theater programs and a copy of the MOMA piano score. He asserted unequivocally that all the sources he had seen pertained to *one* score, that went through only "minor emendations"; also, that the definitive version—"the revised and ultimate score"—was presented in 1921, for a two-week revival of the film at the Capitol Theatre in New York, where he claimed to have heard it.[34]

There are two fundamental reasons for thinking Stern was mistaken. First, the extant sources suggest that there were major rather than "minor" differences between the Breil score and the one that preceded it at Clune's; second, the points of Stern's argument must frequently be called into question. For example, in describing Breil's score, Stern claimed that it contained pieces that are not there, and overlooked several pieces which are. Moreover, he ignored his own evidence concerning the 1921 Capitol score. Contrary to what is implied in the essay, he never found a copy of that score (nor has one been found since); instead, he depended upon two brief references, one in an advertisement for a revival of the film, another in a review. But in these sources the Capitol score was said to be "new," and although four people (including Rothapfel, who was then the manager of the Capitol) were said to be involved in its preparation, neither Elinor nor Breil was listed among them.[35] Granted, we do not know if the Capitol score drew upon material from either Elinor's or Breil's, or was entirely new; but we can be reasonably certain that it has little or nothing to do with a history of the two scores that were presented with the film in 1915.

Apparently the Clune's score was the result of arrangements made during the summer of 1914, when the film was being shot. Griffith and his producers ran out of money, and various sources indicate that Clune, then a leading Los Angeles exhibitor, was one of the individuals whom Griffith persuaded to invest in the production, so that filming could continue. In return, it seems, Clune was given the right to present the film in his theater.

These arrangements are mentioned in the memoirs of three individuals directly involved in the making of the film, Griffith, Roy Aitken, and Lillian Gish. Griffith's version of the story, which was the first to be published, is of particular interest, because it suggests that the director skillfully played upon the exhibitor's pride in the music at his theater. According to Griffith, when Clune came to the studio to see rushes from the film, he was unimpressed until the following incident:

> We had picked up a cheap band . . . about the "corniest" outfit ever gathered together, but as they approached Mr. Clune, they were playing *Dixie*—an air that is hard to kill. Hope started beating its white wings again. He said in his Western drawl, "Say, that war music would sound great in my theater, with *my* orchestra

> playing it." As a part of the bait, we had told him he could have the picture in his theatre. If he had only known it, he could have had it for all the West.
>
> Again I soared—"Can you imagine, Mr. Clune, just picture those soldiers marching to the thrilling music of the best orchestra, not only in Los Angeles but the best in the world—playing *Dixie—Dixie*! Why you would tear them right out of their chairs."[36]

When and if Griffith termed Clune's orchestra "the best in Los Angeles," he was probably not far from the truth. Indeed, if he entrusted control of the presentation of his film to Clune primarily as an act of financial necessity, there were other good reasons for doing so: Clune was known for the quality of his theaters, and under his ownership the Auditorium received much praise for its music. Moreover, Griffith was almost certainly aware of the publicity that would be gained from the association of film and venue, because the Auditorium had opened as a motion picture theater (in May 1914) with the director's Mutual feature, *Home Sweet Home*; according to *MPW*'s reviewer, the film played to a "record-breaking house," which he attributed in no small part to the theater's "grand orchestra and the wonderful pipe organ."[37] Later that year, a report in the *Los Angeles Times* noted the excellence of the music at both Clune's and a rival theater, with particular attention to the way the managers and their music directors set aside a day or more each week to confer "on the subject of fitting the music to each new picture."[38]

The passage just quoted sheds some light on the authorship of the score for *The Clansman* at Clune's, because it implies that the owner regularly delegated responsibility for the music at his theater to the manager and the music director, two individuals identified in the series of weekly theater programs issued at Clune's during the period of *The Clansman*'s exhibitions. As can be seen on the recto side of the program for the week of 24 May 1915 (reproduced as Fig. 28), Lloyd Brown is named as the theater's manager at the top of the page, and in the middle of the page Carli D. Elinor is named as the conductor of the "Musical Program [performed] by Augmented Orchestra."[39] However, there are difficulties in determining precisely how the responsibilities for the creation of the *Clansman* score were divided, because—as is true of accounts of other theatrical collaborations—different sources, each of them important, describe the work in different ways. For example, in an unpublished memoir, Elinor wrote of "his" score for *The Clansman* without reference to anyone else's collaboration.[40] But in the Clune's program, Brown and Elinor are jointly credited with the selection of the "Incidental Music"; and the program also names other musicians, including Ray Hastings, the theater's organist, and J. E. Nurnberger, the composer of a "*Clansman* Overture."[41]

Also to be weighed is a profile of Brown which appeared in *MPW* in May 1915. He is portrayed, in a manner similar to the way Rothapfel is described in the *MPW* articles cited in Chapter Three, as a leading innovator in the field of film exhibition, and attention is called to the *Clansman* score as the most important, and current, evidence of his interest in music. Yet even though he is quoted as taking much of the credit for the *Clansman* score, he also mentions three other collaborators: Clune, Elinor, and an "arranger," whom he does not name.[42]

FIGURE 28. The Clune's Auditorium Program for the week beginning 24 May 1915, recto. (*Film Culture*, no. 36 [Spring–Summer 1965], facing p. 114. I am grateful to the Anthology Film Archives of New York, and especially to Jonas Mekas, for providing me with a copy of this issue of *Film Culture*, and for granting permission to reproduce the Clune's program; for supplementary details, see n. 39.)

55th Week	Starting Monday	May 24th

1915

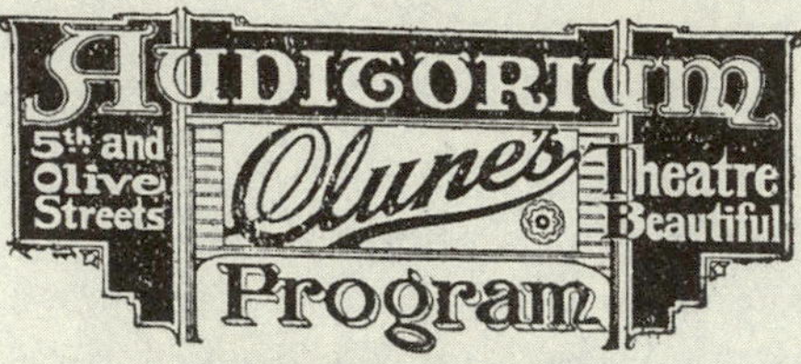

LLOYD BROWN, Manager

MR. W. H. CLUNE presents

THIRTEENTH WEEK

The Clansman

Photo-Drama in Twelve Reels

Amplified from the famous novel of Thomas Dixon, Jr., produced by D. W. Griffith, the world's foremost motion picture director. The greatest motion picture ever staged.

Cost $500,000

Required seven months to stage it

Includes most spectacular battle scenes ever enacted

Presented by the following all-star cast:

Benjamin Cameron	Henry Walthall
His sister Florence	Mae Marsh
His sister Margaret	Miriam Cooper
Mrs. Cameron	Josephine Crowell
Dr. Cameron	Spottiswood Aitken
Austin Stoneman	Ralph Lewis
His daughter Elsie	Lillian Gish
His son Phil	Elmer Clifton
His second son	Robert Harron
Silas Lynch	George Siegmann
Gus	Walter Long
Lydia Brown	Mary Alden
Abraham Lincoln	Joseph Hennaberry
Charles Sumner	Sam de Grasse
Gen. Lee	Howard Gaye
Gen. Grant	Donald Crisp
Jake	Wm. de Vaull
Cyndy	Jennie Lee

Scenic effects in prologue built by J. D. Martin Scenic Co. of Los Angeles, Cal.

Musical Program by Augmented Orchestra
Conducted by CARLI D. ELINOR
RAY HASTINGS, Organist

NOTE—The arrangement and selection of the music for "The Clansman" was accomplished after a diligent search of the music libraries of Los Angeles, San Francisco and New York. To select and cue the scenes it was necessary to run the twelve reels comprising the story eighty-four times; and also to render a perfect score six complete full orchestra rehearsals were necessary.

"The Clansman," Overture	J. E. Nurnberger
"Semiramide," Overture	Rossini
"Tancred," Overture	Rossini
"Light Cavalry," Overture	F. V. Suppe
"Morning, Noon and Night," Overture	F. V. Suppe
"Romantic," Overture	K. Bela
"Stradella," Overture	F. V. Flotow
"Marriage of Figaro," Overture	V. A. Mozart
"Orphee aux Enfers" (Violin Solo Interpreted by Miss Elsa Grosser)	J. Offenbach
"Nabucodonozar"	G. Verdi
"Sinfonia," Giovana d'Arco"	G. Verdi
"First Symphony"	L. V. Beethoven
"Unfinished Symphony"	F. Schubert
"Les Huguenots"	Meyerbeers
"Rienzi"	R. Wagner
"Le Jougleur de Notre-Dame"	J. Masseuet
"L'Arlesienne" (Prelude and Le Carillon)	G. Bizet
"Silent Woe" and "Anathema"	A. V. Fielitz
"Americana" Suite	T. W. Thurban
"Incidental," music selected by	C. D. Elinor L. Brown

SEXTETTE

Miss Helen Becktel	Soprano
Miss Laura Hoebel	Contralto
Mr. Houston M. Dudley	Basso
Mr. Thomas J. Newman	First Tenor
Mr. E. P. Emerson	Second Tenor
Mr. V. A. Campbell	Baritone

Finally, one must consider a 1978 interview with Bernard E. Brown—apparently not related to Lloyd Brown—who identifies himself as the unnamed arranger. This Brown enjoyed a lengthy career as a violinist, music director, and sound engineer at Warner Brothers, beginning in the twenties, and most of the interview concerns the latter work; but at the outset the interviewer poses two questions about the music for *The Birth of a Nation*, to which Brown replies as follows:

> Q: *How were you involved with the music for "The Birth of a Nation"?*
>
> I helped Carli Elinore [*sic*] with the score. He hadn't any previous experience in doing scenes and music together. I had. I wasn't out of my teens yet, for god's sake. In those days we didn't do any writing of music—we didn't have time. We just took standard music—overtures and concert favorites—and took so many bars of this and that and wherever a change occurred, like a change of key, of moods, of one excerpt to another, you know, we'd compose a little bridge or write a little piece to smoothe [*sic*] the transition.
>
> Q: *What was some of the music you used?*
>
> I can remember using Suppé's *Morning, Noon and Night Overture*, Rossini's *Semiramide*, that sort of thing. I remember when D. W. Griffith himself wanted to conduct our makeshift score, his glasses fell off. When I moved to retrieve them for him, he just said, "Never mind, I don't know one sort of note from another."[43]

Bernard Brown's view of the collaboration, as expressed in these replies, runs counter to the information found in the other sources described above. For although his work went uncredited in Elinor's writings and in the sources dating from 1915, in his 1978 interview Brown describes himself and Elinor as more or less equal partners and makes no mention of Lloyd Brown. There is also an ambiguity in Brown's remarks: in answer to the interviewer's first question he implies that he and Elinor created the score for *The Birth of a Nation*, rather than for *The Clansman*. (Elinor sometimes did the same.)

Despite these difficulties, we can be reasonably certain of two points: first, that Elinor was a key participant in the creation of the *Clansman* score, since he is mentioned in all of these sources; second, that Breil was not involved, since he is mentioned in none. Moreover, in a letter to the *Los Angeles Times*, published in December 1915, Breil angrily dissociated himself from the music at Clune's, complaining that even though his *Birth* score had been performed and praised across the rest of the county, it had "never been heard in Los Angeles."[44] Griffith, too, seems to have had little if any influence on the Clune's collaboration, since only Bernard Brown's anecdote connects the director to it at all, and the story is funny but not very informative. By contrast, there are many sources which present vivid pictures of Griffith's collaboration with Breil—though they, too, leave much to be filled in.

The Origin of the Breil Score

Breil is the only individual concerned with providing music for *The Birth* who has left an account of how he came to be associated with that enterprise. He did so in an unpublished (and apparently now lost) fragment of an essay written about five years after the film appeared. Setting out to explain "how it was done," Breil begins by stating that it was the presentations of *Cabiria* in California which brought him to Griffith's attention and which inspired the director to think about a score for his film:

> . . . until he saw *Cabiria* he never thought of developing a big "two dollar regular theatre" show. Billy Bitzer, his cameraman who was with him at our performance, was the first to suggest that a musical score like the one in *Cabiria* would enhance *The Clansman*, as *The Birth of a Nation* was then known. John A. Barry, Mr. Griffith's secretary, seconded the suggestion and ever after that kept assiduously at his principal to do something about it. Mr. McClellan, who was then managing *Cabiria*, also took it upon himself to advise Mr. Griffith in favor of a score—until at last the man had to yield—and he sent me word to come out to his studio and see him.

Breil next states that when he first saw the film he did not like it—indeed, he found the "then much uncut film," in contrast to *Cabiria*, "to lack *detail*"; and the second part, "which was founded on Thomas Dixon's almost fanatical work . . . was so replete with lust, brutality, morbidity, debauchery, rapine and murder" that he believed the film "would be doomed to utter failure." So he refused Griffith's offer to create a score:

> . . . I purposely evinced little further interest, and went on conducting the delightful score of *Cabiria*, and finally in November was back in San Francisco preparing to return to New York when I got a wire from Mr. Griffith asking me to come back to Los Angeles at once and begin work on the score for his film.

After seeing the wire Breil apparently did return to Los Angeles "at once." This time, watching the film over and over, he became convinced of its potential; and so, he states, having accepted Griffith's offer, he was given a contractual deadline of six weeks to complete the score.[45]

In this account there are some surprises, especially the statement that Griffith had given little thought to the music for *The Birth of a Nation* before seeing *Cabiria*. One wonders if Breil overstated the case in order to enhance the importance of the score (that is, the innovative quality of his own work) for the Italian film. It seems reasonable to suppose that Griffith could have had music for the film in the back of his mind long before he arranged to commission a score. The director's anecdote concerning the playing of *Dixie* for Clune provides some slight evidence for this view; so does a statement of Karl Brown, who remembers hearing the director sing one of the score's most distinctive themes—the call of the Klan—over and over during the shooting of the film.[46] Yet even if Griffith had been thinking about music all along, seeing *Cabiria* may have given him ideas about the possibilities of something similar for *The Birth*, and he may have been impressed enough by Breil to want him as a collaborator.

Another unclear aspect of Breil's account is its chronology. If, as he states, he began work on the score in November, the six-week deadline imposed on him would have required its completion sometime before January 1915, well in advance of the opening at Clune's (which Breil does not mention), and three months before the premiere in New York. As it happens, *The Clansman* was given preview screenings in Riverside, California, on the first and second of January, apparently accompanied by a "special seven-piece orchestra";[47] so Breil may have been under pressure to finish the score in time to try it out at these performances, though there is no other indication that he did so.

In fact, contrary to Breil's account, other evidence suggests that Griffith did not really begin to think about a score for his film until very late in the year; also, that as far as he was concerned, regardless of what music was played at Clune's, the opening in New York was the one that counted, and the one for which he became busily involved in musical matters. In support of this view are press notices that place the director in New York in late January and early February (shortly before the premiere at Clune's), hurriedly making arrangements for the opening at the Liberty.[48] Most important is a report in the *Los Angeles Times*, dated 8 February—the day the film opened at Clune's—which gives detailed attention to music for the film. The reporter, a columnist who then wrote regularly about theater and occasionally about film, states that Griffith had returned to Los Angeles from New York only the day before, and, after briefly mentioning the director's interest in the Clune's score, turns to his plans for the opening in New York:

> David Griffith returned from New York yesterday morning, and spent the day down in the projection-room of Clune's Auditorium helping fit the music to *The Clansman*.
>
> Mr. Griffith has decided notions on the arranging of music for pictures.
>
> "Too long," he said, "we've been fitting the pictures to music, rather than the music to pictures. If there's a lady to die, and the orchestra leader happens to want to play *A Hot Time in the Old Town*, the poor lady has to die in two hops, so as to keep time to the music; or if there's a battle on and the orchestra wants to play *Hearts and Flowers*, that battle scene looks like a calisthenic exercise in the 'Old Ladies' Home."
>
> The Russian Symphony Orchestra in New York is to play the music for *The Clansman*. Carl Biel [*sic*], well-known as the author of *The Climax*, is composing music and adapting certain compositions. Mr. Griffith has also written two compositions to be used in displaying the pictures.
>
> A tremendous idea that of Mr. Griffith, no less than the adapting of grand-opera methods to motion pictures! Each character playing has a distinct type of music, a distinct theme as in opera. A more difficult matter in pictures than opera, however, inasmuch as any one character seldom holds the screen long at a time. In cases where there are many characters, the music is adapted to the dominant note or character in the scene.
>
> From now on special music is to be written in this manner for all the big Griffith productions.[49]

This article contains the first appearance of Breil's name (albeit misspelled) in connection with the film. Still, it seems evident, from the great attention given to Griffith and the little given to Breil, that the reporter considered the movie director's name and opinions to be far more newsworthy than the composer's; and her bias makes it difficult to reconcile the information given here with the version of events described in the latter's essay fragment. For one thing, she implies that the composer had begun to work on the score only in late January or early February 1915, rather than in November 1914, as Breil states. (It is intriguing to note that the later starting date, combined with the six-week deadline mentioned by Breil, would place the completion of the score very close to the time of the opening at the Liberty.) Also, the report contains no reference to *Cabiria*, although Breil claimed it to be an important influence on Griffith's thinking.

Thus, the *historical circumstances* of the collaboration's beginning are still very much in doubt; so, too, is its *conceptual basis*, although concerning the latter, at least in the few sources available, Griffith and Breil apparently expressed themselves in similar terms. Compare, for example, Griffith's "idea," as reported in the *Times* article, of giving each character "a distinct type of music, a distinct theme as in opera," with the way the composer described his first thoughts concerning music for the film, in his essay fragment:

> [Watching the film] it finally dawned upon me that the first half of the picture . . . was a most tragic romance, just such as every opera composer is looking for. And right there I decided that the film would be treated as an opera, without a libretto, of course. . . . There, too, it was decided that the principals should be invested with "leitmotifs"; and contrasting ideas, such as lofty love against drunkenness and lust, brutality against the manly determination of Southern gentlemen to protect womankind and their firesides, patriotism against rapacious ignorance—all these were to be contra-distinguished in the score by their own individual motifs.

To be sure, these words were written several years after the score had been completed, but for Breil they were nothing new: more than once, as we have seen, he wrote and spoke of his score for *Queen Elizabeth* in similar terms.[50] It is even possible that Griffith, as quoted above, was merely repeating views which had been previously expressed to him by Breil when discussing the latter's plans for the score. Whether or not such was the case, it does seem that the two shared an interest in the kind of theme to be used, and in making the music fit the film rather than the other way round. Moreover, in their eagerness to create something out of the ordinary, they show little interest in methods of compilation such as were favored by the men at Clune's.

By all accounts the *Clansman* score was almost entirely a compilation of pre-existent music. A note in the Clune's programs calls attention to the "diligent search" of music libraries in three cities for the "arrangement and selection of the music," and during the first twelve weeks of the film's engagement at Clune's, the same programs contained an "Announcement of [a] Musical Contest": members of the audience were invited to guess "the correct name of every musical selection" used in the film.[51] Once the contest ended, the announcement was replaced by a list of pieces (shown in Fig. 28), including nineteen titles of pre-existent music, as well as Nurnberger's "*Clansman* Overture" and an unspecified amount of "Incidental Music." Furthermore, Bernard Brown described the score he and Elinor had created as a "makeshift" one, using "standard music" and "little" original pieces for transitions; Elinor, too, remembered the score as a compilation, though he wrote of it less disparagingly than Brown. He described the contents as: "Music adapted, arranged, and very little compositions. I used a motive from Meyerbeer's *Huguenots* as a theme for the Clansman." And the contents of the Breil score as: "Music original compositions, and arranged. Mr. Breil used Wagner's *The Ride of the Valkyries* as a theme for the Clansman."[52]

The Huguenots vs. *The Ride of the Valkyries* makes for an intriguing opposition, that leaves us wanting to know more (starting with a precise identification of the motive used by Elinor). Unfortunately, our best sources—the list of contents in the Clune's program, and the *MPW* profile of Lloyd Brown—leave much to be found out. The program (though it does include Meyerbeer's *Huguenots* as one of its nineteen titles) indicates neither how much music was borrowed from each piece, nor the number of times each was used. As for Brown, he claimed that the score contained "over a hundred pieces"; also, that "with the six or seven repetitions as motifs or theme music there are 118 arrangements."[53] These divergent figures, along with ambiguous use of such terms as "incidental music," "pieces," "motifs," "theme music," and "arrangements," illustrate the difficulty of discovering what the score of *The Clansman* was actually like.

What is clear is that both the Clune's score and Breil's belonged to the tradition of silent film music as it had evolved over the years, but they appear to have differed in two ways, one of less importance than the other. (1) The borrowed music in each score is different; only two of the pre-existent pieces named in the Clune's program—Suppé's *Light Cavalry Overture* and Wagner's *Rienzi*—appear in Breil's score. (2) There was much less original music in the Clune's score than in Breil's. According to Elinor, the "motifs or theme music" in the *Clansman* score drew on pre-existent pieces (as did the scores prepared under Rothapfel's supervision); but as Breil often stated, most of the recurring themes found in his own score were newly composed. Indeed, in his score even the principal theme for the Klan was original and not—as one might gather from Elinor's description—borrowed from Wagner's *Ride*.

Elinor was not alone in confusing Wagner's theme with Breil's, and he had good reason to do so; but before we consider why, we do well to note that Breil's authorship of this theme, and others, has sometimes been disputed. As noted above, Karl Brown states that it was dictated to the composer by Griffith himself; moreover, he asserts that Breil was a good arranger, orchestrator, and conductor, who "could do just about anything known to music except think up tunes," so it fell on Griffith's shoulders to supply the lack.[54] Others, too, when describing how the score was created, have assigned the starring role to the director. In the *Los Angeles Times* article already cited, the writer depicts Griffith as a controlling figure and reports that he had written two compositions for the score. Aitken—like Brown, relying upon distant memories—does not mention Breil, though he states that "the selection of theme music . . . obsessed Griffith," and that in New York, Griffith "worked tirelessly with the musicians."[55]

Gish's remembrance of the collaboration is rather different and returns us to the Wagnerian theme. She states that the director worked with individual cast members in the selection of particular melodies, apparently chosen from different ones composed by Breil. She also describes the relationship as one of stressful give and take:

> Mr. Breil would play bits and pieces, and he and Mr. Griffith would then decide on how they were to be used. . . . The two men had many disagreements over the

> scoring of the film. "If I ever kill anyone," Mr. Griffith once said, "it won't be an actor but a musician." The greatest dispute was over the Klan call, which was taken from *The Ride of the Valkyries* by Richard Wagner. Mr. Griffith wanted a slight change in the notes. Mr. Breil fought against making it.
>
> "You can't tamper with Wagner!" he protested. "It's never been done!"
>
> This music wasn't *primarily* music, Mr. Griffith explained. It was music for motion pictures. Even Giulio Gatti-Casazza, General Director of the Metropolitan Opera, agreed that the change was fine. Finally Mr. Breil agreed to it.[56]

The anecdote portrays a classic confrontation between a musical purist and a man who better understands the functional nature of film music; yet the story, like the other views of Griffith's role cited above, is open to question. For one thing, virtually all of the symphonic and operatic excerpts in the *Birth* score include "changes in the notes," that is, abridgments, cuts, and reorchestrations; so it is difficult to see why, as Gish states, Breil would have chosen to draw the line at Wagner's *Ride* (which appears near the end of the score). For another, like Elinor and others, Gish seems to have confused one of Breil's original themes with Wagner's—which may have been precisely Breil's intention.

Breil's theme is the last important one to be introduced in the score, midway through Act II, for scenes of the summoning (or "Call") and assembling of the Klan; Wagner's *Ride* comes near the end of the act, and accompanies the Klansmen during their climactic rides and rescues. Though distinct, these scenes are related, just as the two pieces of music have similar cues and features, which can be seen by comparing Figs. 26 and 27. Like the main theme of Wagner's *Ride*, the second part of Breil's theme (mm. 5 ff.) contains ascending arpeggios which outline minor triads, and dotted figures that suggest galloping horses; also, at the beginning (in mm. 1–4) there is a progression from an augmented chord to a major triad, similar to a progression found in the continuation of the excerpt from the *Ride*, the "Hojotoho" theme (not shown in Fig. 27—it comes on the next page of the score).

It should be noted that Breil subsequently designated the music given in Fig. 26 to be one of his own compositions, as part of the published collection of "incidental music" from the score;[57] yet the same music seems to match what Karl Brown remembered hearing Griffith sing: "two notes of different spacings . . . in a bewildering variety of improvisation." Distinctive patterns of two notes—or three, to be precise—can be seen in mm. 1 and 2 (C and A oscillate by way of G♯), 6 and 8 (F♯ and B, preceded by the upbeat G), 9 and 10 (G and E, with upbeat F♯), and so forth. Perhaps Brown had in mind another version of this music, heard earlier in Act II, for scenes in which various Klansmen on horseback sound the call: here the C–A motive is played alternately by a solo trumpet in the orchestra and by a muted trumpet "on stage" (that is behind the screen). This arrangement of the Klan music seems far removed from Wagner's *Ride*; indeed, in 1915 various commentators noted its "weird" quality and rated it one of the score's most impressive moments.[58]

Perhaps Griffith did dictate some version of the theme, and perhaps he demanded, as Gish states, that Wagner's music be used as well. Even so, it was Breil who put the pieces together, and their resemblances are ones that a trained composer would be more likely to provide (or find significant) than a director. We are left to wonder whether the claim that Griffith composed music for the *Birth* score—a claim first stated in the *Los Angeles Times* article early in 1915 and repeated many times since—was an exaggeration, made for the sake of publicity value, which later came to be remembered as fact. The actual facts seem to be that Griffith loved vocal music and may have known much of the operatic repertoire, but possessed little musical training.[59] (As Bernard Brown tells the story, he "didn't know one note from another.") Indeed, rather than being the ideal *Gesamtkunstler*, Griffith seems to have resembled Rothapfel and Lloyd Brown—and Chaplin in years to come—in possessing strong musical intuitions, and in depending upon various musicians for the realization of scores for his films. Moreover, he was apparently so pleased by the *Birth* score that he sought to repeat such collaborations many times thereafter: having taken little or no interest in the music for any of his previous productions, after this epic he and his producers commissioned orchestral scores for fourteen more silent films, including four by Breil.[60]

In short, Breil was an experienced musician of the theater, Griffith was not, and much of what is most interesting in the music for *The Birth of a Nation*, as well as what is not so interesting, should almost certainly be credited to him. He composed more than half of it, arranged and collaborated in selecting the borrowed material, and conducted the orchestra at the New York premiere. For these reasons, we are justified in calling it "the Breil score," even as we recognize that its contents were born of an unusual collaboration, difficult to sort out at this date, between a well-known director and, in the larger scheme of twentieth-century music, an obscure composer—one whose music we now shall undertake to know better.

Relationships of Film and Music

Overview

The length and structure of *The Birth of a Nation* probably challenged Breil as a composer far more than did *Queen Elizabeth*, a stage-bound production in four reels; and far more than Saint-Saëns was challenged by *L'Assassinat du Duc de Guise*, a film of five "tableaux," focused on one historical incident, or Simon by *An Arabian Tragedy*, with its conventional, quick-paced story. *Birth*, shown complete and at the proper speed, lasts about three hours—in 1915, the longest American film ever made. Its twelve reels contain more than 1,350 shots and 230 titles; and its sequences (that is, groups of shots constituting distinct segments of the narrative) vary significantly in length and style. Adding to Breil's labor, Griffith continued re-editing the film for months, even after it had begun to be shown in various cities, inserting, deleting, and reordering titles and footage.[61]

By the time the film was unveiled at the Liberty it had been divided into two "acts," so different in their narrative strategies that they suggest the director gradually invented *The Birth of a Nation* as he went along. The first act can be likened to a string of one-reelers subdivided into discrete scenes that trace the history of the Civil War. It contains the following segments, reel by reel: an introduction, with scenes of life in the South before the war begins, and of meetings between members of the Stoneman and Cameron families (Reel 1); the beginning of the war and the departures of the Stoneman and Cameron sons to fight (Reel 2); escalating violence and tragedy, represented by a guerrilla raid on Piedmont, the death of sons from each family and the destruction of Atlanta (Reel 3); the Battle of Petersburg, the war's climactic event as far as the film is concerned, and the occasion for Ben Cameron to emerge as a hero (Reel 4); Ben's convalescence, his acquaintance with Elsie Stoneman, and homecoming (Reel 5); and Lincoln's assassination (most of Reel 6). Act II is more truly a multiple-reel feature than Act I: the narrative moves faster and has greater continuity, the sequences tend to be longer, and editing techniques more complex. The viewer's attention is focused, first, on the interrelationships of fictional characters, then, in the film's final half-hour, on non-stop action.

It appears that Breil worked on his score for this epic segment by segment, according to varied methods necessitated by the evolving structure and content of the film. By the time he was finished, the music had taken shape in a series of "numbers": twenty-eight in Act I, thirty-one in Act II. (However, as stated above, there are inconsistencies in the way the acts and numbers are labeled both within and between different versions of the score.[62]) Following Griffith's lead, he laid out most of the numbers of Act I in short segments, and they include many borrowed tunes, associated with the story's time period, locales, and historical events. In Act II, he tended to tie numbers together into larger units, by means of transitional passages; and from the beginning to the middle of the act the music is all by Breil, the emphasis falling on his "leitmotifs" for the leading characters; on the other hand, for the action segments that conclude the film, the score mainly contains extended borrowings from the symphonic repertoire. (See Appendix part 8 for an outline of the score's structure and contents, as well as parts 9–11 for indexes of the score's borrowed tunes, symphonic excerpts, and recurring themes.)

The differences between the music of Acts I and II are matters of degree, rather than of hard and fast distinctions. For example, twenty-five borrowed tunes appear in Act I, but only five are found in Act II. Three extended symphonic excerpts appear in Act I, widely separated, twelve in the second half of Act II, many of them strung together. Eighteen of Breil's recurring themes are introduced in the first half of Act I, for scenes which present the main characters; four new themes appear in the middle of Act II, for key scenes concerning the death of Flora and the creation of the Klan.

If there is a logic to be found in these figures, it derives from the score's subservience to the film—subservience so great that the result is one of fascinating discontinuity. True, Breil attempts to provide unity by means of thematic relationships: examples in the themes for the Klan have already been discussed, and others are to come; and in various ways he may have sought to give his work the cumulative power of Wagnerian opera or even the qualities of fluidity and balance found in the music of Saint-Saëns. But inevitably, if measured against these composers, his work will be seen to fall short (just as his opera, *The Legend*, does not stand up well in comparison to its European models). The deepest impression made by the *Birth* score is that of a sprawling, kaleidoscopic pastiche, and, as is also true of most other American silent film scores, its pieces do not always fit together in a manner pleasing to the musician's or music-lover's ear. It might be termed a Simon score writ large, or a Rothapfel score, or the Clune's score, polished and transformed. What holds our interest are the many ways by which Breil fit music to the film's individual scenes, using a broad range of types and forms with varied interpretive functions. Scene by scene, number by number, Breil reached into the film composer's bag of tricks and pulled out whatever music seemed most appropriate. Thus, his work offers one of the first great exemplars of the film composer's craft; moreover, within the conventions of film music in 1915, the score often matches the epic character and dramatic intensity of Griffith's moving, disturbing images.

Types of Music

BORROWED TUNES. As shown in Appendix part 9, twenty-six tunes have been identified in the score. They can be classified in six different categories: traditional tunes (these include *Auld Lang Syne* and *Comin' thro' the Rye*); parlor songs (*Home! Sweet Home!*, *Listen to the Mocking Bird*); minstrel music (that is, black-face theater tunes such as (*De*) *Camptown Races* and *Zip Coon*); Civil War songs and marching tunes (*The Bonnie Blue Flag*, *Tramp, Tramp, Tramp [The Boys Are Marching]*); military calls (*Assembly*, *Taps*); and national airs (*America*, *Hail to the Chief*). But such categories were not always hard and fast; indeed, because many of these tunes belonged to more than one genre, their significance was apt to be enhanced. *Old Folks at Home*, for example, was both a parlor song and a minstrel tune, and its dual nature is perhaps reflected in the way Breil used it in his score. It begins the third number of Act I, which accompanies the film's first Southern scene. The title which cues the number reads as follows: "In the Southland. Piedmont, South Carolina, the home of the Camerons, where life runs in a quaintly way that is to be no more."[63] Responding to the title, Breil chose a well-known song whose lyrics, appropriately, depict a Southern scene in acutely nostalgic terms; also appropriate is the song's three-fold reference to "old folks," a phrase that accords well with the film's fond presentation of the elder Camerons. However, the lyrics are in black dialect, which may seem ironic when associated with members of this family; and there is only a loose connection between the song's implied locale ("Way down upon de Swanee Ribber") and the film's (Piedmont, South Carolina).

Whether or not Breil had this ambiguity in mind, the example of *Old Folks at Home* suggests that he counted on audience recognition of the words associated with these tunes. The songs he (and Griffith) chose were from the standard repertoire for home and community singing, and their words, though not heard, reflect on the film's action in ways that audiences could easily understand.[64] For another example, one may consider the traditional tune *Auld Lang Syne*. Like *Old Folks at Home*, only the opening portion of the tune is used, and it is found in only one number of the score (Act II, no. 23), where it interrupts the music of the previous number, a frantic agitato which accompanies a prolonged chase sequence. Members of the Cameron family, together with their faithful ex-slaves and Phil Stoneman, are being pursued by black soldiers and seek refuge in a little cabin occupied by two Union veterans; when they are welcomed into the cabin, *Auld Lang Syne* suddenly rings out as this title appears on screen: "The former enemies of North and South are united again in common defence of their Aryan birthright."[65] The song's text contains a nostalgic appeal to "old acquaintance" that reflects the coming together of the Stoneman and Cameron families in this scene. At the same time, the song's traditional association with communal celebrations of the New Year underscores the idea that this moment in the film is a turning point: as "former enemies" unite, the "birth" of a new nation has begun.[66]

Some tunes are used more than once, with varied associations. Of these, perhaps the most notable example is *Dixie*, which is inserted whole into the score three times. First it accompanies a parade of Confederate troops through Piedmont as they prepare to leave for war (Act I, no. 11C). This is in part a jubilant scene with jubilant music (and probably the one that sold Clune on *The Birth*, according to the passage cited from Griffith's autobiography); yet for many audience members in 1915 the song was also a sad one, owing to its association with the passing of the Old South and the defeat of the Confederacy. These mixed emotions were surely sought by Griffith, who shows us both the marching soldiers, full of optimism, and also members of the Cameron family (Flora, Margaret, and their parents), watching the departure of the three sons with excitement and wistfulness. Later in Act I (no. 20B), within the sequence depicting the Battle of Petersburg, *Dixie* accompanies a scene that evokes similarly mixed feelings. Ben Cameron leads a charge against a company under Phil Stoneman; though wounded, he continues to run forward until he reaches the Union line, then rams the Confederate flag into the mouth of a Union cannon and collapses. Both the heroic gesture and the song call to mind the words "to live and die for Dixie." The third time the song appears (in Act II, no. 27), it accompanies the parade of the Klan, with Margaret Cameron, Elsie Stoneman, and Ben Cameron in the lead and continues as we see the Klan stand guard over polling booths during the next election, to insure that blacks will not vote. Thus *Dixie* comes to symbolize the triumph of whites over blacks, in spite of its words, which, in dialect, look back to "old times" supposedly untroubled by racial conflict.

The twenty-six song titles listed in Appendix part 9 represent *tunes*, borrowed in whole or in part, rather than pieces of music; as arranged by Breil, elements of rhythm, harmony, texture, and timbre help determine the music's relationship to the film. For example, according to the MOMA piano score, a solo clarinet and oboe are to play the melody of *Old Folks at Home*, "Moderato con espressione." As Allen's recording demonstrates, their tone colors and dynamic shading impart feelings of warmth and intimacy to the scene—just as the solo harp, used for the first presentation of *In the Gloaming* (Act I, no. 4 1/2 [Fig. 16]), renders a scene of slaves picking cotton into a serene pastoral, presumably what Griffith wanted for a background setting that leads into a love scene. Allen's recording also shows that *Dixie*, in its last appearance, is arranged to sound like it is being played by a marching band, such as Piedmont might have mustered for the Klansmen's parade.

These treatments are not particularly surprising, perhaps, but they are what the scenes require; elsewhere in the film Breil responds with more imaginative treatment of the borrowed tunes. Perhaps the one he uses most effectively is

Comin' thro' the Rye, heard twice in Act I, in numbers 10 and 25 1/2 (Figs. 20 and 21). The first time it is turned into dance music, for scenes of celebration in Piedmont following the first Battle of Bull Run, probably just as it was used across America during much of the nineteenth century. Breil gives detailed instructions (at the top of the page in the piano score) for changing the rhythm of the music from a "Valse lento" to 6/8, when the scene shifts from ballroom dancers to bonfire revelers. In this way the number, analogous to the final appearance of *Dixie*, reflects the rhythms of these scenes almost in a diegetic, or "source music" manner (as if it were coming from musicians playing at the ball and in the streets of the town)—though one may also note a less obvious association between the sexual connotations of the lyrics ("When a body meets a body," and so on) and the dancing couples and crowds seen on screen. The second time the song appears, in accompaniment to the scene of Ben's homecoming, it relates more to mood than movement, in a completely non-diegetic manner. In contrast to the earlier scenes, Ben now stands pensive and alone on the sidewalk, surveying the desolate street and his ruined home. Although Griffith cross-cuts more than once to shots inside the home, where Flora and the others expectantly await him, the music remains focused on Ben and emphasizes his solitude: played by two solo horns in simple thirds and sixths and in gentle triple meter (andante), the tune echoes like a wistful, tenuous memory of the dance—by extension, of the world that has been lost; and now there is an intentional, bittersweet irony (though not sexual) in the association of the song's words with the scene of an impending meeting.

When Ben and his family come together, two other poignant tunes are heard: first *Home! Sweet Home!*, and then a brief quotation from *My Old Kentucky Home*. The latter, perhaps Griffith's choice since he came from Kentucky, was at times a minstrel song whose words might seem out of place for the scene (as was the case with *Old Folks at Home*); but the present medley, harmonized very simply, in C major throughout, and marked to be played progressively softer ("p," "pp," and "ppp"), defers to the quiet yet emotional scene, and is thus a perfect match to Griffith's poetic restraint. Indeed, Ben's homecoming was one of the moments remembered by Agee for its "dreamlike absoluteness"; it is still remembered, because here Griffith shows both his deep sympathy for these characters and also, in the final shot, as the son is drawn off-screen into his mother's outstretched arms, his sense of where to let the camera draw the line.

As these examples suggest, most of the tunes listed above can evoke feelings of sadness, nostalgia, and regret, both in the particulars of their lyrics and in the general fact that in 1915 they were widely known and traditional, and thus reminded audiences of their own past. Breil, in the essay fragment quoted earlier, termed *Birth* "a tragic romance." In his use of borrowed tunes, he did much to make it seem so.

SYMPHONIC EXCERPTS. Excerpts from ten works are found in the score, all but one from the nineteenth-century concert repertoire, from Beethoven to Tchaikovsky. (See Appendix part 10: one excerpt is from a mass formerly attributed to Mozart.) These, of course, are not simple tunes; they are complex pieces, which Breil used primarily in prolonged action sequences. They give heightened impact to portions of the film in which tension is at its peak, and in which the cross-cutting and movement are so rapid that it would be difficult to match the details of individual scenes with a musical mosaic.

The first such excerpt, from the *molto vivace* section of the *Freischütz* Overture (Act I, no. 13), runs through scenes depicting the guerrilla raid on Piedmont, the invasion of the Cameron home, the terror and resistance of its occupants, a counterattack by Confederate army units, and the rescue of the Camerons. Of course the story of *Freischütz*, and in particular its supernatural elements (drawn from German folktales), is irrelevant to the film's narrative. One wonders, however, whether Breil turned to this music partly because he thought of the guerrilla raiders, most of whom are black, in demonic terms. (In one brief shot, a black soldier and a black girl jeer at a dead white man.[67]) More likely it was the frantic syncopated rhythms at the start, the surging and tumbling scales and arpeggios of the opening themes, the anxious *pianissimo* passages, tremolos, and diminished seventh chords (clichés of much movie music of the period), the violent outbursts, the heroic fanfares, and the see-sawing "battle" of fragments in the development section that led Breil to his choice of Weber's overture. In short, this music is used as a glorified "hurry," of the sort recommended by Lang and West in their 1920 manual, *Musical Accompaniment of Moving Pictures*: the *Freischütz* is one of twenty "standard overtures" which they list in their suggestions for repertoire, stating that they "contain brilliant and lively passages which will fit scenes in the wild West, hurries, chases, fights, and mob scenes," just as they list Wagner's *Ride of the Valkyries*, the last of the score's symphonic excerpts, in another group of pieces useful for "Speed (Hurries)."[68]

Having already noted some particulars of the latter piece, we do well to examine it further in these generic terms; for in fact, Wagner's *Ride* functions as the score's ultimate "hurry," and as such is well suited for a sequence which brings together shots of the galloping riders, those in peril, and those who besiege them, through cross-cutting at dizzying speed. The music's combination of swirling string and wind figures with the principal theme in the brass paints a vivid picture of heroic figures in motion; the theme's modulations phrase by phrase, as well as those heard during the "Hojotoho" portion of the excerpt, reflect the turmoil depicted on screen; and after these modulations, the grandiose restatement of the Valkyrie theme, now in B major, gives resounding emphasis to the moments when the Klansmen triumph.

As the example of Wagner's *Ride* suggests, one may sometimes find points of correspondence between the form of a symphonic excerpt and the content of the sequence it accompanies. The overture to *Freischütz* is no less suggestive: as used by Breil, the exposition apparently coincides with the attack of the Northern guerrillas, the recapitulation with the counterattack of the Southern troops. Breil may have intended to signal these particular correspondences with two cues placed relatively close together, in a long number that contains only four internal cues overall: one cue appears near the end of the development section, just before the beginning of the retransition to C minor, the other appears in the recapitulation, at the point where the arpeggio theme returns explosively. Yet we cannot be sure that he intended for these cues to be taken as anything more than general guides to keep the musicians on track. For in *Freischütz*, as in all of these excerpts, the music has been made to "fit" the sequence by means of cut-and-paste methods that distort the original form. There are four substantial modifications: (1) in place of the overture's *adagio* introduction, Weber's music is preceded by one of Breil's themes; (2) a passage has been cut from the exposition; (3) repeat signs have been placed around a segment of the recapitulation; (4) at the end of the sequence the overture gives way to *Maryland, My Maryland* (once it becomes clear that the Cameron household has been saved). The song, which Breil was careful to set in C major, provides a resolution of sorts, but one that is far less jubilant than the overture's; its function here is to arrest the (musical) action and focus the audience's attention on the heroism and poignancy of the Southern cause—just as it did earlier in the film, by being played when Ben took leave of the family and prepared to ride off to war. In short, Weber's truncated music may help to shape the sequence, but the borrowed tune gives it larger significance.

The music from *The Ride of the Valkyries* is likewise inserted into the score by means of scissors and paste. Breil joins two distinct passages from the beginning of Act III of Wagner's opera (mm. 13–25 and 45–78) and compresses two of Wagner's measures (18 and 19) into a single one of his own. He places repeat marks around the concluding portion of the excerpt, and indicates that the whole excerpt, and some of the preceding segments of number 26 1/2, are to be played twice, for each of the Klansmen's two rescues, the first in Piedmont, the second at the cabin. Moreover, when Wagner's music is played the second time, it may well break off in mid-phrase: the performer is instructed, first, to watch for the next cue ("Disarming the blacks," a title which the drummer is to "catch" on the snare drum), and second, to segue to *Dixie*.

We shall return to this music once more at chapter's end, with further attention to Breil's jarring manipulation of form; for the moment let us retreat to another familiar piece, Grieg's *In the Hall of the Mountain King* (Act I, no. 17B), which of all the symphonic excerpts has been altered the least. Indeed, Stern claims that in the sequence which this music accompanies, the destruction of Atlanta, Griffith repeated some of his footage so as to allow a portion of the music to be played complete—and there is evidence to support his claim, since footage is indeed repeated.[69] But even in this excerpt, Breil changed the form of the music, by cutting sixteen bars from the middle of this piece and placing repeat marks around its ending portion, including the coda. Still, these changes do not in any way alter the character (and associations) of Grieg's music, which may well seem a puzzling choice, drawn from the realm of the grotesque. Lang and West list the piece as appropriate for scenes of "villainous characters, robbers (in comedy)";[70] yet the sequence it accompanies presents shots of Sherman's army on the march and of crowds of refugees fleeing Atlanta in panic, as fire spreads. For Breil (and Griffith), some elements that may have made the music seem suitable are its relentless ostinato and repeated phrases suggesting an unstoppable force; its long crescendo, for the growing fire and panic; and perhaps even its original association, in Ibsen's play, with a murderous assault—comparable to the actions of Sherman's army, which might be construed as "villainous." Moreover, like several other symphonic excerpts, this one has a driving force that complements the sequence's epic character. Though we see the death of the second Cameron son, the moment passes quickly, as one incident within a larger tragedy, and the music evokes horror in response to the episode as a whole rather than to the death of an individual. In any case, at the beginning of the film this character is but sketchily drawn, so Griffith does well here not to linger. (By contrast, in an earlier Civil War scene Griffith focused our full attention on the deaths of the youngest Cameron and Stoneman sons—whose characters he had etched more deeply—in a brief vignette. For this moment Breil composed his own music to match the scene's details.[71])

Well after the period of his pioneering work on *Cabiria* and *Birth*, Breil expressed regret that it was necessary to use the music of past composers in film accompaniment, once terming such adaptations, forced upon him and other musicians by lack of time, "the greatest fault in motion picture production."[72] But though he claimed to dislike the method, and certainly did not invent it, he followed it well: the impact of this score's symphonic excerpts was very great, in part because of the power of the scenes they accompany, the apt correspondences such as were described above, and the freshness which the music still retained in 1915. (We do well to remember that some of the pieces used by Breil had entered the concert repertoire not long before *Birth* was made: the *1812* Overture was published in 1882, *In the Hall of the Mountain King* in 1888.[73]) Only as film musicians imitated Breil's achievement, with cue sheets and manuals to guide them, did the repertoire quickly became shopworn. Indeed, it did not take long for some of the war horses in the *Birth* score to be ridden into the ground—so deeply, as it were, that within recent decades the same pieces have been resurrected by film-makers chiefly for purposes of irony or caricature, utterly removed from Griffith's and Breil's lofty intentions.[74]

BREIL'S MUSIC. More than half the music in the score is Breil's—the amount might have been greater, had he been given more time—and it is of many types. The simplest consists of functional bits and pieces, including several that are used to make transitions, like the fragments Elinor and Bernard Brown composed for the Clune's score (according to the latter's comments, cited above). Such a transitional passage is given in Example 16: a three-bar chord progression, it connects the end of an excerpt from Wagner's *Rienzi*, in D major, to the beginning of one from Weber's *Freischütz*, in C minor.

Out of context, this music has little meaning; in relationship to the film, it emphasizes a turning point in the action. The film jumps from shots of the assembled army of the Klan riding off to its mission of rescue, to a scene between Stoneman and Lynch, who announces his intention to marry Elsie—this is the scene accompanied by the bridge passage, as indicated by the cue given above—and then to scenes in which blacks riot in the streets of Piedmont, while Elsie and her father try to escape from Lynch. For this violent eruption, Breil could have simply cut from Wagner's music to Weber's; instead he decided upon a transition passage both to give the music continuity and to heighten the impact of the scene. The transition prepares the violence by wrenching the music brutally from one key to another, then pausing in suspense, and the chords underscore Lynch's words with the force of hammer-strokes.

EX. 16. Breil, *Birth of a Nation*, Act II, no. 26 1/2, mm. 42–44

In a few places Breil composed short fragments not for transitions, but simply to accompany single shots of special import. One example is found in the middle of the sequence depicting the Battle of Petersburg. When Griffith intercuts two brief glimpses of the Cameron family in prayer, amid scenes of continued fighting, Breil supplies quick changes to match. As can be seen in Example 17, he separates two identical series of "religioso" chords (containing "amen" cadences), with the instruction to "fake buglers and drums." To mimic bits of action with disconnected fragments in this manner was more Simon's trademark than Breil's. (It anticipates methods later associated with animated cartoons, thus dubbed "Mickey Mousing" by Hollywood professionals.) True, we have seen how he used a similar procedure with a borrowed tune, for the dance scene accompanied by *Comin' thro' the Rye*; but for the most part, he preferred to work out the music in longer, less fragmented segments—a wise thing to do, given a film with over a thousand shots—and to relate the music to the film in other ways.

Where Breil most resembles Simon is in his reliance on *familiar styles* to comment variously on action, mood, and character. For example, in Act II he uses a series of light-hearted minstrel tunes for comic scenes among blacks, and some standard "misterioso" and "agitato" segments for sequences of intense action; also, his love theme for Ben Cameron and Elsie Stoneman is nothing other than a conventionally styled parlor song—hence its success in sheet music, as the "perfect" song. But of all the music in familiar styles, perhaps the most interesting examples are Breil's themes for Flora Cameron, which relate to her character in both obvious and subtle ways, a mixture seemingly beyond Simon's reach.

Flora's themes are introduced in the middle of Act I, in accompaniment to the first scene in which she takes a leading role: two and a half years have passed since she was last seen, and though she is now a "big girl" (as she writes to her brother Ben), she is full of mischievous changes of mood and unable to keep still. To match her vivacity and impulsiveness, Breil gives her three themes, one after the other, in contrasting rhythmic styles; all contain sudden starts and stops as well as slow downs. The first is an introductory fragment, scherzo-like, enlivened by hemiola (Ex. 18a, mm. 6–9); the remaining themes partake of the rhythms of popular dances, one in the style of a tango (Ex. 18a, mm. 10 ff.), the other a "hesitation" waltz (Ex. 18b). What is striking is that in 1915 both the tango and the hesitation waltz were generally thought of as seductive dances, with sexual connotations. Breil thus seems to have used these rhythmic styles to foreshadow Flora's attractiveness to Gus, the "renegade" who pursues her, and he may also have intended to hint at the danger she faces by building tension in the continuation of the two

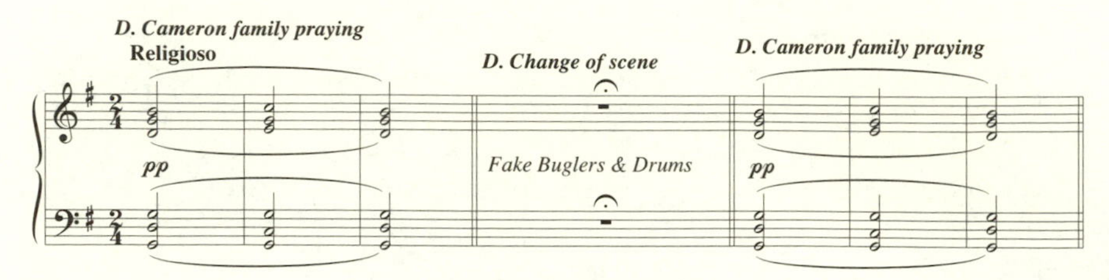

EX. 17. *Birth*, Act I, no. 19 1/2, mm. 12–18

themes. Each is led to augmented sixth chords that modulate away from the tonic (from A minor to C major) and avoid cadences; moreover, the second time this happens, at the end of the number, two sudden chords bring the music to a crashing stop. (The same passage reappears at the end of Act I, no. 25, which can be seen in Fig. 21.) In context, the effect of this music is comic but unsettling; in hindsight, the entire number can be heard to contain omens of Flora's misfortune.

The darker implications of Flora's themes are increased when one observes their relationship to two earlier themes by Breil, each associated with another character. The first to be introduced is Austin Stoneman's. Though his theme is in a different meter from Flora's, it begins with a melodic sequence of stepwise rising thirds that is very similar to the pattern found in Flora's second theme. (Compare Ex. 18a, mm. 14–17, with Ex. 19.) The other character is Lydia Brown, Stoneman's mulatto servant: her principal melody, which Breil labeled "Lust and Passion" in the 1916 Chappell collection, is in a tango rhythm, though more heavily accented and sustained at greater length than Flora's (Ex. 20). These relationships are especially significant because Breil uses them to connect characters of very different types, and thereby to probe beneath the surface of the narrative. Stoneman never appears in any scenes with Flora in the course of the film; but during Reconstruction, this "master of Congress" indirectly controls her fate, and

EX. 18a. *Birth*, Act I, no. 12, mm. 6–17 (Flora's themes, R10a and R10b)

EX. 18b. *Birth*, Act I, no. 12, mm. 30–37 (R10c)

(in Griffith's view) is responsible for her death: such at least is the point foreshadowed by Breil's thematic relationship. As for the link between Brown's theme and Flora's, its effect is to point up their opposite natures: one character is jaded, arrogant, and humorless, the other innocent, devoted, and mischievous; one makes conscious use of her sexuality (her tango, as it were) to control Stoneman and Lynch; the other cannot control Gus after having unknowingly aroused him.

We come, by way of Breil's music for Stoneman, Lydia Brown, and Flora, to what might be termed the heart of the *Birth* score—the part which occurred to him first, according to Breil's fragment of a memoir, and which he hoped would enable him to create an "opera without a libretto." Altogether, he employed fifteen recurring themes and theme groups to represent the film's principal characters and ideas. They are listed below (the letter "R" simply signifying that they recur); functional labels have been assigned to them, some quoted from Breil's Chappell publications, some inferred from context; and also given is the score number in which each theme first appears. (One of the themes listed here, *In the Gloaming*, is not by Breil; it is included because he treats it as one of his own. Further details about the appearances of each theme can be found in Appendix part II.)

EX. 19. *Birth*, Act I, no. 2, mm. 1–4 (Austin Stoneman's theme, R2)

EX. 20. *Birth*, Act I, no. 6, mm. 5–18 (Lydia Brown's theme, R7b)

Act I

R1 "The Motif of Barbarism" (no. 1)
R2 Austin Stoneman ("and Lydia Brown, the Mulatto") (no. 2)
R3 "The Elsie Stoneman Motif" (no. 2 1/2)
R4 The Cameron Family (no. 3)
R5 The Love of Margaret Cameron and Phil Stoneman (= *In the Gloaming*, no. 4 1/2)
R6 The Love of Ben Cameron and Elsie Stoneman (= *The Perfect Song*, no. 4 1/2)
R7a-g Ambition, "Lust and Passion," "The Pride of Ignorance," "Anger," "Violent Anger," "Fury," "Fury Allayed" (no. 6)
R8 The Old South (no. 7)
R9 Elsie's Sorrow (no. 11D)
R10a-c Flora Cameron (no. 12)
R11 "Marcia Funebre" (no. 16)

Act II

R12 The Rape of Flora (no. 9)
R13 Agony (no. 10)
R14 Fear (no. 10)
R15 "The Ku Klux Clansmen's Call" (and Ride) (no. 11)

Like most of the rest of Breil's music, these themes are modeled on conventional types; what distinguishes them is (1) the ways in which he interrelates them, as in the examples discussed above; and (2) his methods of thematic development, to which our attention now turns. To illustrate Breil's methods, we shall consider four instances of his treatment of the theme for Austin Stoneman (R2), from its first appearance early in Act I, to its final transformation, midway through Act II.

In its original version, as part of Act I, no. 2 (given in Fig. 14), the theme accompanies the scene in which Stoneman is introduced, and immediately helps to establish him as the film's principal villain or "heavy" (a slang term perhaps justified by the tempo marking "Pesante energico"). The music is cued to begin with these sentences, which Griffith places one above the other in a single title card:

> In 1860 a great parliamentary leader, whom we shall call Austin Stoneman, was rising to power in the National House of Representatives.
>
> We find him with his young daughter, Elsie, in her apartments in Washington.[75]

The first four bars of this number constitute Stoneman's theme (Ex. 19): set in a minor key, the melody rises sequentially, then plummets an octave, moves toward a distant harmony, and pauses—musical elements which symbolize Stoneman's rising power, as well as the dangerous potential of his ambitions, apt to lead him astray. Just as suggestive is the theme's continuation (shown in Fig. 14). After the title, Stoneman appears, as heavy in body as he is stern in spirit; he sits stiffly, while Elsie moves easily about and shows great affection, kneeling to wipe her father's

EX. 21. *Birth*, Act I, no. 2 1/2, mm. 1–8 (Elsie Stoneman's theme, R3)

brow. While this brief scene unfolds, a repeat of the melody begins, but now it modulates and prepares the introduction of Elsie's theme (R3, Ex. 21). The elision seems to symbolize the kinship between father and daughter, while the contrasting themes—like the separation of sentences in Griffith's title, as shown above—emphasize their sharp differences of character: his is a sombre, open-ended fragment, played by strings in low registers; hers is an animated eight-measure tune ("light, bright and sparkling," as it were) given to flute and violins.

When Stoneman's theme next appears (in number 5 1/2, Fig. 17), Breil makes it stronger than before, in part because Elsie is absent, in part because the father has become more assertive. The scene is set in his library, where he receives Senator Sumner; and while they argue, Stoneman pounds his fist angrily on his desk and overwhelms Sumner's objections. Accordingly, this time his theme reaches an emphatic full cadence in the dominant (G minor), and between the first and second phrase, Breil enriches it with a new and portentous phrase, consisting of alternating A♭ major and C minor triads. Moreover, as can be seen by comparing Examples 22a and 22b, the new phrase is reminiscent of one found in R1, Breil's "motif of barbarism," associated throughout the film with various black characters.[76]

The similarity between these two chord progressions points the way toward Stoneman's dangerous exploitation of the blacks later in the film, for the sake of political power; more immediately, the progression takes on added potency in the very next number, for a scene focused on Lydia Brown. One of her themes contains a passage clearly reminiscent of the earlier ones, transposed downward to the key of B♭ minor (Ex. 23; for the complete number, see Figs. 17–19). Stoneman is sexually attracted to Brown, by whom he is easily manipulated, and Breil's manipulation of this progression—he treats it as an autonomous motive, which can be moved from theme to theme—comes to symbolize her power over him, as well as his power over the blacks.

In Act II, in which Stoneman now rules the South as its "uncrowned King," the range of these associations continues to widen, until it includes the power and

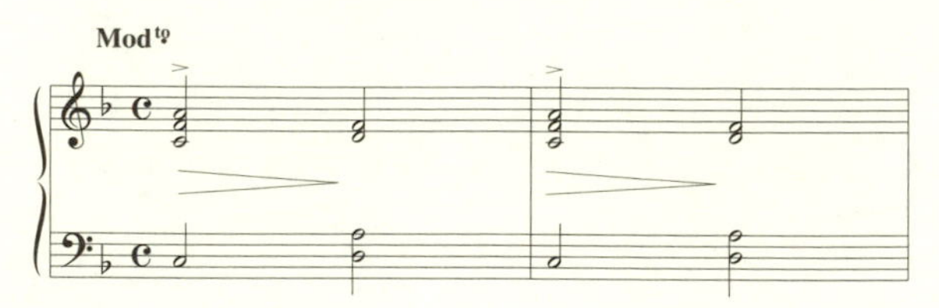

EX. 22a. *Birth,* Act I, no. 1, mm. 3–4 (portion of R1)

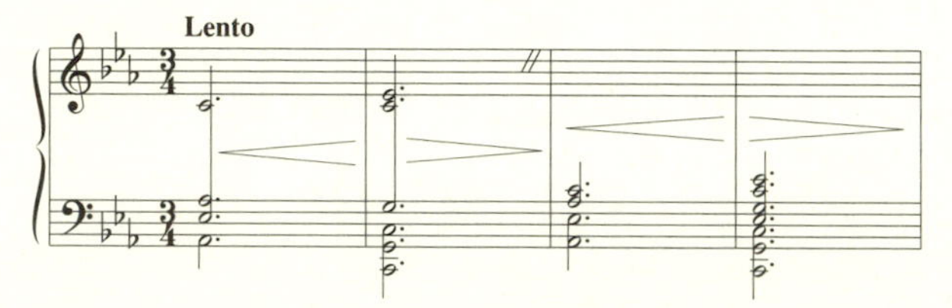

EX. 22b. *Birth,* Act I, no. 5 1/2, mm. 5–8 (portion of R2, new version)

passions of all the film's villainous characters. At the outset Stoneman's theme, Brown's themes, and the "motif of barbarism" are all joined together, for scenes depicting the activities of Stoneman, Brown, and Silas Lynch, his mulatto "protégé." (The latter sets his sights on Elsie, whom he eyes lasciviously.) More interesting, however, is the way Stoneman's theme is applied to the blacks in general, as part of a segment accompanying the scene in the South Carolina state legislature, the so-called "riot in the Master's Hall."[77] At first the tone of the sequence seems comic (albeit in a blatantly racist manner), as we watch the antics of uncouth black legislators, supported by simple tunes in minstrel style. But the mood quickly darkens: accompanied by a very slow and ominous version of R1 (the "barbaric" motive), the legislature takes up a bill legalizing interracial marriage, while "white visitors in the gallery" look on; once the bill is passed and the blacks rise to their feet in jubilation, Breil presents an agitated version of Stoneman's theme (Ex. 24). Reflecting the turbulence on screen, the theme has been turned upside down: that is, the melody is placed in the bass with tremolos of diminished harmonies above, the original fall of an octave has been changed to a seventh, and the music modulates wildly (from B♭ minor to G major)—all en route to a brutally joyous dance tune which concludes the number and the sequence. In this way Breil editorializes: for although Stoneman is not present in the scene, the appearance of his theme

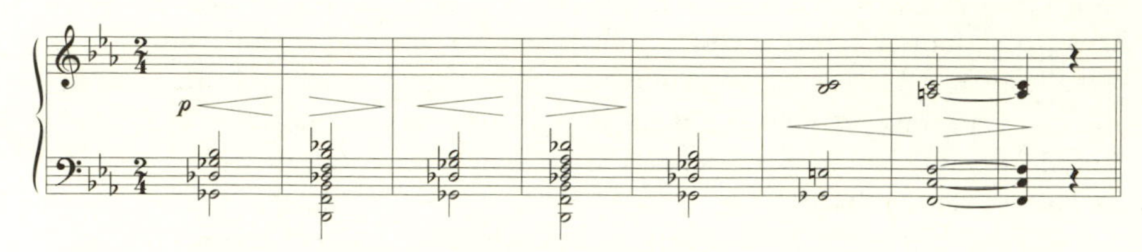

EX. 23. *Birth,* Act I, no. 6, mm. 79–86 (R7g)

EX. 24. *Birth*, Act II, no. 8, mm. 49–55 (transformation of R2)

suggests that this "riot" among the blacks, triggered by their attainment of new sexual freedom, is a chaotic result of his rule.

The last appearance of Stoneman's theme (in Act II, no. 11) has the strongest impact of all. Now back in its original key, it has again been placed in the bass, this time with a counter-melody, generally moving in contrary motion, set above it. The treble and bass melodies hammer against one another, reinforced by thick chords that increase the power of the music (Ex. 25). In all previous appearances, the theme was heard only once or twice within a single strain, but in this number it is repeated four times, always with the same counter-melody above, and the performer is instructed to play the whole segment three times (with cues for the second and third playing). In short, there are twelve repetitions of the theme in all, really too many for comfort, but they serve the narrative effectively. The music accompanies a scene of violent action, in which Lynch's supporters, led by Gus, ambush and kill three Klansmen. At the end of this sequence, news of the Klan's "rebellion" is brought to Lynch and Stoneman, and the latter, when told what has happened, angrily pounds the floor with his cane and asserts: "We shall crush the white South under the heel of the black South."[78] The words and actions recall Stoneman's behavior in previous arguments with Sumner and Lincoln, and show him at a peak of arrogance and power; in response, Breil has created his most powerful version of the theme, in its most extended form. The music, insistently contrapuntal, also suggests the struggles which Stoneman's policies have unleashed—and by which he (and his daughter) will nearly be destroyed. Given these factors, Breil must have found it necessary to make this the last appearance of the theme: for one thing, it had been heard enough; for another, from this point in the story, events move beyond Stoneman's control.

EX. 25. *Birth*, Act II, no. 11, concluding segment, mm. 1–5 (final version of R2)

In 1921, at a pioneering conference devoted to film music as it was then practiced across America, Breil read a paper on the "perfect motion picture score," in which he noted the influence of his own music for *The Birth of a Nation*:

> Ever since [this production], it has been the slogan of music writers for the screen to promulgate the motif or the theme—and now they do it often in the progress of the play [*sic*]—but not always wisely.

From here he proceeded to offer advice on the best ways to use such motifs; though confining himself to generalities, one passage could be taken as a partial summation of Breil's approach to the film, demonstrated by the examples discussed above:

> The composer must remember that a character whom he has labeled with a theme at his first entrance does not appear in the same condition—in the same surroundings—nor in the same psychological mood at each re-appearance. Therefore the motif must in its further presentations be varied to suit the new situations. And the greatest development of the theme must not appear in the early part of the score, but towards the end where is the climax of the whole action.[79]

These maxims are apt, but they apply to only some of Breil's music, which is in turn only part of the *Birth* score and does not include its so-called "climax of the whole motion." (Stoneman's theme last appears only midway through Act II.) Breil, were he to discuss his achievement in more general terms, might have told his audience what we have observed: that his score offers many instances of the use of borrowed tunes, symphonic excerpts, *and* recurring themes to illustrate details of the narrative, to relate similar and dissimilar characters, and to interpret some of the film's principal ideas. What remains to be considered—in what might be called the climax of this whole chapter—is the way all three types of music function within the score's dizzying variety of musical forms. In order to consider this topic properly, some of the same musical ground already explored must be crossed anew, but now with an eye toward a different subject: the degree to which form and function unite to create, if not a "perfect" score, at least one that is greater than the sum of its parts.

Function and Form

SEGMENTATION: NUMBERS FOR REELS 1 AND 2. The first sequence of the film begins with a title, "The bringing of the African to America planted the first seed of disunion," followed by a shot of a group of slaves being blessed by a New England minister. The second sequence shows a meeting of Abolitionists.[80] Breil matched the first with seven bars reminiscent of a Negro spiritual (the opening four bars becoming R1, "The Motif of Barbarism"), the second with nine bars in the style of a Protestant hymn. (See Fig. 14.) His aim, it seems, was to mirror the conflicting attitudes toward slavery expressed in these scenes with two types of religious music, the first simpler in style than the second. (The spiritual is heard over repetitions of the note D played by a tom-tom, which was probably meant to evoke the "barbarism" of the slaves.) Breil also created parallels between the two segments, so as to tie these introductory scenes together: both begin in D minor and end with the same reverent cadence formula in F major. Together the two segments demonstrate the film composer's ability to convey a lot of information in a short space of time, and to match separate sequences with discrete musical forms.

Reel 1 continues with several more sequences showing the introduction of the Stoneman and Cameron families and the visit of the Stoneman sons to Piedmont. The numbers which accompany them, all similarly divided into short, discrete segments, take varied forms, which are outlined in Appendix part 12.

In some of these numbers the sectional forms do not correspond to clear divisions in the sequences they accompany, as, for example, in numbers 2 and 2 1/2. As noted above, the cue for number 2 is a title, introducing Austin Stoneman and his daughter Elsie; but for number 2 1/2, the cue is an action (she kneels beside him) which occurs in mid-shot. Then, as the latter number continues, a new sequence begins, introduced by these sentences:

> Some time later.
> Elsie and her brothers at the Stoneman country home in Pennsylvania.[81]

This sequence is longer than the previous one: it shows the brothers discussing a letter they plan to send to the Camerons accepting their invitation, Elsie's interruption of their discussion, and the playful interchanges between them. There are no cues to indicate whether the music of number 2 1/2 is supposed to reflect these actions. Possibly Breil intended for the number's second strain, which is in B minor, and quite distinct from Elsie's theme, to be associated with the shift of scene to the Stoneman country home. (Such a correlation is possible if the first strain, Elsie's theme, is performed, with its repeat, quite fast.) Possibly Breil also intended for the repetition of her theme to be heard when she comes to the foreground of the scene to speak with her brothers, and for it to conclude the number, since Elsie is the last one to exit from the scene.

The problem is that none of these relationships is indicated in the score, and even if Breil had them in mind, some other factors (continuity? emphasis on a favorite theme for a favorite character?) must have motivated him to repeat this music as number 3 1/2, for the scenes depicting the arrival of the Stoneman brothers in Piedmont. Here the form of the number does not seem to match the content of the sequence in any obvious way, especially because Elsie, despite the presence of her theme, is absent from the scene. Moreover, though the "Trio" heading in number 2 1/2 suggests that Breil might have thought of this music as a self-contained, rounded (dance) form, the heading is lacking in the later number, and both contain instructions for performers to repeat the music "Da Capo" until the next cue. Thus, these numbers, along with 3 and 5, are best considered as examples of open-ended mood music: form follows content, leaving the musicians to decide questions of tempo, repetition, and so on.

In contrast, numbers 4 and 4 1/2 are not open-ended, and they match many details of the sequences they accompany. Number 4 (partially given in Fig. 15) contains lively action music for scenes of horseplay between the youngest Stoneman and Cameron sons, and each segment is cued, including the four repetitions of the principal strain (A). Number 4 1/2 (Figs. 15 and 16) matches lyrical melodies to Griffith's idyllic imagery of prewar life in the South, again with careful cueing: a pastoral theme (apparently modeled on the "Morning" music of Grieg's *Peer Gynt*) accompanies a view of a plantation landscape, first seen in a long shot; next, *In the Gloaming* (R5), played by the aforementioned harp, matches a closer shot of slaves picking cotton; Breil's principal love theme (R6) begins when we see Ben look at a photograph of Elsie—"He finds the ideal of his dreams," a title states—and her picture is seen in close-up;[82] it ends with a full cadence, as Ben, transformed in spirit, departs from the scene. Thus, with the exception of the brief opening numbers (1, 1B, 2), 4 1/2 is the only one in the film's first reel which might be termed through composed. Each segment is heard only once and tailored to fit the length of a part of the sequence, and the music reaches a climax at the end of the scene, with the first appearance of a phrase from "The Perfect Song."

A similar close relationship between music and film occurs with number 6, at the beginning of reel 2 (Figs. 17–19). Longer than its predecessors, the number provides an example of a rounded form which, in the manner of an operatic *scena*, is closely matched to a scene of intense dramatic action. The music consists of seven motifs (R7a–g), as shown in Table 4.1. This music accompanies a sequence focused on Lydia Brown, and each of the motifs can be related to her changing moods and actions, as indicated in part by the labels Breil attached to all but the first of them, when reproduced in Chappell's theme collection of 1916. A title introducing "Lydia Brown, Stoneman's housekeeper," is the cue for theme *a*, a solemn melody, whose profile in certain respects recalls the score's opening theme.[83] When first seen, she expresses her disdain for housekeeping by arrogantly giving orders to another servant; the melody for this portion of the sequence, *7b*, is the one in tango-style discussed above ("Lust and Passion"), which intimates both her restlessness and her sexuality. When Sumner, who has been seen arguing with Stoneman, orders her to get his hat and thus interrupts her "ambitious dreamings" (as a title states), a more agitated theme (*c*, "The Pride of Arrogance") begins; it continues while Lydia, rather than hand the hat to him, lets it drop to the floor. Sumner orders her to pick it up; she does so, then offers to brush it off, but he pushes her away (*d*, "Anger"). Once he has departed, Lydia reacts melodramatically by spitting in his direction and slamming the door (*e*, "Violent Anger"), then sinks to her knees, spits twice more, tears at her blouse and throws her head back, sobbing (*f*, "Fury"). Her fury is "allayed" (as Breil's label suggests), when she thinks of Stoneman (*g*, the theme derived from chords in number 5 1/2, as discussed above). Having regained self-control, she turns her attention to drawing sympathy from Stoneman by seducing him: she is, according to a title, "the great leader's weakness that is to blight a nation."[84] At this point Breil brings back the theme of "lust and passion" exactly as it appeared the first time, its sexual implications now made explicit. The scene closes with Stoneman and Brown's embrace, accompanied by a variation of the powerful opening theme.

Number 6 is clearly in rounded form; yet at the same time the music is harmonically open-ended, because the restatement of theme *a* has been transposed up

TABLE 4.1

6: Andante moderato	Andante	-----	Energico		Allegro		Andante moderato	Moderato vigoroso
C	2/4							C
3♭	4♭				3♭		4♭	
4			:16:		|8	26	8	8	8			:16:			6
R7a	b	c	d	e	f	g	b	a'

a third, from C minor to E♭ minor (though the key signature contains four flats), and it lacks a close on the tonic chord. Through this open ending Breil may be seen to link the music to number 7 (Fig. 19), with a bit of harmonic sleight-of-hand: the new melody, a variation on *In the Gloaming* in G major, harmonized in thirds, begins on the same pitch (D, though raised an octave) with which number 6 concludes. This tune (combined with another theme, similar in character) accompanies a slow, sentimental scene of departure: the Stoneman sons take their leave of the Camerons, now that war has come, and the magical shift from the previous number to this one conveys a feeling of impermanence—a suggestion, perhaps, that the pleasant holiday is part of a make-believe world (compared with the darker scenes we have just witnessed) that will soon disappear.

A rather subtle interpretation, perhaps; still, the link can be seen as one example of Breil's attempt to give the score's segmented forms coherence, despite shifts in the narrative which demanded changes in musical style. There are others, such as these two instances, which follow soon after. (1) *We are Coming, Father Abraham* (no. 8), which accompanies the "Historical Facsimile" of Lincoln's signing of the "First Call" for volunteers,[85] begins with a sixth (B above D); the two notes are an inversion of the pair (D above B) with which number 7 begins, and which concludes its second segment. (2) In number 11, a trumpet plays the *Assembly* call in A major (following an excerpt from Suppé's *Light Cavalry* Overture in A♭), to summon troops from their homes in Piedmont; in (11)B, which accompanies a scene inside the Cameron household, *Maryland, My Maryland* begins with the same leap heard in the previous trumpet solo, from E up to A.

In both of these examples, of course, the numbers are in the same key, so such links are easily made. (Indeed, by keeping nos. 7–9 all in G major, Breil may have meant to sustain the sweet mood described above, despite the war's outbreak, to enhance the pathos of the scenes.) Between numbers in different keys Breil more commonly found ways to link them through devices such as melodic bridges or half cadences. But there are plenty of numbers that simply come to a full stop, followed by an abrupt change of key, and sometimes the break is warranted by the action on screen, as between numbers 12 and 13: Flora's music cadences abruptly in A minor, and theme R1, in altered form, takes off in C minor, reflecting the surprise and panic occasioned by the guerrilla raid on Piedmont.

Breil clearly valued coherence, at least in the abstract: "there is nothing so disagreeable in picture presentations," he wrote, in the 1921 paper cited above, "as the blunt breaking off from one passage of music and the immediate taking up of another, entirely foreign to it both in construction and atmosphere." And further on, he returned to the same point, first with criticism of what was then common, next with a view of the ideal:

> Today some of the finest and greatest pictures have musical scores that are not units—they are rather a jumble of incoherent musical hodge-podge. . . . Just as in a great picture play the many scenes are all correlated, so too must its score be a collection of logical and correlative musical sequences that melt into each other.[86]

Whether the *Birth* score more resembles a "hodge-podge" or a "collection of logical and correlative musical sequences" is a question that cannot be decided on the basis of introductory numbers alone; one must look further on, into those tailored to Griffith's most powerful scenes, rich in "construction and atmosphere."

COHERENCE AND COMPILATION: LONG NUMBERS IN ACT II. Within the film's second half, in response to lengthy sequences, Breil expands the numbers and gives them more complex forms. One impressive example is to be seen in numbers 5 and 5A–C (partially given in Figs. 22–24), which together constitute a closed and rounded form with more coherence—more "musical sequences that melt into each other"— than those from early in Act I.

Number 5 seems utterly peaceful in terms of melody and harmony, as well as in form. It begins in C major, moves to the subdominant (F major) for 5A, and after a modulating segment in the first part of 5B, returns to C major, where it remains until the end, with elisions between all segments of 5B and 5C. This music is predominantly lyrical (therein it differs from surrounding numbers, which contain lively minstrel tunes), and emphasizes the score's two love themes through repetition and extension. As can be seen in Table 4.2, number 5 begins with a short introduction based on Elsie's theme (R3), then moves to Elsie and Ben's love theme (R6), which Breil extends into the song form A A'; number 5A contains Margaret and Phil's theme (*In the Gloaming*, R5), which he turns into a rounded form, A B A'. (The extended form of the latter theme does not appear elsewhere in the score.) In number 5B a new melody is heard, which was later published in the sheet-music version of *The Perfect Song* as the introductory "verse"; it leads to a return of the "chorus," R6, again in extended form; and the second strain, A', is heard once more, at the end of number 5C.

These numbers are rounded so as to match a sequence which contains four scenes between Elsie and Ben, surrounding one between Margaret and Phil, and the change from theme to theme mirrors the way in which, scene by scene, romantic relationships established earlier in the film alter. Number 5 accompanies the scene in which Elsie and Ben go for a walk and, as a token of his love, he presents her with a dove; he also attempts to kiss her, but she playfully rebukes him. Then Elsie is seen alone in her room, where she fondles and kisses the dove. Number 5A accompanies a contrasting scene in which Margaret, haunted by "bitter memories" of the war, rejects Phil Stoneman. Griffith cuts from this scene to a second meeting between Elsie and Ben, again out for a walk, and now it is the "verse" of the

TABLE 4.2

Number	5		5A	5B		5C	
Tempo	Lento	Amoroso	Lento	Andante	And. mod.	All. viv.	Mod.
T.S.	C		2/4	C		2/4	C
K.S.	0		1♭			0	
Bars	3 3	8 9	‖:8:‖ 8 8	9 8	8 8	‖:8:‖	9
Theme	R3	R6	R5		R6	R3	R6
	(intro.)	A A'	A B A'	verse	A A'		A'

song which accompanies the lovers. They embrace until Elsie, tormented like Margaret by memories of the war, first pulls back in tears, then holds out her arms to Ben. Through all of this the verse modulates and builds up tension, until there comes a return of the love theme, once they sit together; it continues while Ben escorts her home, and reaches its cadence phrase with the scene's culminating moment, when they finally kiss before parting. Number 5C accompanies the conclusion of the sequence: Elsie is seen once more alone in her room, subject, as an introductory title states, to "love's rhapsodies and love's tears." Such contrast is evident in the way she first skips joyfully around the room, accompanied by her playful theme (R3), then presses her face to the bedpost, tears running down her face, while the concluding strain of the love theme is heard once more.[87]

Never again in the *Birth* score did Breil achieve such a convincing fusion of form and function. (Perhaps he was always at his best with sentimental tunes: it was the *Song of the Soul*, for *The Climax*, which had established him as a dramatic composer.) After this point in the film, sequences become more complex and forms increasingly problematic, as can be seen by examining numbers 14 and 15, which accompany the scenes of Flora's death and the mourning that follows. Table 4.3 illustrates that these are the longest numbers yet discussed, and filled with contrasting segments. They contain both recurring themes and new material, and they end differently from the ways in which they begin.

Despite their lack of coherence, each of these two numbers contains some of Breil's most effective music, in varied styles. Flora is first seen at home with her family, and Breil opens number 14 with restatements of all three of her themes, including the tango and waltz in their original versions (R10b and R10c); but when she goes into the woods, where she is spied on by Gus, Breil breaks the music into fragments, some derived from the tango theme, others imitative of bird calls. (See Fig. 25.) Here, for once, the music continues to change shot by shot, indicating that Breil, like most observers, found this to be one of Griffith's most powerful sequences, deserving of special treatment. (Breil's approach to number 5 differed: intent on sustaining the romantic mood, he kept the love theme going, even though Griffith intercut three quick shots of Lynch spying on Elsie and Ben.) Most effective is the way he increases the tension of the scene through repetition of a falling half-step from F to E, a motive derived from the chords which support Flora's tango theme (as in Ex. 18a, above), for every shot of Gus. The music no longer dances: it has become an emblem of stillness and danger. When Flora sits

TABLE 4.3

No.	*14:*	All'tto	And'te	All'o graz.	Valse brillante
T.S.		3/4 C	3/4	2/4	3/4
K.S.		2♭	0		
Bars		4 4	18	22	38
Theme		R10a	R13	R10b	R10c
		Moderato		§Andante	
		2/4		C	
		0		3♯	
		16 12		|| :4: || :4: ||	D.S. till cue.
		R10b (fragments)		*Listen to the Mockingbird*	
	15:	Agitato		Allegro	(All of this portion of no. 15 is written out a second time, with a § sign at the start.)
		¢ C 3/4		12/8	
		0 3♭		0	
		8 8 10		9 + 8	
		R7e R7f R11			
		And'te doloroso		Funebre	
		3/4		4/4	
		1♭		4♭	
		|| :8: ||		10 16 6 || :9: ||	
				(Laments)	

on a log and playfully talks to a squirrel, Breil eases the tension by shifting to the major key and introducing a quotation from *Listen to the Mockingbird.* The passage borrowed from the tune is lyrical and mirrors Flora's innocence, as well as the natural setting; but its effect is laden with irony and pathos, because the chorus of the song concludes with the words "singing o'er her grave." Breil must have wished to emphasize the point. Though Griffith continues to intercut shots of Gus, the music no longer mirrors the editing: the song is repeated ad lib, until the next cue.

Compared with number 14, the music of number 15 seems more conventional, and its relationship to the action less precise. Except at the beginning, for the moment when Flora is accosted by Gus, there are no cues in the number, and for the extended chase scenes, which include much cross-cutting between Gus's pursuit of Flora and Ben's attempt to rescue her, we hear open-ended repetition of a few familiar themes (though two of them, R7e and f, may be of interest on account of their association with Lydia Brown), plus a new agitato strain. The latter, comprised of a chromatic sequence of rising and falling triplet figures based on broken chords (an outgrowth of R12, which is in turn evidently derived from Gluck's music for the Furies in *Orfeo ed Euridice*), can be heard to imitate Flora's attempt to escape by climbing a cliff and then leaping to the rocks below. But the score contains no indication of where in the number the leap appears, and one cannot be sure whether Breil intended for performers to continue playing through the climactic action or to stop (without a cadence, since none is written?) for her fall.

EX. 26a. *Birth*, Act II, no. 15, concluding music

Overall, then, number 15 is a loose series of segments of two distinct types: agitato strains for the chase and laments for the death and mourning scenes that follow. Both parts of the number lack cues and cadences, and both call for open-ended repetition.[88]

At the same time, the final lament can be interpreted as one of Breil's strongest attempts to give coherence to his score, because it recalls music associated with earlier tragic scenes. As can be seen by comparing the passages given above and below, a portion of the lament (the bracketed bars in Ex. 26a) is similar to the melody that concludes Act I, used to accompany scenes that follow Lincoln's assassination (Ex. 26b). Moreover, in their use of arresting harmonies both of these segments recall music heard when the youngest Cameron and Stoneman sons die side by side on the battlefield (Ex. 26c). The shifts of key during Flora's scene (from F minor to A♭ major to an implied G major tonic that is never reached) echo the shifts from F minor to A♭ major during the scene of Lincoln, and from B major to A♭ major to a half cadence in C minor during the scene on

EX. 26b. *Birth*, Act I, no. 28D, concluding music

EX. 26C. *Birth*, Act I, no. 15, concluding music

the battlefield. Taken together, these three scenes represent what might be called the film's tragic arch—the deaths of youthful innocents surrounding the death of a statesman—supported by musical pillars of increasing strength. Thus, with rather subtle thematic links across long intervals of time, coupled with rich modulations and avoided cadences, Breil apparently sought to give his music Wagnerian power and pathos and to overcome the discontinuity inherent in his own music's segmented musical forms.

CULMINATION AND CLOSE. After Flora's death Gus is captured by the Klan, and the narrative turns from tragedy toward its triumphant conclusion. Likewise, to match the action-packed scenes that bring the victory of the Klan in the final reels, Breil turned from original to borrowed music. With one exception—the "Storm" movement of Beethoven's Sixth Symphony, which Breil inserts into number 17 to accompany the vivid scene of Gus's trial and execution—all of the symphonic excerpts come close to the end. As can be seen in Appendix part 13, four of them are used in the course of number 26 1/2, drawn from the overtures to *Zampa*, *Freischütz*, and *Rienzi*, and from *The Ride of the Valkyries*; these are repeated and intermixed with shorter segments, of which all but one, *In the Gloaming*, are by Breil.

The length of number 26 1/2, far greater than that of any other in the score, and its medley of borrowed music, leads us to regard it as a textbook example of cue-sheet accompaniment, to which Breil simply sought to give continuity as best he could. First, he contributed short bridges between three of the symphonic excerpts (one being the passage shown in Ex. 16, discussed above. Second, he elided some other segments: for example, the excerpt from *Freischütz* breaks off on a dominant seventh chord that leads to *In the Gloaming*, which begins on the tonic chord of the same key (Ex. 27). Third, he seems to have taken care to select some excerpts whose themes are in related keys and have similar shape and character. Those of *Zampa* and *Rienzi* both begin with brass fanfares in D major (Exs. 28a and 28b), and the *Valkyrie* theme enters in the relative key of B minor. Moreover, throughout the sequences which this number accompanies, all three themes are repeatedly associated with scenes of the Klansmen on horseback; and the *Valkyrie* theme, as noted above, recalls Breil's own theme, heard for the last time in number 25 (Fig. 26), when Klansmen begin to assemble.

The last three pieces of this impossibly long "number" do their work well, and they are the ones people tend to remember; but we should also note Breil's effective use of two other segments, the overture to *Freischütz* and *In the Gloaming*. Inserted to accompany scenes which direct attention away from the actions of the

EX. 27. *Birth*, Act II, no. 26 1/2, end of excerpt from *Der Freischütz*, followed by R5 (*In the Gloaming*)

Klan, they stand apart from the other segments in key and character. The music from *Freischütz*, of course, is a partial reprise of the excerpt heard in Act I, which accompanied the attack by black raiders on Piedmont, as described above. Breil probably decided to reuse it here because the scene again depicts mobs of blacks assaulting white citizens of the town, more ferociously than before; certainly he decided to jump from the overture to *In the Gloaming*—the only calm bit of music in the number—because in the middle of the action Griffith intercuts a few brief shots of Margaret among the besieged in the cabin, tears rolling down her cheek,

EX. 28a. *Birth*, Act II, no. 26 1/2, beginning of excerpt from *Zampa* Overture

EX. 28b. *Birth*, Act II, no. 26 1/2, beginning of excerpt from *Rienzi* Overture

a little girl by her side. Moreover, because Phil Stoneman is also present in the cabin, the return of their love theme, and the words which it recalls—"Will you think of me and love me, as you once did long ago?"—is apt to remind us that Phil had previously been spurned by Margaret, despite his pleas for a reconciliation. For this reason the song imparts psychological intensity to the vignette, as well as a welcome respite from the hectic music.

In short and as always, Breil did what he could with a daunting task: making the music fit an unprecedented sequence of pictures. Still, we may well ask why, at the end of the *Birth* score, he relied on other people's music so much more than his own. One reason may be that Griffith insisted he do so: Gish implied as much, in the anecdote cited above. Another may be that he decided that he had not the time to do otherwise: six weeks, according to his own account. Or perhaps he found the action sequences at the end of the film too long, too complex, or too alike in character to be mirrored with original music in short segments. Whatever the explanation, we have seen that most of the excerpts in number 26 1/2 are well suited for the scenes they accompany; so, too, are the numbers that follow, in which brief restatements of the love themes, for two shots of the married couples (a "double honeymoon," states the title), are the only bits of music by Breil to be heard.[89] From *Dixie* onward, each segment of the score makes an effective contribution to the film's grandiose conclusion, and in 1915, the final combination of a rousing fragment from a movement of a late eighteenth-century mass and the complete national anthem must have guaranteed an enthusiastic audience response.

Like other parts of the score, the closing numbers are not without unifying aspects. Some parts of number 26 1/2 are related to others, and some echo earlier numbers, as has been noted; moreover, from the second half of number 27 onward —with the exception of the *Cocoanut Dance*, which accompanies a sequence that Griffith inserted for some early screenings, and then deleted—all segments are elided and remain in C major. Still, neither these relationships nor any others which have been observed can entirely counter the "hodge-podge" effect that such a mammoth compilation is bound to produce. That is why, when we finally close the book on the *Birth* score, we remember it best as a gloriously big and well-wrought example of the type of "Musical Accompaniment of Moving Pictures" described in manuals of the day. Breil may have had the ambition to match the epic film with music of Wagnerian grandeur, but limitations of time, the collaborative nature of film-making (the Griffith factor), and his own limitations as a composer were against it. For all that, the score is a major achievement of the period, and was recognized as such by Breil's contemporaries.

Hare, the Boston critic who in 1915 described what he saw and heard as a "marriage of music and spectacle," might better have reversed his phrase: the film came first and will always do so. Yet he was correct in spirit if not in the letter. *The Birth of a Nation* remains a spectacular, moving, and deeply troubling marriage of image and music. From the evening of its first performance at the Liberty until today, as an object of contemplation, its example has been found to offer hope for more perfect unions, waiting to be born.

FIVE

Erik Satie's Score for Entr'acte

Significance

Entr'acte is the first original film score of consequence by an avant-garde composer; it has been highly praised and, in one published study, even termed a model of film music.[1] In the following analysis, the case is made for hearing it not so much as a "model," but as a unique solution to the problems posed by a nonnarrative film. In some respects the music recalls earlier scores discussed above, for, like *L'Assassinat*, *Entr'acte* is a unified, continuous piece, composed for a small orchestra and lasting about twenty minutes. But the film's unconventional nature forced Satie (or rather, reinforced his customary desire) to compose unconventional music; and his score called into question the prevailing film music aesthetic of its time—as exemplified by *The Birth of a Nation*—on behalf of an avant-garde that was seeking new forms and meanings in the artful combination of music and image.

The film, directed by René Clair, was originally an integral part of *Relâche*, a work created for the Ballets Suédois (under the stewardship of Rolf de Maré), and given its premiere, with the film presented between the ballet's two acts, at the Théâtre Champs-Elysées, on 4 December 1924. Satie composed the music, Francis Picabia outlined the "action" for both ballet and film and designed the decor, and he and Jean Börlin were responsible for the production. These men were conspicuous figures in the world of the Parisian avant-garde. Satie was their elder statesman, widely known for his unconventional theater pieces (beginning with *Parade* in 1917), as well as for his role as mentor to the so-called "Six" (one critic's label for a "group" of prominent young composers);[2] Picabia was perpetually active as a painter, poet, publisher, and patron of Dada;[3] Börlin was a leading dancer in the Ballets Suédois, a company known for its sponsorship of provocative new works.[4]

Relâche, it was hoped, would be no exception. When Picabia was invited to collaborate on the project, in January 1924, the invitation came at Satie's behest, in a letter from Pierre de Massot, who wrote that *Relâche* could spark "a true revolution . . . a new DADA."[5] To his young friend Milhaud, Satie wrote playfully in September 1924 of the impending "tornado."[6] Audience excitement was heightened by means of a publicity campaign promising an evening of anarchic spectacle: for example, shortly before the premiere, in Picabia's final issue of *391*, an advertisement announced the ballet with the exhortation to "Bring dark glasses and something to plug your ears. . . . Ex-Dadaists are invited to come riot and especially to cry 'Down with Satie! Down with Picabia! Long live the *Nouvelle revue française*!'"[7] On the night when the premiere was supposed to take place (27 November), the gala audience was kept milling in front of the theater until the announcement came that the premiere would be postponed for a week because Börlin was ill: since *relâche* in theatrical parlance means "no show tonight," there was suspicion that the "false" premiere was a Dada joke and that the ballet did not really exist.[8]

When the premiere did take place (on 4 December), the joke turned out differently. *Relâche*, seen to contain minimal action, failed to arouse its audience. The ballet was performed a dozen or so times before the Ballets Suédois disbanded (in the spring of 1925); since then the work has rarely been revived.[9] But *Entr'acte* has not slipped from view. The film is continually rescreened; its script has been published in several versions; and it has been analyzed with some frequency.[10] Among film intelligentsia, critical opinion is clear: *Entr'acte* remains one of the most delightful works to emerge from France in the decade of experimental film-making that followed World War I.

Yet it is easier to appreciate *Entr'acte* and to enjoy its humor and vitality than to explain what it is about. Though the film lasts less than twenty minutes, it is crammed with well over 300 motion-filled shots, which bewilder us with their speed, fantasy, and technique.[11] (There are no titles to explain the film's content or to divide it into sequences.) Non sequiturs abound: one moment we behold a paper boat sailing over the roofs of Paris; next, the legs of a ballerina leap in a darkened studio. There are illogical jokes in abundance, too: for example, when the camera pans up the ballerina's body, "she" is revealed to be a bearded man; when it pans down from the tips of her upstretched hands, the dancer's true face comes into view. Later in the film, while assembling for a funeral procession, one mourner breaks a piece of bread from a loaf hanging on the back of the hearse. He eats it, incurring the disapproval of his companion. The hearse, we discover, is drawn by a camel; the mourners, leaping in slow motion, follow it into the Luna amusement park (in Paris), and circle a diminutive model of the Eiffel Tower.

With incidents like these in view, *Entr'acte* appears to be a Dadaist farce, and Picabia characterized it as such. He called the film "a true entr'acte, an intermission from life's monotony and from all hypocritical and ridiculous conventions."[12] If the film shows disrespect for art (as personified by the ballerina) and for the dead, the reason, as Picabia put it, is that "*Entr'acte* respects nothing, if not the wish *to burst out laughing*."[13] But the film takes off its hat to more than humor. *Entr'acte* was Clair's second picture, the work of a young man in love with the camera and what it could do. He treated it like a newfound toy, and organized his playful images with a remarkable array of effects: complex rapid-fire editing, dense superimpositions, rhythmic manipulations from slow to fast motion and back, all in the interest of developing a new language for cinema. For during the years following World War I, among the intermingled circles of Clair, Picabia, and Satie, there had developed a "New Spirit" of appreciation for the unique properties of the film medium.[14] Those artists who wrote about film (like Clair himself) placed great emphasis on the need to develop "pure" cinema—that is, cinema based on inherently visual styles, divorced from literature and theater, and shaped into anti-narrative (often dreamlike) forms. "Thus came *Entr'acte*," wrote Clair, "claiming to give the [cinematic] image new value."[15]

Thus, too, came Satie's score, which many claim gave new values and functions to film music. During the final dozen years of the silent period (from about 1915 on), most films were products of an industry geared to supplying audiences with entertaining stories; music was expected, as in Breil's score, to underline and interpret the narratives, by reflecting settings, characters, actions, and moods. Clair's film came out of an altogether different world; the "story" it tells is at best a puzzle; and Satie's music has its share of puzzles, too. Rather than compile or compose a series of mood or action pieces in conventional styles, or a series of leitmotifs in a pseudo-Wagnerian manner, Satie built the score out of brief repetitive patterns strung together in units of four and eight measures. (See, for example, the opening measures of the score, given in Ex. 29.) For the most part, commentators have found only the most general relationship between the music's crazy-quilt style and the film's anarchic torrent of images; and in the composer's departure from convention, in his apparent refusal to "interpret" the film, they have asserted that Satie understood the true nature of "good" film music. *Entr'acte* has repeatedly been praised for being unpretentious and unobtrusive; and the score has also been seen as a prime example of what Satie called "*musique d'ameublement*," or "furniture music."[16]

This was a term Satie employed occasionally during his final years—the earliest known references seem to date from 1917—usually in a semi-parodistic manner.[17] He used the term to describe a type of functional music to be "furnished" on specification like an industrial product, designed (like furniture) to provide comfort and support for some other activity. Here is how the composer described furniture music in a letter to Jean Cocteau (ca. 1918):

> What we want is to establish a music made to satisfy "useful" needs. Art does not enter into this. "Furniture music" creates a vibration: it has no other goal; it fills the same role as light and heat—as comfort in all its forms.[18]

Satie's commentators have observed that unobtrusive background music is now often heard in public environments: supermarkets and waiting rooms, for example, which are filled with soothing Muzak; and they have placed film theaters into the same category, likening a film's "background music" to "furniture music"—or "wallpaper music," as it has also been called.[19] In making the connection between furniture music and movie music, these observers echo those historians and theorists (cited in Chapter Two), who assert that film music originated in response to basic "useful" needs (for example, the "noise problem"). The claim that early film music fulfilled its basic functions with little relevance to the screen images it accompanied is similar to the claim that Satie's music does not interpret the images of *Entr'acte*.

One can counter these assertions in a general way by noting that even the most "unobtrusive" film accompaniment (however that intangible quality is to be measured) is likely to play a much more active role than ambient "light and heat." In the specific case of *Entr'acte*, one can also point out that there are good reasons for *not* considering the score to be an example of furniture music. In the first place, as a source for the style of *Entr'acte*, one need not look to the idea of furniture music: Simon's music for *An Arabian Tragedy* resembles Satie's in that it, too, is divided into units of two, four, and eight measures, and is full of repetition and abrupt changes. Remove the "modernism," and some of Satie's music could pass for Simon's; Satie's intention may have been to imitate, in a playful manner, the clichéd types of music he heard in the movie theaters and music halls of his day.

Furthermore, Satie himself never related the term *musique d'ameublement* explicitly to *Entr'acte*, or even to film music in general. Indeed, the one performed work to which he did apply the term was a set of pieces for piano duet and a few other instruments, in which themes from *Mignon* and the *Danse Macabre* were mingled with his own. As described by Templier and Lambert, the music was played on 8 October 1920 in the foyer of the Galerie Barbazanges, during the intermission of a Max Jacob play, and people were asked, without success it seems, to pay the music no heed.[20]

Entr'acte is not just a few scraps of music; it certainly does not sound like Muzak; and it is not meant to be ignored. It is an extended, challenging composition to be listened to in silence. At best we might say that a furniture music style—detached, repetitive, tuneless—was a starting point for this score, and for many others by Satie as well. But the music of *Entr'acte* as a whole enjoys a dynamic relationship with a complex film. Though it does not interpret the narrative in a conventional manner, it does support the film, help to elucidate its structure, and extend its range of meanings. Deservedly, the music claims the foreground of our attention.

Musical Sources and Structure

There are four published versions of the score, all of them bearing the awkward, but accurate, full title, *Cinéma: Entr'acte symphonique de "Relâche"*:

1) The orchestral score for flute, oboe, clarinet, bassoon, two horns, two trumpets, trombone, strings and percussion (Paris: Rouart-Lerolle, 1926);
2) A four-hand piano reduction made by Darius Milhaud (Paris: Rouart-Lerolle, 1926), plate number 11573;
3) A two-hand piano reduction (Paris: Salabert, 1972), plate number 17061; and
4) A revised orchestral score (Paris: Salabert, n.d.), plate number 17.207.[21]

Another important source of information about the score consists of two loose pages containing Satie's handwritten list of its cues, together with key signatures and numbers of measures. There is uncertainty as to the purpose of these "cue sheets," but they appear to be the composer's only "sketches" for the score.[22]

While these sources leave many questions relating to the performance of the score unanswered, the cues they contain provide some indication of how to fit the music to the film. There are ten of these cues, to which I have added Roman numerals, as follows:

I. Chimneys; deflating balloons
II. Boxing gloves and matches
III. Scenes from the air; chess game and boats on roof
IV. The female dancer and figures within water
V. The hunter and the beginning of the funeral
VI. Funeral march
VII. Funeral procession in slow motion
VIII. The chase
IX. The coffin's fall and the emergence of Börlin
X. The End (Screen bursts and The End).

These can be taken as an outline of the film's content, and they show that *Entr'acte*, for all its craziness, gradually develops a comic "plot." The images within the first two sections are the most fragmented, and the objects on screen (chimneys, boxing gloves, and so on) have no narrative context. In the third and fourth sections, the director changes his approach and offers teasing glimpses of stories: first a chess game between Marcel Duchamp and Man Ray, next a scene of a ballerina. Section V marks a major shift in *Entr'acte* toward a relatively continuous narrative. A hunter (Börlin), as if he were in a fairground booth, attempts to shoot an egg balancing on a jet of water. A mock funeral procession follows (in Sections VI and VII), with the hearse, as previously mentioned, led by a camel and the mourners following behind, first at a normal pace, then in slow motion. Normal motion resumes, until the hearse comes loose from the camel's reins. It begins to roll away, faster and faster, and a runaway chase accelerates into a parody of a Mack Sennett comedy, climaxing with an upside-down ride on a roller coaster (Section VIII). Suddenly the coffin falls from the hearse and tumbles to rest. A few of the panting mourners (still in pursuit!) catch up, and out pops Börlin (Section IX). With a magician's wand he makes everyone, himself included, disappear. "Fin," says the screen, only to be turned into one more joke. Börlin bursts through the canvas sign to tell us that this not the end, as indeed it is not, since the second act of *Relâche* is to follow. De Maré enters angrily, remonstrates to his "star," then knocks him down and kicks him in the head. Börlin hurtles backward through the ripped canvas, which heals itself into the final conclusive "FIN."

Just as Satie's cues indicate ways in which the film's images can be divided into "sequences," they also can be seen to divide the score into distinct sections. Altogether, *Entr'acte* contains 58 musical units, mostly lasting eight bars each. These units are numbered consecutively in Appendix part 14, with indications of their interrelationships, lengths, and key signatures; also shown is the way Satie has grouped these units into larger sections, cue by cue, that is, film segment by film segment. Cues I and II correspond to the first 14 units of the score. (On Satie's cue sheet, the layout and corrections suggest that he originally intended these two sections to be linked under a single heading, perhaps because of their similar images.) Thereafter, each new cue marks the beginning of a new section of music, sometimes with a change of meter and tempo, usually with a cadence or a pause, and always with a change of theme and key. Section VIII is subdivided into two parts by these same means.

It seems, then, that, like all the scores discussed in previous chapters, the structure of *Entr'acte* was shaped in response to the content of the film, in detailed ways, as well as in a general fashion. To be sure, the score is a coherent whole, and the style of the music is consistent; moreover, within the framework of this structure and style the music changes from section to section in relationship to the images. A study of those relationships follows.

Music and Film

Affinities are apparent from the outset. At the beginning we hear a series of oscillating patterns. The music "creates a vibration"—Satie's description of furniture music—or rather, one pattern of vibration after another. As can be seen in Example 29, the patterns heard in the first, third, fourth, and fifth units occupy single measures; the second unit's pattern occupies two measures.[23]

Overall, the characteristics of this music are *buoyancy*, suggested by the bouncing and dissonant figures which blithely refuse to resolve; *momentum*, sustained by the constant tempo and the lack of cadences; and *discontinuity*, caused by the abrupt shifts which isolate each unit in terms of "theme," key area, and orchestration. No two units are scored alike. Unit by unit, various soloists and small ensembles take turns, often in parodies of popular musical styles: in the fourth unit, for example (mm. 21–28 of Ex. 29) an oscillating two-note "melody" for oboe and horn sits above an "oom-pah" pattern in the low strings, while a wood block jauntily canters in dotted rhythm. The effect is comic; at the same time the music has a peculiarly neutral quality, owing to its detachment from the surrounding music and its motion that reaches no goal.

The six units represented in Example 29 extend from the score's first cue to the second, and accompany the following 23 shots:

1. Fade in to coruscating dots of light with halos. The halos fade and the dots recede.

2–11. Fade in on a series of eleven different long shots of houses and roofs seen diagonally or completely upside down. The shots are all very short and one dissolves rapidly into the next. (Shots 3–5 are superimposed on other, fainter shots of similar roofs.)

12. Medium close-up of three little dolls—one male, two female, against a background of painted flowers. Their heads are balloons with faces painted on them. Through an aperture behind them, which looks like the back window of a car, roofs and houses can be seen passing rapidly from left to right.

13. Long shot of houses and chimneys upside down.

EX. 29. Satie, *Entr'acte*, opening measures (units 1–6)

14. Resume on the three dolls.
15. Close-up of one of the female dolls, whose head slowly deflates and flops onto its shoulder.
16. Resume on medium close-up of the dolls, all their heads deflated.
17. Close-up of the male doll whose head re-inflates and swells to its original size.
18. Medium close-up of a ballerina in a tutu, shot directly from below, twirling round on a sheet of glass.
19. Resume on the three dolls, all their heads re-inflated.
20. Extremely fast tracking shot, looking directly upward from beneath some trees, with rays of sunlight sparkling through the branches.
21. Resume on the three dolls again with their heads deflated. Fade out.
22. Fade in to another shot of dots of light; they expand and contract as they move in and out of focus. Amorphous moving shapes fade in behind them.
23. Close-up of white boxing gloves on a black background.[24]

...

As this shot analysis indicates, *Entr'acte* begins with a jerky series of disconnected images. It pictures a world of objects in constant flux (as in shots 1, 22, and

23), a world turned upside down (shots 2–11, 13) and a world seen from the "ground up" (shots 18 and 20). We also see, in a kind of mini-narrative, a caricature of a complacent family threesome out for a ride (shots 12, 14–17, 19); and when their heads deflate, re-inflate, and deflate again, we may take the sequence to symbolize the puffed-up pretensions of the *bourgeoisie*. Thus, within the world of *Entr'acte*, nothing is fixed; many images provoke the audience in comic fashion; and the beginning comes close to realizing one of Picabia's happiest phrases for the cinema: "an evocative invitation, as rapid as the thought of our brain."[25]

For the most part, the music does not respond to these imagistic flashes of thought by changing from one shot to the next; such a method would be all but impossible, given the speed with which the shots fly by, and Satie did not cue such rapid changes in the score. Instead, the music matches the film's content by means of the characteristics emphasized above. The buoyancy of the first theme, for example, seems perfectly suited to the bouncing dots of light it accompanies at the start. The film's fast-paced movement is mirrored by the music's quick tempo and unflagging momentum. The fragments of music are as discontinuous, and as subject to unpredictable recurrences, as the images they accompany.

Music and film also share a common *tone*, both detached and humorous. It might be said that both chords and pictures have been abstracted from normal positions and meanings for the purpose of comic disorientation. We can hear, for example, the harmonic basis of each musical unit: A major in the first, F in the second, C in the third, and so on; but no cadences confirm these keys or resolve the "wrong" notes. Indeed, so many notes sound out of place, and so many key areas are abruptly juxtaposed, that the chords tend to lose their functional meaning in terms of harmonic relationships. One might say that chords have been "liberated" from such relationships, just as Clair explicitly sought to liberate the film's images.[26] (Some images have even been detached from what they really represent. For example, the dots of light in shots 1 and 22 are in fact the street lights of Paris, as we later discover, altered and made to move by changing the position of the camera lens.)

The point was made above that the film's beginning is also "liberated" from any semblance of a conventional narrative: it is the film's most abstract portion. Satie's response was to join the score's first 14 musical units into a continuous section, separated from what follows. As can be seen in Appendix part 14, several of the oscillating patterns introduced in Section I are repeated in Section II (an intriguing procedure which Satie also followed in linking the two acts of *Relâche*). Among the units that recur, the first is the most prominent. It is heard three times, in such a way as to delineate the sectional structure: first at the beginning of the score (unit 1), next in correspondence with the second cue (unit 6—that is, Ex. 29, m. 37), then at the end of Section II (unit 14). The third time there is a difference: after six bars the downbeat chord "freezes" like a photographic frame; the music "cadences" simply by coming to a stop (Ex. 30).

The sudden halt serves two purposes. First, it gives punch to the joke that ends the second section: superimposed images of matches spin and blaze in a man's hair; he scratches his head, then looks at the camera in surprise, and it is as if the music stops short in surprise along with him. The sudden pause also emphasizes the dominant role played by the opening music—the "theme" of *Entr'acte*.

EX. 30. *Entr'acte*, end of Section II (unit 14). (Mm. 1–5 of this unit are identical to mm. 1–5 of Ex. 29.)

There is a unity to all the images this theme accompanies: bouncing lights, bouncing white boxing gloves, matches moving in a man's hair. They are all of a type: inanimate objects made animate, defying gravity and the natural order, moving in air or hair. Like these images, the opening theme defies musical "gravity" by refusing to come to rest on the solid ground of an A major chord. Its melody keeps bobbing back up to the pitch just above the tonic; its buoyancy sets the pace and character for all the music of the first two sections; and only when the film is about to change does Satie bring this unit (and the section) to a halt.

In Section III, the film begins to depart from its purely abstract character to tell its first little "story."[27] Pillars in front of a building are shown at various angles, then superimposed in a criss-cross pattern that leads metaphorically to the shot of a chess board. A camera tracks across the pillars, first to the left, then to the right. The two players, Duchamp and Man Ray, are shown together, then one after another.

We sense in this imagery a greater degree of stability and balance than at the beginning, and these qualities are reflected in Satie's music. The first unit of Section III oscillates like all the earlier ones, but the pattern has been made to fit into two sub-phrases—an antecedent and a consequent of three-plus-one bars each (Ex. 31). This new phraseology is quickly parodied by the third unit of the section: a twelve-bar (!) unit, subdivided into phrases of seven and five bars each (Ex. 32). With their perky cadences, these units are at once balanced and comically out of kilter, a playful ambiguity driven home by the end of this sequence. The game, it turns out, is on no more solid ground than the rest of the film. Indeed, it is being played on a parapet, vulnerable to attack, and suddenly a stream of water blows the

EX. 31. *Entr'acte*, beginning of Section III (unit 15)

EX. 32. *Entr'acte,* middle of Section III (unit 17)

players and the game away. While a paper boat floats dreamily across the roofs of Paris, the music floats with it; but in this last unit of Section III there is another unbalanced outburst. Four loud chords bring Section III to a halt (Ex. 33).

Once again, a cadence both emphasizes a joke and divides two sections. The close is far stronger (though no less abrupt) than the one which ended Section II, and it articulates a division between images which the film interconnects. Clair cuts back and forth between shots of the paper boat and the ballerina who holds center stage in Section IV.[28] His point is to stress a resemblance in their movements, as he did with a pictorial resemblance between crossed pillars and chess board earlier, and thereby to establish a sense of continuity despite the film's choppiness. Thus we perceive the boat as a transitional image: its voyage is launched by the stream of water that breaks up the game; its goal is the ballerina's studio.

It was difficult for Satie to duplicate such a dreamlike visual continuity in music, particularly in music so full of shifting fragments as the *Entr'acte* score. When the composer introduces cadences, he awakens us to shifts in the film, ignoring the hidden logic that holds the images together. The cadence at the end of Section III calls attention to itself with the force of an alarm clock; yet, having granted this, we also recognize that the "boat music" *does* subtly prepare the music to come. Its triplets (the only such figures in the score) anticipate the triple meter

EX. 33. *Entr'acte,* end of Section III (unit 19)

EX. 34. *Entr'acte*, beginning of Section IV (unit 20)

of Section IV; its angular, oscillating line, which may be taken to reflect the boat's angular movement, hints at the arch-like melody that follows (Ex. 34).[29]

These are subtle anticipations, however, apt to impress us only subliminally, perhaps only after analysis. What we are more likely to respond to are the difference between Section IV and all that preceded it, since there is unexpected visual beauty in the camera-play. As at the beginning of the film (in shot 18), in Section IV the ballerina is seen many times from below, a surprising point of view, which demonstrates film's ability to depict the art of dance in new perspectives. (The sequence reminds us that the film originally was to be seen in the middle of a non-narrative ballet.) The ballerina's exercises become a study in rhythm; owing to the shot's use of light and shade, her tutu seems to open and close like a flower's white petals.[30]

The music for Section IV is appropriately lyrical: the meter changes to waltz time (though there is no clear triple-meter pattern to the dancer's exercises), the tempo slows, and one hears the first real tune of the score. Even though it lasts only four bars, it sets a gentle mood that suffuses the whole section. The line's melodic arch well suits the graceful motions of the dancer. All the succeeding patterns are light and smooth; all are eight measures long, neatly divided in half. Neither harmony nor orchestration jars. Satie also rounds off this section smoothly, with a return of its opening melody, and as we might by now expect, a cadence brings Section IV to a close (Ex. 35).

Like the cadence that ended Section III, this one is unconventional in its chord progression, and ironic in effect. As the waltz theme returns, we behold a puzzling set of superimposed images so intricate that our sense of a "reality" behind them all but collapses.[31] Various pairs of eyes, a ballerina's tutu, a face upside down that merges into a mirror image of itself—these and other pictures melt into one another and into a rippling layer of water "behind" them. In response, the music builds to a loud, fully orchestrated restatement of the section's opening theme, and then stops firmly in E major (Ex. 35, mm. 5–8), as if attempting to supply a foundation missing in the film.

Stability is not to be had. Suddenly the opening music returns, as we see an egg balancing on a jet of water, and Börlin, the "hunter," preparing to shoot it. By being as unstable an element here as it has been all along, the water disturbs his game: the jet bobs up and down, as does the egg. Indeed, while the hunter stands vexed, the egg bounces and multiplies unpredictably. When finally the water and egg stabilize, the hunter pulls the trigger, only to have this sequence explode (like all the others) with jokes. The egg hatches a dove that comes to rest on the brim

EX. 35. *Entr'acte*, end of Section IV (unit 23)

of Börlin's hat. While the hunter cheerfully converses with the bird, he is himself stalked and shot by one of his "creators," Picabia. After Picabia fires, Börlin plummets from a roof and out of the picture.

The score's opening theme dominates Section V even more than it did the first two, but in an altogether new way. While Börlin, exasperated, watches the egg, performers are instructed to repeat this same musical unit ad lib and to stop only when he is shot. Heeding these instructions, performers must play at least sixty measures of a pattern by now quite familiar.[32] Did Satie devise this approach to the sequence because he discovered, too late for new music to be inserted into the score, that what he had composed for this section was too short? Perhaps; yet this music, too, closely parallels the effect of the film. With its high level of dissonance and rhythmic agitation, especially in comparison to the music of Section IV, the music helps keep this episode up in the air, on edge so to speak, until the hunter is brought down. The double shooting is thus tied together with a single musical thread, and the music does not give away the joke on Börlin. The more the music is repeated, the more it generates tension, first as a reflection of the hunter's impatience, then of the audience's.

But the ultimate effect of this section of the score is somewhat more complicated. It would be difficult to imagine film music more obtrusive than a segment repeated so many times, although in performance some of its vexing quality could be softened.[33] Confronted by the exasperating repetitions, we may find ourselves "tuning out" both music *and* film. Such a distancing effect may have been precisely Satie's intention, to keep us from taking anything in the world of *Entr'acte* seriously. Thus the music seems to be calling attention to itself and mocking the film, at a point where one could claim that it follows the story closely. Satie being Satie, he must have enjoyed these contradictory effects; *Entr'acte* being *Entr'acte*, the contradiction is not resolved. When Börlin falls, the music breaks off and both music and image move in new directions.

As remarked previously, the opening theme is heard at the beginning, in the middle, and at the end of the score segment covered by the first two cues. Something like the same design governs the score as a whole, since the theme dominates beginning, middle, and end sections. The whole mirrors the part; and the sum of the parts, as others have observed, makes the whole seem very much like a rondo. That is, the opening music reappears in Sections II, V, VII, and X, while the other sections provide various kinds of contrast. Section III has the character of a scherzo, Section IV possesses lyric repose. Section III moves to the subdominant side of the opening key area (D major in relation to A major), Section IV centers on the dominant (E major). These are common key relationships for rondo episodes, although the order of the contrasting key areas and their characters seem to have been reversed, as if to parody conventional expectations.

If this interpretation is correct, one may ask why Satie gave his score the simple structure of a rondo. A general answer is that the complicated "modern" music of the twenties was often cast into simple (neo-)classical molds; another is that Satie eschewed formal complexity in most if not all of his compositions. In more specific terms, the structure fits the content of the film. For as was stated above, the appearances of the opening theme in Sections I and II reflect similarities in the images the music accompanies, and further similarities can be traced through the rest of the score. When the opening music returns at the beginning of Section V, it seems to bring us home; but of course, "home" in *Entr'acte* is up in the air—with bouncing discs, boxing gloves, a paper boat, and an egg on water. The same music accompanies all but one of these images, and that one (the boat) has special "airborne" music of its own (that is, Ex. 33). Thus the structure of the score can be intimately linked to a fundamental—and simple—pattern of imagery within the film.[34]

This pattern is sustained through the remainder of *Entr'acte*, in the context of a narrative that seems more continuous than before. Accordingly, Satie adheres to the rondo structure while bringing a succession of new and old techniques into play. Section VI, for example, like Section IV, is a slow, dance-like episode, a march rather than a waltz. The music begins in the tonic minor (a common key for a contrasting episode in the center of a rondo); and for the first time the composer parodies conventional silent-film music in an obvious way, by alluding to Chopin's Funeral March.[35] Satie quotes Chopin's theme in the key of A minor (a semitone below the original), and then, somewhat disrespectfully, imposes his own tune on the warhorse's back (Ex. 36).

This music sets a mock-somber mood for the dreamlike procession on screen, and similar patterns are heard through much of the rest of Sections VI and VII. The bar-long rhythmic pattern in Chopin's theme, with a dotted eighth note on the second beat, is heard in the next two units of VI (29 and 30); when the score's opening theme returns in a slow tempo at the beginning of VII (32), its dotted rhythmic pattern, though it falls on the first beat of the bar, sounds as funereal as Chopin's. The cue for the return of the opening theme is "Cortège du ralenti," the moment when the mourners begin to move ahead by leaping off the ground in slow motion. Thus, the theme once again accompanies objects—or rather, people—up in the air.

EX. 36. *Entr'acte*, beginning of Section VI (unit 28)

At the beginning of Section VIII, the procession turns into a chase, and to mark the transformation, Satie devised the two most complex units of the second half of the score (Exs. 37a and 37b). In the first of these units, the opening chords have the rather aimless quality of the music in VII, and the music is partially derived from unit 38, heard earlier in that section; but the timbre is darker than before (the low brass dominate), the harmonies are more dissonant, and the music accelerates through rhythmic diminution into a counterpoint of lines that move in opposite directions (mm. 5–8). Thus the music creates tension and builds momentum while the hearse begins to slip away, and the rhythmic acceleration (driven by the snare drum introduced in m. 6) pushes the music into a surprising chase theme: a modal-sounding, hymn-like line that covers seven (!) duple-time measures. The new theme, as indicated in Ex. 37b, is rhythmically

EX. 37a. *Entr'acte*, beginning of Section VIII (unit 40)

EX. 37b. *Entr'acte*, continuation of Section VIII (unit 41)

ambiguous enough to be heard in triple meter, with an incomplete final bar; its metrical instability is one way that the theme seems to comment ironically on what we see: the male mourners, black-frocked and hatted, stepping faster and faster until they reach a furious fast-motion run.[36] Three times this dignified theme is repeated, moving no faster despite the mourners' ever-quickening strides. With each repetition the solemnity of the music is increased by an enrichment of instrumentation and harmony. Thus the acceleration on screen is matched by an expansion of texture rather than by an increase of tempo, and the music makes the beginning of the chase seem as dreamlike and as comic as the previous sequence.

Once the chase is under way, this sophisticated music is followed by a series of eight units as simple as any in the score. All are eight measures long, and all contain one-measure patterns (as in Ex. 38). The music becomes less assertive, in deference to Clair's visual structures, which are most fully developed in this portion of the film; however, as the chase builds, the music builds with it. Both the pitch and the dynamic levels rise, and the number of instruments steadily increases until the last of these units (Ex. 39). This music accompanies the climactic roller-coaster ride, an ever more confused blur of several dozen shots, and once more Satie instructs the performer to repeat a single unit ad lib. As was the case the first time, the repeated pattern is highly dissonant, and may seem to create tension; but now we are not waiting for an action to transpire (like the shooting of the egg and Börlin) so much as for an *end* to the action. Film can move no faster than it does here, and the repetitive music, fixed on one chord, pulls against it: the syncopated rhythms feel like brakes on the runaway hearse. The longer the sequence and the musical repetitions continue, the more the sense of friction builds. Thus the same irony is in force as before: an obtrusive, seemingly autonomous piece of music increases the film's dramatic effect. Moreover, resolution is again denied, since the music simply stops when the coffin, with Börlin inside, falls to the ground.[37]

EX. 38. *Entr'acte*, Section VIII, the first "chase" unit (44)

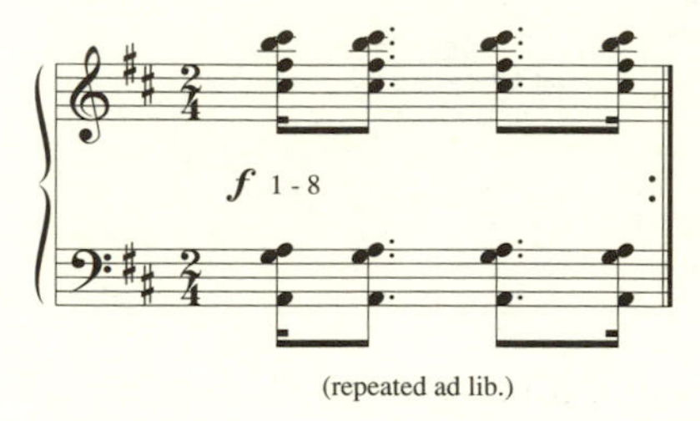

EX. 39. *Entr'acte*, Section VIII, the last "chase" unit (51)

A slower section ensues; like the mourners, the music must pause to catch its breath. Section IX presents a series of units in triple time that vaguely recall the music of the ballerina's section, with similar circular patterns that gently move through very small ranges. In this section, however, the patterns do not arch and float; they rise chromatically and weakly, depicting post-chase exhaustion. The first of them also sounds a bit exotic, owing to the use of a tambourine on the third beat of every bar (Ex. 40). The scene of this sequence is the countryside, seemingly far from Paris, where the film began; yet Börlin jumps out and hops and dances about in a manner that recalls the ballerina in her studio. Perhaps this explains why Satie chose to make the music of Sections IX and IV similar. Börlin acts as if he were still on stage, where in fact he shortly would be, were *Relâche* to resume, and once again we are reminded of the theatrical context of the film.

From here to the end, the theatricality of the action is maintained, with music to match. First Börlin ends his "show" by using a magic wand to make his companions—and himself—disappear, one by one. For accompaniment, the music repeats a soothing pattern that seems to close on a dominant chord, softened by an added sixth (Ex. 41). The film fades out, and the music fades away, with little energy remaining. But there is one more explosion: Satie repeats the energetic opening theme, as "Fin" appears and Börlin bursts through the screen. We feel the half-humorous bow to classical symmetry contained in this gesture; we also sense the appropriateness of the return, since Börlin has placed *Entr'acte* once again up in the air.

This time, a true ending is achieved, for the music, if not the film. In units 55 and 56 the opening theme undergoes its first transformations in the score: thirds are piled up into an augmented triad that itself augments the tension of the argu-

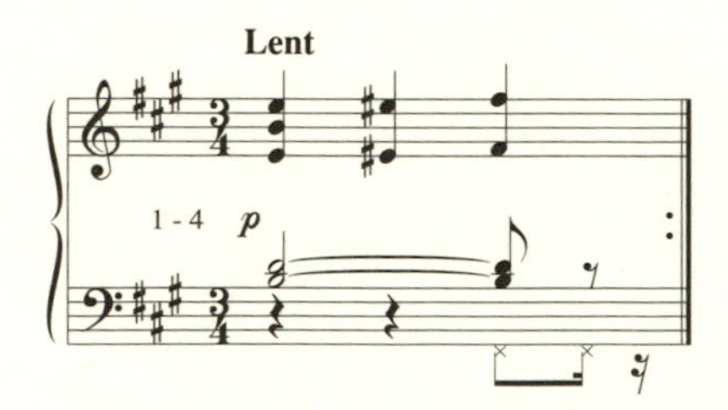

EX. 40. *Entr'acte*, beginning of Section IX (unit 52)

EX. 41. *Entr'acte*, end of Section IX (unit 54)

ment between Börlin and de Maré. When Börlin is knocked to the ground, for the third time in the film, the music crashes down, too, with brutal chords matched to the kicks at the dancer's head (Ex. 42). While de Maré tells us not to go away, an A major triad holds the floor, triumphantly sounded by the entire orchestra, which plays together only in the last twelve measures of the score. This is the music's final joke: though the film points ahead without coming to a true end, the opening theme, after bouncing in the air over a period of twenty minutes, has finally come to rest on what is presumed to be stable ground.

On what ground does this analysis come to rest? How do we assess Satie's achievement as a composer of film music?

Entr'acte is lively, puzzling, and funny: from its opening bursts of light to the closing kicks in the head the film challenges and delights us by hanging in the air, on a screen far above us all. With his score, Satie sought likewise to lift us out of this world into the world of film. Satie's score is "good" film music, not for being unobtrusive or subordinate, but because it is so evenly matched to its film in both large and small ways, in both style and structure.

Yet we should not claim for the score, for all its success, the status of a "model" of film music. It has too much wit and subtlety to serve as one either for its own time or ours. Nor should we hail it as the "supreme example" of Satie's furniture music. Furniture comes in models, but good film music does not; and while the same piece of furniture, or the same wallpaper design, might work well in many

EX. 42. *Entr'acte*, concluding unit (58)

rooms, combined with many kinds of decor, the best film scores—including all those we have studied in previous chapters—show off their virtues in the light of the films they accompany. Indeed, a piece of furniture may be appreciated even standing alone in an otherwise empty room; but the *Entr'acte* score, heard on its own in the concert hall, might well leave us bored, indifferent, or at best mildly curious. To say the score has no independent musical life, therefore, is not to equate it with furniture music; rather, the point is to stress how much the music requires the film for its peculiar and very striking characteristics to be understood. We may question, moreover, whether any film score—or any kind of music, however "minimalist" it may seem—is *by nature* so lacking in presence that its sole function is to remain in the background of some airport, restaurant, supermarket, or theater. Is furniture music hollow, or is the concept? Does the music's supposed vacuity exist merely in the ear of the beholder, to be filled in by analysis and close attention?

Picabia hailed the *Entr'acte* score as a masterpiece and pronounced it inseparable from the film.[38] We may not be carried so far in our judgment, but analysis supports the view that the film should be presented with the score whenever possible. By extension, both should be restored to their original positions, in the middle of *Relâche*; for there are relationships between ballet and film as vital as those here discerned between film and score. The set of *Relâche* in Act I provides one example. It consisted of hundreds of metallic discs, made to reflect and shine like automobile headlights; at the beginning of *Entr'acte* similar discs are seen to move. Thus a visual element of the non-narrative ballet launches an abstract dance on film. These larger patterns of music and movement, design and dance, await further study. The object here has been to demonstrate the shared meanings of film and score.

To read what the three principal creators had to say about *Entr'acte* is to be told that the film and the music resist analysis. The film is like a dream, wrote Clair, with all the incoherence of true dreams.[39] Any attempt to interpret the images threatens the "liberation" and purity the director claimed for them. And Satie? Though his comments on the music of *Entr'acte* have not been recorded, he repeatedly described *Relâche* in terms that do not invite scholarly interpretation. In a letter to Milhaud, written while Satie was working on *Relâche*, he called it a "ballet obcène" (*sic*); in an interview given before the premiere, he termed the music "pornographic"; yet in the ballet program, he was characteristically both modest and cryptic: "I would not want [my music] to make a lobster blush, nor an egg."[40] We have already observed that according to Picabia an essential element of the film is its lack of respect, its laughter at the pretensions of humankind. But what could be more open to ridicule than the attempt to impose rational order on irrational experience? The more systematic the order—that is, the more consistent the analysis—the more it will beg a fundamental question inscribed by Picabia beneath a caricature of Satie on the frontispiece of the *Relâche* score: "When will we lose the habit of explaining everything?"[41]

An attack on the will to explain things was a fundamental aspect of Dada; yet during the 1920s, even seemingly inexplicable phenomena (including dreams) were believed more and more to contain hidden coherencies of their own. Witness the efforts of such dissimilar explainers as Freud and Breton: the former gave us psychoanalysis, the latter surrealism, a movement officially proclaimed during the same period that saw the creation of *Entr'acte*.[42] *Entr'acte* could be said to mix elements of all three movements, because both film and score are filled with dreamlike nonsense, inviting yet resisting interpretation. The patterns and relationships described above may inspire the ghosts of Picabia, Clair, and Satie with laughter; but so long as we do not take ourselves too seriously, we are justified in the view that Satie's score for *Entr'acte*, while not illustrative music in the conventional sense, is one of the most illustrious examples of music for silent film.

It appeared at a time rich in both present achievement and future promise for the silent medium, but suddenly that time was cut short; thus, fittingly, *Entr'acte* brings our study of an obsolete genre to a close. Like Agee's *Birth*, this film, too, has an aura of dreamlike absoluteness, now that silent films seem so much a part of the past—an intermission, as it were, within an unfolding history that links spoken (and musical) theater to the sound film. Perhaps irrevocably, our experience with the latter has radically altered the way we look at silents and, when given the opportunity, hear their music. All the same, the contemplation of *Entr'acte*, together with all the other scores and motion pictures described above, leaves us to dream further of the wondrous possibilities offered by film music, whether presented in live performance or through mechanical reproduction, to artist and audience alike.

Appendix

PART 1. Inventory of Music for the Skladanowsky Bioskop Presentations, 1895–96

A. Summary list of pieces, as identified in extant parts

INTRODUCTION. E major. 6/8, Andante mosso.

1. POLKA. D major. 2/4.
2. GALOPP. F major. 2/4.

VALSE. B♭ major. 3/4.

The only extant music for this piece appears on a sheet pasted to the back of the Violin part for no. 2. The music is taken (without attribution) from *Loin du bal*, a piano piece by Ernst Gillet (1856–1940).

3. GALOPP. A major. 2/4.

Violin part has "Jongleur" written above the music; so does another copy of the same part, inserted into the folder for Clarinet 2.

4. DER STIERKÄMPFER. SPANISCHER MARSCH. D major. ¢.

All surviving parts have written "für Orch. bearbeitet von [arranged for orchestra by] Herm. Reh."

5. MASKEN-GALOPP. A major. 3/4.

Violin part has "Jongleur" written above the music.

6. KAMARINSKAYA. D major. 2/4.

The music is a compressed arrangement of the "Tanzlied" found in Glinka's *Kamarinskaya*, mm. 46–125.

7. MARSCH. C major. ¢.

Bassoon part has "Ringkampf" written above the music.

Though no music has been found for the next four numbers, song-titles are penciled into various parts beneath the music for no. 7: *"Lang, lang ist[s] her, C dur,"* in the Violin part [fig. 3]; *Lang ist's her* and *Unter den Linden* in the parts for Trumpets I and II. The latter titles also appear penciled on the outside of the folded sheet containing the Flute part for nos. 12–13.

8.–11. [No music found.]

12. FEUERWEHR-GALOPP AUS "FLICK UND FLOCK." D major. 2/4.

Printed music; all parts attribute the music to P. Hertel, Op. 33.

PART 1. (*continued*)

13. EISENBAHN-DAMPF-GALOPP. B major. 2/4.
    Printed music, published by Bote & G. Bock, Berlin; all parts attribute the music to Jos. Gung'l, Op. 5. Trumpet II part has "Film 13" penciled above the music.
14. [No music found.]
    Several parts indicate a percussion solo: e.g., Flute part has "Erst Schlagzeug solo" penciled above music for no. 15; trombone has "No. 14 Shlagzeug" [*sic*] penciled above music for no. 13. Other parts with similar comments, harder to read, include Clarinet II and Trumpet II.
15. MIT BOMBEN UND GRANATEN: MARSCH. G major. ¢.
    Printed music, published by Bote & G. Bock, Berlin: all parts attribute the music to B. Bilse, Op. 37.

    FINALE. D major. C, Maestoso.

B. Inventory of extant parts

Parts were examined at the Deutsche Film- und Fernsehakademie, Berlin, March 1978. Except for those numbers designated above as "printed music" (i.e., nos. 12, 13, and 15), all parts are in manuscript. In this table, a single x indicates a part for one instrument; xx indicates parts for two instruments (e.g., Flute and Piccolo, Oboes I and II, etc.). Parts for additional instruments are indicated in supplementary notes. When an individual part has been crossed out, the x is in brackets.

Pieces for which music survives, as numbered above.
(I = Introduction; V = Valse; F = Finale.)

Instruments	I	1	2	V	3	4	5	6	7	12	13	15	F
Violin[a]	[x]	x	x	[x]	[x]	x	x	x	x	x	x	x	x
Flute and Pic.	x	x	x	t[b]	[xx]	xx	x	xx	xx	x	x[c]	xx	x
Oboes	[xx]	xx	xx	t	xx			x	xx	x		xx	xx
Clarinets		x	xx	[t]	[xx][d]	xx	xx	[x]	x	xx	x	x[e]	x
Bassoons	xx	xx				xx	x	xx	xx	x		xx	xx
Horns	xx	xx	xx	[t]	xx	xx	xx	xx	xx	xx		xx[f]	
Trumpets	[xx]	xx	xx	[t]	xx	x	xx	xx	xx[g]	x	x	xx[h]	
Trombones							x	x		x	x	xx[i]	

[a] Parts in the Violin folder for nos. 12, 13, and 15 are marked for Violino II; all others for Violino I.
[b] "t" = "Serpentintanz tacet."
[c] The Flute folder contains a Piccolo part only for no. 13.
[d] The Clarinet II folder contains both its own part and a duplicate of the Violino I part for no. 3.
[e] There is a Clarinet II part but no Clarinet I part for no. 15.
[f] The Horn folder also contains parts for Horns III & IV, as well as Cornets à Piston I & II, for no. 15.
[g] The Trumpet folder contains a sheet with Trumpets I & II parts in F for no. 6, another sheet with Trumpets I & II parts in B for no. 7. The folder also contains a copy of a Trumpet I part in B for nos. 6 and 7 on a single page, ditto a part for Trumpet II in B.
[h] The Trumpet folder also contains parts for Trumpets III & IV for no. 15.
[i] The Trombone folder contains printed parts for Trombones I, II, III, and Tuba, as well as a revised handwritten part for Trombone, for no. 15.

PART 2. The Structure of Saint-Saëns' Score for *L'Assassinat du Duc de Guise*

Note. Score segments and cues, as well as meter and tempo markings, are given as they appear in the piano score arranged by Léon Roques (Paris: A. Durand & Fils, 1908). The labels given to subsections of each segment ("Intro" for introduction, A, B, "Trans" for transition, etc.) are of course my own. Measures are counted separately within each seg-

PART 2. (*continued*)

ment. Themes are identified in two ways: boldface nos. are themes that recur in more than one segment; letters in italics designate themes that appear only within a single tableau. The symbol ≈ is used to suggest that a seemingly new theme is closely related by its intervallic or harmonic profile to one already encountered. Keys are given for the start of each subsection only; I do not chart the subsequent modulations. "End" keys are those marked by full cadences or pauses, heard at the end of each segment and occasionally at the end of a subsection. Lowercase and uppercase letters denote minor and major keys.

Segment or Cue	*Measures*	*Meter*	*Tempo*	*Theme*	*Key*	
INTRODUCTION					*beg.*	*end*
A	1–11	4/4	Allegro	**1 – 2**	f♯	
	12–20			**1 – 2**	D	
l'annonce						
B	21–33			**3**	f♯	
Trans	34–38					f♯
TABLEAU 1						
A	1–16	3/4	All^{to} mod.	*a*	D	
Entrée du Page						
B	17–20	4/4	Allegro	*b*	A	
	21–30			**1 – 2**	b	f♯
Trans	31–36					
Entrée du Duc						
C	37–49		Andantino	**4**	C	
B	50–62		Allegro	**1**	a	
	63–73		a Tempo	*b* – **4**	C	C
	73–88		Animé	≈ **2**	c	C
Départ du Duc						
Coda	89–97		Andantino	**4**	(F)	
	98–104		Allegro	**1**	c	C
TABLEAU 2						
Quatre heures sonnent						
Intro	1–20	4/4	And^{te} sos.	*c*	c♯	
A	21–44	3/4	All^{to}	*d*	g♯	
B	45–50			*e* (≈ **1**)	mod	
	51–72		. . . M^{olto} all^{o}	**2**	c	
A	73–92		All^{to}	*d*	mod	c♯
Coda	93–121			. . . *d*	C♯	c♯
TABLEAU 3						
Intro	1–2	4/4	Modéré . . .			f
A	3–22			*f*	f – F	(f)
B	23–31			*g* (≈ **1** + **2**)	A♭	
A	32–43			*f*	f	F
Coda	44–49			≈ **4**	F	
Trans	50–55			≈ **1**		D♭(VI/f)
TABLEAU 4						
Intro	1–2	4/4	ad^{gio} sost.	**2**	f♯	
A	3–17			*h*	f♯	
L'Assassinat						
B	18–57		Presto . . . Animé	**2 – 3 – 2**	c	

PART 2. (*continued*)

Segment or Cue	*Measures*	*Meter*	*Tempo*	*Theme*	*Key*	
					beg.	*end*
C	58–85		Andante	2 – *i* (≈ 4)	c	
D	86–126			*j*	f	F
Coda	127–138				F	F
L'Escalier (*)						
A	139–150		Lent	*h*	f	C♯(V/f♯)
TABLEAU 5						
A	1–12	4/4	Allegro	1	f	
	13–18			2	f♯	
On met une croix sur le corps du Duc						
B	19–28		Le double plus lent	*k*	f♯	
On place le corps dans la cheminée						
C	29–44		Allegro	3	c♯	
	45–68			4	e♭	f♯
A	69–80	2/2	Più allegro	2	f♯	
Coda	81–101		Presto			f♯

(*)Dans le cas où la bande cinématographique ne contiendrait pas la scène de "L'ESCALIER," passer de suite au 5e Tableau. (See Chapter Two, n. 65.)

PART 3. Film Scores in America, 1910–14

Note. Films are listed by title in chronological order, according to the date of the initial reference to a special score for the film in *Moving Picture World.* If no *MPW* reference has been found for a copyrighted score, the film is entered in the table according to the *CCE* date of registration. (In a very few cases the *CCE* date precedes the earliest *MPW* reference to the same score. If so, the *CCE* date has priority.) Following the film title, each entry contains in parentheses the name of the film's production company or distributor and the number of reels as given in *MPW.* Any film longer than two reels was unusual, and often designated a "special" release or a "feature." Initial *MPW* references to special scores are cited with a brief quotation. These references come from articles, advertisements, or reviews; some are discussed in the text of Chapter Three. An asterisk has been placed beside each film title for which at least one copy of a score has been found. The composer's name is given when known. Copies of scores can be seen in the Library of Congress (LC), the New York Public Library (NYPL), or UCLA, as indicated. For the Kalem film scores of 1912 and 1913, cross-references are made to Appendix part 4, where additional information can be found.

1910

1 *Il Trovatore* (Pathé; 1). "Music and the Picture," 31 Dec., 1518–19: "Pathé engaged the services of a competent man to prepare the music of the opera when the film is projected."

1911

2 *Faust* (Pathé; 2). Sinn, "Music for the Picture," 17 June, 1370: "A splendid musical setting has been arranged for this picture by a musician who certainly understands his business."

3 *Dante's Inferno* (Milano; 5). Sinn, "Music for the Picture," 22 July, 116: "Milano Film Company has motiographed *Dante's Inferno,* with special music by 'Signor Caravaglios, composer of some note' (in Naples, Italy)."

PART 3. (*continued*)

4 *Arrah-Na-Pogue* (Kalem; 3). "Special Music for *Arrah-Na-Pogue*," 18 Nov., 536: "Walter C. Simons [*sic*] has been engaged by the Kalem Company to write a complete piano score for *Arrah-Na-Pogue*."

1912

5 *Mignon* (Solax; ?). Review of *Mignon*, 27 Jan., 288: "We are advised that special music, adapted from the music of the opera, has been prepared for this picture and will be distributed by the exchanges."

6 *Camille* (Film d'Art; 2). "Bernhardt and Rejane," 10 Feb., 468. See no. 7.

7 *Madame Sans-Gêne* (Film d'Art; 3). Ibid.: "Appropriate music has been prepared for these subjects and a fine line of advertising will accompany the pictures."

8 **A Spartan Mother* (Kalem; 1). "Special Music for *A Spartan Mother*," 17 Feb., 570: "The Kalem Company announces that it has prepared special music for its release of March 11, *A Spartan Mother*." Walter C. Simon. Score in LC. See part 4, no. 3.

9 *Homer's Odyssey* (Monopol; 3). Advertisement, 24 Feb., 706: "Grecian music, overture and scene music, written by Mr. Edgar Selden, general manager, Shapiro Music Co., of New York City . . . ."

10 **The Fighting Dervishes of the Desert* (Kalem; 1). "Kalem Announces Egyptian Pictures," 20 April, 208: "Special music and a large variety of special advertising matter will be available for the Egyptian pictures, obtainable at exchange or advertising supply houses." Walter C. Simon. Score in LC. See part 4, no. 8.

11 **Fighting Dan McCool* (Kalem; 1). Advertisement, 4 May, 402: "Special piano music." M. Komroff. Score in LC. See part 4, no. 6.

12 *The Coming of Columbus* (Selig; 3). Review by James S. McQuade, 4 May, 407–10: "A special musical program for the presentation of the films [*sic*] is being prepared for Mr. Selig by S. L. Rothapfel, the widely known manager of the Lyceum theatre, Minneapolis."

13 **Under a Flag of Truce* (Kalem; 1). Advertisement, 11 May, 544: "Special music, complete piano score." Walter C. Simon. Score in LC. See part 4, no. 7.

14 *Missionaries in Darkest Africa* (Kalem; 1). Advertisement, 25 May, 702: "Special piano music." Walter C. Simon? See part 4, no. 9.

15 **The Drummer Girl of Vicksburg* (Kalem; 1). Ibid.: "Special piano music." Walter C. Simon. Score in LC. See part 4, no. 10.

16 **The Spanish Revolt of 1836* (Kalem; 1). Ibid.: "Special piano music." Walter C. Simon. Score in LC. See part 4, no. 4.

17 *War's Havoc* (Kalem; 1). Ibid.: "Special piano music." Walter C. Simon? See part 4, no. 5.

18 *The Colleen Bawn* (Kalem; 3). Sinn, "Music for the Picture," 25 May, 717: "I know of some who are still using numbers from *Colleen Bawn* [etc.] . . . . It pays to get this special music." See part 4, no. 1.

19 **An Arabian Tragedy* (Kalem; 1). "Manufacturer's Advance Notes: *An Arabian Tragedy*," 8 June, 836: "Special piano music." Walter C. Simon. Score in LC. See part 4, no. 11.

20 *Fra Diavolo* (Solax; 3). Advertisement, 15 June, 988: "Advertising matter includes . . . musical accompaniment."

21 **Captured by Bedouins* (Kalem; 1). Advertisement, 15 June, 1002: "Special piano music." Walter C. Simon. Score in LC. See part 4, no. 12.

22 **Tragedy of the Desert* (Kalem; 2). Advertisement, 29 June, 1241: "Special music." Walter C. Simon. Score in LC. See part 4, no. 13.

23 **The Bugler of Battery B* (Kalem; 1). Advertisement, 29 June, 120: "Special piano music." Walter C. Simon. Score in LC. See part 4, no. 14.

PART 3. (*continued*)

24 **Hungry Hank's Hallucination* (Kalem; 1). Ibid.: "Special piano music." Walter C. Simon. Score in LC. See part 4, no. 15.

25 **A Prisoner of the Harem* (Kalem; 1). No *MPW* ref. found. *CCE*, 6 July. Walter C. Simon. Score in LC. See part 4, no. 16.

26 **Egyptian Sports* (Kalem; 1). No *MPW* ref. found. *CCE*, 6 July. Walter C. Simon. Score in LC. See part 4, no. 17.

27 **The Siege of Petersburg* (Kalem; 2). Advertisement, 6 July, 63: "Special piano music with suggestions for effects." Walter C. Simon. Score in LC. See part 4, no. 18.

28 **The Soldier Brothers of Susanna* (Kalem; 1). No *MPW* ref. found. *CCE*, 19 July. Walter C. Simon. Score in LC. See part 4, no. 19.

29 *Queen Elizabeth* (Histrionic Film—Famous Players; 4). *CCE*, 15 Aug.: "*Queen Elizabeth*, composed by Joseph Carl Breil; musical accompaniment to Sarah Bernhardt's play. 4to." *MPW*: "Sarah Bernhardt's *Queen Elizabeth* in Chicago," 17 Aug., 656: "The exhibition will be billed like a high-class legitimate road attraction and will be presented with special music and lecture."

30 **The Confederate Ironclad* (Kalem; 1). *CCE*, 1 Sept. Walter C. Simon. Score in LC. See part 4, no. 20.

31 *From the Manger to the Cross* (Kalem; 5). Review by W. Stephen Bush, 20 Oct., 324: "A musical program has been compiled which has some merit."

32 *The Miracle* [*Sister Beatrice*] (Continental Kunstfilm—New York Film Co.; 4). Review by W. Stephen Bush, 2 Nov., 443–44: "The owners of the American rights have recognized the musical opportunities of the play and have provided a complete musical score said to have been composed by a competent musician."

33 *Siegfried* (Ambrosio; 3). Advertisement, 2 Nov., 477: "Specially arranged music."

34 *Historical Pageant of 1912* (Historical Pageant Film Co.; ?). Advertisement, 9 Nov., 574–75: "We have a seventy-two page book of music for each and every scene in the film."

35 *The Miracle* (Joseph Menchen—Woods & Aborn; ?). Advertisement, 23 Nov., 803: "*The Miracle*, as presented at the Olympia, London, with music by Professor Englebert Humperdinck, is owned and controlled by us exclusively."

36 *The Shaughraun* (Kalem; 3). Advertisement, 7 Dec., 954: "Special piano music." Walter C. Simon? See part 4, no. 21.

37 *Cleopatra* (Helen Gardner—U.S. Film Co.; 6?). Advertisement, 7 Dec., 996–97: "Special music."

38 *The Life of John Bunyan* (F. W. Hochstetter; 5). "Symphony Orchestra Interprets Pictures," 21 Dec. 1309: "Modest Altschuler, the conductor of the [Russian Symphony] orchestra, had specially composed, selected and adapted music for the occasion."

1913

39 *The Prisoner of Zenda* (Famous Players; 4). "*The Prisoner of Zenda* Is Completed," 1 Feb., 477: "Joseph Carl Briel [*sic*], author of *The Climax* and the composer of the music for the Bernhardt *Queen Elizabeth* picture, is now writing music for *The Prisoner of Zenda*."

40 *Dick Whittington and His Cat* (Solax; 3). Advertisement, 8 March, 1038–39: "Three reels with a musical accompaniment . . . . Advertising matter includes . . . musical score."

41 *Hiawatha* (F. E. Moore; 4). Advertisement, 15 March, 1127: "Also a reading to fit the action, and a specially arranged score of Ojibway Indian music." *CCE*, 13 May: "*Hiawatha*, the Indian passion play, in four parts, by John J. Braham: 11 instrumental parts."

42 *The Strength of Men* (Vitagraph; 2). Advertisement, 22 March, 1193: see no. 43.

43 *The Modern Prodigal* (Vitagraph; 2). Ibid.: "Special release, *The Strength of Men* . . .

PART 3. (*continued*)

released Wednesday, March 19th; special release, *The Modern Prodigal*, released Friday, March 28th. . . . Special music (piano score) for all specials." (NB. All Vitagraph advertisements cited below have texts similar to the one quoted here.)

44 *The Golden Hoard* [or *Buried Alive*] (Vitagraph; 2). Advertisement, 29 March, 1309: see no. 43.
45 *The Web* (Vitagraph; 2). Advertisement, 5 April, 21: see no. 43.
46 *The Artist's Great Madonna* (Vitagraph; 2). Advertisement, 12 April, 137: see no. 43.
47 *Hearts of the First Empire* (Vitagraph; 2). Advertisement, 19 April, 253: see no. 43.
48 *The Cheyenne Massacre* (Kalem; 2). Advertisement, 27 April, 409: "Special music, complete piano score." See part 4, no. 22.
49 *The Deerslayer* (Vitagraph; 2). Advertisement, 3 May, 461: see no. 43.
50 *The Vampire of the Desert* (Vitagraph; 2). Ibid.
51 *The Still Voice* (Vitagraph; 2). Ibid.
52 *The White Slave* (Vitagraph; 2). Advertisement, 17 May, 677: see no. 43.
53 *The Battle for Freedom* (Kalem; 2): Advertisement, 17 May, 678: "Special piano music." See part 4, no. 23.
54 *The Tragedy of Big Eagle Mine* (Kalem; ?): Advertisement, 24 May, 786: "Special piano music." Walter C. Simon. See part 4, no. 24.
55 *A Regiment of Two* (Vitagraph; 2). Advertisement, 31 May, 893: see no. 43.
56 *The Snare of Fate* (Vitagraph; 3). Advertisement, 14 June, 1109: see no. 43.
57 *The Tiger Lily* (Vitagraph; 3). Advertisement, 21 June, 1225: see no. 43.
58 *Quo Vadis* (Kleine-Cines; 8). "Facts about *Quo Vadis*," 28 June, 1366: "*Quo Vadis* . . . will have fully fifteen companies touring the United States and Canada . . . and special music has been arranged and composed for the performance."
59 *The Diamond Mystery* (Vitagraph; 2). Advertisement, 5 July, 21: see no. 43.
60 *A Prince of Evil* (Vitagraph; 2). Ibid.
61 *The Intruder* (Vitagraph; 2). Advertisement, 26 July, 401: see no. 43.
62 *The Lineup* (Vitagraph; 2). Ibid.
63 **Schuldig* (Messter; ?). No *MPW* ref. found. *CCE*, 29 July: piano score by "G[iuseppe] Becce." Score in LC.
64 *[*The Life (and works) of the Composer*] *Richard Wagner* (Messter; 4). *CCE*, 15 August: piano score, arranged and composed by "Dr. G[iuseppe] Becce." Cf. the advertisement in *MPW*, 13 Dec., 1307, referring to the special score. Score in LC.
65 *The Feudists* (Vitagraph; 2). Advertisement, 23 Aug., 817: see no. 43.
66 *The Call* (Vitagraph; 2). Advertisement, 30 Aug., 933: see no. 43.
67 *When Women Go on the Warpath* (Vitagraph; 2). Ibid.
68 *The Lost Millionaire* (Vitagraph; 2). Advertisement, 13 Sept., 1149: see no. 43.
69 *Our Wives* (Vitagraph; 2). Advertisement, 20 Sept., 1257: see no. 43.
70 *Under the Daisies* (Vitagraph; 2). Advertisement, 27 Sept., 1365: see no. 43.
71 *The Mystery of the Silver Skull* (Vitagraph; 2). Advertisement, 4 Oct., 21: see no. 43.
72 *Protea* (Eclair—World Special Films Corp.; 5). Advertisement, 11 Oct., 125: "A world beater in five reels with 80 pages of specially written music."
73 *The Test* (Vitagraph; 2). Advertisement, 11 Oct., 129: see no. 43.
74 *The Pirates* (Vitagraph; 2). Advertisement, 18 Oct., 239: see no. 43.
75 **Comtesse Ursel* (Messter; ?). No *MPW* ref. found. *CCE*, 24 Oct.: piano score by G[iuseppe] Becce. Score in LC.
76 *The Next Generation* (Vitagraph; 2). Advertisement, 25 Oct., 353: see no. 43.
77 *The Warmakers* (Vitagraph; 2). Advertisement, 1 Nov., 469: see no. 43.

PART 3. (*continued*)

78 *The Diver* (Vitagraph; 2). Advertisement, 8 Nov., 585: see no. 43.

79 *The Last Days of Pompeii* (Kleine-Ambrosio; 6). "Special Music for Kleine's *Pompeii*," 8 Nov., 598: "The well-known Chicago music composer, Palmer Clark, has prepared a fifty-page score, written especially for *The Last Days of Pompeii*."

80 *Jenny's Mother in Law* (Vitagraph; 2). Advertisement, 15 Nov., 709: see no. 43.

81 *The Hero of a Nation: Bar Cochba* (Supreme Feature Film Co.; 6). Advertisement, 6 Dec., 1217: "Special music."

82 **The Legend of Provence* (Thanhouser; 4). "Musical Score for *Provence*," 13 Dec., 1270: "A composer for regular musical show productions, E. A. Price, has been engaged to do a score for the *Provence* picture." Score in UCLA Music Library, Capitol Theatre Collection.

83 **Frou Frou* (Thanhouser; 4). "Is Daly Version of *Frou Frou*," 13 Dec., 1288: "Special musical accompaniment, prepared by the Tams Music Library, is furnished exhibitor readers of this journal free on request to the Thanhouser people." Score in UCLA Music Library, Capitol Theatre Collection.

1914

84 *Joseph in the Land of Egypt* (Thanhouser; 4). "Change of Thanhouser *Joseph* Title," 3 Jan., 30: "Special music is again offered by the Thanhouser Company."

85 **Antony and Cleopatra* (Kleine-Cines; 8). "Special Music for *Antony and Cleopatra*," 10 Jan., 185: "George Kleine has assigned a well-known Chicago composer [George Colburn] to the task of preparing appropriate music for *Antony and Cleopatra*." Score in LC and NYPL.

86 *The Marriage of Figaro* (Kleine-Ambrosio; 2). Advertisement, 24 Jan., 381: "Music adapted from the famous Opera will be supplied gratis through the General Film Company."

87 **Soldiers of Fortune* (All-Star; 6). Advertisement, 31 Jan., 556: "An especially written musical score by Manuel Klein, Musical Director of the New York Hippodrome." Score in LC.

88 **Samson* (Universal; 6). No *MPW* ref. found. *CCE*, 25 Feb. Music by Noble Kreider. Score in LC and NYPL.

89 **Paid in Full* (All-Star; 5). Advertisement, 28 Feb., 1109: "Original music score by Manuel Klein." Score in LC.

90 **America* (All-Star; 7). George Blaisdell, "Hippodrome's *America* in Pictures," 21 March, 1510: "Accompanying the production, which will be marketed as a theatrical proposition, will be the music composed by Manuel Klein."

91 *Sealed Orders* (De Luxe Attractions Film Co.; 6). Advertisement, 28 March, 1709–10: "Musical score by Prof. Sol. P. Levy."

92 **In Mizzoura* (All-Star; 5). No *MPW* ref. found. *CCE*, 31 March. Music by Manuel Klein. Score in LC.

93 *Quincy Adams Sawyer* (Puritan Special Features Co.; 4). Advertisement, 4 April, 117: "Special music for the whole picture."

94 *The Life and Works of Giuseppe Verdi* (Arias Film Co.—Int. Film Traders; 6). Advertisement, 9 May, 891: "Specially arranged music."

95 *Spartacus* (Pasquali—Kleine; 8). James S. McQuade, "*Spartacus* at the [Chicago] Auditorium," 16 May, 972: "One of the most attractive features of the presentation was the accompanying music . . . by Modest Altschuler."

96 **Pierre of the Plains* (All-Star; ?). No *MPW* ref. found. *CCE*, 25 May. Music by Manuel Klein. Score in LC.

PART 3. (*continued*)

97 **The Jungle* (All-Star; 5). No *MPW* ref. found. *CCE*, 8 June. Music by Manuel Klein. Score in LC.

98 *Cabiria* (Itala; 12). "*Cabiria* Shown on Broadway," 13 June, 1517: "The specially written music was interpreted by an orchestra of fifty or more pieces."

99 **Dan* (All-Star; 5). No *MPW* ref. found. *CCE*, 10 July. Music by Manuel Klein. Score in LC.

100 *The Nightingale* (All-Star; ?). "Manuel Klein Music for *The Nightingale*," 11 Aug., 975. "The musical score . . . has been compiled for the accompaniment of the picture by Manuel Klein, the musical director and leader of the New York Hippodrome, whose compositions for All Star productions are now becoming so well known."

101 *The Patchwork Girl of Oz* (Oz Films–Paramount Program; 5). Advertisement, 19 Sept., 1598–99: "Every advertising aid worthy of this wonderful picture is supplied the exhibitor, together with a complete Orchestra, Piano and Organ Score of GOTTSCHALK'S ORIGINAL MUSIC, composed to fit each scene."

102 *The Seats of the Mighty* (Colonial Motion Picture Corp.—World Film Corp.; 6). "*Seats of the Mighty* at [New York] Casino," 28 Nov., 1246: "Special music has been written for this picture by Professor Harper Garcia Smyth and Ludwig Marum."

Sources: *Moving Picture World*, the U.S. *Catalogue of Copyright Entries*, Part 3: *Musical Compositions* (*CCE*), new series (issued annually 1906–41), and individual published scores.

PART 4. Kalem Film Scores, 1911–13

Note. If a score has been located in the Library of Congress (LC), its number appears in italics; if Simon has been positively identified as the composer, the letter S follows the number. Films are listed chronologically, according to their release dates (as given in *MPW*). Included under each title, again in chronological order, are references to the score in *MPW*, as well as the copyright number and publication date assigned to the music in the *Catalogue of Copyright Entries* (*CCE*). (In a few cases *CCE* gives an earlier date for receipt of the score than for its publication; when this occurs, the date of receipt is given first, followed by the publication date in parentheses.) When a copy of the score has been found in LC, its page length is given, along with the number of musical segments. (I have been unable to verify the number of segments in scores 18–19.) One important Kalem film of this period, *From the Manger to the Cross*, is discussed separately in Chapter Three.

1 *The Colleen Bawn*: 16 Oct. 1911. Suggestions for music offered by Sinn in "Music for the Picture" (henceforth MfP), *MPW* 21 Oct., 200; special score mentioned by Sinn in "MfP," 25 May 1912, 717. No *CCE* entry found. No copy in LC.

2 S *Arrah-Na-Pogue*: 4 Dec. 1911. Piano score and 4-piece orchestration by "W. C. Simons" announced in *MPW* 18 Nov., 536; both versions advertised at a cost of 50 cents in *MPW* 25 Nov., 613 (see Fig. 9); reference to the score by Sinn, in the second "MfP" column cited under no. 1. No *CCE* entry found. No copy in LC.

3 S *A Spartan Mother*: 11 March 1912. Piano score announced (25 cents) in *MPW* 17 Feb.; music advertised in same issue, p. 554; "Special music . . . complete piano score" advertised in *MPW* 2 March, 754; description of private screening with music performed by Walter C. Simon in "Splendid Kalem Feature," ibid., 770; *CCE* E 279506, 6 March; reference to score by Sinn, in the second "MfP" column cited under no. 1. LC copy: music by Walter C. Simon, pp. [1]–10; introduction + 24 numbered and cued segments.

PART 4. (*continued*)

4 S *The Spanish Revolt of 1836*: 3 April 1912. *CCE* E 282718, 28 March; "Special piano music" (25 cents) advertised in *MPW* 25 May, 702. LC copy: music by Walter C. Simon, pp. [1]–10; introduction + 19 numbered and cued segments.

5 *War's Havoc*: 15 April 1912. "Special piano music" (25 cents) offered in the advertisement cited under no. 4. No *CCE* entry found. No copy in LC.

6 *Fighting Dan McCool*: 13 May 1912. *CCE* E 283733, 20 April (pub. 21 April); "Special piano music" advertised in *MPW* 4 May, 402. LC copy: music by M. Komroff, pp. [1]–10; introduction + 25 numbered and cued segments.

7 S *Under a Flag of Truce*: 24 May 1912. "Special music, complete piano score" (25 cents) advertised in *MPW* 11 May, 544; *CCE* E 284965, 16 May. LC copy: music by Walter C. Simon, pp. [1]–11; 23 cued segments.

8 S *The Fighting Dervishes of the Desert*: 27 May 1912. Announcement of "special music" for this and other Kalem "Egyptian Pictures" in *MPW* 20 April, 208; *CCE* E 284864, 13 May (pub. 17 May); "Special piano music" advertised in *MPW* 25 May, 702; description of a private screening for New York exhibitors, at which "the composer, W. C. Simon, presided at the piano," in *MPW* 1 June, 826. LC copy: music by Walter C. Simon, pp. [1]–10; overture + 12 1/2 numbered and cued segments.

9 *Missionaries in Darkest Africa*: 3 June 1912. "Special piano music, 25 cents" advertised in MPW 25 May, 702 (see Fig. 10); mentioned in private screening report cited under no. 8. No *CCE* entry found. No copy in LC.

10 S *The Drummer Girl of Vicksburg*: 5 June 1912. "Special piano music, 25 cents" advertised in *MPW* 25 May, 702 (see Fig. 10); *CCE* E 285244, 25 May. LC copy: music by Walter C. Simon, pp. [1]–9; 20 cued segments.

11 S *An Arabian Tragedy*: 19 June 1912. "Special piano music, 25 cents" advertised in *MPW* 1 June, 836; *CCE* E 297641, 4 June (pub. 19 June); separate "suggestions" for music offered by Sinn, "MfP," *MPW* 13 July, 150. LC copy: music by Walter C. Simon, pp. [1]–10; 14 cued segments. (For portions of the score, see Figs. 11–13.)

12 S *Captured by Bedouins*: 26 June 1912. *CCE* E 296671, 6 June; "Special piano music, 25 cents" advertised in *MPW* 15 June, 1002. LC copy: music by Walter C. Simon, pp. [1]–14; 22 cued segments.

13 S *Tragedy of the Desert*: 1 July 1912. *CCE* E 288569, 26 June. "Special music . . . complete piano score, 25 cents," advertised in *MPW* 29 June, 1241. LC copy: music by Walter C. Simon, pp. [1]–25; divided into two parts—introduction + 17 cued segments, and introduction + 15 cued segments.

14 S *The Bugler of Battery B*: 10 July 1912. Together on one reel with

15 S *Hungry Hank's Hallucination*. *CCE* E 288312, 20 June; "Special piano music . . . complete score, 25 cents," advertised in *MPW* 29 June, 1202. LC copy: music by Walter C. Simon, *Bugler*, pp. [1]–10, *Hungry*, pp. 11–13; 14 + 7 cued segments.

16 S *A Prisoner of the Harem*: 19 July 1912. Together on one reel with

17 S *Egyptian Sports*. *CCE* E 297642, 6 July. LC copy: music by Walter C. Simon, *Prisoner*, pp. [1]–11, *Egyptian*, pp. 12–13; 15 + 1 cued segments.

18 S *The Siege of Petersburg*: 22 July 1912. "Special piano music, with suggestions for effects," advertised in *MPW* 6 July, 63; *CCE* E 288953, 15 July (pub. 16 July). LC copy: music by Walter C. Simon, pp. [1]–26; divided into two parts, pp. [1]–15 and 15–26.

19 S *The Soldier Brothers of Susanna*: 31 July 1912. *CCE* E 289142, 19 July. LC copy: music by Walter C. Simon, pp. [1]–13.

20 S *The Confederate Ironclad*: 5 Oct. 1912. *CCE* E 293449, 1 Sept. "Special piano music for this feature, 25 cents," advertised in *MPW* 28 Sept., 1298. LC copy: music by Walter C. Simon, pp. [1]–18; 25 cued segments.

PART 4. (*continued*)

21 *The Shaughraun*: 23 Dec. 1912. "Special piano music" (50 cents) advertised in *MPW* 7 Dec., 1054; "splendid special music" mentioned in review of film by W. Stephen Bush, ibid., 1065. No *CCE* entry found. No copy in LC.

22 *The Cheyenne Massacre*: 9 May 1913. "Special music, complete piano score" (15 cents) advertised in *MPW* 26 April, 409; separate suggestions for music offered by R. J. Bessette in letter to Sinn, "MfP," *MPW* 7 June, 1020. No *CCE* entry found. No copy in LC.

23 *The Battle for Freedom*: 17 May 1913. "Special piano music" (15 cents) advertised in *MPW* 17 May, 678. No *CCE* entry found. No copy in LC.

24 S *The Tragedy of Big Eagle Mine*: 7 June 1913. "Special piano music by Walter C. Simon" (15 cents), advertised in *MPW* 24 May, 786. No *CCE* entry found. No copy in LC.

PART 5. The Structure of Simon's Score for *An Arabian Tragedy*

(*Note.* In the diagrams of the forms of individual numbers, "v" signifies a vamp.)

<table>
<tr><th>#</th><th>Meter</th><th>Tempo</th><th>Mm.</th><th>Form</th><th>Key</th></tr>
<tr><td>1</td><td>3/4</td><td>Adagio</td><td>9</td><td>a a b
2 2 5 (= 1 + 1 + 3)</td><td>C minor</td></tr>
<tr><td>2</td><td>3/4</td><td>Andante Quasi Turca</td><td>19</td><td>A A' [D.S.]
v a a b a a b'
2 2 2 4 2 2 5</td><td>C minor</td></tr>
<tr><td>3</td><td>3/4</td><td>Moderato Decide [*sic*]</td><td>18</td><td>A B D.S.
a b c d d
4 4 6 2 2</td><td>C minor</td></tr>
<tr><td>4</td><td>3/4</td><td>Moderato Grazioso</td><td>22</td><td>A B D.S.
v ||: a a' a" :|| b
2 4 4 4 8</td><td>F major</td></tr>
<tr><td>5</td><td>3/4</td><td>Andante Affet[u]oso</td><td>16</td><td>A A'
a b c d a b c d'
2 2 2 2 2 2 2 2</td><td>D.S.
F major</td></tr>
<tr><td>6</td><td>2/4</td><td>Moderato Quasi Turca</td><td>16</td><td>A A'
a a a' a'
4 4 4 4</td><td>D minor</td></tr>
<tr><td>7</td><td>3/4</td><td>Andante Affetuoso</td><td>10</td><td>a b (= a'?)
5 5</td><td>F major</td></tr>
<tr><td>8</td><td>2/4</td><td>Andante Quasi Turca</td><td>42</td><td>A B C D.S.
v a a' v' b b' b" b'" c
6 6 6 4 4 4 4 4 4</td><td>C minor</td></tr>
<tr><td>9</td><td>3/4</td><td>Andante</td><td>16</td><td>a a' a" b
4 4 4 4</td><td>A♭ major</td></tr>
<tr><td>10</td><td>2/4</td><td>Moderato</td><td>16</td><td>A A'
a a' a" a'" :||
4 4 4 4</td><td>F minor</td></tr>
<tr><td>11</td><td>[= 8]</td><td></td><td></td><td></td><td>C minor</td></tr>
<tr><td>12</td><td>[= 1]</td><td></td><td></td><td></td><td>C minor</td></tr>
</table>

PART 5. (*continued*)

#	Meter	Tempo	Mm.	Form	Key
13	[= 8]				C minor
14	3/4	A[n]dante Affetuoso	18	A A' a a' b a a' b' : ‖ 2 2 4 2 2 6	A♭ major

PART 6. A checklist of *MPW* Literature on S. L. Rothapfel, 1910–15, with Headings to Indicate His Positions of Employment

Employed by United Booking Office

(1) S. L. Rothapfel. "Music and Motion Pictures." 16 April 1910, 593.

Manager of the Alhambra, Milwaukee

(2) "A Progressive Exhibitor"—under Sinn, "Music for the Picture" ("MfP") 2 Sept. 1911, 618.

Manager of the Lyric, Minneapolis

(3) James S. McQuade. "The Belasco of Motion Picture Presentations." 9 Dec. 1911, 796–98.
(4) McQuade. "A De Luxe Presentation of *Cinderella*." 27 Jan. 1912, 288.
(5) Rothapfel. "Music for Cines Subject *Josephine*"—under Sinn, "MfP," 20 April 1912, 210–11.
(6) McQuade. Review of "*The Coming of Columbus*." 4 May 1912, 407–10.

Manager of the Shubert Circuit, including the Lyric, Chicago

(7) McQuade. "Chicago Letter," 15 June 1912, 1012.
(8) Sinn. "MfP," 6 July 1912, 49.

Manager of the Regent, New York

(9) W. Stephen Bush. "The Theatre of Realization." 15 Nov. 1913, 714–15.
(10) J. A. A. "Regent Theatre, New York City." 20 Dec. 1913, 1401–2.
(11) "Crowds at Rothapfel's Regent." 24 Jan. 1914, 394.
(12) "Rothapfel Sails for Europe." Ibid., 398. (A trip of six weeks, to look over exhibition in various European cities.)
(13) "Rothapfel Will Sail." 31 Jan. 1914, 557. (Corrects previous item: Rothapfel has not sailed yet, but will do so at the end of February.)
(14) J. A. A. "*Quo Vadis* at the Regent." 7 Feb. 1914, 680.
(15) Bush. "Rothapfel Rehearsing" (*Quo Vadis*). 14 Feb. 1914, 787.
(16) "Rothapfel Back from Europe." 21 March 1914, 1526.
(17) "Eduards [i.e., Carl Edouarde, conductor] to Remain at the Regent." 28 March 1914, 1693.

Manager of the Strand, New York

(18) Bush. "Opening of the Strand." 18 April 1914, 371.
(19) "Rothapfel To Leave Strand." 10 Oct. 1914, 201. (An announcement which proved incorrect.)
(20) Bush. "The Art of Exhibition: Rothapfel's Ideas . . . ." 17 Oct. 1914, 323–24.
(21) Bush. "The Art of Exhibition" (2). 31 Oct. 1914, 627–28.
(22) Bush. "The Art of Exhibition" (3). 21 Nov. 1914, 1063–64.
(23) "Special Showing of *Rose of the Rancho*." 28 Nov. 1914, 1241.
(24) Bush. "The Art of Exhibition" (4). 12 Dec. 1914, 1511–12.
(25) "Notable Showing of *The Eternal City*." 9 Jan. 1915, 199.
(26) Bush. "The Art of Exhibition" (5). 16 Jan. 1915, 355–56.
(27) "Great Film [*The Eternal City*] Plays for Long Runs." 13 Feb. 1915, 958.
(28) Bush. "The Art of Exhibition" (6). 5 June 1915, 1613.

PART 7. Select Biographical Data on Joseph Carl Breil, through 1913

1870	born Pittsburgh, 29 June to Joseph and Margaret A. (Frohnhoefer) Breil
1910	married Jean Frances Stevenson of North Adams, Mass.
	education: Pittsburgh College, St. Fidelis College, Curry University, University of Leipzig, Leipzig Conservatory, studied voice in Leipzig with Ewald, in Milan, and in Philadelphia with Del Puente
1887?	age 17, his opera *Orlando of Milan* performed by amateurs under his direction in Pittsburgh
1891–92	principal tenor of Emma Juch Opera Co.
1892–97	tenor soloist and choir director, St. Paul's Cathedral, Pittsburgh
1897–1903	theatrical conductor, Pittsburgh, also on tour
1903–1910	reviser and editor of music publications: T. B. Harms Co., 1903–4; Francis Day & Hunter, 1904–5; Leo Feist, 1905–8; J. H. Remick, "since" May 1909—supervisor of the Remick "Library Edition"; head of the Remick "department of art and classical songs"
	vocal compositions: a requiem and two other masses, vesper service, sacred songs and anthems, and popular songs including *The Song of the Soul*, *If Dreams Came True*, *A Toast to Angeline*, *Boatman's Love Song*
	dramatic works
1909	incidental music for *The Climax*, at Weber's in New York; subsequently at Powers' in Chicago, at the Nixon in Pittsburgh, etc.
1910	opera, *Love Laughs at Locksmiths*, produced by the New Opera Co. (Breil, managing director), at the Kingston Opera House in Kingston, N.Y.; on tour in New England and elsewhere, 1910–11
1912	*Queen Elizabeth* ("first score ever written for a moving picture play") at Powers' Theatre, Chicago; *Camille*, with Sarah Bernhardt; *Mme. Sans-Gêne*, with Réjane
1913	film scores: *The Prisoner of Zenda*, with Hackett; *Tess of the D'Urbervilles*, with Mrs. Fiske; *In the Bishop's Carriage*, with Pickford
	comic operas (book and music): *Professor Tattle*, in New York; *The Seventh Chord*, at the Empire Theatre in Chicago

Sources: *An Encyclopedia of Notable Men and Women in Music and the Drama*, Dixie Hines and Harry Prescott Hanaford, eds. (New York: H. P. Hanaford, 1914); *International Who's Who in Music and Musical Gazetteer*, Cesar Saerchinger, ed. (New York: Current Literature, 1918); materials in the Breil collection at UCLA: "Hypnotic Art in *The Climax*," (New York) *Morning Telegram* 13 April 1909, p. 12; "Joseph C. Breil's Views," *Music Trade Review* 18 Sept. 1909, p. 31; "Publishing New American Songs: Joseph Carl Breil's Important Work," *Musical America* 5 March 1910, n.p.; "Composer Married," *New York Dramatic Mirror* 5 March 1910, n.p. (*International Who's Who* gives the year of Breil's marriage date as 1911; *Who Was Who in America, Vol. 1: 1897–1942* gives the date as 21 Feb. 1910); "Grand Opera in Kingston," *Kingston Daily Leader* n.d., n.p. (Hipsher, *American Opera and Its Composers*, incorrectly states that *Love Laughs at Locksmiths* was first performed in Portland, Maine; so does *Who Was Who in America*); "Amusements: The New Opera Company," *Daily Eastern* 19 Nov. (1910? 1911?), n.p., and "Amusements: New Opera Company at the Empire," *Lewiston Evening Journal* n.d., n.p.; playbill from the Empire Theatre, Chicago, March 1913.

PART 8. The Structure of Breil's Score for *The Birth of a Nation*

Note. Each entry in the table contains the following information: score number, the content of the corresponding film sequence(s), identification of the composer and music, and the key(s).

Score numbers. Contents are numbered as they appear in the MOMA-LC version of the piano score. A few numbers have been corrected with figures in brackets.

Film sequences. The brief descriptions of the content of each sequence are partly my own, and partly based on the sequence outline in Cuniberti's shot analysis (pp. 29–31).[a] In particular, some of his descriptions of sequence have been expanded, and some strung together in a single entry, so as to match the succession of numbers in Breil's score. The sequence numbers in Cuniberti's outline are given in brackets following the entries in part 8 to which they correspond.

Composers and music. When a segment is based on pre-existent music, the name of the composer is given, along with the title of the music in italics; however, for segments based on popular or traditional tunes which were given new words or published in different arrangements during the nineteenth century—e.g., *America*—no composer's name is given, even when the author of the original is known. Much of the music by Breil is easily identifiable; a few problematic attributions are indicated here. A large part of Breil's music consists of his recurring themes (R1–15), indexed separately in part 11.

Keys. The initial key and other principal keys of each number are given. Uppercase letters designate major, and lowercase letters minor keys. A hyphen between two keys indicates that they are connected by continuous music and a modulation. When a segment ends without a full close—that is, with a half-cadence or with a transition leading into the next segment—the final key of the segment is followed by a hyphen.

No.	*Film Sequence [and Sequence Number in Cuniberti].* *Composer*	*Music*	*Key*
	ACT I [Reel 1]		
1	*A New England minister blesses captive slaves [1]*		
	Breil	First Presentation of R1	d-F
1B	*An Abolitionist meeting [2]*		
	Breil	Hymn	d-F
2	*Title and scene introducing Austin Stoneman and Elsie [3]*		
	Breil	First presentation of R2	f-
2 1/2	*Scene between father and daughter [3, cont.], and scene of the Stoneman sons and Elsie at their country home [4]*		
	Breil	First presentation of R3, &	D
	Breil	Two strains alternating with R3	b D G D
3	*Introduction of the Camerons of Piedmont, South Carolina [5]*		
	Foster	*Old Folks at Home*, refrain, alternating with	F
	Breil	First presentation of R4	F
3 1/2	*The arrival in Piedmont of the Stoneman sons [6]*		
	Breil	Same music as in 2 1/2, above	D
4	*Horseplay between Tod Stoneman and Duke Cameron*		
	Sullivan	*Where Did You Get That Hat?* title phrase &	D-
	Breil	R3 beginning, as introduction to	D-
	Breil	Two strains of comic action music (a b a)	D G D
4 1/2	*A walk through the cottonfields: romance begins [7]*		
	Breil	Pastoral theme, with bridge to	F-
	Harrison	First presentation of R5 (= *In the Gloaming*)	A
	Breil	Bridge to	-
	Breil	First presentation of R6	D

PART 8. (*continued*)

No.	Film Sequence [and Sequence Number in Cuniberti]. Composer	Music	Key
5	*A visit to the slave quarters [8]*		
		Zip Coon (*Turkey in the Straw*)	D
		[Reel 2]	
5 1/2	*The newspaper report—a gathering storm [9]*		
	Weber	*Der Freischütz* Overture, mm. 1–2, 26–36	c-
5 1/2 [B]	*Sumner and Stoneman argue in Stoneman's library [10]*		
	Breil	R2, expanded version	c-g
6	*Scenes of Lydia Brown, Sumner, and Stoneman*		
	Breil	First presentation of R7a–g ending with	c; f-c-
		Restatement of R7b & R7	f-e♭-
7	*The departure of Phil and Tod Stoneman from Piedmont [11]*		
	Breil	R5 extended, alternating with	G
	Breil	First presentation of R8	G
8	*Lincoln signing the proclamation calling for volunteers [12]*		
	Emerson	*We Are Coming, Father Abraham*	G
9	*Elsie bids her brothers goodbye [13]*		
	Breil	Playful march	G
10	*Piedmont's farewell ball and a bonfire celebration [14]*		
		Comin thro' the Rye, in alternating meters	E♭
10 1/2	*Cheering the Confederate flag brought back from Bull Run*		
		The Bonnie Blue Flag	E♭
11	*Summoning the troops at daybreak*		
	Suppé	*Light Cavalry* Overture, mm. 60–93	A♭
		Assembly March (bugle call, first phrase)	A
[11]B	*The Cameron sons bid the family farewell*		
		Maryland, My Maryland	A
	Kinkel	*Soldier's Farewell*, refrain	A
[11]C	*The troops parade through Piedmont and march away*		
	Emmett	*Dixie*	D
		[Reel 3]	
[11]D	*Elsie returns to Washington from the Stoneman home [15]*		
	Breil	R3 beginning, leading to	D-
	Breil	First presentation of R9	b♭-
12	*Ben in the field with a letter from Flora [16]*		
	Breil	Bridge (sad and ominous)	-a
	Flora, Margaret, and Mrs. Cameron at home [17]		
	Breil	First presentation of R10a–c (Flora)	a-C-a
13	*An attack on Piedmont by Union guerrillas*		
	Breil	R1 as introduction to	c
	Weber	*Der Freischütz* Overture, Molto vivace, excerpts	c-E♭-c-
13[1/2]	*The Camerons in their home, after the rescue*		
		Maryland, My Maryland	C

PART 8. (*continued*)

No.	*Film Sequence [and Sequence Number in Cuniberti].* *Composer*	*Music*	*Key*
14	*Ben in the field, with Elsie's portrait [18]*		
	Breil	R6, without close	G-
15	*The battlefield deaths of Tod and Duke [19]*		
	Breil	Fragments, including	g-
	Sullivan	*Where Did You Get That Hat* title phrase	A♭-G
16	*The families receive news of the deaths [20–21]*		
	Breil	First presentation of R11 (Funeral March)	g
	The Cameron women's last donations to the cause, and Elsie's departure from home to become a nurse [22–23]		
	Breil?	Sentimental song	D
17	*Sherman's march through a Georgia valley [24]*		
	Work	*Marching through Georgia*, two phrases	B♭-
	Breil	March, with a bridge to	d-
17B	*The destruction of Atlanta and Wade Cameron's death [25]*		b
	Grieg	*In the Hall of the Mountain King*, mm. 1–49, 66–88	
		[Reel 4]	
18	*Corn rations for the Confederate lines before Petersburg, and a Confederate food train behind Union lines [26–27]*		
	Suppé	*Light Cavalry* Overture, mm. 155–70	a
19	*The Battle of Petersburg begins [28]*		
		Reveille (bugle call), developed	A-
	Breil?[b]	Two extended segments of "battle" music	a-f♯-
	Breil	Fragments intermixed, including *Tramp! Tramp! Tramp!* (Root), *Dixie* (Emmett), *Hail, Columbia*, and *The Bonnie Blue Flag*, with a bridge to	D-
	Breil	March tune, followed by a "Hurry" segment	G-
19 1/2	*A charge led by Ben, and the Camerons in prayer*		
	Breil	Hurry segment from no. 19, and	-
	Breil	"Fake buglers and drums," alt. with "Religioso" chords	G-
19 1/2B	*Ben's company in battle*		
	Breil	March tune & Hurry segment from no. 19	G-
20	*The battle continues; Ben aids a wounded Union soldier*		
		The Bonnie Blue Flag, with	D-
	Breil	March-like coda	D
20B	*Ben's final charge and wounding*		
	Breil	Introduction to	D-
	Emmett	*Dixie*, followed by	D-
	Breil	Coda from no. 20, & "fake" cornets & drums	D-
20C	*Scenes of dead soldiers, alternating with battle scenes*		
		Taps (bugle call, first half); tpt. & drums	A♭-
20D		*Taps* complete; tpts. & drums	A♭-

PART 8. (*continued*)

No.	*Film Sequence [and Sequence Number in Cuniberti].* Composer	Music	Key
20E	*The Union army breaks through the Confederate lines*		
		The Star-Spangled Banner, concluding portion	D
21	*The Camerons get news of Wade and Ben*		
	Breil	R11 reprise, alt. with an Agitato fragment	g-g
		[Reel 5]	
22	*Ben, wounded in a Union hospital, sung to by Elsie [30]*		
	Work	*Kingdom Coming*	B♭
22B	*The two become acquainted*		
	Breil	R3 beginning, as introduction to	D-
	Breil	R6 expanded to two strains, without close	G-
22C	*Mrs. Cameron's visit, and her appeal to Lincoln for a pardon for her son [31]*		
	Breil	R8, R4, R11, & R6 fused & developed	G-g-G-e-G
22 1/2	*Mrs. Cameron and Elsie's return to the hospital, and Mrs. Cameron's return home [32–33]*		
	Work	*Kingdom Coming* (same as no. 22)	B♭
23	*The surrender at Appomattox [34]*		
		America	G
24	*Ben's discharge and leave-taking from Elsie [35]*		
		The Girl I Left Behind Me	E♭
25	*Preparations for Ben's return home [36]*		
	Breil	R10a–c (as in no. 12)	a-C-a
25 1/2	*The homecoming*		
		Comin thro' the Rye, first half	C
	Bishop	*Home! Sweet Home!* complete	C
	Foster	*My Old Kentucky Home*, fragment	C
		[Reel 6]	
26	*Stoneman's meeting with Lincoln [37]*		
	Breil	R2 beginning–R7d-g (as in no. 6)	f-c-b♭-
		America	B♭
27	*The rebuilding of the South under Lincoln [38]*		
	Foster	*Camptown Races*	D
28	*Lincoln's assassination: Elsie and Phil depart for Ford's Theatre, and the play begins [39–40]*		
	Bellini	*Norma* Overture, mm. 1–41, with	g-
	Breil	Continuation and pause (5 mm.)	
	Lincoln enters the theater box		
		Hail to the Chief	B♭
	The assassination		
	Bellini	*Norma* Overture, mm. 89–139, with	B♭-g-
	Breil	Continuation and pause (3 mm.)	g-
	Breil	R2 developed	g-
28B	*Pandemonium after the shot is fired*		
	Breil	3 fragments: Vivace–Agitato–Lento doloroso	g-A♭

PART 8. (*continued*)

No.	*Film Sequence [and Sequence Number in Cuniberti].* *Composer*	*Music*	*Key*
28C	*The report to Stoneman of the assassination [41]*		
	Breil	R2 beginning & the last two fragments of no. 28B	c-A♭
28D	*The report to Piedmont of the assassination [42]*		
	Breil	The last two fragments of no. 28B	-A♭
	ACT II		
29	*Stoneman, "the uncrowned king," in Washington [43]*		
	Breil	R2, extended version (same as no. 5 1/2[B])	c-g
29B	*The introduction of Silas Lynch; Sumner's visit to Stoneman and the arrogance of Lydia Brown; Stoneman's assignment of Lynch to the South; Lynch's arrival in Piedmont [44–45]*		
	Breil	R1 (as in no. 1)	d
	Breil	R7b, d-g, b (as in no. 6)	f-c-f
	Breil	R1 (as in no. 1), and R2 in a new form	d
	[Reel 7]		
1	*The beginning of Lynch's campaign of disruption; the Freedman's Bureau; Ben Cameron's first encounter with Silas Lynch [46–48]*		
	Breil	Minstrel tunes (a b c a) leading to	G-g G G-g-
	Breil	R1 with coda	e-A
2	*The Stoneman family's departure from Washington, and their arrival in Piedmont [49–50]*		
	Breil	R3 and R8, as in I, no. 11D, with new ending	D-A
2A	*Comedy scene between Mammy and Northern servant*		
	Breil	Simple phrase, sequenced, with extension	A
2B	*The meeting of Elsie and Flora*		
	Breil	R3 complete, as in I, no. 2 1/2	D
2C	*Second comedy scene between Mammy and servant*		
	Breil	Abridged version of no. 2A, above	G-
2D	*Flora, Elsie, and Ben*		
	Breil	R10b, as in I, no. 12	a-
3	*Ben's second encounter with Lynch*		
	Breil	Fragments, partly based on R2	A♭-
3A	*Lynch alone, showing his fury*		
	Breil	R1, as in I, no. 1, with ending from R7g	d-b♭-
	Breil	R7c, with bridge to next number	f-
4	*The Southern Union League rally, addressed by Lynch; and scenes showing the enrolling of the black vote [51–52]*		
	Breil	An Agitato strain, alternating with R2	a-f a-F
	Breil	Two minstrel tunes	F
5	*Ben Cameron's presentation of a dove to Elsie [53]*		
	Breil	R3 beginning, as introduction to	C-
	Breil	R6, two strains	C
5A	*Margaret Cameron's rejection of Phil Stoneman [54]*		
	Breil	R5, with new second strain	F

PART 8. (*continued*)

No.	*Film Sequence [and Sequence Number in Cuniberti].* *Composer*	*Music*	*Key*
5B	*Elsie's rejection of Ben, and her change of heart [55]*		
	Breil	A new romantic strain (= the "verse" from the sheet music version of R6), leading to	F-
	Breil	R6, as in no. 5 above, but without close	C-
5C	*Elsie's "rhapsodies of love," alone in her room*		
	Breil	R3 complete, and R6 second strain	C
6	*Election day: incidents at the polls [56]*		
	Breil	Minstrel tune, with additional fragments	G
	The returns: Lynch's election as Lieut. Governor [57]		
	Breil	R1–Hurry music–Jubilant dance tune	e-G
7	*Ben's narration of "a series of outrages" [58]*		
	Breil	Misterioso, alt. with Agitato segments and Coda	a-f
	[Reel 8]		
7	[Conclusion of the same sequence]		a-f
8	*The riot in the S. Carolina House of Representatives [59]*		
	Breil	2 tunes (the second from II, no. 4)	D-C
	Breil	The Agitato strain from II, no. 4, with bridge to	a-
	Breil	R1–R2 developed–Jubilant tune from II, no. 6	c-G
9	*Gus and Lynch encounter Flora, Elsie, and Ben [60]*		
	Breil	R1, R7e, R10a, & R10b, developed culminating in	a-
	Breil[c]	First presentation of R12	c-e
10	*Ben's agony, and his inspiration for the Klan [61]*		
	Breil	First presentation of R13	a-
	Breil	First presentation of R14, with extension and grand cadential passage	- -E♭
11	*The Klan goes into action [62]*		
	Breil	First presentation of R15	e-
	Breil	R14 and its extension transposed, leading to	-
	An ambush of Klansmen by Lynch's forces [63]; Lynch's report to Stoneman [64]		
	Breil	R2 developed	f
12	*Stoneman angry with Elsie over her love for Ben*		
	Breil	R3 and R9, with hint of R13 (cf. I, no. 11D, and II, no. 2)	F-B♭
	[Reel 9]		
13	*Elsie's meeting with Ben; the engagement broken [65]*		
	Breil	Restless phrases, with fragment of R10b	d-
	Breil	R6, two strains, but without close	G-
14	*Ben talks with Flora concerning Klan costumes, and she attempts to console him [66]*		
	Breil	R10a, R13, & R9 developed; R10b & R10c	g-a-C-a

PART 8. (*continued*)

No.	*Film Sequence [and Sequence Number in Cuniberti].* *Composer*	*Music*	*Key*
	Flora alone in the woods, observed by Gus [67]		
	Breil	R10b, with interpolated fragments	a-
	Milburn	*Listen to the Mockingbird*	A
15	*Gus's pursuit of Flora*		
	Breil	R7e, R7f, & R12 with development and repetition	c-
	Flora's death, and the mourning of her family; Phil Stoneman's argument with his father [68]		
	Breil	3 laments, with development of R10b and the doloroso theme from I, no. 28B	f-A♭-
16	*Gus seeks to hide in Joe's gin-mill*		
		[Reel 10]	
	A townsman searching for Gus is killed at Joe's [69]		
	Breil	R1 & R14 developed, with interpolation	d-
17	*Gus's capture, trial and execution by the Klan*		
	Beethoven	Symphony No. 6, mvt. 4, mm. 64–136	D?-C-
	Breil	Reprise of first lament from II, no. 15	e
18	*The discovery of Gus's body by Lynch, Lynch's yearning for vengeance, and Stoneman's departure [70]*		
	Breil	R14 developed; R7f, R7g, & a new Agitato	c-b♭
19	*Ben performs rites to honor Flora, as the Klan prepares for action [71]*		
	Breil	R15, R10a, & R10b fragments developed	e-
20	*Lynch's spies dispatched; Lynch alone, in drunken fury [72]*		
	Breil	Misterioso; fragment of R1; R7f & R7g	g♯-c-b♭-
21	*Elsie alone, in sorrow*		
	Breil	R13 briefly developed, leading to next number	f-
22	*The arrest of Dr. Cameron: Margaret goes to Elsie to ask her to intervene; the flight of the Camerons and Phil Stoneman*		
		[Reel 11]	
	Elsie told of her brother's crime; Lynch celebrates; the fugitive group arrives at a cabin [73–74]		
	Breil	A series of agitato and hurry fragments from the first half of II, no. 7, and the second half of II, no. 16, all repeated several times	a-d-
23	*Two Union veterans in the Cabin welcome the group*		
		Auld Lang Syne	E♭
24	*Elsie in Lynch's power [75]*		
	Breil	Fragments from II, no. 7 (and II, no. 22), leading to	a-f-
	Breil	A new Agitato, with development of R1, R7a, R13, & R3	c♯-e-

PART 8. (*continued*)

No.	*Film Sequence [and Sequence Number in Cuniberti].*[a] *Composer*	*Music*	*Key*
25	*The assembling of the Klansmen begins [76]*		
	Breil	R15 complete version	e-
26	*Lynch's struggle with Elsie, intercut with shots of Klansmen, and of Stoneman's arrival at Lynch's home*		
	Tchaikovsky	*1812* Overture, mm. 161–202, with bridge	F♯-e♭-
	Breil?	"Heavy Dramatic"[d] themes in triple meter	E♭-C-
	Breil	R7e, R7f, and R7d	c-f
26 1/2	*Ben's orders to the assembled Klansmen*		
	Hérold	*Zampa* Overture, mm. 272–312, with bridge to	D-
	Lynch announces his intentions to Stoneman; a riot begins in Piedmont		
	Weber	*Der Freischütz* Overture, mm. 37–122 (cf. I, no. 13)	c-E♭-
	Inside the cabin, Margaret grieves		
	Breil	R5 briefly developed	E♭
	Helpless whites and rioting blacks in Piedmont; the siege of the cabin; and		
	[Reel 12]		
	the veterans' refusal to let Cameron surrender [77–78]		
	Breil?	"Heavy Dramatic" from II, no. 26, with bridge	E♭-C-
	Wagner	*Rienzi* Overture, mm. 346–94	D-
	The battle in the streets of Piedmont; an attempt by Klansmen to aid the cabin; Elsie's rescue and the ride of the Klansmen to rescue those in the cabin [79–81]		
	Hérold	*Zampa* Overture, mm. 272–312	D-
	Wagner	*Rienzi* Overture, as above, with bridge added	D-
	Wagner	*The Ride of the Valkyries*, excerpts[e]	b-B
27	*The aftermath: disarmament of the blacks and the Klansmen's parade; the jubilation of white families; the next election; a double honeymoon [82–85]*		
	Emmett	*Dixie*	D
	Breil	R5, R6 fragment	C-
28	*Documentary footage of two black schools*[f]		
	Hermann	*Cocoanut Dance*	G
29	*Allegorical visions of war and peace*		
	["Mozart"]	*Mass in G* [Anh. 232], *Gloria*, mm. 1–24	C-
30	*Quotation from Daniel Webster: "Liberty and Union," etc.*		
		The Star-Spangled Banner	C

[a] John Cuniberti, "*The Birth of a Nation*"*: A Formal Shot-by-Shot Analysis Together with Microfiche*, Cinema Editions on Microfiche (n.p.: Research Publications, 1979).

[b] Two extended "battle" segments in no. 19 are perhaps not by Breil. (1) Mm. 41–59: Allegro, 4/4, common time, A minor—some of the same music appears in Elinor's compiled score for Griffith's film *Hearts of the World* (1917) as no. 20, following a passage from Rossini's *Semiramide* Overture. (2) Mm. 68–107: Allegro vivace, 3/4, F♯ minor—like a stormy passage from a nineteenth-century operatic overture.

[c] The music of R12 is similar to Gluck's music for the first chorus of Furies in *Orfeo ed Euridice*, Act II, scene 1: see the Vienna version (1762), ed. Anna Amalie Albert and Ludwig Finscher (Cassel: Bärenreiter, 1963), pp. 61–65—especially mm. 61–90.

PART 8. (*continued*)

[d] I take the term "Heavy Dramatic" from Erno Rapée, *Encyclopedia of Music for Pictures* (New York: Belwin, 1925; rpt., Arno, 1970): see Rapée's list of pieces under the heading "Dramatic," pp. 181–83. This segment of I, no. 26, seems likely to have been borrowed from a nineteenth-century work, but no source has been identified.

[e] Performers are instructed to play the three concluding concert works of no. 26 1/2 twice. The repeat begins after Elsie's rescue.

[f] The documentary footage at the end of the film does not survive; it was apparently inserted into the film for presentations in a few Eastern cities in early 1915. See Cuniberti, *Birth*, 168.

PART 9. An Index of Borrowed Tunes in Breil's Score for *The Birth of a Nation*

Note. Entries are listed by the tune's principal *Title*. Alternate titles are given in parentheses. Locations of each title are given with the following information: "Act" (I or II), score number, and page (MOMA-LC piano score), plus the extent of the tune. Though references are sometimes made to song verses and refrains, and so on, the tunes are printed in the score without words. I list the appearance of these tunes in four published sources (as abbreviated below): Rapée's anthology and the *New Brown Book* show how these tunes were known and used during the silent period; Crawford's and Jackson's collections provide useful contextual details.

CWSB *The Civil-War Songbook*. Comp. Richard Crawford. New York: Dover, 1977.
MPM *Motion Picture Moods*. Comp. Erno Rapée. New York: G. Schirmer, 1924; rpt., Arno, 1974.
NBB *Twice 55 Plus Community Songs: The New Brown Book*. Eds. Peter W. Dykema et al. Vocal edition, rev. and enl. Boston and New York: C. C. Birchard, n.d. [1920?].
PS *Popular Songs of the Nineteenth Century*. Comp. Richard Jackson. New York: Dover, 1976.

1 *America* (*My Country, 'tis of Thee*) (*MPM*, 262; *NBB* no. 1; *PS*, 6)
a) I, 23 (p. 55): complete
b) I, 26 (p. 60): first six measures
Assembly: see *Bugle Call I*
2 *Auld Lang Syne* (*MPM*, 439; *NBB*, no. 37)
II, 23 (p. 121): mm. 1–8
3 *The Bonnie Blue Flag* (*CWSB*, 17; *PS*, 35)
a) I, 10 1/2 (p. 13): introduction, verse, and refrain
b) I, 19 (p. 42): last phrase of refrain
c) I, 20 (pp. 45–46): introduction, verse, and chorus
4 *Bugle Call I: Assembly March* (*MPM*, 277)
I, 11 (p. 15): complete?
5 *Bugle Call II: Reveille* (*MPM*, 273)
I, 19 (p. 35): complete
6 *Bugle Call III: Taps* (*MPM*, 274; *NBB*, no. 2)
I, 20C and 20D (p. 49): first half and complete
7 (*De*) *Camptown Races* (*Gwine to Run All Night*) (*PS*, 39)
I, 27 (p. 61): complete
8 *Comin' thro' the Rye* (*MPM*, 443; *NBB*, no. 36)
a) I, 10 (p. 12): complete
b) I, 25 1/2 (p. 57): first half
9 (*I Wish I Was in*) *Dixie* (*Dixie's Land*) (*CWSB*, 13; *MPM*, 281; *NBB*, no. 62; *PS*, 61)
a) I, 11c (pp. 16–17): complete
b) I, 19 (pp. 41–42): opening fragment, then first half
c) I, 20b (pp. 47–48): complete
d) II, 27 (p. 146): complete

PART 9. (*continued*)

10 *The Girl I Left Behind Me* (*Continental Army*)
I, 24 (p. 55): complete
11 *Hail Columbia* (*MPM*, 262)
I, 19 (p. 41): first four measures
12 *Hail to the Chief* (*The President's March*)
I, 28 (p. 65): complete
13 *Home! Sweet Home!* (*MPM*, 304; *NBB*, no. 23)
I, 25 1/2 (p. 58): complete
14 *In the Gloaming* (*NBB*, no. 98)
I, 4 1/2 (p. 6): first eight measures (*Note*: This is used by Breil as a recurring theme; see part 11, no. R5)
15 *Kingdom Coming* (*CWSB*, 145; *PS*, 106)
a) I, 22 (pp. 50–51): complete
b) I, 22 1/2 (p. 54): complete
16 *Listen to the Mockingbird* (*MPM*, 309; *PS*, 110)
II, 14 (p. 102): complete, but first half altered
17 *Marching Through Georgia* (*CWSB*, 34, *PS*, 126)
I, 17 (p. 29): first phrase
18 *Maryland, My Maryland* (*CWSB*, 21; *PS*, 130)
a) I, 11B (p. 15): complete
b) I, 13 (p. 26): complete
19 *My Old Kentucky Home* (*MPM*, 282; *NBB*, no. 22; *PS*, 134)
I, 25 1/2 (p. 58): chorus
20 *Old Folks at Home* (*Way Down upon the Swanee River*) (*MPM*, 283; *NBB*, no. 16; *PS*, 163)
I, 3 (p. 3): first eight measures (verse)
Reveille: see *Bugle Call II*
21 *The Soldier's Farewell* (*NBB*, no. 105)
I, 11B: refrain
22 *The Star-Spangled Banner* (*MPM*, 261; *NBB*, no. 3)
a) I, 20E (p. 49): end portion ("say does that star-spangled banner yet wave," etc.)
b) II, 30 (p. 151): complete
Swanee River: see *Old Folks at Home*
Taps: see *Bugle Call III*
23 *Tramp, Tramp, Tramp* (*The Boys Are Marching*) (or *The Prisoner's Hope*) (*CWSB*, 45; *MPM*, 269; *PS*, 214)
I, 19 (p. 41): title phrase (chorus, mm. 1, 2)
24 *We Are Coming, Father Abraham* (*CWSB*, 30)
I, 8 (p. 11): fist sixteen measures of verse
25 *Where Did You Get That Hat* (See Sigmund Spaeth, *Read 'em and Weep: A Treasury of American Songs*, rev. ed. [New York: Arco, 1945], 137–38.)
a) I, 4 (p. 4): title phrase
b) I, 15 (p. 27): title phrase
26 *Zip Coon* (*Turkey in the Straw*) (*PS*, 258)
I, 5 (p. 7): complete

PART 10. An Index of Symphonic Excerpts in Breil's Score for *The Birth of a Nation*

Note. Excerpts are listed alphabetically by composer. Score locations are identified as in part 9. Descriptions of borrowed material refer to measures numbers from standard editions.

1 Beethoven. Symphony No. 6 in F Major, mvt. 4
II, 17 (pp. 111–15), m. 4 ff. = mm. 64–136 of mvt. 4. Mm. 1–3 of no. 17 contain tremolos on D;

PART 10. (*continued*)

mm. 62 and 63 of the symphony mvt. contain tremolos on A. The number continues with original music by Breil.

2 Bellini. *Norma* Overture [Sinfonia}
I, 28 (pp. 62–64) = mm. 1–41 of the overture, to which Breil adds 5 mm. The music stops for *Hail to the Chief,* then resumes with the overture, mm. 89–139, to which Breil adds 3 mm. The number continues with original music by Breil.

3 Grieg. *Peer Gynt Suite* I, No. 4: *In the Hall of the Mountain King*
I, 17B (pp. 30–33) = mm. 1–49 and 66–88. Breil cuts mm. 50–65 and places repeat marks around mm. 66–88.

4 Hérold. *Zampa* Overture
a) II, 26 1/2, beginning (pp. 131–32) = mm. 272–312 from the overture. Breil adds a repeat of the final 12 borrowed measures, then a transition to Weber's *Freischütz* Overture.
b) Same number, middle (p. 140) = the first 28 mm. from the same portion of the overture. This music is preceded and followed by an excerpt from Wagner's *Rienzi* Overture.

5 [Mozart]. Mozart's Celebrated Twelfth Mass, in G Major [Anh. 232]
II, 29 (p. 150) = Gloria, mm. 1–24, first beat. This mass, published by Novello et al. in the nineteenth century under the title above, is no longer believed to be by Mozart. See Ludwig Ritter von Köchel, *Chronologicsch-thematisches Verzeichnis . . . Mozarts*, 6th ed. (Wiesbaden: Breitkopf and Härtel, 1964), Anhang C 1.04 (Anh. 232), p. 812.

6 Suppé. *Light Cavalry* Overture
a) I, 11 (p. 14) = mm. 60–93. (Original key A major, transposed to A♭ major)
b) I, 18 (p. 34) = mm. 155–70, to which Breil adds 1 m. cadence in A minor.

7 Tchaikovsky. *1812* Overture
II, 26 (pp. 126–27) = mm. 161–202, except that Breil changes C flat to C natural in the last 4 mm. (preparing a modulation to the next segment).

8 Wagner. *Rienzi* Overture
II 26 1/2, middle (pp. 138–39 & 141–42) = Assai stretto (𝅗𝅥 = 160), mm. 346–94. The first time the excerpt leads into a repeat of music from Hérold's *Zampa*; the second time it cadences and is followed by a transition (2 mm.) into Wagner's *Ride of the Valkyries.*

9 Wagner. *The Ride of the Valkyries*
I, 26 1/2, end (pp. 143–45) = mm. 13–25 and 45–78. Breil compresses mm. 18–19 into his m. 6, and changes the figuration in Wagner's mm. 15–17 and 23–25. *Dixie* follows.

10 Weber. *Der Freischütz* Overture
a) I, 5 1/2 (p. 7) = mm. 1–2 and 26–36 (beginning and end of Adagio)
b) I, 13 (pp. 19–26), following Breil's introduction (mm. 1–6) uses the following segments of the Molto vivace: A-B = mm. 37–122; C-E = mm. 145–278
c) II, 26 1/2, middle (pp. 133–35) = mm. 37–122, followed by a version of *In the Gloaming*

PART 11. An Index of Recurring Themes in Breil's Score for *The Birth of a Nation*

Note. Themes are entered as they first appear. Score locations are identified as in part 9. Name tags in quotes are taken from the *Selection of Themes from the Incidental Music to "The Birth of a Nation"* (London: Chappell, 1916); other name tags have been inferred from their context. Recurrences of each theme, when the same as the original version, are listed without comment; changes are briefly noted.

R1 "The Motif of Barbarism." I, 1 (p. [1]):

PART II. (*continued*)

Recurrences

I	13	(p. 19)	Allegro vivo, C minor.
II	29B	(pp. 72 and 75)	
	1	(p. 76)	E minor.
	3A	(p. 79)	Close to original form.
	6	(p. 88)	E minor.
	8	(p. 92)	Lento, C minor.
	9	(pp. 93, 94, and 95)	E minor (twice) and G minor
	16	(pp. 108–10)	D minor, repeated and transformed
	22	(p. 120)	Same music as on p. 110
	24	(pp. 122–24)	E minor, as on p. 110

R2 "Stoneman and Lydia Brown, the Mulatto." I, 2 (p. [1]), mm. 1–4:

Recurrences

I	5 1/2[B]	(p. 8)	Deciso, C minor, new continuation
	26	(p. 59)	
	28B	(p. 69)	Lento, G minor, 1 m.
	28C	(p. 70)	Same as 5 1/2, mm. 1–4
II	29	(p. 72)	Same as 5 1/2, complete
	29B	(p. 75)	D minor, new cadence
	3	(p. 79)	A♭ major, free transformation
	4	(p. 80)	
	8	(p. 92)	B♭ minor, theme in bass
	11	(p. 98)	Theme in bass

R3 "The Elsie Stoneman Motif." I, 2 1/2 (p. 2), mm. 1–4:

Recurrences

I 3 1/2 (p. 4)

	4	(p. 5)	Beginning only (to m. 2)
	11D	(p. 17)	Moderato, cont. with R9
II	2	(p. 77)	Molto moderato, cont. R9
	2B	(p. 78)	
	5	(p. 82)	Lento, C major, intro. to R6
	5C	(p. 86)	Allegro vivace, C major

PART II. (*continued*)

12	(p. 98)	Doloroso moderato, F major
24	(p. 124)	Molto lento, E minor

R4 The Cameron Family. I, 3 (p. 3), mm. 9–16:

Recurrence

I	22C	(pp. 52–53)	G major, new harmonies.

R5 The Love Theme of Margaret Cameron and Phil Stoneman. I, 4 1/2 (p. 6), mm. 9–12 (*In the Gloaming*, opening phrase):

Recurrences

I	7	(pp. 10–11)	G major
II	5A	(p. 83)	Lento, F, duple, complete song
	26 1/2	(p. 135)	Moderato, duple, E♭ major, 8 mm.
	27	(p. 146)	Andante, C major, 8 mm.

R6 The Love Theme of Elsie Stoneman and Ben Cameron ("*The Perfect Song*"). I, 4 1/2 (p. 6):

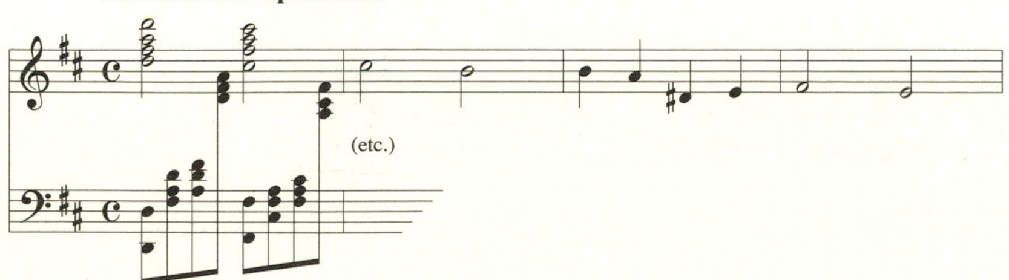

PART II. (*continued*)

Recurrences

I	14	(p. 27)	G major
	22B	(p. 51)	G, 9 + 8 mm.
	22C	(p. 53)	G, variation of mm. 1–4
II	5	(p. 82)	Amoroso, C major, 9 + 8 mm.
	5B	(p. 85)	As in no. 5
	5C	(p. 86)	C, last 9 mm. of no. 5
	13	(p. 99)	Same as in I, 22B
	27	(p. 146)	C, mm. 1–4 only

R7 I, 6 (pp. 8–10)—seven themes

a) Ambition:

b) "Lust and Passion":

c) "The Pride of Ignorance":

d) Seething "Anger":

PART II. (*continued*)

e) "Violent Anger":

f) "Fury":

g) "Fury Allayed":

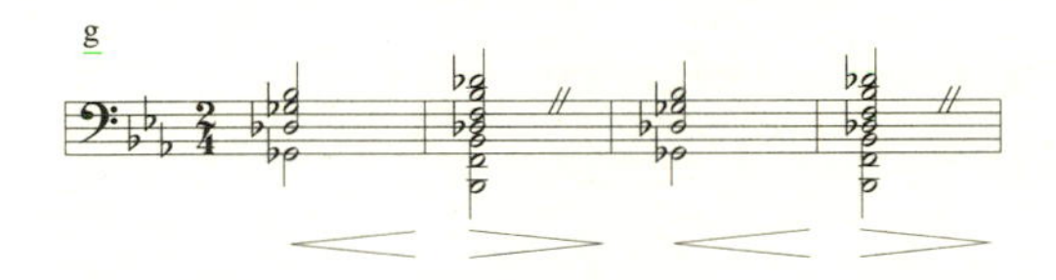

Recurrences

I	26	(pp. 59–60)	7d-g
II	29B	(pp. 72–4)	7b-g
	3A	(p. 80)	7c
	9	(pp. 93–95)	7e, *passim*
	15	(pp. 103–5)	7e-f, *passim*
	18	(pp. 115–16)	7f-g
	20	(p. 118)	7f-g
	24	(p. 123)	7a, in B♭ and E♭ minor, to R13
	26	(pp. 129–30)	7e-f, then 7d

R8 The Old South
I, 7 (p. 11):

PART II. (*continued*)

Recurrence

I 22C (pp. 52–53)	Extended and fused with R4

R9 Elsie's sorrow
I, 11D (p. 17):

Recurrences

II 2 (p. 77)	Molto moderato, mod. to A major
12 (p. 98)	Doloroso, mod. to B♭ major
14 (p. 100)	Follows R13

R10 Flora Cameron
I, 12 (pp. 17–19), three themes:
a and b:

c:

Recurrences

I 25 (pp. 56–57)	10a-c
II 2D (p. 79)	10b
9 (pp. 93–95)	10a and b in various keys with other themes 10a also transformed in meter
13 (p. 99)	10b fragment in G minor
14 (pp. 100–101)	

PART II. (*continued*)

R11 "Marcia Funebre."
I, 16 (p. 27):

Recurrences

I 21 (p. 49)
22C (pp. 52–53) Fragment

R12 The Rape of Flora (See part 8, note c)
II, 9 (p. 95):

Recurrence

II 15 (pp. 103, 105)

R13 Agony.
II, 10 (p. 95):

Recurrences

II 12	(p. 98)	Fragment, modulating
14	(p. 100)	New continuation
21	(p. 118)	F minor
24	(p. 123)	Furioso, duple meter, G major

R14 Fear
II, 10 (p. 95):

PART 11. (*continued*)

Recurrences

II 11 (p. 97)	Transposed
16 (p. 109)	Developed with R1
18 (p. 115)	Transposed

R15 "The Ku Klux Clansmen's Call" (and Ride)
II, 11 (p. 97):

Recurrences

II 19 (pp. 116–17)	Developed with R10a & 10b
25 (p. 125)	

PART 12. The Forms of the Opening Numbers of Breil's Score for *The Birth of a Nation*

(♯ = a sharp; ♭ = a flat; D.C. = Da Capo; D.S. = Dal Segno; § = a "Da Capo" or "Dal Segno" sign.)

No., etc.	*1*:	Moderato (C)	*B*:	Moderato (C)
Key sig.		1♭		2♭
Bars		7 (4 + 3)		10 (2 + 2 + 2 + 3)
Section		a b		c c' c" b'
		(R1)		
	2:	Pesante energico (3/4)		
		4♭		
		10 (4 + 6)		
		a a'		
		(R2)		

2 1/2: Allegro jocoso (2/4) Trio
2♯ 1♯
| | : 8 : | | : 8 : | | : 16 : | | : 16 : | | D.C.
A B A C till cue.
(R3)

§
3: Moderato con espr. (C)
1♭
8 | | 16 (8 + 8) | | D.S. Repeat 1st strain
A B after D.S.
(Old Folks (Breil)
at Home)

§
3 1/2: Allegro gracioso (2/4)
2♯ 1♯
| | : 8 : | | : 8 : | | : 16 : | | : 16 : | | D.C.
A B A C till cue.
(This music is the same as in number 2 1/2.)

PART 12. (*continued*)

4:	Andante	§ Vivace	Più Lento (2/4)
	2♯		1♯
	2 2	|| : 16 : || : 8 : ||	D.S. al Fine (= end of A)
	* (R3)		
	Intro.	A	B
	(**Where Did You Get That Hat* title phrase)		

4 1/2:	Andante Pastorale (6/4)	And. (3/4)	And. (C)
	1♭	3♯	2♯
	|| : 4 : ||	12 ||	5 || 10
	Intro.	R5	bridge R6

5:	§ Allegro (2/4)	
	2♯	
	8 || : 8 : ||	D.S. till cue
	A B	
	(*Zip Coon*)	

PART 13. The Forms of the Closing Numbers of Breil's Score for *The Birth of a Nation*

No.	*25*:	Energico
T.S.		C
K.S.		O
Bars		16
		(R15)

26:	Moderato con molto espr.	
	C	
	6♯	
	42	
	1812 Overture	

26 1/2:	Più animato		Molto Vivace	Moderato
	¢			2/4
	2♯		3♭	
	12 || : 16 : || :12 : ||	4	86	8
	Zampa -----------	bridge	*Freischütz*	*In the Gloaming*
				(R5)

Andante	Allegro	Molto più stretto 𝅗𝅥 = 160
3/4	¢	
o		2♯
42	4	48
Breil?	bridge	*Rienzi*

§Più animato 𝅗𝅥 = 116				Allegro
C				9/8
2♯				
|| : 28 : || *	32	18	2	26 || : 20 : || D.S. till cue.
Zampa	*Rienzi*------		bridge	*Ride of the Valkyries*

(*Repeat first time only.)

PART 13. (*continued*)

27:	§Marcia Allegro 2/4 2♯ | | : 8 : | | : 16 : | | D.S. till cue. *Dixie*	Andante 0 8 4 R5 R6
[*28*:	Allegretto] 2/4 1♯ 16 | | : 8 : | | 16 | | : 8 | | 16 Dal Segno [no sign visible] a b a c d *Cocoanut Dance*	
29:	Allegro moderato C 0 25 *Mass in G, Gloria* (attrib. Mozart)	
30:	Maestoso 3/4 0 24 *Star-Spangled Banner*	

PART 14. The Structure of Satie's Score for *Entr'acte*

Note. Cues are underlined and given as they appear in all versions of the score, except for the tenth cue which does not appear in the four-hand piano reduction. C.N. = cue number, in Roman numerals. Score units are listed in Arabic numerals, and letters have been used to indicate relationships between units. T.S. = time signature. T.M. = tempo marking. K.S. = key signature. A zero indicates a key signature with no sharps or flats. An empty line between two units indicates that they are separated by a cadence or an interruption (as described in Chapter Five). Note that the Roman numerals within this outline are indications of cues (and the main divisions of structure); they do not correspond to the placement of Roman numerals within the score as rehearsal numbers.

C.N.	*Cue* *T.S.* (*T.M.*)	*Unit*		*Bars*	*K.S.*
I	*Cheminées; ballons qui explosent*	1	A	8	3♯
	2/4 (Pas trop vite)	2	B	4	1♭
		3	C	8	0
		4	D	8	3♯
		5	E	8	3♯
II	*Gants de boxe et allumettes*	6	A	8	3♯
		7	F	4	3♯
		8	E'	4	3♯
		9	B'	4	3♯
		10	B"	4	1♭
		11	D'	8	2♯
		12	F'	4	2♯

PART 14. (*continued*)

C.N.	Cue T.S. (T.M.)	Unit			Bars	K.S.
		13	G		4	2♯
		14	A		8	3♯
III	*Prises d'air, jeux d'échecs et ballons sur les toits*	15	H	H'	4 + 4	2♯
		16	I		4	2♭
		17	J	J'	7 + 5	1♭
		18	H	H'	4 + 4	2♯
		19	K		6 + 2	2♯
IV	*La danseuse; et figures dans l'eau*	20	L	M	4 + 4	4♯
	3/4	21	N	O	4 + 4	1♯
		22	P	Q	4 + 4	0
		23	R	L'	4 + 4	4♯
V	*Chasseur; et début de l'enterrement*	24	A		12	3♯
	2/4	25	B'''		4	0
		26	S		8	1♭
		27	A		8	3♯
VI	*Marche Funèbre*	28	T		8	0
	C (Plus Lent)	29	U		8	1♭
		30	V	W	4 + 4	0
		31	X		8	3♯
VII	*Cortège du ralenti*	32	A		8	3♯
	2/4	33	D''		8	0
		34	X	Y	4 + 4	3♭
		35	Z		8	1♯
		36	AA		8	2♯
		37	A		8	3♯
		38	BB		8	1♭
		39	CC		8	0
VIII	*La poursuite*	40	BB'		8	3♯
	¢ [Beg. in unit 41]	41	DD		7	3♯
		42	DD'		7	3♯
		43	DD''		7	3♯
	2/4	44	EE		8	2♯
		45	EE'		8	2♭
		46	EE''		8	1♭
		47	FF		8	0
		48	GG		8	0
		49	HH		8	1♯
		50	II		8	2♭
		51	JJ		8	2♯
IX	*Chûte du cerceuil et sortie de Börlin*	52	KK		8	3♯
	3/4 (Lent)	53	LL		8	0
		54	MM		8	4♯
X	*Final: Écran crevé et Fin*	55	A		8	3♯
	2/4	56	A'		8	3♯
		57	NN		8	3♯
	6/8 (Large et lourd en retenant)	58	OO		4	3♯

Notes

LIST OF ABBREVIATIONS

AMPAS	Academy of Motion Picture Arts and Sciences, Los Angeles
BN	*Bianco e nero*
CJ	*Cinema Journal*
CQ	*Cinema Quarterly*
CS	*The Cue Sheet* (Society for the Preservation of Film Music)
FIR	*Films in Review*
HQ	*Hollywood Quarterly*
LC	The Library of Congress
MM	*Modern Music*
MOMA	The Museum of Modern Art, New York
MPW	*Moving Picture World*
MQ	*Musical Quarterly*
NYT	*New York Times*
QRFS	*Quarterly Review of Film Studies*
SS	*Sight and Sound*

PREFACE AND ACKNOWLEDGEMENTS

1. Don DeLillo, *The Names* (1982; rpt. New York: Vintage Books Edition [Random House], 1983), 200.

2. *The Film Index: A Bibliography*, by the Works Project Administration, Writer's Program (New York), covers English-language sources through 1935 in 3 volumes: vol. 1, *The Film as Art*, Harold Leonard, ed. (MOMA and H. W. Wilson, 1941; rpt. New York: Arno, 1966), vols. 2 and 3, *The Film as Industry* and *The Film in Society* (New York: Krause International, 1986).

CHAPTER 1. FILM AND MUSIC

1. This chapter is a revision of my article "Film Music: The Material, Literature and Present State of Research," *Notes: The Quarterly Journal of the Music Library Association* 36 (1979), 282–325. The article was reprinted with a few changes in the *Journal of the University Film and Video Association* 34, no. 1 (Winter 1982), 1–40.

2. The premiere of the *cinématographe* in Paris on 28 December 1895 (by inventors August and Louis Lumière) was the first "effective" projection of motion pictures for public amusement, according to Kenneth Macgowan, *Behind the Screen: The History and Techniques of the Motion Picture* (New York: Dell, 1965), 80–81. The presence of a pianist at this premiere is asserted in many books: see, e.g., the eyewitness reminiscences of René Jeanne, *Cinéma 1900* (Paris: Flammarion, 1965), 8. (Sources on the earliest films and their music are discussed at length in Chapter Two.)

3. Peter Odegard, review of the *Dictionary of Contemporary Music*, John Vinton, ed. (New York: Dutton, 1974), and the *New Oxford History of Music, Vol. X: The Modern Age, 1890–1960*, Martin Cooper, ed. (London: Oxford, 1974), in the *Journal of the American Musicological Society* 19 (1976), 155.

4. Typically, music has received more attention from theorists than from historians: see, e.g., the chapter "Music" in Siegfried Kracauer, *Theory of Film: The Redemption of Physical Reality* (London: Oxford, 1960), 133–56; and the chapter "(Recorded) Sound" in Gerald Mast, *Film/Cinema/Movie: A Theory of Experience* (New York: Harper & Row, 1977), 206–37.

5. Charles Seeger defines these idioms in "The Music Compositional Process as a Function in a Nest of Functions as in Itself a Nest of Functions," a revision of a 1966 essay in his *Studies in Musicology* (Berkeley and Los Angeles: Univ. of California Press, 1977), 139–67. On the problems of using words to describe music, see his "Speech, Music, and Speech about Music," 16–30.

6. In Daniel Kingman's *American Music: A Panorama* (New York: Schirmer, 1979), film scores of Copland, Bernstein, and Thomson are discussed. In the *Schirmer History of Music*, Léonie Rosenstiel, ed. (New York: Schirmer, 1982), only Copland's film scores are mentioned. William W. Austin's *Music in the 20th Century* (New York: W. W. Norton, 1966) indexes the following names under "film music": Auric-Cocteau, Chaplin, Copland, Eisler, Hindemith, Honegger, Milhaud, Prokofiev, Shostakovich, and Stravinsky.

7. Walter Benjamin, "The Work of Art in the Age of Mechanical Reproduction," in *Illuminations*, Hannah Arendt, ed., Harry Zohn, trans. (New York: Schocken, 1969), 238. The essay originally appeared in the *Zeitschrift für Sozialforschung* 5 (1936).

8. Pauline Kael, "Movies on Television," in *Kiss Kiss Bang Bang* (New York: Little, Brown, 1968), 269–70.

9. Raymond Spottiswoode, *A Grammar of the Film: An Analysis of Film Technique*, rev. ed. (Berkeley and Los Angeles: Univ. of California Press, 1969), 3.

10. Raymond Bellour, "The Unattainable Text," *Screen* 16, no. 3 (Autumn 1975), 20, cited by Claudia Gorbman in "Vigo/Jaubert," *Ciné-Tracts* 1, no. 2 (Summer 1977), 65–80.

11. The distinction comes from Roger Manvell, "Screenwriting," in *The International Encyclopedia of Film*, Manvell, ed. (New York: Crown, 1972), 449.

12. Even the writer's best ideas may not be written down: Gore Vidal describes his comical adventure in Hollywood and illustrates the serious difficulties involved in answering the question "Who Makes the Movies?," *New York Review of Books* 23, no. 19 (25 Nov. 1976), 35–39.

13. Vlada Petric, "From a Written Film History to a Visual Film History," *CJ* 14, no. 2 (Winter 1974–75), 21. This issue is given over to a "Symposium on the Methodology of

Film History," eds. Piers Handling and Peter Morris, sponsored by the International Federation of Film Archives in Montreal, 1974; in the "Transcript of Discussion" (pp. 47–64), several participants challenge Petric's point of view.

14. For examples of sound film cue sheets, see these manuals: Robert Emmett Dolan, *Music in the Modern Media* (New York: G. Schirmer, 1967); Earle Hagen, *Scoring for Films: A Complete Text* (New York: EDJ Music, 1971); Milton Lustig, *Music Editing for Motion Pictures*, Communication Arts Books (New York: Hastings House, 1980); Marlin Skiles, *Music Scoring for TV and Motion Pictures* (Blue Ridge Summit, Pa.: Tab Books, 1976); and Frank Skinner, *Underscore* (Los Angeles: Skinner Music, 1950; rpt. New York: Criterion, 1960). In the most recent and comprehensive manual, by Fred Karlin and Rayburn Wright, *On the Track: A Guide to Contemporary Film Scoring*, with a "Complete Click Book" by Alexander Brinkman (New York: Schirmer Books, 1990), these materials are called "spotting notes" and "timing sheets"; examples of several types are given on pp. 53–65.

15. Charles Berg, *An Investigation of the Motives for and Uses of Music to Accompany the American Silent Film, 1896–1927*, Dissertations on Film Series of the Arno Press Cinema Program (New York: Arno, 1976), 158.

16. For a revealing example of what words both can and cannot convey, see Marie-Claire Ropars-Wuilleumier, "The Disembodied Voice: *India Song*," *Yale French Studies*, no. 60 (1980), 241–68; the author analyzes the film's first nine shots with a detailed "tableau" of image and sound track side by side; see also Gorbman, "Vigo/Jaubert," in which she takes up the problem of transcription and assesses various attempted solutions.

17. See Ken Sutak, "The Investment Market in Movie Music Albums," *High Fidelity* 22 (July 1972), 62–66; but the prices quoted by Sutak are now out of date, and many soundtrack albums that had gone out of print are being reissued on compact disc.

18. Clifford McCarty's *Published Screenplays: A Checklist*, Seriff Series [of] Bibliographies and Checklists, no. 18 (Kent, Ohio: Kent State Univ. Press, 1971), lists 388 films, with an introductory survey of screenplay publications. Manvell, "Screenwriting," lists seven complete shot-by-shot analyses. Two impressive new scholarly collections are: Tino Balio, ed., *Wisconsin/Warner Bros. Screenplay Series* (Madison: Wisconsin Center for Film and Theater Research [Univ. of Wisconsin], 1979–); and Charles Affron et al., eds., *Rutgers Films in Print* (New Brunswick and London: Rutgers Univ. Press, 1984–).

19. Gillian B. Anderson, comp., *Music for Silent Films (1894–1929): A Guide* (Washington: Library of Congress, 1988). Prior to the publication of Anderson's *Guide*, published references to film music holdings in LC were limited to such brief notices as "Early Film Music Collections in the Library of Congress," *Main Title* (publ. Entr'acte Recording Society) 2, no. 2 (Fall–Winter 1976), 8. Further discussion of the significance of Anderson's *Guide* is contained in this chapter's survey of the literature.

20. See Linda Harris Mehr, comp., *Motion Pictures, Television, and Radio: A Union Catalogue of Manuscript and Special Collections in the Western United States* (Boston: G. K. Hall, 1977)—the first book in which film music holdings of many institutions are systematically indexed. A second publication of still greater scope and value is *Resources of American Music History: A Directory of Source Materials from Colonial Times to World War II*, D. W. Krummel et al., comps. (Urbana, Chicago, & London: Univ. of Illinois Press, 1981): it lists 30 institutions under the heading "Silent Film Music." A few acquisitions of California State and LC are mentioned in *Notes* 33 (1977), 577–79, and those in the Free Library are described in Arthur Cohn, "Film Music in the Fleischer Collection of the Free Library of Philadelphia," *Film Music Notes* 7, no. 4 (March–April 1948), 11–13. For more recent descriptions of archival holdings, see n. 24.

21. Page Cook assesses the Newman Library in "The Sound Track," *Films in Review* (*FIR*) 17 (1976), 369–72. In 1981 Brigham Young University acquired the library of Max

Steiner; included are sketches for virtually all of his film scores, as well as scrapbooks and personal memorabilia.

22. See Robert Fiedel, "Saving the Score—Wanted: A National Film Music Archive," *American Film* 3, no. 1 (Oct. 1977), 32 and 71.

23. A list of the world's film archives is included in the annual *International Film Guide*, Peter Cowie, ed. (London: Tantivy Press; New York: A. S. Barnes, 1964–). An excellent, though now dated guide to several important American archives and libraries is "Our Resources for Film Scholarship," *Film Quarterly* 16, no. 2 (Winter 1962–63), 34–50.

24. Statement at the head of the society's newsletter, *CS* 1, no. 1 (Jan. 1984), 1; see also William H. Rosar, "The S.P.F.M.—History and Goals," *CS* 3, no. 1 (Jan. 1986), 1–2. Several issues of the newsletter contain inventories of archival holdings: e.g., Stephen M. Fry, comp., "UCLA Music Library: Guide to the Archival Film and TV Music Collections," 1, no. 3 (July 1984), 4–5; Rudy Behlmer, "Film Scores at the Academy," 1, no. 4 (Oct. 1984), 3–4; and Behlmer, "Film Scores at USC," 2, no. 1 (Jan. 1985), 1–2. Most important is vol. 9, no. 1 (Jan. 1992), a special issue published as "A Preliminary Directory of Film Music Collections in the United States," H. Stephen Wright, comp. Beginning in 1990, *CS* was supplemented by a separate bulletin, "News from the Executive Director," which contains up-to-date information on the status of its publication projects. Another important publication of the society is its anthology of writings about film music by composers, performers, and scholars: *Film Music 1*, Clifford McCarty, ed. (New York: Garland, 1989).

25. Roger Manvell, "The Explosion of Film Studies," *Encounter* 37, no. 1 (July 1971), 67–74; Jean Cohen, "A Visual Explosion: The Growth of Film Literature," *Choice* 10 (1973), 26–40.

26. Roy Prendergast, foreword to *A Neglected Art: A Critical Study of Music in Films* (New York: New York Univ. Press, 1977), xiii. (In the same year, Norton published a paperback edition under the title *Film Music: A Neglected Art*, and a second edition of the latter was issued by Norton in 1991. References to Prendergast will henceforth be to the 1991 edition.) Prendergast's claim that his book is the first to attempt a "comprehensive look" at film music should be qualified: cf. the subtitle of a much earlier book by Kurt London, *Film Music: A Summary of the Characteristic Features of Its History, Aesthetics, Technique and Possible Developments*, Eric S. Bensinger, trans. (London: Faber, 1936; rpt., Literature of Film, New York: Arno, 1970). Other comprehensive books which antedate Prendergast are discussed in the text of this chapter, as is Lawrence Morton's own view of the literature.

27. Two helpful compilations are: (1) Win Sharples, Jr., "A Selected and Annotated Bibliography of Books and Articles on Music in the Cinema," *CJ* 17, no. 2 (Spring 1978), 36–67; abridged rpt. in Tony Thomas, comp. and ed., *Film Score: The View from the Podium* (South Brunswick and New York: A. S. Barnes; London: Thomas Yoseloff, 1979), 260–66; (2) Claudia Gorbman, "Bibliography on Sound in Film," *Yale French Studies*, no. 60 (1980), 269–86. The former is now surpassed by Steven D. Westcott, *A Comprehensive Bibliography of Music for Film and Television*, Detroit Studies in Music Bibliography, no. 54 (Detroit: Information Coordinators, 1985).

28. Zofia Lissa cites about 50 mainly theoretical works in "Literatur über den Tonfilm," a chapter of her *Aesthetik der Filmmusik* (Berlin: Henschel, 1965), 9–16; Harry M. Geduld offers an uncritical introduction to a few books on music and musicals, and also soundtracks, in "Film Music: A Survey," *Quarterly Review of Film Studies* 1 (1976), 186–204; Alicja Helman presents a thoughtful discussion of much theoretical literature in "Probleme der Musik in Film," *Film* (Frankfurt) 5 (1964), 687–707.

29. For extended discussion of the history of synchronized sound, see Geduld, *The Birth of the Talkies: From Edison to Jolson* (Bloomington: Indiana Univ. Press, 1975) and David A. Cook, *A History of Narrative Film*, 2nd ed. (New York: W. W. Norton, 1990),

253–89. Kurt London reviews some of the experimental devices used in the silent period to achieve synchronization in *Film Music*, 66–70; see also Samuel Peeples, "The Mechanical Music Makers Brought Sound to the Silents," *FIR* 24 (1973), 193–200.

30. For an indication of how rapidly silent film theaters developed their own richly varied traditions of design and decor, compare Hans Schliepmann, *Lichtspieltheater: Eine Sammlung ausgeführter Kinohaüser in Gross-Berlin* (Berlin: Ernst Wasmuth, 1914), and Fritz Wilm, *Lichtspieltheater*, Neues Werkkunst (Berlin: Friedrich Ernst Hübsch, 1928). Of the many recent studies of movie-theater architecture, these three cover the silent period in the greatest detail: Dennis Sharp, *The Picture Palace and Other Buildings for Movies* (London: Hugh Evelyn, 1969); David Naylor, *American Picture Palaces: The Architecture of Fantasy* (New York: Van Nostrand Reinhold, 1981); and Francis Cloche, *Architectures des cinémas*, Collection Architecture "Les Bâtiments" (Paris: Moniteur, 1981). Ben M. Hall's *The Best Remaining Seats: The Golden Age of the Movie Palace* (New York: Bramhall House, 1961) is less technical than these volumes and gilds the subject with nostalgia, but it is by far the most informative on music in the "palaces."

31. Berg sketches the early history of cue sheets (to about 1915) in his *Investigation*, 102–12; five examples are printed in Charles Hofmann, *Sounds for Silents* (New York: Drama Book Specialists, 1970); Max Winkler explains his own important role in their development (though he was not, as he claims, their inventor), in "The Origins of Film Music," *FIR* 2, no. 10 (Dec. 1951), 34–42, rpt. in James Limbacher, comp. and ed., *Film Music: From Violins to Video* (Metuchen, N. J.: Scarecrow, 1974), 15–24. Early cue sheets are also discussed in Chapter Three.

32. An annotated list of 24 anthologies and indexes published between 1909 and 1929 is given in the appendix to my article in *Notes*, 316–19.

33. Prior to the *Encyclopedia*, Rapée (b. Budapest 1891–d. New York 1945) prepared the anthology *Motion Picture Moods* (New York: G. Schirmer, 1924; rpt. New York: Arno, 1974); there he refers to his "six years' experience in the Motion Picture game" (p. iii). He had played the game in illustrious arenas: the theaters in which he conducted include the Rivoli and Capitol in New York and the UFA Palast in Berlin; from 1926 to 1931 he served as music director at the Roxy in New York, and subsequently for NBC and at Radio City Music Hall. Biographies of this important figure are limited to brief entries in standard reference works—e.g., various editions of *Baker's Biographical Dictionary of Musicians* and the *ASCAP Biographical Dictionary of Composers, Authors and Publishers*—but there are several references to his career in literature of the period: see George W. Beynon, *Musical Presentation of Motion Pictures* (New York: G. Schirmer, 1921), 118; "Erno Rappe [*sic*], Conductor at Capitol, Joins Synchronized Music Company," *MPW* 50 (May–June 1921), 526; Eugene Bonner, "Sunday Morning at 'Roxy's,'" *Outlook*, 16 May 1928, 102; "Those Who Wield the Batons in New York's Principal Motion-Picture Houses," *Theatre Magazine* 48 (Sept. 1928), 47; and Rapée, "The Future of Music in Moviedom" *Etude* 47 (1929), 649–50, 699. Westcott cites an additional source which I have not seen: Hans Erdmann, "Eine Unterhaltung mit E. Rappee [*sic*]," *Reichsfilmblatt*, no. 13 (1926), 17.

34. Eighteen manuals are listed in the appendix to my article in *Notes*, 319–20.

35. The first editorials in the *World* on film music were "The Musical End" and "Musical Accompaniments for Moving Pictures," *MPW* 3 July and 23 Oct. 1909, 7–8 and 559. Chapter Three contains many more citations from the early years of *MPW*.

36. The first column of "Music for the Picture" is in *MPW* 26 Nov. 1910, 1227; the last is in 8 March 1919, 1359–63. Clarence Sinn edited all columns published through 18 Dec. 1915; from 25 Dec. until 26 Jan. 1918, he collaborated variously with S. M. Berg, Norman Stuckey, and Frank E. Kneeland; beginning on 7 Feb. 1918, all columns were edited by George W. Beynon.

37. J[ohn] M. B[radlet], Introduction to "Music for the Picture," *MPW* 26 Nov. 1910, 1227.

38. Sharp, *Picture Palace*, 70.

39. *MPW* contains many articles that establish a correlation between innovative management and music—e.g., James S. McQuade's account of Samuel L. ("Roxie") Rothapfel, "The Belasco of Motion Picture Presentations," 10 (Oct.–Dec. 1911), 796–98. Other early *MPW* references to Rothapfel are discussed in Chapter Three.

40. See, e.g., Carl Van Vechten, "Music for the Movies," in *Music and Bad Manners* (New York: Knopf, 1916), 44–54; K. Sherwood Boblitz, "Where 'Movie Playing' Needs Reform," *Musician* 25 (June 1920), 8, 29; and Richard Holt, "Music and the Cinema," *Musical Times* 65 (1924), 426–27. Van Vechten wanted a new kind of music, but he was not specific as to what kind it should be; Boblitz stressed the value of playing classical accompaniments as a means to educate the young; Holt lambasted nearly all movie music, with kind words only for an original score (film not named) by Eugene Goosens.

41. Giuseppe Becce was the composer of a number of original scores and of the popular *Kinothek* anthologies; his career is traced in Hans Alex Thomas, *Die deutsche Tonfilmmusik: von den Anfängen bis 1956*, Neue Beiträge zur Film- und Fernsehforschung, vol. 3 (Gütersloh: Bertelsmann Verlag, 1962), 81–83. Hans Erdmann wrote many articles for *Filmtechnik* and *Reichsfilmblatt* between 1926 and 1930 (indexed in Westcott, *Comprehensive Bibliography*, like the one cited in n. 33). Music and literature by Becce and Erdmann, as well as by Ludwig Brav, is indexed in Herbert Birett, *Stummfilm-Musik: Materialsammlung* (Berlin: Deutsche Kinemathek, 1970). See also Ulrich Eberhard Siebert, *Filmmusik in Theorie und Praxis: Eine Untersuchung der 20er Jahre und frühen 30er Jahre anhand des Werkes von Hans Erdmann*, Europäische Hochschulschriften, Reihe XXXVI, Musikwissenschaft, Bd. 53 (Frankfurt: Peter Lang, 1990).

42. On the plight of silent film musicians, see Maurice Mermey, "The Vanishing Fiddler," *North American Review* 227 (1929), 301–7; on publishers, see Winkler, "Origins."

43. "A Complete Record of the Musical Score, as It Appears in the [Warner Bros.] Studio Files" is given in Robert L. Carringer, ed., *The Jazz Singer*, Wisconsin/Warner Bros. Screenplay Series (Madison: Univ. of Wisconsin Press, 1979), 182–83. The list includes 85 separate numbers—mostly arrangements of pre-existent music, such as *East Side, West Side* (*The Sidewalks of New York*), *Give My Regards to Broadway*, and Tchaikovsky's *Romeo and Juliet*; seven numbers are termed "original" compositions by Louis Silvers.

44. Harry Alan Potamkin, "Music and the Movies," *MQ* 15 (1929), 281–96. This is the first article on film music to appear in *MQ*, one example of how the sound film brought forth literature from new quarters and quarterlies; for others, see nn. 51, 60, and 61, below.

45. The phrase is Marian Hannah Winter's, in "The Function of Music in the Sound Film," *MQ* 27 (1941), 153. As an example of a "manifesto," Winter cites Guido Bagier, *Der kommende Film: Eine Abrechnung und eine Hoffnung* (Stuttgart: Deutsche Verlag-Anstalt, 1928). Compare Thomas's overview of the period, "Zwischen Stummfilm und Tonfilm," in *Die deutsche Tonfilmmusik*, 11–17.

46. Sergei Eisenstein, *Film Form: Essays in Film Theory*, Jay Leyda, trans. and ed. (1947; rpt. New York: Harcourt, n.d.), 257–60. According to Leyda, the original "Statement on the Sound Film" appeared in *Zhisn Iskustva*, 5 Aug. 1928.

47. See the bibliography of writings by Eisenstein that have been translated into English in *The Film Sense*, Jay Leyda, trans. and ed. (1947; rpt. New York: Harcourt, 1970), 269–76; in the same book see also the essay "Form and Content: Practice," 155–216. This concerns Prokofiev's score for *Alexander Nevsky*, and in it Eisenstein focuses on examples of audio-visual parallelism rather than counterpoint—with what many consider to be faulty musical understanding. (See n. 50, below.) Vsevelod Pudovkin's essays from the thir-

ties are gathered in *Film Technique and Film Acting*, rev. ed., Ivor Montagu, trans. and ed. (1958; rpt. New York: Grove, 1970). "Asynchronism as a Principle of Sound Film," 183–93, and "Dual Rhythm of Sound and Image," 308–16, show Pudovkin's continuing interest in an independent soundtrack.

48. See Rudolf Arnheim's chapter, "The Sound Film," in *Film*, L. M. Sieveking and Ian F. D. Morrow, trans. (London: Faber, 1933), 201–8.

49. See the chapter "Tonfilm" in Béla Balázs, *Der Geist des Films* (1930; rpt. Frankfurt: Makol, 1972), 142–85. Balázs's first book on film, *Der sichtbare Mensch, oder die Kultur des Films* (Vienna: Deutsch-Österreichische Verlag, 1924), also contains a brief section on "Musik ins Kino," 143–44; ideas from both books are incorporated, in revised form, into *Theory of the Film: Character and Growth of a New Art*, trans. Edith Bone (1952; rpt. New York: Dover, 1970), 194–241. (Some of the sources listed in nn. 46–48 are reprinted either in whole or in part, along with other texts fundamental to "Classical Sound Theory," in the anthology *Film Sound: Theory and Practice*, Elizabeth Weis and John Belton, eds. [New York: Columbia Univ. Press, 1985], 75–144.)

50. Balázs wrote the libretto for Bartok's *Bluebeard's Castle*, and Eisenstein worked closely with Prokofiev on *Alexander Nevsky* and *Ivan the Terrible*. The Russian director's analysis of a sequence from the former film (cited in n. 47) has been sharply criticized for its musical shortcomings. For example, Hanns Eisler rejects the essay's underlying assumptions, and likens Eisenstein's "high-sounding aesthetic arguments" to "heavy artillery [used] to shoot sparrows"—*Composing for the Films* (New York: Oxford Univ. Press, 1947), 152–57; in *Film Music*, Prendergast states that the "support of Eisenstein's concept of an 'audiovisual score' on the part of film theoreticians is a result of their highly limited and superficial knowledge and understanding of music" (p. 226). See also Douglas Gallez, "The Prokofiev-Eisenstein Collaboration: *Nevsky* and *Ivan* Revisited," *CJ* 17, no. 2 (Spring 1978), 13–35.

51. The following are theoretical articles from *Die Musik*: Ali Weyl-Nissen, "Stilprinzipien des Tonfilms—Versuch einer Grundlegung," 21 (Sept. 1929), 905–7; Walter Gronostay, "Die Technik der Geräuschanwendung im Tonfilm," 22 (Oct. 1929), 42–44; A. Lion, "Erreichtes und Erreichbares: Zur Frage der Natürlichen Klangwiedergabe im Tonfilm," 22 (March 1930), 473–74; and Franz Benedict Biermann, "Tonfilm und Musik," 24 (Dec. 1931), 250–54. In *Melos*, see Hanns Gutman, "Der tönende Film," 7 (1928), 163–66; Hans Luedtke, "Filmmusik und Kunst," 7 (1928), 166–70; Becce, "Der Film und die Musik: Illustration oder Komposition?" 7 (1928), 170–72; W. Mechback, "Grundgedanken zur Filmmusik," 8 (1929), 24–29; Adolf Raskin, "Grundsätzliches zum Klangfilmproblem," 8 (1929), 249–51; Gronostay, "Die Möglichkeiten der Musikanwendung im Tonfilm," 8 (1928), 317–18; Kurt London, "Kinoorchester und Tonfilm: Organisationsfragen der Filmmusik," 9 (1930), 247–50, and "Filmstil und Filmmusik," 11 (1932), 404–6; and Leonhard Fürst, "Filmgestaltung aus der Musik," 12 (1933), 18–22.

52. Cf. André Coeuroy, ed., "La Musique mécanique," a collection of articles in *La Revue musicale*, no. 106 (July 1930), 1–74; Constant Lambert, "Mechanical Music and the Cinema," in *Music, Ho! A Study of Music in Decline* (London: Faber and Faber; New York: Scribner's, 1934), 256–68; and Albert Richard, ed., "La Musique mécanisée," articles in *Polyphonie*, series 2, no. 6 (1950). See also n. 63.

53. See, e.g., these reviews of the 1928 and 1929 Baden-Baden Music Festivals, where many films with avant-garde scores were screened: Heinrich Ströbel, "Film und Musik: Zu den Baden-Baden Versuchen," *Melos* 7 (1928), 343–47; Oscar Thompson, "More Fun, Less Music," *MM* 6, no. 1 (Nov.–Dec. 1928), 38–40; and Ströbel, "Die Baden-Baden Kammermusik, 1929," *Melos* 8 (1929), 395–400. Other reviews from *Melos* during this period are: Hans Mersmann, "*Der blaue Engel*," 9 (1930), 188; H[ellmuth] G[ötze], "Vier Tonfilme," 10

(1931), 371–72; and Kurt London, "*L'Arlésienne*: Ein Tonfilm mit Musik von Bizet," 11 (1932), 53–54. For a very good discussion of the avant-garde's approach to film music during the late silent and early sound periods, see Dietrich Stern, "Komponisten gehen zum Film," in *Angewandte Musik der 20er Jahre*, Stern, ed. (Berlin: Argument, 1977), 10–38.

54. Paul Valéry, "The Conquest of Ubiquity," essay in his *Aesthetics*, Ralph Mannheim, trans. (New York: Pantheon, 1964), 225. The essay appeared in Valéry's *De la musique avant toute chose* (1928), and Benjamin cited a passage from it at the head of "The Work of Art in the Age of Mechanical Reproduction."

55. My overview of the early sound period follows Thomas, *Die deutsche Tonfilmmusik*, 11–30; and Roger Manvell and John Huntley, *The Techinque of Film Music*, Focal Press Library of Communication Techniques (London: Focal Press, 1957); 2d ed., rev. and enl. by Richard Arnell and Peter Day (New York: Hastings House, 1975), 31–53. See also Miles Krueger, comp., *The Movie Musical: From Vitaphone to "42nd Street," as Reported in a Great Fan Magazine* (i.e., *Photoplay*, from 1926 to 1933) (New York: Dover, 1975).

56. Leonhard Fürst, "Musikkritik und Tonfilm," *Melos* 12 (1933), 92–97.

57. Newly recorded excerpts from Max Steiner's score for *King Kong* can be heard on the album *King Kong: Original Motion Picture Score*, Fred Steiner conducting the National Philharmonic Orchestra (Entr'acte Recording Society, 1976, ERS 6504; CD reissue, Southern Cross 901); the liner notes include commentary by Fred Steiner, with analysis of the score's leitmotifs.

58. See "Academy Award Winners and Nominees for Music: 1934–1972," in Roger D. Kinkle, ed., *The Complete Encyclopedia of Popular Music and Jazz: 1900–1950*, vol. 4 (New York: Arlington House, 1974), 2029–39. The new awards were themselves granted recognition in the article "Music in the Movies Wins New Place," *Musician* 40, no. 1 (Jan. 1935), 14. In the early years, awards went to the studio's music department, rather than to composers: see Frank Verity, "The Sound Track," *FIR* 15 (1964), 295–97, 300.

59. See "Radio, film, grammofono" and "La musica e il film" in *Atti del primo congresso internazionale di musica, Firenze, 30 aprile–4 maggio 1933* (Florence: Felice Le Monnier, 1935), 43–100 and 209–21. Ten papers were published from these two sessions, of which the most pertinent are Adriano Lualdi, "Due novi vie per la musica: Radio e film," 43–52; Massimo Mila, "Musica e ritmo nel cinematografo," 209–16; and Leonhard Fürst, "Prinzipien musikalischer Gestaltung im Tonfilm," 216–21 (a reworking of the *Melos* article cited in n. 51, above).

60. André Coeuroy and Léon Kochnitzky, eds., "Le Film sonore: L'Écran et la musique en 1935," a collection of articles in *La Revue musicale*, [no. 151] (Dec. 1934). There are 19 articles under four headings: "Esthétique," "Technique," "Dessin animé," and "L'Écran pédagogique." More than a third of the issue is given over to these articles by composer Arthur Hoérée: "Essai d'esthétique du sonore," 45–62; "Le Travail du film sonore," 63–69; and, with Artur Honegger, "Particularités du film *Rapt*," 88–91.

61. *Sight and Sound*, founded in 1932, was published by the British Film Institute from 1934; at that time it began to run articles on film music, including Ernest J. Borneman, "Sound Rhythm and the Film: Recent Research on the Compound Cinema," 3, no. 10 (Summer 1934), 65–67; John Grierson, "Introduction to a New Art," 3, no. 11 (Autumn 1934), 101–4; and M. D. Calvocoressi, "Music and the Film: A Problem of Adjustment," 4, no. 14 (Summer 1935), 57–58. *Cinema Quarterly* (Edinburgh) ran from 1933 to 1935, then merged with the monthly *World Film News* (*WFN*); under both titles it featured many articles by composers, including: Alexander Hackenschmied, "Film and Music," Karel Santar, trans., 1 (1933), 152–55; Walter Leigh, "The Musician and the Film," 3 (1935), 70–74; and Hanns Eisler, "Music and the Film: Illustration or Creation?," 1, no. 2 (May 1936), 23. (Cf. Becce's article, n. 51.) *Bianco e nero* began in 1937, at the *Centro sperimentale di cine-*

matografia in Rome; it offered many theoretical studies, starting with Sebastiano Luciani, "La musica e il film," 1, no. 6 (June 1937), 3–17.

62. London did not explicitly connect the *Allgemeines Handbuch* to his own work: in *Film Music*, all he says of the former is that it "dealt with directions for cinema conductors playing musical accompaniments to silent films, which soon after became superfluous . . ." (p. 12).

63. "Film music," wrote Walter Leigh, "must be written specifically for performance through the microphone, with full regard to its various needs and possibilities"—from "Music and Microphones," *WFN* 1, no. 5 (Aug. 1936), 40; Benjamin Britten gave Walton's score for *As You Like It* a negative review, complaining that "one cannot feel that the microphone has entered very deeply into Walton's scoring soul," in *WFN* 1, no. 7 (Oct. 1936), 46. Other examples: Eric Sarnette, "Musique et électricité," *La Revue musicale*, [no. 151] (Dec. 1934), 80–87; Libero Innamorati, "I problemi della registrazione musicale," in *Atti del secundo congresso internazionale di musica* (Florence: Felice Le Monnier, 1940), 261–64; Carlos Chavez, *Toward a New Music: Music and Electricity*, Herbert Weinstock, trans. (New York: W. W. Norton, 1937); and, from more technical points of view, W. F. Elliott, *Sound Recording for Films: A Review of Modern Methods* (London: Isaac Pitman & Sons, 1937), and Ken Cameron, *Sound and the Documentary Film* (London: Isaac Pitman & Sons, 1947).

64. London's book, though published one year after Sabaneev's, became obsolete sooner, because it was based on developments prior to 1933; cf. George Antheil's reviews of Sabaneev, in "Good Russian Advice about Movie Music," *MM* 13 (1936), 53–56, and of London, in "On the Hollywood Front," *MM* 14 (1937), 107–8.

65. Nine papers on film music are contained in the *Atti* of the second ICM (n. 63); its other theme was "Il pubblico e la musica."

66. In chronological order: Friedrich G. Robbe, *Die Einheitlichkeit von Bild und Klang im Tonfilm: Untersuchung über das Zusammenwirken der vershiedenen Sinnesorgane und seine Bedeutung für die tonfilmische Gestaltung* (Diss., Hamburg, 1940; Hamburg: Niemann & Moschinski, 1940); Wilhelmine Fey, *Die Verwertung musikschöpferischer Werke (insbes. bei Funk, Film und Schallplatte)* (Diss., Munich, 1941; Würzberg: Triltsch, 1941); and Konrad Ottenheym, "Film und Musik bis zur Einführung des Tonfilms" (Diss., Berlin 1944). Of the three works I have thus far been able to consult only Ottenheym.

67. See, e.g., "Music in the Movies Wins New Place" (n. 58); Douglas Moore, "Music and the Movies," *Harper's* 171 (June–Nov. 1935), 181–88; and Antheil, "Hollywood Composer," *Atlantic Monthly* 165 (Jan.–June 1940), 160–67; also, Prendergast cites many articles from the *NYT* and *Herald Tribune*.

68. The titles of the anthologies containing these essays contrast as sharply as the essays themselves: Jaubert's "Music on the Screen" appears in *Footnotes to the Film*, Charles Davy, ed. (New York: Oxford, 1937), 101–15; Steiner's "Scoring the Film" in *We Make the Movies*, Nancy Naumburg, ed. (New York: W. W. Norton, 1937), 216–38. (Cf. Herbert Stothart, "Film Music," in *Behind the Screen*, Stephen Watts, ed. [New York: Dodge Publishing, 1938], 139–44.) Jaubert's essay is said by many scholars to have originated as a lecture, delivered (whether in French or English is not clear) in London on 10 Dec. 1936, and excerpts were subsequently published in French and Italian: see Westcott, *Comprehensive Bibliography*, items 3466a–d. However, prior to the lecture Jaubert expressed some of the same ideas in at least two articles: "Music and Film," *WFN* 1, no. 4 (July 1936), 31; and "La Musique," an essay in the series "Le Cinéma: Petite école du spectateur," *Esprit*, no. 43 (April 1936), 114–19.

69. See these articles in *MM*: Oscar Thompson, "More Fun, Less Music"; Darius Milhaud, "Experimenting with Sound Films," 7, no. 2 (Feb.–March 1930), 11–14; Hans Hansheimer, "Film Opera—Screen vs. Stage," 8, no. 3 (March–April 1931), 10–14; Richard

Hammond, "Pioneers of Movie Music," ibid., 35–38; Virgil Thomson, "A Little More about Movie Music," 10 (1932–33), 188–91; Ernst Toch, "Sound-Film and Music Theatre," 13 (1935–36), 15–18; and John A. Gutman, "Casting the Film Composer," 15 (1937–38), 216–21.

70. "On the Hollywood Front" ran in *MM* through vols. 14–16 (1936–39). It continued as "On the Film Front" under Paul Bowles, 17–18 (1939–41), and Jean Latouche and Leon Kochnitzky, 19 (1941–42); as "Films and Theatre" and then as "Theatre and Films," under Bowles and Elliot Carter, 20–21 (1942–44); and, with the title changed back to "On the Hollywood Front," under Lawrence Morton, 21–23 (1943–46). Morton gives a summary of Antheil's views in 22 (1944–45), 135–37.

71. Antheil, "On the Hollywood Front," *MM* 14 (1936–37), 105–8, and 15 (1937–38), 48–51. See also Prendergast's discussion of Antheil's columns, as well as of Schoenberg, Stravinsky, and Morros, in *Film Music*, 45–48.

72. See the credits for these composers in Clifford McCarty, *Film Composers in America: A Checklist of Their Work* (Glendale, Calif.: John Valentine, 1953; rpt. New York: Da Capo, 1972).

73. Antheil, *Bad Boy of Music* (Garden City, N.Y.: Doubleday, 1945), 314; Levant, *A Smattering of Ignorance* (New York: Doubleday, 1940), 111. Both autobiographies, along with Hans W. Heinsheimer's *Menagerie in F Sharp* (Garden City: Doubleday, 1948), are highly entertaining, and tell a great deal about Hollywood during the thirties and forties.

74. Antheil's association with Hecht, and the latter's frequent screen-writing partner Charles MacArthur, began in 1935, when he scored his first two films, *Once in a Blue Moon* and *The Scoundrel.* The first was written, produced, and directed by MacArthur, the second was co-written by the pair and directed by Hecht. See Antheil's accounts of "Ben and Charlie" in *Bad Boy of Music*, 271–72 and 308–11; and also Linda Whitesitt, *The Life and Music of George Antheil, 1900–1959*, Studies in Musicology, no. 70 (Ann Arbor: UMI Research Press, 1983), 49–50. Item no. 67 in Whitesitt's "Catalogue of Antheil's Music" (p. 201) is titled "The Ben Hecht Valse" (1943).

75. "United Artists provides an efficient and one of the few channels for film distribution to meet the requirements of the showman-entrepreneurs—the producer, actor or director who is willing (and able) to match his wits and purse against the strongly entrenched major companies. . . . United Artists long ago justified its place in the film industry as a dominant influence for the production of better pictures." *Variety*, 25 Dec. 1940, p. 5; cited in Tino Balio's *United Artists: The Company Built by the Stars* (Madison: Univ. of Wisconsin Press, 1976), 161. Copland's first two feature-film scores were *Of Mice and Men* (1940) and *Our Town* (1941), produced for United Artists by Hal Roach and Sol Lesser, respectively. Copland described his approach to music for the first film, and noted the freedom to experiment granted him by both the producer and the director (Lewis Milestone), in "The Aims of Music for Films," *NYT*, 10 March 1940, sec. 11, p. 7. Eisler's first Hollywood film score, composed for *Hangmen Also Die!* (1943), a UA Picture produced by Arnold Pressberger, was discussed by Walter Rubsamen in "A Modern Approach to Film Music: Hanns Eisler Rejects the Clichés," *Arts and Architecture* 61, no. 11 (Nov. 1944), 20, 38—and by Eisler himself in *Composing for the Films*, 27–28 and 37–38.

76. Kubik wrote that "composers in the documentary field have more often been allowed the luxury of writing what they have felt than have our colleagues in the more commercial films," in "Music in the Documentary Film," *Writers' Congress: Proceedings of the Conference Held in October 1943 under the Sponsorship of the Hollywood Writers' Mobilization and the University of California* (Los Angeles: Univ. of California Press, 1944), 256. Before coming to Hollywood, Copland composed music for an innovative documentary, *The City* (1939), direction by Ralph Steiner and Willard Van Dyke, scenario by Henwar Rodakiewicz; see the latter's notes, published as "Treatment of Sound in the *The City*," in *The*

Movies as Medium, Lewis Jacobs, comp. and ed. (New York: Farrar, Straus & Giroux; paperback rpt., Noonday Press, 1970), 278–88; see also Copland and Vivian Perlis, *Copland, 1900 through 1942* (New York: St. Martin's/Marek, 1984), 288–91 for discussion of *The City*, and 295–304 for *Of Mice and Men* and *Our Town*.

77. See Copland, "Music in the Film," in *Our New Music* (New York: McGraw-Hill, 1941), 260–75, the third of three chapters devoted to "New Musical Media," following those on radio (232–42) and phonograph (243–64). (Cf. the literature on "mechanical music" and "music for the microphone," cited in nn. 51, 52, and 63, above.) An earlier version of the chapter on film music appeared in *MM* 17 (1939–40), 141–47, under the ambivalent title "Second Thoughts on Hollywood"; Copland removed all three from the revised edition, *The New Music, 1900–1960* (New York: W. W. Norton, 1968), terming them "superannuated." The last major essay in which he sought to explain film music to the lay audience appeared as "Tips to Moviegoers: Take off Those Earmuffs," *NYT Magazine*, 6 Nov. 1949, pp. 28–32; to some degree this overlaps earlier writings, but also contains comments on his and other composers' scores of the late forties; it was reprinted intact in *What to Listen for in Music*, rev. ed. (New York: McGraw-Hill, 1957), 152–57.

78. The history of *Composing for the Films* is complex. The text was originally written in German, by Eisler and Theodor W. Adorno, in 1944. For publication by Oxford in 1947 it was translated—with significant changes—by Eisler in collaboration with George MacManus and Norbert Guterman. Adorno withdrew his name from this edition with Eisler's consent, seeking to avoid the kinds of political problems the latter was experiencing with the United States government. After Eisler returned to Germany, he brought out a German edition (Berlin: Henschel, 1949), much revised in accordance with anti-American and pro-Soviet doctrine, along with a desire to make the language more popular in style. Subsequently, however, Eisler gave Adorno publication rights to the book, and the latter brought it out as *Komposition für den Film* (Munich: Rogner & Bernhard, 1969). What Adorno was in fact publishing was the original German version, for the first time, with both authors named; and he explained the book's complicated history in a postscript, "Zum Erstdruck der Originalfassung" (pp. 212–13). An edition published in 1971 by Books for Libraries Press contains a translation of this postscript, but the text remains identical to the 1947 Oxford version. For further information on the different versions, see the preface to the "Textkritische Ausgabe," Eberhardt Klemm, ed., in *Hanns Eisler: Gesammelte Werke*, series 3, vol. 4 (Leipzig: VEB Deutscher Verlag für Musik, 1977).

79. See Albrecht Betz, *Hanns Eisler: Musik einer Zeit die sich eben bildet* (1976), published in English as *Hanns Eisler Political Musician*, Bill Hopkins, trans. (Cambridge: Cambridge Univ. Press, 1982)—especially the sections "Practice and Theory: The Project for Film Music" and "Hollywood: A Temporary Refuge," 169–94. See also Jürgen Schebera, *Hanns Eisler im USA-Exil: Zu dem politischen, ästhetischen und kompositorischen Positionen des Komponisten 1938 bis 1948*, Literatur und Gesellschaft (Meisenheim am Glan: Hein, 1978).

80. Eisler, "Film Music—Work in Progress," *MM* 18 (1940–41), 250–54.

81. In ch. 2, "Function and Dramaturgy," in *Composing for the Films*, Eisler comments on his scores for *No Man's Land*, *Hangmen Also Die!*, *La Nouvelle Terre*, *Kuhle Wampe*, and *Dans les Rues*.

82. For an excerpt from the appendix to *Composing for the Films* concerning Eisenstein, see n. 50. On pp. 65–71, Eisler offers a critique of Eisenstein's "basic law" governing the relation between music and the picture.

83. See Lawrence Morton's review, "Hanns Eisler: Composer and Critic," *Hollywood Quarterly* (*HQ*) 3 (1947–48), 208–11.

84. Louis Levy, *Music for the Movies* (London: Sampson Low, 1948); Frank Skinner,

Underscore (cited in n. 14, above). The film *The Fighting O'Flynn* was released by Universal in 1949; in the book it is titled *The Irishman.*

85. Nathaniel Finston, "The Screen's Influence in Music," in *Music and Dance in California*, Jose Rodriguez, ed., William J. Perlman, comp. (Hollywood: Bureau of Musical Research, 1940), 124. Cf. the claim that "the great and the near-great of the musical world are finding their way to Hollywood to try their skill in the new medium"—from an anonymous pamphlet, *The Men Who Write the Music Scores* (Hollywood: Motion-Picture Producers and Distributors of America, 1943), 2.

86. "On the Hollywood Front," *MM* 15 (1937–38), 48.

87. Keller, *The Need for Competent Film Music Criticism* (London: British Film Institute, 1947), 21; for other Kellerian thrusts, see "Film Music: Some Objections," *SS* 15, no. 60 (Winter 1946–47), 136; "Hollywood Music: Another View," *SS* 16, no. 64 (Winter 1947–48), 168–69; and the sources cited in nn. 88 and 90.

88. In America criticism was written on a regular basis by Antheil et al. for "On the Hollywood Front" (n. 70); Kurt London, "Film Music of the Quarter," *Films*, nos. 1, 2, and 4 (1939–40); Walter Rubsamen, "Music in the Cinema," *Arts and Architecture* 61–64 (June 1944 to Jan. 1947); and Lawrence Morton, "Film Music of the Quarter," *HQ* 3–7 (1947–53). (Also, *Film Music Notes* contained criticism in every issue from 1941 to 1957: see n. 92.) In England the most prolific critic was Keller, whose columns included "Film Music" and "Film Music and Beyond," *Music Review* 9–17 and 19–20 (1948–56 and 1958–59); "Film Music," *Music Survey* 1–3 (1949–51); "Recent Film Music" and "Film Music," *Musical Times* 96–97 (1955–56). Other practitioners were Ernest Irving, "Film Music," *Tempo*, n.s., nos. 1–3 (1946–47); Antony Hopkins, "Music" and "The Sound Track," *SS* 18–19 (1949–51); and John Huntley, "The Sound Track," *SS* 19–24 (1950–55).

89. Among Lawrence Morton's essays, see, especially, the balanced perusal of both sides of the question, "Film Music: Art or Industry?" *Film Music Notes* 11, no. 1 (Sept.–Oct. 1951), 4–6.

90. Two examples of trans-Atlantic debates: (1) Morton's "Rule, Britannia!" *HQ* 3 (1947–48), 211–14, was a negative review of both John Huntley's *British Film Music* (London: Skelton Robinson, 1947) and Gerald Cockshott's pamphlet on *Incidental Music in the Sound Film* (London: British Film Institute, 1946), to which Cockshott responded with "Comments on a Review," *HQ* 3 (1947–48), 326–27. (2) Antony Hopkins described American film music as "orchestration run riot" in "Music: Congress at Florence," *SS* 19 (1950–51), 243–44; Morton replied to the charge in his column on "Film Music of the Quarter," *HQ* 5 (1950–51), 282–88; the reply was reprinted (incomplete) with a rebuttal by Hopkins, "Film Music: Orchestration Run Riot," *SS* 20 (1951), 21–23; Keller got into it with "Film Music and Beyond: The Dragon Shows His Teeth," *Music Review* 12 (1951), 221–25; and Morton showed his teeth once more with "Composing, Orchestrating, and Criticising," *HQ* 6 (1951–52), 191–206. Within the United States, similar exchanges also took place, among composers and others: see, for example, Erich Leinsdorf's negative view of "Film Music and the Screen," *NYT*, 17 June 1945, sec. 2, p. 3, which prompted, the following week, a mild response from Bosley Crowther, "Heard Melodies: Some Comments by a Strictly Average Listener on the Uses of Film Music," *NYT*, 24 June 1945, sec. 2, p. 1, and a sharp one from Bernard Herrmann, "Music in Films: A Rebuttal," ibid., p. 3. (Excerpts from the Leinsdorf-Herrmann debate were quoted, along with views of Aaron Copland, in "Is It Bad to Be Good?" *Newsweek* 26 (9 July 1945), 90. Subsequently, Leinsdorf's article appeared in revised form as "Some Views on Film Music," in *Music Publishers' Journal* 3, no. 5 (Sept.–Oct. 1945), 15 and 53–54; Herrmann's was reprinted intact as "Music in Motion Pictures—A Reply to Mr. Leinsdorf," ibid., 17 and 69.)

91. Sternfeld analyzed Hugo Friedhofer's score for *The Best Years of Our Lives* in

"Music and the Feature Films," *MQ* 33 (1947), 517–32; Miklós Rózsa's for *The Strange Love of Martha Ivers* in "The Strange Music of Martha Ivers," *HQ* 2 (1946–47), 242–51; "Gail Kubik's Score for *C-Man*," *HQ* 4 (1949–50), 360–69; and "Copland as a Film Composer" (for *The Heiress*), *MQ* 37 (1951), 161–75.

92. Grace Widney and Mabee Constance Purdy edited this periodical, published under various titles: *Film Music Notes* 1–10 (1941–51); *Film Music* 11–15 (1951–55); and *Film and TV Music* 16–17 (1955–57). Contents include news items, general articles, and many reviews of current film scores, frequently with score excerpts, and more often than not by the composer. An index to vols. 6–11 (1947–52) is in 11, no. 5; 12 is indexed in 13, no. 1; 15 in 16, no. 1; and 16 in 17, no. 1.

93. Paulo Milano, "Music in the Film: Notes for a Morphology," *Journal of Aesthetics and Art Criticism* 1, no. 1 (Spring 1941), 89–94; [Claude] Roland-Manuel, "Rhythme cinématographique et musical," in *Cinéma: Cours et conférences d'IDHEC* (L'Institut des hautes études cinématographiques), no. 2 (1945), 30–35; Robert U. Nelson, "Film Music: Color or Line?" *HQ* 2 (1946–47), 57–65; Pierre Schaeffer, "L'Élément non-visuel au cinéma," *La Revue du cinéma*, n.s., 1, nos. 1, 2, and 3 (Oct.–Dec. 1946), 45–48, 62–65, and 51–54; and Nazareno Taddei, "Funzione estetica della musica nel film," *BN* 10, no. 1 (Jan. 1949), 5–11.

94. Each composer explains how he wrote his score: see Herrmann, "Score for a Film" (*Citizen Kane*), *NYT*, 25 May 1941, sec. 9, p. 6, and Deutsch, "*Three Strangers*," *HQ* 1 (1945–46), 214–23. (Cf. Copland, "The Aims of Music for Films," cited in n. 75.) Herrmann's article was reprinted as "*Citizen Kane*" in *Film Music Notes* 1, no. 1 (1941), and as "Score for a Film" in *Focus on "Citizen Kane*," Ronald Gottesman, ed. (Englewood Cliffs, N.J.: Prentice-Hall, 1971), 69–72.

95. "Music in Films: A Symposium of Composers," *Films*, no. 4 (Winter 1940), 5–20; *Music and Dance in California*, Jose Rodriguez, ed. (1940); "Music and the War," in *Writers' Congress* (1944), 241–79; *Music Publishers' Journal* 3, no. 5 (Sept.–Oct. 1945)—entire issue devoted to film music; *Music and Dance in California and the West*, Richard Drake Saunders, ed. and comp. (Hollywood: Bureau of Musical Research, 1948); and Luigi Chiarini, ed., with Enzo Masetti, comp., *La musica nel film: Quaderni della Mostra internazionale d'arte cinematografica di Venezia* (Rome: Bianco e nero editore, 1950)—also published, with one additional paper, in *BN* 11, nos. 5–6 (May–June 1950). Both in the editor's introduction and also in the concluding acknowledgment signed by the directors of the Venice exhibition (pp. 146–47) the publication of *La musica nel film* is tied to the seventh "Congresso internazionale di musica" (ICM) in Florence, where film music was the principal topic of papers and discussion; but the large majority of papers presented at the ICM were not the same as those published in this volume: most of the ICM participants were composers and critics from abroad, most of the contributors to *La musica nel film* were Italian. See Antony Hopkins, "Film Music: Congress at Florence" (n. 90), and also Bianca Becherini, "À Firenze, il VII Congresso Internazionale di Musica," *Rivista musicale italiana* 52, no. 3 (July–Sept. 1950), 296–99. A volume of *Proceedings* of the seventh ICM is listed in the bibliography appended to the article by Irving, Keller, and Wilfred Mellers on "Film Music," in *Grove's Dictionary of Music and Musicians*, 5th ed., Eric Blom, ed. (1954), but I have seen no other evidence that such a book was ever published; however, a later anthology of papers from the so-called 1959 "Congresso internazionale 'Musica e film'"—again, linked to the Venice exhibition, this time in conjunction with the "Festival internazionale di musica contemporanea"—also contains seven papers from the 1950 Florence Congress, including Ildebrando Pizzetti's closing address: see S. G. Biamonte, ed., *Musica e film* (Rome: Ateneo, 1959)—especially the preface ("Presentazione") by the director of the Venice exhibition, F. L. Ammannati, and pp. 197–233 for the Florence papers.

96. Probably the best scholarly works of the forties are Ottenheym's dissertation (n. 66), and these three ground-breaking bibliographies: *The Film Index: A Bibliography* (1941), entries on silent and sound film music, pp. 202–11; Robert U. Nelson and Walter Rubsamen, comps., "Literature on Music in Film and Radio," *HQ: Annual Communications Bibliography*, supp. to vol. 1 (1946), 40–45, along with Rubsamen, "Literature on Music in Film and Radio: Addenda (1943–48)," *HQ* 3 (1947–48), 403–5—both reprinted in *Hinrichsen's Musical Yearbook* 6 (1950), 318–31; and John V. Zuckerman, comp., "A Selected Bibliography on Music for Motion Pictures," *HQ* 5 (1950–51), 195–99. Also, Alberto Cavalcanti wrote a concise and useful history of "Sound in Films," *Films*, no. 1 (Nov. 1939), 25–39, rpt. in *Film Sound*, 98–111 (see n. 49), and Marian Hannah Winter wrote one of film music, misleadingly titled "The Function of Music in the Sound Film," *MQ* 27 (1941), 146–64 (cf. the citations in nn. 45 and 49).

97. Morton, foreword to McCarty, *Film Composers in America*, xi.

98. Contrast, e.g., Page Cook's damning of composers who write "noise" instead of music (Neil Hefti, Quincy Jones, et al.) in *FIR* 19 (1968), 162–63 and 166, with his effusive praise of Scott Lee Hart in 26 (1975), 235–39. Principal contributors to "The Sound Track"—a column of unsurpassed longevity—have been Gordon Hendricks, *FIR* 3–5 (1952–54); Edward Connor, 6–10 (1955–59); T.M.F. Steen, 11–13 (1960–62); and Page Cook, 14–43 (1963–93). Illuminating examples of this type of literature are also to be found in the soundtrack review columns and occasional special articles written throughout the 1980s by Frederic Silber and Royal S. Brown for *Fanfare*: see, especially, Brown, "Film Musings," the title for all of his columns beginning with vol. 7, no. 2 (Nov.–Dec. 1983). (In various issues of earlier volumes, Silber and Brown contributed jointly to such columns as "Soundtracks and Shows." Thereafter, Silber's columns appeared somewhat less frequently than Brown's, mostly under the title "Reel Music" and/or "Silber's Consumer's Guide to Soundtracks and Film Music.")

99. *FIR* articles on silent film music include: Winkler, "The Origins of Film Music" (n. 31); John Griggs, "The Music Masters: The Days of the Piano and Organ Are Recalled by One Who Played Them," 5 (1954), 338–42; McCarty, "Filmusic for Silents," 8 (1957), 117–18, 123, and "Victor Herbert's Filmusic," ibid., 183–85; John Ripley, "Song Slides: Helped to Unify US Communities—and Sell Sheet Music," 22 (1971), 147–52; Peeples, "The Mechanical Music Makers" (n. 29); and a column by Cook on "authoritative" source material, "Films on 8 and 16," 27 (1976), 493–94, 499. For studies of American composers, see Theodor Huff, "Chaplin as Composer," 1, no. 6 (Sept. 1950), 1–5; Dimitri Tiomkin, "Composing for Films," 2, no. 9 (Nov. 1951), 17–22; Jack Jacobs, "Alfred Newman," 10 (1959), 403–14; Harry Hauer and George Raborn, "Max Steiner," 12 (1961), 338–51; Anthony Thomas, "David Raksin," 14 (1963), 38–41, and "Hugo Friedhofer," 496–502; Ken Doeckel, "Miklós Rózsa," 16 (1965), 536–48; Rudy Behlmer, "Erich Wolfgang Korngold," 18 (1967), 86–100; Cook, "Bernard Herrmann," 18 (1967), 398–412, "Franz Waxman," 19 (1968), 415–30, and "Ken Darby," 20 (1969), 335–56.

100. From the fifties to the present, the principal encyclopedic surveys of film music are: Ernest Irving, Hans Keller, and Wilfrid Mellers, "Film Music," in *Grove's Dictionary of Music and Musicians*, 5th ed. (1954); Edmund Nick and Martin Ulner, "Filmmusik," *Die Musik in Geschichte und Gegenwart* (1955); Georges Van Parys, "Film (Musique de)," *Encyclopédie de la musique* (1959); Mario Verdone, "Musica per film," *Enciclopedia dello spettacolo* (1960); Olivier Clouzot, "La Musique de film," *Encyclopédie de la Pléiade, 6: Histoire de la musique, II: Du XVIIIe Siècle à nos jours* (1963); Maurice Bessy and Jean-Louis Chardans, "Musique," in *Dictionnaire du cinéma et de la télévision* (1966); Roman Vlad, "Musica per film," *La musica, 1: Enciclopedia storica* (1966); Christopher Palmer and John Gillett, "Film Music," *The New Grove Dictionary of Music and Musicians* (1980); Frederick Steiner and Martin Marks, "Film Music," in *The New Grove Dictionary of American Music* (1986); and

2 articles by Marks and 1 by Royal S. Brown in *A History of the Cinema, 1895–1995*, forthcoming from Oxford Univ. Press (Oxford).

101. The only notable predecessor to McCarty was Claire Reis, comp., *Composers in America: Biographical Sketches of Contemporary Composers with a Record of their Works*, rev. ed. (New York: Macmillan, 1947; rpt. New York: Da Capo, 1977), a book praised by Morton as the first reference work to put "Film Music in the Mainstream," *HQ* 3 (1947–48), 101–4; but it is a general work, with some errors and limited space afforded to film musicians. McCarty's most comprehensive successor is James L. Limbacher, ed. and comp., *Film Music* (1974—see no. 31), a more inclusive book, covering credits through 1971; but it must be used with the greatest caution. McCarty, though obviously not an unbiased judge, nonetheless wrote a devastating review of Limbacher for *Notes* 31 (1974), 48–50. Revisions, corrections, and new credits are contained in Limbacher, comp., *Keeping Score: Film Music, 1972–1979* (Metuchen, N.J.: Scarecrow Press, 1981); and in Limbacher and H. Stephen Wright, comps., *Keeping Score: Film and Television Music, 1980–1988 (with Additional Coverage of 1921–1979)* (Scarecrow Press, 1991). See also Steven C. Smith, comp. and ed., *Film Composers Guide* (Beverly Hills, Calif.: Lone Eagle, 1990), the first volume in an ongoing series, continually updated.

102. See n. 55. The bibliography in *The Technique of Film Music* is extensive, and, owing to its chronological ordering, was very useful in the writing of this survey; but it contains minor errors and inconsistencies, not corrected in the second edition. Some examples: McCarty's *Film Composers in America* is dated 1954 instead of 1953; Skinner's *Underscore* is dated from its 1960 reprint, rather than the 1950 original; Biamonte appears to be the author of *Musica e film*, rather that the editor; and a whole 1971 issue of *Filmmaker's Newsletter* is said to be "devoted to the subject of film music," but it contains only a few articles on sound.

103. See Gorbman, "Vigo/Jaubert." The transcriptions in *The Technique of Film Music* are from *Henry V*, *Louisiana Story*, *Julius Caesar*, and *Odd Man Out*.

104. Colpi, *Défense et illustration de la musique dans le film*, Collection Panoramique (Lyons: SERDOC [Société d'Éditions de Recherches et de Documentation Cinématographiques]); Porcile, *Présence de la musique à l'écran*, 7ème Art, no. 49 (Paris: Les Éditions du CERF, 1969); Lacombe and Rocle, *La Musique du film* (Paris: Éditions Francis Van de Velde, 1979). A more concise work than these is their predecessor, Hacquard, *La Musique et le cinéma*, Bibliothèque internationale de musicologie (Paris: Presses universitaires de France, 1959); it now seems dated and superficial, though it draws attention to some of the most interesting French postwar literature (by Schaeffer, Hoérée, and Baudrier), as well as film scores (by Grémillon and Messiaen).

105. Bazelon, *Knowing the Score: Notes on Film Music* (New York: Van Nostrand Reinhold, 1975). The composers interviewed are John Barry, Richard Rodney Bennett, Elmer Bernstein, Paul Glass, Jerry Goldsmith, Bernard Herrmann, Gail Kubik, Johnny Mandel, Alex North, David Raksin, Leonard Rosenman, Laurence Rosenthal, Lalo Schifrin, Bernardo Segáll, and John Williams. Score excerpts, including a few interspersed through the book's first half, are drawn from Bazelon, *Survival—1967* (pp. 61–72); Bennett, *Secret Ceremony* (55–60); Bernstein, *Men in War* (103) and *To Kill a Mockingbird* (345); Gene Forrell, *To Be Alive* (298–300); Glass, *Interregnum* (335–36); Goldsmith, *Planet of the Apes* (103, 302) and *Seconds* (317–23); Kubik, *Gerald McBoing Boing* (338–40) and *The Desperate Hours* (346–47); Mandel, *Point Blank* (326–29); North, *Viva Zapata* (308–11), *2001* (rejected score, 330–32), and *Cleopatra* (342–44); Raksin, *What's the Matter with Helen?* (312–14); Rosenman (unidentified cue, 73), *The Cobweb* (tone row, apparently with a misprint, 99), and *The Savage Eye* (333–34 and 341); Rosenthal, *The Miracle Worker* (315); Schifrin, *The Hellstrom Chronicle* (301); Segáll, *The Luck of Ginger Coffey* (324–25);

Thomson, *Louisiana Story* (337); Dimitri Tiomkin, *Cyrano de Bergerac* (125); and Williams, *Images* (303–7).

106. Thomas, *Music for the Movies* (South Brunswick, N. J.: A. S. Barnes, 1973; paperback rpt., 1977); Evans, *Soundtrack: The Music of the Movies*, Cinema Studies Series, Lewis Jacobs, ed. (New York: Hopkinson & Blake, 1975; paperback rpt., New York: Da Capo, 1979); Prendergast, *A Neglected Art/Film Music*.

107. Prendergast, original edition (1977), viii. (This phrase does not appear in the second edition.) The composers and films that receive by far the most attention from Prendergast are Scott Bradley (*The Cat Concerto*, *The Cat Who Hated People*, *Heavenly Puss*), Hugo Friedhofer (*The Best Years of Our Lives*, *Broken Arrow*, *Joan of Arc*), Goldsmith (*Chinatown*, *The Wind and the Lion*), Herrmann (*Citizen Kane*, *Psycho*), Raksin (*Carrie*, *Force of Evil*, *Forever Amber*, *Laura*, *The Redeemer*, *Will Penny*), Rózsa (*Julius Caesar*, *Quo Vadis*, *Spellbound*), and Rosenman (*The Cobweb*, *East of Eden*).

108. Prendergast's very heavy dependence upon *The Technique of Film Music* and other sources is obscured by the absence of notes. For example, though *Technique* is listed in the bibliography for chapter two, the reader is not informed that it is (apparently) the source for paragraphs in *Film Music* on pp. 20, 24–25, and 32. (The corresponding pages in Manvell and Huntley [2d ed.] are 33, 46–47, and 41–42.) At times, moreover, a source is not listed in the bibliography: e.g., large portions of Lawrence Morton's "Film Music: Art or Industry?" are restated almost word for word in Prendergast, pp. 36 and 38, without acknowledgment. Inconsistency is also apparent: Prendergast criticizes both Gerald Mast (on pp. 25–26 and 167) and Hanns Eisler, whose book, as stated above, he calls "testy and relatively valueless" (p. 3); yet he refers repeatedly to Mast as an authority on film history, and he paraphrases Eisler's testy and valuable critique of Eisenstein (pp. 223–26—see n. 50). These criticisms of *Film Music* are elaborated in my review, "Focus!" *Pro Musica Sana* (Miklós Rózsa Society) 6, no. 4 (1978), 14–18.

109. See nn. 28 and 41.

110. La Motte-Haber and Emons, *Filmmusik: Eine Systematische Beschreibung* (Munich: Carl Hanser Verlag, 1980). Cf. La Motte-Haber, "Fünf Thesen zur Filmmusik," *Melos/Neue Zeitschrift für Musik*, NS, vol. 4, no. 2 (March–April 1978), 111–13.

111. Thiel, *Filmmusik in Geschichte und Gegenwart* (Berlin [DDR]: Henschelverlag Kunst und Gesellschaft, 1981).

112. See Miceli, *La musica nel film: arte e artigianato*, Contrappunti 11 (Fiesole: discanto edizioni, 1982), part 3, "Il rapporto Rota-Fellini: Analisi di un 'caso,'" 249–305, and the Appendix, "Il musicista nel cinema d'oggi: Colloquio con Ennio Morricone," 307–30. Part 3 presumably reworks Miceli's "Musica e film: proposta per un'analisi audiovisiva attraverso il rapporto Rota-Fellini" (Ph.D. diss., Florence, 1976).

113. Schmidt, *Filmmusik: Für die Sekundar- und Studienstufe*, Musik aktuell: Analysen, Beispiele, Kommentare, no. 4 (Kassel: Bärenreiter Verlag, 1982); accompanying albums issued by Bärenreiter-Musicaphon, BM 30 SL 5104/5105.

114. The following paragraphs list key works published ca. 1960–1990 in five categories.

Reference works. Limbacher, *Film Music* (1974); David Meeker, comp., *Jazz in the Movies: A Guide to Jazz Musicians, 1917–1977* (London: Talisman, 1977); Ermanno Comuzio, *Film music lexicon* (Pavia: Amministrazione provinciale, 1980); Limbacher, *Keeping Score* (1981); Alain Lacombe, *Des compositeurs pour l'image (cinéma et télévision)* (Paris: Musique et promotion, 1982); Westcott, *Comprehensive Bibliography* (1985); Linda J. Sandahl, comp., *Encyclopedia of Rock Music on Film: A Viewer's Guide to Three Decades of Musicals, Concerts, Documentaries and Soundtracks 1955–1986* (Poole, Dorset, U.K.: Blandford Press, 1987); Smith, *Film Composers Guide* (1990); and Limbacher and Wright, *Keeping Score* (1991).

Manuals. See the sources listed in n. 14; of these, Karlin and Wright's *On the Soundtrack* is the most wide-ranging, and lavishly supplemented with score excerpts and comments by composers—thus indispensable for the study of Hollywood film music in recent decades.

Biographies. Dimitri Tiomkin and Prosper Buranelli, *Please Don't Hate Me* (Garden City, N.Y.: Doubleday, 1959); Luzi Korngold, *Erich Wolfgang Korngold: Ein Lebensbild*, Österreichishe Komponisten des XX. Jahrhunderts, vol. 10 (Vienna: Verlag Elisabeth Lafiti/Österreischischer Bundesverlag für Unterricht, Wissenschaft und Kunst, 1967); Porcile, *Maurice Jaubert: Musicien populaire ou maudit?* (Paris: Les Éditeurs français réunis, 1971); Christopher Palmer, *Miklós Rózsa: A Sketch of His Life and Work* (London and Wiesbaden: Breitkopf & Härtel, 1975); Betz, *Hanns Eisler* (1976); Rózsa, *Double Life: The Autobiography of Miklós Rózsa* (Tunbridge Wells, Kent, U.K.: Midas Books; New York: Hippocrene Books, 1982); Whitesitt, *George Antheil* (1983); Aaron Copland and Vivian Perlis, *Copland, 1900 through 1942* (1984) and *Copland since 1943* (1989); Palmer, *Dimitri Tiomkin: A Portrait* (London: T.E. Books, 1984); Lyn Murray, *Musician: A Hollywood Journal* (Secaucus, N.J.: Lyle Stuart, 1987); and Steven C. Smith, *A Heart at Fire's Center: The Life and Music of Bernard Herrmann* (Berkeley and Los Angeles: Univ. of California Press, 1991). (See also n. 120 for dissertations by Bruce and Steiner, and n. 121 for oral histories of composers in Hollywood.)

Anthologies. Heinrich Lindlar and Reinhold Schubert, eds., *Die drei grossen "F": Film-Funk-Fernsehen*, Musik der Zeit: Eine Schriftenreihe zu Musik und Gegenwart, NS, vol. 2 (Bonn: Boosey & Hawkes, 1958); Biamonte, comp., *Musica e film* (1959); Hartmut Engmann, comp., *Filmmusik: Eine Dokumentation* (Munich: Wolfgang Gielow, 1968); Limbacher, comp., *Film Music* (1974), part 1; Hans-Christian Schmidt, ed., *Musik in den Massenmedien Rundfunk und Fernsehen: Perspektiven und Materialen* (Mainz: B. Schotts Söhne, 1976); Tony Thomas, comp. and ed., *Film Score* (1979), revised as *Film Score: The Art and Craft of Movie Music* (Burbank, Calif.: Riverwood Press, 1991); Luc Van de Ven, comp. and ed., *Motion Picture Music* (Michelen, Belgium: Soundtrack, 1980); Iris Newsom, ed., *Wonderful Inventions: Motion Pictures, Broadcasting, and Recorded Sound at the Library of Congress* (Washington, D.C.: LC, 1985); Weis and Belton, comps. & eds., *Film Sound* (1985); Hans-Klaus Jungheinrich, ed., *Oper-Film-Rockmusik: Veränderungen in der Alltagskultur*, Musikalische Zeitfragen no. 19 (Kassel: Bärenreiter, 1986); and McCarty, ed., *Film Music 1* (1989).

Special issues of periodicals. See the following (page numbers are given when only a part of the issue is devoted to film music): untitled collection in *Musik und Gesellschaft* 12, no. 2 (Feb. 1962), 66–87; Jacques Rivette et al., eds., "La Bande-Son," *Cahiers du Cinéma*, no. 152 (Feb. 1964), 19–44; Glauco Pellegrini and Mario Verdone, eds., "Colonna Sonora," *BN* 28, nos. 3–4 (March–April 1967); Enrico Ghezzi, ed., "Cinema musica cinema (2)," *Filmcritica* 30, nos. 296–97 (Aug. 1979), 242–300; Jean Pierre and Connie Tadros, eds., "Music for the Movies," *Cinéma Canada*, nos. 60–61 (Dec. 1979), 13–54; Alain Lacombe, ed., "Cinéma et musique, 1960–1975" *Écran*, no. 39 (Sept. 1975), 3–59; Philippe Carcassonne, ed., "Dossier: La musique de film," *Cinématographe*, no. 62 (Nov. 1980), 1–44; John L. Fell, ed., "Film Music," *CJ* 17, no. 2 (Spring 1978); Clemens Kühn, ed., "Musik und Medien," *Musica* 32 (1978), 229–55, and "Musik im Fernsehen," vol. 34, no. 1 (Jan.–Feb. 1980), 1 and 9–35; Rick Altman, ed., "Cinema/Sound," *Yale French Studies*, no. 60 (1980); Mandy Merck, ed., "On the Soundtrack," *Screen* 25, no. 3 (May–June 1984), 2–98; Kathleen Hulser and Reynold Weidenaar, eds., "The Composer and the Moving Image," *Ear Magazine* 9, no. 5/10, no. 1 (Fall 1985); Steven Fore, ed., "Film/Music/Video," *Wide Angle* 10, no. 2 (1988); Krin Gabbard, ed., "Jazz and Film," *University of Hartford Studies in Literature* 21, no. 3 (Nov. 1989), 3–46; and Jim Aikin and Robert L. Doerschuk, eds., "Film Scoring," *Keyboard* 16, no. 3 (March 1990), 32–98.

115. *Hollywood Studio Musicians: Their Work and Careers in the Recording Industry* (Chicago: Aldine-Atherton, 1971), a revision of "Studio Musicians: Their Work and Career Contingencies in the Hollywood Film Industry" (Ph.D. diss., UCLA, 1968); *Music on Demand: Composers and Careers in the Hollywood Film Industry*, New Observations Series (New Brunswick, N.J.: Transaction Books, 1983).

116. Birett, *Stummfilm-Musik: Materialsammlung*; Walter Seidler et. al., eds., *Stummfilmmusik gestern und heute: Beiträge und Interviews anlässlich eines Symposiums im Kino Arsenal am 9. Juni 1979 in Berlin* (Berlin: Verlag Volker Spiess, for the Stiftung Deutsche Kinemathek, 1979); Hansjörg Pauli, *Filmmusik: Stummfilm* (Stuttgart: Kletl-Cotta, 1981); Ulrich Rügner, *Filmmusik in Deutschland zwischen 1924 und 1934*, Studien zur Filmgeschichte, vol. 3 (Hildesheim: Georg Olms, 1988). Articles by Prox in the Seidler anthology include his opening remarks at the symposium, "Perspektiven einer Wiederaufbereitung von Stummfilmmusik" (pp. 9–25) and an important discussion of performance practice and modern-day presentation of silent films, "Stummfilmvertonungen deutscher Fernseh-Redaktion" (pp. 27–34) (a reworking of "Musik zu alten Filmen: Stummfilmvertonungen der Fernsehanstalten," *Musica* 34, no. 1 [1980], 35–41—part of the special issue on "Musik im Fernsehen" cited earlier). For further discussion of performance practice, see, in the anthology, "Aus der Praxis junger Stummfilmpianisten" (pp. 83–94), a pair of interviews by Gerhard R. Koch and Berndt Heller with pianists Joachim Bärenz and Albert Lévy, who performed at the symposium. Note that five additional German monographs have recently appeared. Three are studies of music in select groups of sound films: Josef Kloppenburg, *Die dramaturgische Funktion der Musik in Filmen Alfred Hitchcocks* (Munich: Wilhelm Fink, 1986); Norbert Jürgen Schneider, *Handbuch Filmmusik I: Musikdramaturgie im Neuen Deutschen Film*, Kommunikation audiovisuell: Beiträge aus der Hochschule für Fernsehen und Film, München, Bd. 13 (Munich: Ölschläger, 1986); and Schneider, *Handbuch Filmmusik II: Musik im Dokumentarischen Film*, same series, Bd. 15 (1989). Two others are concerned with the silent period: Siebert, *Filmmusik in Theorie und Praxis* (1990), and Rainer Fabich, *Musik für den Stummfilm: Analysierende Beschreibung originaler Filmkompositionen*, Europäische Hochschulschriften, Reihe XXXVI, Musikwissenschaft, Bd. 94 (Frankfurt: Peter Lang, 1993). The latter came to my attention too late to be of use in the writing of this book.

117. See n. 15. Prior to Berg's *Investigation*, the only American book on the subject was Hofmann's brief *Sounds for Silents* (1970), a source of many fascinating photographs and facsimiles. Also of interest, mainly for the numerous illustrations of theaters and mechanical instruments, is Q. David Bowers, *Nickelodeon Theatres and Their Music* (Vestal N.Y.: Vestal Press, 1986).

118. "Introduction: A Warming Flame—The Musical Presentation of Silent Films," in *Music for Silent Films*, xii–xlix; cf. two other major essays by Anderson, "The Presentation of Silent Films, or, Music as Anaesthesia," *Journal of Musicology* 5 (1987), 257–95, and "'No Music until Cue': The Reconstruction of D.W. Griffith's *Intolerance*," *Griffithiana*, no. 38/39 (Oct. 1990), 154–71; and also, by Donald R. Hunsberger, "Orchestral Accompaniment for Silent Films," *Image* 25, no. 1 (March 1982), 7–16.

119. The "Literature of Film" series published by Arno Press (New York) includes six reprints of books on film music: Edith Lang and George West, *Musical Accompaniment of Moving Pictures* (Boston: Boston Music, 1920; 1970); London, *Film Music* (1936; 1970); Rapée, *Encyclopedia* (1925; 1970); Huntley, *British Film Music* (1947; 1972); Rapée, *Motion Picture Moods* (1924; 1974); and Sabaneev, *Music for the Films* (1935; 1978).

120. For example, Douglas Gallez, "The Effect upon Cognitive Learning of Background Music in Instructional Films" (Berkeley, 1975); Esther Hanlon, "Improvisation: Theory and Application for Theatrical Music and Silent Film" (Cincinnati, 1975); James C.

Hamilton, "Leith Stevens: A Critical Analysis of His Works" (Missouri-Kansas City, 1976); Malcolm Eugene Bowes, "Eurhythmics and the Analysis of Visual-Musical Synthesis in Film: An Examination of Sergei Eisenstein's *Alexander Nevsky*" (Ohio State, 1978); Claudia Gorbman, "Film Music: Narrative Functions in French Films" (Washington, 1978); Regie Rae Wintle, "Emotional Impact of Music on Television Commercials" (Nebraska, 1978); Philip Tagg, "Kojak—50 Seconds of Television Music" (Göteborg, 1979)—pub. under the same title, in the series Studies from the Dept. of Musicology, no. 2 (Göteborg, 1979); Fred Steiner, "The Making of an American Film Composer: A Study of Alfred Newman's Music in the First Decade of the Sound Era" (USC, 1981); Whitesitt, "The Life and Works of George Antheil" (Maryland, 1981); Graham Bruce, "Bernard Herrmann: Film Music and Narrative" (NYU, 1982)—pub. in revised form, under the same title, in the series Studies in Cinema, no. 38 (Ann Arbor: UMI Research Press, 1985); Kathryn Kalinak, "Music as Narrative Structure in Hollywood Film" (Illinois, 1982); and Frances McKay, "Movement in Time and Space" (Peabody Conservatory, 1982).

121. Tapes and transcripts of composers' seminars and oral histories have been collected at the AFI Center for Advanced Film Studies (Feldman Library, Los Angeles) since 1967, and many are available on microfiche: see *The American Film Institute Seminars and Dialogues on Film*, part 1 (1–199), and *The American Film Institute/Louis B. Mayer Foundation Oral History Collection*, part 1 (1–25), both in the New York Times Oral History Program (Glen Rock, N.J.: Microfilming Corp. of America, 1977). Composers included in the former are E. Bernstein (no. 16), Goldsmith (no. 66), and Mancini (nos. 118 and 199); in the latter are contained lengthy interviews by Irene Kahn Atkins with Friedhofer ("Arranging and Composing Film Music," no. 7), Joseph Gershenson ("Reminiscences," no. 9), Bronislau Kaper ("Scoring Hollywood Movies," no. 13), and Harry Warren ("Hollywood Song Writer," no. 24), as well as with several sound technicians and music editors: for indexes to these microfiche publications, see the *New York Times Oral History Program . . . Guide No. 2: A Bibliographic Listing of the Memoirs in the Micropublished Collections* (Sanford, N.C.: Microfilming Corp. of America, 1979). Other publications containing material based on AFI seminars with Hollywood composers are Donald Chase, ed., *Filmmaking: The Collaborator's Art* (Boston: Little, Brown, 1975)—see pp. 271–91 ("The Composer") for comments by E. Bernstein, North, Goldsmith, and John Green; and Joseph McBride, ed., *Filmmakers on Filmmaking: The American Film Institute Seminars on Motion Pictures and Television* (Los Angeles: J. P. Tarcher, 1981), vol. 1, pp. 111–24 (Rosenman), and vol. 2, pp. 133–46 (Goldsmith). The *Quarterly Journal of the Library of Congress* (*QJLC*), now defunct, published seven articles on film music between 1977 and 1983, the majority based on materials held in the Music Division. The first five were reprinted in the Library's beautiful anthology, I. Newsom, ed., *Wonderful Inventions*, 59–185: Jon Newsom, "'A Sound Idea': Music for Animated Films"; Ross B. Care, "Threads of Melody: The Evolution of a Major Film Score—Walt Disney's *Bambi*"; J. Newsom, "David Raksin: A Composer in Hollywood"; Raksin, "Life with Charlie [Chaplin]"; and Wayne Shirley, "'A Bugle Call to Arms for National Defense': Victor Herbert and His Score for *The Fall of a Nation*." The remaining two articles are Fred Steiner, "Keeping Score of the Scores: Music for *Star Trek*," *QJLC* 40, no 1. (Winter 1983), 4–13, and William H. Rosar, "Music for the Monsters: Universal Pictues' Horror Film Scores of the Thirties," 40, no. 4 (Fall 1983), 390–421. Also published by LC is a compact disc recording, *Our Musical Past*, vol. 2, containing excerpts from scores for two silent films, *Fall of a Nation* by Herbert (see Shirley's article, above) and *Gloria's Romance* by Jerome Kern, recorded by the MusicCrafters Orchestra, conducted by Frederick Fennell, with notes by Shirley and John McGlinn (recording #OMP-103, available from the Motion Pictures, Broadcasting and Recorded Sound Division). LC's most recent relevant publication is Anderson, *Music for Silent Films*.

122. Many such essays are found in the foreign-language anthologies and special issues cited in n. 114. Other important examples, published both in Europe and the U.S., include Pierre Schaeffer, "Les Nouvelles techinques sonores et le cinéma," *Cahiers du Cinéma* 7, no. 37 (July 1954), 54–56, and "Le Contrepoint du son et de l'image," *C. du C.* 18, no. 108 (June 1960), 7–22; Lissa, "Formprobleme der Filmmusik," in *Festschrift Karl Gustav Fellerer*, Heinrich Hüschen, ed. (Regensburg: G. Bosse, 1962), 321–35; Helman, "Probleme der Musik in Film" (1964); Rolf Urs Ringger, "Filmmusik sucht sich selbst," *Melos* 33 (1966), 313–19; Hanns Jelinek, "Musik in Film und Fernsehen: Einige Bemerckungen zu einem aktuellen Thema," *Öst. Musikzeitschrift* 23 (1968), 122–35; Leonard Rosenman, "Notes from a Sub-culture," *Perspectives of New Music* 7 (1968), 122–35; William Johnson, "Face the Music," *Film Quarterly* 22, no. 4 (Summer 1969), 3–19; Hans Heinrich Eggebrecht, "Funktionale Musik," *Archiv für Musikwissenschaft* 30 (1973), 1–25; Jean Mitry, "Musique et cinéma," *Revue d'esthétique* 26 (1973), 311–28; H. Pauli, "Filmmusik," continued as "Musik im Film," *Schweizerische Musikzeitung* 114, nos. 5 and 6 (1975), 265–70 and 326–31; W. Sharples, Jr., "The Aesthetics of Film Sound: The Importance of Being Audible," *Filmmaker's Newsletter* 8, no. 5 (March 1975), 27–32; Mast, "(Recorded) Sound," in *Film/Cinema/Movie* (1977); Miceli, "Musica e film: La colonna sonora ha cinquant'anni. È possibile un bilancio?," *Nuova Rivista musicale italiana* 11, no. 3 (July-Sept. 1977), 349–63; H.-C. Schmidt, "Autonomie und Funktionalität von Musik: Gedanken zu einer aesthetischen Polarisierung und ihrer didaktische Bedeutung," *Schweiz. Mus.* 117, no. 5 (Sept.–Oct. 1977), 267–72; Stern, "Komponisten Gehen zum Film" (1977); la Motte-Haber, "Fünf Thesen zur Filmmusik" (1978); and Robbert Van Der Lek, "Filmmusikgeschichte in systematischer Darstellung: Ein Entwurf," *Arch. für Mus.* 44 (1987), 216–39.

123. For some of the best examples of such case studies, see the essays by J. Newsom and Care cited earlier (n. 121), and the following: H.-C. Schmidt, "Wesenmerkmale und dramaturgische Funktion der musik in Roman Polanski's Film *Rosemaries Baby*," in *Musik in den Massenmedien*, 250–75; Lucy Fischer, "René Clair, *Le Million*, and the Coming of Sound," *CJ* 16, no. 2 (Spring 1977), 34–50; Kristin Thomson, chapters on "Simple Sound Relations" and "Vertical Montage" in her book *Eisenstein's 'Ivan the Terrible': A Neoformalist Analysis* (Princeton: Princeton Univ. Press, 1981), 202–60; Epi Wiese, "The Shape of Music in *The Rules of the Game*," *QRFS* no. 3 (Summer 1982), 199–209; R. S. Brown, "Herrmann, Hitchcock, and the Music of the Irrational," *CJ* 21, no. 2 (Spring 1982), 14–49; Samuel Chell, "Music and Emotion in the Classic Hollywood Film: The Case of *The Best Years of Our Lives*," *Film Criticism* 8, no. 2 (Winter 1984), 27–38; William Penn, "The Music for David O. Selznick's Production No. 103 [*Duel in the Sun*]," in *Perspectives on Music: Essays on Collections at the Humanities Research Center*, Dave Oliphant and Thomas Zigal, eds. (Austin, Texas: H.R.C, Univ. of Texas, 1985), 157–87; K. Kalinak, "The Text of Music: A Study of *The Magnificent Ambersons*," *CJ* 27, no. 4 (Summer 1988), 45–63; Kalinak, "Max Steiner and the Classical Hollywood Film Score: An Analysis of *The Informer*," in *Film Music 1* (1989), 123–42; S. Westcott, "Miklós Rósza's *Ben-Hur*: The Musical-Dramatic Function of the Hollywood Leitmotiv," ibid., 183–207; and Michael Walter, "Die Musik des Olympiafilms von 1938," *Acta musicologica* 62 (1990), 82–113.

124. *Gallez.* "Theories of Film Music," *CJ* 9, no. 2 (Spring 1970), 40–47; "Facing the Music in Scripts," *CJ* 11, no. 1 (Fall 1971), 57–62; "Satie's *Entr'acte*: A Model of Film Music," *CJ* 16, no. 2 (Fall 1976), 36–50; and "The Prokofiev-Eisenstein Collaboration," (1978). *Steiner.* "Herrmann's 'Black and White' Music for Hitchcock's *Psycho*," *Film Music Notebook* 1, nos. 1 and 2 (1974), 28–36 and 26–46; "An Examination of Leith Stevens' Use of Jazz in *The Wild One*," *F.M.N.* 2, nos. 2 and 3 (1976), 26–34 and 27–34; "Fred Steiner on Film Music," in *Film Score* (1979), 178–86; "Keeping Score of the Scores: Music for *Star Trek*" (1983); "Foreword" to Robert Faulkner, *Music on Demand*, 1–8; with Marks, "Film Music"

in the *New Grove Dictionary of American Music* (1986); and "What Were Musicians Saying about Movie Music during the First Decade of Sound? A Symposium of Selected Writings," in *Film Music 1* (1989), 81–107. *Gorbman*. "Music as Salvation: Notes on Fellini and Rota," *Film Quarterly* 28, no. 2 (Winter 1974–75), 17–25; "Clair's Sound Hierarchy and the Creation of Auditory Space," in *Film Studies Annual*, Ben Lawton et al., eds. (West Layfayette, Ind.: Purdue Research Foundation, 1976), 113–23; "Teaching the Soundtrack," *QRFS* 1, no. 4 (Nov. 1976), 446–52; "Vigo/Jaubert," (1977); "Film Music," *QRFS* 3, no. 1 (Winter 1978), 105–13; "Narrative Film Music" and "Bibliography on Sound in Film," *Yale French Studies*, no. 60 (1980), 183–203 and 269–86; "*Cléo from Five to Seven*: Music as Mirror," *Wide Angle* 4, no. 4 (1981), 39–49; and "The Drama's Melos: Max Steiner and *Mildred Pierce*," *Velvet Light Trap*, no. 19 (1982), 35–39.

125. In "Satie's *Entr'acte*," Gallez refers to a portion of a sketch for the score; see my discussion in Chapter Five for details.

126. *Unheard Melodies: Narrative Film Music* (Bloomington: Indiana Univ. Press, 1987).

127. Gorbman also contributed an impressive "Bibliography on Sound in Film," 269–86.

128. See, for example, two subsequent anthologies with similar wirtings: the special issue of *Screen*, "On the Soundtrack" (1984); and *Film Sound* (1985), sections on "Modern Sound Theory" and "Practice and Methodology," 145–209 (including reprints of essays by Metz and Doane from *Yale French Studies*, no. 60). Ohter recent work of this type, mostly in French—showing the influence of such thinkers as Saussure, Derrida, and Metz—includes Charles Lafayette Boilès, "La Signification dans la musique de film," *Musique en jeu*, no. 19 (June 1975), 71–85; Dominique Chateau, "Projet pour une sémiologie des relations audi-visuelles dans le film," ibid., no. 23 (April 1976), 82–98; Jean-Rémy Julien, "Éléments méthodologiques pour une typologie de la musique de film," *Revue de musicologie* 66, no. 2 (1980), 179–202, with an English summary, p. 260; Gérard Blanchard, *Images de la musique de cinéma*, Collection Médiathèque (Paris: edilig, 1984); Michel Chion, *Le Son au cinéma* (Paris: Éditions de L'Étoile/Cahiers du cinéma, Seuil, 1985); Chion, "Cinéma et musique acousmatique: Centrement et linéarisation," in *Recherche musicale au GRM* (Groupe de Recherches Musicales, Institut National de la Communication audiovisuelle), M. Chion and François Delalande, eds. (special issue of *La Revue musicale*, nos. 394–97) (Paris: Éditions Richard-Masse, 1986), 135–43; and Carol Flinn, "The Most Romantic Art of All: Music in the Classical Hollywood Cinema," *CJ* 29, no. 4 (Summer 1990), 35–50. Concerning Chion and Flinn, see n. 132.

129. The 1975 edition of *The Technique of Film Music* contains discussion of "Four films since 1955," chosen for their different approaches toward film music: *The Devils*, with both seventeenth-century French music and original work by Peter Maxwell Davies; *2001: A Space Odyssey*, with prerecorded works by Johann and Richard Strauss, Khatchaturian, and Ligeti; *Second Best*, with a somewhat more traditional score by Richard Arnell; and *Zabriskie Point*, with an amalgam of popular music by groups such as the Rolling Stones and Pink Floyd. Two recent essays which explore widely different types of film music are Frederic Silber, "The State of the Art: The Film Soundtrack as Contemporary Music, Contemporary Music as Film Score," *Fanfare* 4, no. 1 (Sept.–Oct. 1980), 309–17—a very fine discussion of many pop soundtracks; and John Rockwell, "*Musique concrète* and Composition beyond Music: Walter Murch," in *All American Music: Composition in the Late Twentieth Century*, Rockwell, ed. (New York: Knopf, 1983), 154–63. (In conjunction with the latter, see also Frank Paine, "Sound Mixing and *Apocalypse Now*: An Interview with Walter Murch," in *Film Sound*, 356–60.) Some recent, celebrated scores that demonstrate today's "multi-cultural" variety include: the "Minimalist" music composed by Philip Glass for *Koyaanisqatsi* (1983), *Mishima* (1985), *Hamburger Hill* (1987), *The Thin Blue Line* (1989),

and so on; the Oscar-winning music credited to Ryuichi Sakamoto, David Byrne, and Cong Su (and also to "Music Associate" Hans Zimmer) for Bertolucci's *The Last Emperor* (1987); the compilation of traditional American songs and instrumental music featured on the soundtrack (so rich in texture!) of Ken Burns's *The Civil War* (1990); and the fascinating mixture of rock songs, Pygmy songs, and music by Graeme Revell heard in Wim Wenders's *Until the End of the World* (1991).

130. Such allusions first became common in the mid-seventies—a consequence of the increasing number of films that were themselves tied self-consciously to earlier pictures: e.g., *Obsession* (1974), in which Bernard Herrmann deliberately echoed his own score for the film's double, *Vertigo* (1958); *L'Histoire d'Adèle H.* (1975), for which François Porcile constructed a score entirely from compositions by film composer Maurice Jaubert (a pairing discussed by Annette Insdorf in her essay in *Yale French Studies*, No. 60); *Star Wars* (1977), in which one hears John Williams's unmistakable imitations of Korngold's swashbuckler style (a tribute acknowledged by Williams in his notes for the soundtrack album); and, to leap ahead, *Dead Men Don't Wear Plaid* (1982), which cleverly integrates footage from many forties "*films noirs*," just as Rózsa's music pays homage to his own scores of that style. (A recent example is Scorsese's 1991 remake of *Cape Fear*, which contains a score by Elmer Bernstein based on Herrmann's music for the 1962 original.) Moreover, some Hollywood composers today seem intent on continually borrowing from the past, in new and not-so-new contexts: perhaps the most affecting examples are those by Danny Elfman in collaboration with Tim Burton, beginning with *Pee-Wee's Big Adventure* (1985).

131. The Society for the Preservation of Film Music is the most significant organization of its kind: see the list of its publications in n. 24. American-based predecessors include the Max Steiner Music Society (est. 1965), the Miklós Rózsa Society (1971), the Entr'acte Recording Society (1974), and the Elmer Bernstein Film Music Collection (1975). All five of these societies did or do offer journals—*The Max Steiner Music Society Newsletter* (and other similar titles), *Pro Musica Sana*, *Main Title*, *Film Music Notebook*, and *The Cue Sheet*—and all but the SPFM issued recordings. Some foreign societies, clubs, and soundtrack newsletters are listed by Sharples in his 1978 bibliography for *CJ*. Of these, *Soundtrack: The Collector's Quarterly*, Luc Van de Ven, ed. (formerly *SCN* and *Soundtrack!*) is the most detailed in matters of discography; the anthology *Motion Picture Music* (n. 114) draws much of its content from this magazine. In recent years, the company Varèse-Sarabande has become the most active producer of soundtrack recordings, and many items in its catalogue are either reissues or rerecordings of "classic" Hollywood scores: see, e.g., R. S. Brown, "The Sea Hawk Sails Again: Varèse-Sarabande's New Recording Documents One of Hollywood's Supreme Efforts in Film Scoring," *Fanfare* 11, no. 4 (March-April 1988), 52–55; the company has also produced two nostalgic series, both superbly engineered and annotated: music from *The Twilight Zone* (five albums since 1983), and *Star Trek* (three albums since 1985).

132. Since 1990 the number of textual and theoretical studies has risen more quickly than ever: new English-language monographs include William Darby and Jack Du Bois, *American Film Music: Major Composers, Techniques, Trends, 1915–1990* (Jefferson, N. C.: McFarland, 1990); Christopher Palmer, *The Composer in Hollywood* (London and New York: Marion Boyars, 1990); Caryl Flinn, *Strains of Utopia: Gender, Nostalgia, and Hollywood Film Music* (Princeton: Princeton Univ. Press, 1992); Kathryn Kalinak, *Settling the Score: Music and the Classical Hollywood Film*, Wisconsin Studies in Film (Madison: Univ. of Wisconsin Press, 1992); Michel Chion, *Audio-Vision: Sound on Screen*, Claudia Gorbman, trans. and ed. (New York: Columbia Univ. Press, 1994); George Burt, *The Art of Film Music: Special Emphasis on Hugo Friedhofer, Alex North, David Raksin, Leonard Rosenman* (Boston: Northeastern Univ. Press, 1994); and Royal S. Brown, *Overtones and Undertones:*

Reading Film Music (Berkeley: Univ. of California Press, 1994). See also the landmark review-essay, focused on the books of Flinn and Kalinak, by James Buhler and David Neumeyer in the *Journal of the American Musicological Society* 47 (1994), 364–85; much has changed in the twenty years since the same journal published the review by Odegard (cited in n. 3, above), in which he complained of film music's neglect!

CHAPTER 2. FIRST STAGES, DIMLY LIT

1. Key pioneering works on film's prehistory include: Georges-Michel Coissac, *Histoire du cinématographe: De ses origines à nos jours* (Paris: Éditions du *Cinéopse*, 1925); Terry Ramsaye, *A Million and One Nights: A History of the Motion Picture through 1925*, 2 vols. (New York: Simon & Schuster, 1926; rpt. in 1 vol., 1986); Georges Sadoul, *Histoire générale du cinéma*, vol. 1: *L'Invention du cinéma, 1832–1897* (Paris: Denoël, 1946); Gordon Hendricks, *The Edison Motion Picture Myth* (1961), *Beginnings of the Biograph: The Story of the Invention of the Mutoscope and the Biograph and Their Supplying Camera* (1964), and *The Kinetoscope: America's First Commercially Successful Motion Picture Exhibitor* (1966), all three studies reprinted in his *Origins of the American Film* (New York: Arno Press, 1972); C. W. Ceram, *Archaeology of the Cinéma*, 1st American ed., Richard Winston, trans. (New York: Harcourt, Brace & World, 1965); and Jacques Deslandes, *Histoire comparée du cinéma*, vol. 1: *De la cinématique au cinématographe, 1826–1896* (Paris: Casterman, 1966).

Other useful sources: Martin Quigley, *Magic Shadows: The Story of the Origin of Motion Pictures* (Washington, D.C.: Georgetown Univ. Press, 1948); Heinrich Fränkel, *Unsterblicher Film: Die grosse Chronik von der Laterna Magica bis zum Tonfilm* (Munich: Kindler, 1956); Kenneth MacGowan, "Many Inventors and Inventions," *Behind the Screen* (1965), 25–84; Gianni Rondolino, "Archaeologia del cinema," in *Storia del cinema*, vol. 1 (Torino: Unione Tipografico, Editrice Torinese, 1977), 3–37; Michael Chanan, *The Dream That Kicks: The Prehistory and Early Years of Cinema in Britain* (London: Routledge & Kegan Paul, 1980); and Brian Coe, *The History of Movie Photography* (London: Ash and Grant, 1981).

Ramsaye prefaces his history with a fanciful 11,000-word essay on "The Prehistory of the Screen"—perhaps the earliest use of the word in this context. In his view, motion pictures were truly prehistoric and "overdue many, many centuries ago" . . . "the realization of the age-old Wish of the world" (pp. xxxvii and xxxviii). The "Wish," while never precisely defined, would seem to represent elemental human desire: see the passage from this essay cited in n. 9.

2. Some valuable studies are by E. I. Sponable, "Historical Development of Sound Films," *Journal of the Society of Motion Picture [and Television] Engineers* (*SMPE Journal*) 48, nos. 4 and 5 (April and May 1947), 275–303 and 407–22; Edward W. Kellogg, "History of Sound Motion Pictures," *SMPE Journal* 64, nos. 6, 7, and 8 (June, July, and Aug. 1955), 291–302, 356–74, and 422–37; MacGowan, "The Coming of Sound to the Screen," *Quarterly Journal of Film, Radio and Television* 10, no. 2 (Winter 1955), 136–45, rpt. as "The Inventive Struggle, 1906–1926," in *Behind the Screen*, 275–86; Peter Ford, "The History of Sound Recording, Part IV: Motion Picture and Television Sound Recording," *Recorded Sound* 2, no. 12 (Oct. 1963), 146–54; Geduld, *The Birth of the Talkies* (1975); John G. Frayne et al., "A Short History of Motion Picture Sound Recording in the United States," *SMPTE Journal* 85, no. 7 (July 1976), 515–28; and Douglas Gomery, "The Coming of Sound: Technological Change in the American Film Industry," in Weis and Belton, *Film Sound*, 5–24. See also Raymond Fielding, ed., *A Technological History of Motion Pictures and Television: An Anthology from the Pages of the Journal of the Society of Motion Picture and Television Engineers* (Berkeley and Los Angeles: Univ. of California Press, 1967; rpt. 1979); and Gorbman, "Annotated Bibliography on Film Sound," in Weis and Belton, *Film Sound*, 427–45.

3. In addition to works cited in n. 1, the following surveys of early cinema, published between 1945 and 1975, have been helpful in writing this chapter: Sadoul, *Histoire générale du cinéma*, vol. 2: *Les Pionniers du cinéma (De Méliès à Pathé), 1897–1909* (Paris: Éditions Denoël, 1947); Rachel Low and Roger Manvell, *The History of the British Film, 1896–1906*, and Low, *The History of the British Film, 1906–1914* (London: George Allen & Unwin, 1948 and 1949); Deslandes and Jacques Richard, *Histoire comparée du cinéma*, vol. 2: *Du cinématographe au cinéma, 1896–1906* (Paris: Casterman, 1966); and Jerzy Toeplitz, *Geschichte des Films, 1895–1928* (Munich: Rogner & Bernhard, 1975).

Important recent scholarly work on early cinema can be found in these anthologies and special issues: *Cinema 1900/1906*, 2 vols. (Brussels: International Federation of Film Archives (FIAF), 1982), a collection of papers from a seminal conference in Brighton, England, spring 1978, with a filmography compiled by André Gaudreault; Peter Lehman, ed., "Silent Film: History, Aesthetics & Exhibition," *Wide Angle* 3, no. 1 (1979); John L. Fell, ed., *Film before Griffith* (Berkeley and Los Angeles: Univ. of California Press, 1983), containing reprints of articles from several English and American journals; "Archives, Document, Fiction: Films before 1907/Le cinéma devant 1907," *Iris* (Paris) 2, no. 1 (1er semestre 1984); Marcel Ohms et al., "Les Pionniers du cinéma," *Les Cahiers de la cinémathèque*, no. 41 (Winter 1984); Claude Beylie et al., "1895–1910: Les Pionniers du cinéma français," *L'Avant-scène cinéma*, no. 334 (Nov. 1984); Tino Balio, ed., *The American Film Industry* (1985), especially 3–102 ("Part I: A Novelty Spawns Small Businesses, 1894–1908"); Thomas Elsaesser, ed., with Adam Barker, *Early Cinema: Space, Frame, Narrative* (London: BFI Publishing, 1990); and Tom Gunning, ed., "Early Cinema: From Origins to 1913," *Persistence of Vision*, no. 19 (1991). See also the various items published since 1981 in conjunction with the annual festivals at Pordenone ("Giornate del cinema muto di Pordenone"), many edited by Paulo Cherchi Usai, replete with articles and filmographies: e.g., *Vitagraph Co. of America: Il cinema prima di Hollywood*, Usai, ed., in collaboration with LC et al. (Pordenone: Edizione Studio Tesi, 1987).

Of importance, too, are the following individual works: John Barnes, *The Beginnings of the Cinema in England* (London: David & Charles; New York: Barnes & Noble, 1976); Anthony Slide, *Aspects of American Film History Prior to 1920* (Metuchen, N.J.: Scarecrow Press, 1978); Aldo Bernardini, *Cinema muto italiano*, 3 vols., Grandi opere series (Rome & Bari: Laterza, 1980–81); and Kemp R. Niver, *Early Motion Pictures: The Paper Print Collection in the Library of Congress*, Bebe Bergsten, ed. (Washington, D.C.: LC (Motion Picture, Broadcasting and Recorded Sound Division), 1985). The following recent monographs by two of our foremost scholars are indispensable: Charles Musser, *The Emergence of Cinema: The American Screen to 1907*, History of the American Cinema, vol. 1 (New York: Charles Scribner's Sons, 1990); Musser, *Before the Nickelodeon: Edward S. Porter and the Edison Manufacturing Company*, the UCLA Film and Television Archive Studies in History, Criticism and Theory (Berkeley and Los Angeles: Univ. of California Press, 1991); Musser, with Carol Nelson, *High-Class Moving Pictures: Lyman H. Howe and the Forgotten Era of Traveling Exhibition, 1880–1920* (Princeton: Princeton Univ. Press, 1991); and Gunning, *D. W. Griffith and the Origins of American Narrative Films: The Early Years at Biograph* (Urbana: Univ. of Illinois Press, 1991). Finally, at the same time as Musser's *Emergence of Cinema*, Scribner also published vols. 2 and 3 in the History of the American Cinema series: Eileen Bowser, *The Transformation of Cinema, 1907–1915*, and Richard Koszarski, *An Evening's Entertainment: The Age of the Silent Feature Picture, 1915–1928*.

4. *The Technique of Film Music* (1975), 15–21. The essay by O'Neill is "Music for Stage Plays," *Proceedings of the [Royal] Musical Association* 37 (1910–11), 85–102; from the same source Manvell and Huntley also cite George Bernard Shaw, "The Reminiscences of a Quinquagenarian" 17–27.

5. See Berg, *Investigation*, 6–8, and Pauli, *Filmmusik: Stummfilm*, 39–40.

6. Erdmann and Becce, *Allgemeines Handbuch der Filmmusik* (1927); London, *Film Music* (1936); Eisler, *Composing for the Films* (1947); Kracauer, *Theory of Film* (1960); Lissa, *Aesthetik der Filmmusik* (1965). Berg cites only those writers published in English. Pauli uses German sources when available, including the Adorno and Eisler edition of *Komposition für den Film* (1969), but he is equally familiar with English sources, including Berg. Both writers also refer to brief passages in Ernest Lindgren, *The Art of the Film*, 2d ed. (London: George Allen & Unwin; New York: Macmillan, 1963; rpt. New York: Collier Books, 1970), and to Manvell and Huntley, *The Technique of Film Music.*

7. *Unheard Melodies* (1987), chap. 2, pp. 31–52, and see the summary of "arguments" given on p. 53.

8. *Investigation*, 43. Cf. the following statements: "At the outset . . . there was little or no connection between music and the film it accompanied"—London, *Film Music*, 40. "Any music would do if it were only music and fairly popular at that. The important thing was musical accompaniment as such"—Kracauer, *Theory of Film*, 133. "From the very beginning, music was regarded as an indispensable accompaniment. . . . [But] at first, the music played bore no special relationship to the films; an accompaniment of any kind was sufficient"—Lindgren, *The Art of the Film*, 183.

It should be noted that London, the earliest author cited in the group above, placed his statement within an elaborate schematic overview of film music's early history, quite similar to the one presented by Erdmann and Becce. As these men saw it, film music progressed through a series of stages based on its performing medium: first, mechanical instruments (e.g., barrel organ, orchestrion, and phonograph, used—with seeming appropriateness—to cover the mechanical noises made by projectors); next, the pianist (sometimes aided or replaced by a lecturer)—an intermediary stage; and finally, the silent film orchestra, used to "illustrate" films. The initial stages (Erdmann and Becce called them "vor-Episoden") were said to have lasted until 1912 or 1913; thereafter, orchestral accompaniments took over. This outline possesses clarity, but lacks any real factual basis. One does better to regard these various "stages" as coexistent from one end of the silent period to the other.

9. *Film Music*, 35. Cf. Ramsaye's poetic explanation of film's psychological power: "In the twilighted theatre, lulled with music's emotional and motional rhythms, we see our day-dream wishes ethereally materialized before us at the screen's window, which opens on the land of heart's desire"—*A Million and One Nights*, LXX.

10. Mayer's writings include: *Harlequin in His Element: The English Pantomime, 1806–1386* (Cambridge, Mass.: Harvard Univ. Press, 1969), appendix B, "Pantomime Music" (pp. 337–62); "The Music of Melodrama," in *Performance and Popular Drama: Aspects of Popular Entertainment in Theatre, Film and Television, 1800–1976*, David Bradby, Louis James, and Bernard Sharratt, eds. (Cambridge: Cambridge Univ. Press, 1980), 49–63; and "Nineteenth Century Theatre Music," *Theatre Notebook* 30 (1976), 115–22. By Shapiro, see, especially, "Action Music in American Pantomime and Melodrama, 1730–1913," *American Music* 2, no. 4 (Winter 1984), 49–72; articles on "Melodrama" and "Pantomime" in *The New Grove Dictionary of American Music* (1986); and "Nineteenth-Century Melodrama: from *A Tale of Mystery* to *Monte Cristo*," in "Bits and Pieces: Music for Theater," Lowell Lindgren, ed., *Harvard Library Bulletin*, NS, 2, no. 4 (Winter 1991), 54–73, with a response by Laurence Senelick, pp. 74–77; also her introduction to *The Touchstone, or Harlequin Traveller* (1779), by Charles Dibdin, Music for London Entertainment 1660–1800, series D, vol. 1 (London: Stainer & Bell, 1990), ix–xix. See also Frank Rahill, *The World of Melodrama* (University Park, Penn., and London: Pennsylvania State Univ. Press, 1967), chapter 16: "The Opera and Music in Melodrama" (pp. 120–28); and Marian Smith, "Borrowings and Original Music: A Dilemma for the Ballet-Pantomime Composer," *Dance Research* 6, no. 2 (Autumn 1988), 3–29.

11. David Mayer (text) and Matthew Scott (musical arrangements), *Four Bars of "Agit": Incidental Music for Victorian and Edwardian Melodrama* (London: Samuel French, 1983). Included in the collection are 60 melos which the editors have mostly indexed (p. 14), in two large categories: *character signatures* (Female [heroine, comic, villainess/adventuress], Male [hero, comic, villain], Lovers, Children, and Elderly persons); and *emotional states/attitudes/affects* (comedy, cheer/merriment, distress/depression/tragedy, sentiment, pathos, fear, expectation/excitement/danger, military, storm, death, lively/comic bustle, violence/pursuit/struggle [hurries and agits], and evil/sinister/suspense/impending danger/mysteriosos). The remaining categories are more formal than narrative: *curtain rise, curtail fall, segue*. As in various silent film anthologies, many pieces are assigned multiple functions: e.g., no. 1, consisting of 8 bars in common time, *moderato*, in F major, is indexed under curtain rise, pathos, military, and lively/comic bustle.

12. *Music of the Shadows/Musica delle ombre: The Use of Musical Accompaniment with Silent Films, 1896–1936*, Le Giornate del cinema muto (di Pordenone), "Supplemento a *Griffithiana*, n. 38/39 (ottobre 1990)," See pp. 20–23, containing lists of items under the headings "Forerunners: Music in the Live Theater," "Forerunners: Music and Pre-Cinema Shows," and "Music and Cinema: The First Years."

13. See Robinson, *World Cinema: A Short History* (London: Eyre Methuen; New York: Stein & Day, 1973), 1.

14. Muybridge's Zoopraxi (no) scope lectures of the 1880s and 1890s, in America and Europe, are prime examples of music-less optical shows: see the accounts in Gordon Hendricks, *Eadweard Muybridge: The Father of the Motion Picture* (New York: Grossman Publishers, 1975), 149–76 and 213–18; and in Robert Haas, *Muybridge: Man in Motion* (Berkeley and Los Angeles: Univ. of California Press, 1976), 127–58 and 167–73. See also the drawing of lecturer Albert Smith's "Mont-Blanc Show" (1852), in Detlev Hoffmann and Almut Junker, *Laterna Magica: Lichtbilder aus Menschenwelt und Götterwelt*, Winfried Ranke, ed. (Berlin: Verlag Frölich & Kaufmann, 1982), 67, plate 64: no musicians are present. But in Georges Sadoul's *Histoire générale du cinéma*, vol. 1, pp. 205–6, a program for l'abbé Moigno's "séances" at his *Théâtre de la Science illustrée* includes music before, between, and after the lectures. (Sadoul's source for the program is presumably Moigno's *Traité de projections* (1872), which he cites in his bibliography. Note that on p. 205 he dates these shows 1877; the correct date, 1872, is given on p. 95.)

15. Here is a list of six works, produced between the early eighteenth and mid-nineteenth centuries, that depict lantern shows at which musicians are present: (1) Engraving after Schenau, ca. 1765, in Hoffmann and Junker, *Laterna magica*, 10, plate 2; also in Arthur Pougin, "Fantasmagorie," *Dictionnaire historique et pittoresque du théâtre* (Paris: Firmin-Didot, 1885; rpt. in 2 vols., Plan-de-la-Tour [Var]: Éditions d'Aujourd'hui, 1985), 357; and in Samuel McKechnie, *Popular Entertainments through the Ages* (London: Sampson, Low, Marston, 1931), plate facing p. 176. (2) Oil painting ascribed to Trautmann, ca. 1765, in Hoffmann and Junker, *Laterna magica*, 35, plate 22. (3) French late eighteenth-century drawing in Helmut Zeraschi, *Drehorgeln* (Bern: Hallwag, 1979), plate 20; also in Fränkel, *Unsterblicher Film*, 211. (4) English late eighteenth-century drawing in "Laterna Magica," *Enciclopedia dello spettacolo*, vol. 6 (1959), plate 176, facing p. 1218. (5) Illustration from *The Magic Lantern*, 1822, in Ceram, *Archaeology of the Cinema*, plate 34. (6) Victorian illustration in Coe, *The History of Movie Photography*, 91. Nos. 1–5 are all set in drawing-rooms and show musicians standing alongside lanternists, playing small mechanical instruments; no. 6 shows a theatrical performance, with a woman seated at a harmonium and a lecturer standing beside her, both to the left of the screen.

Other items depict itinerant lanternists outdoors, some carrying or playing small mechanical instruments themselves, some with companion musicians: (1) Engraving after

Bouchardon entitled "L'orgue de Barbarie ou plutost d'Allemagne," one of a series produced between 1737 and 1746, in Hoffmann and Junker, *Laterna magica*, 6, plate 1; also in Zeraschi, *Drehorgeln*, 45. (2) Porcelain figure by Kandler (one of a series produced between 1756 and 1763) in ibid., plate 1. (3) Oil painting by Seekatz ca. 1760 in Hoffmann and Junker, 34, plate 21. (4) A pair of engravings from a series by Deisch (1763) in Zeraschi, plates 22–23. (5) An engraving by Bartolomeo Pinelli, 1809, in Rondolino, *Storia del cinema* (1977), vol. 1, p. 13. Finally, see Quigley, *Magic Shadows*, 112–14, and Ceram, *Archaeology of the Cinema*, 88, for information about "posed motion photographs" of dance scenes shown at the Philadelphia Academy of Music, 5 Feb. 1870, with orchestral accompaniment.

16. Cecil Hepworth, *Came the Dawn: Memories of a Film Pioneer* (London: Phoenix House, 1951), 31–32; cited in Manvell and Huntley, *The Technique of Film Music*, 20. Hepworth does not make clear whether only two pieces were played or more than two; if only two, his sister might have changed her manner of playing in an improvisatory fashion, to make the first piece seem increasingly more "threatening" as a build-up to the second piece. Also, if he correctly remembers the composers, the piece by Jensen might have been "Am Meeresstrand," from the composer's *Romantische Studien*, Op. 8, vol. 2, no. 8: the music, marked "Leidenschaftlich bewegt" begins softly and builds to "wild" passionate climaxes.

17. Four compositions by Schumann are in Rapée, *Motion Picture Moods* (1924): "Andante Pathétique No. 1," an excerpt from the slow movement of the Piano Quintet, Op. 44, arr. Otto Langey (under "Funeral," pp. 161–62); *Jagdlied*, from *Waldszenen*, Op. 82, Max Vogrich, ed., and *Jägerliedchen*, from *Album für die Jugend*, Op. 68 (under "Hunting," pp. 186–89 and 191); and *Träumerei*, from *Kinderszenen*, Op. 15 (under "Quietude and Purity," p. 596). Two pieces by Jensen are included: *Happy Wanderer*, rev. by William Scharfenberg (under "Joyfulness or Happiness," pp. 202–5); and *The Mill/Die Mühle* (under "Railroad," pp. 608–11).

18. "On observera combien le musicien a suivi de près le 'découpage' de la pantomime d'Émile Reynaud"—*Histoire comparée du cinéma*, vol. 1, p. 293, caption to fig. 94, containing music for *Un bon Bock*; here Deslandes also emphasizes the historical significance of these scores: "Il s'agit de la première *musique de film* jamais écrite." For the cover to *Pantomimes lumineuses* (Paris: G. Ducrotois, n.d.) and the first page of *Pauvre Pierrot*, see pp. 291–92, figs. 92–93. For detailed history of Reynaud's work, including a list of all his film programs presented at the *Théâtre Optique* through 28 Feb. 1900 (when the series concluded), and also a photographic portrait of Paulin, see Gérard Talon, "Émile Reynaud, 1844–1918," *L'Anthologie du cinéma*, no. 69 (Oct. 1972), supplement to *L'Avant-scène du cinéma*, no. 129. Whether Paulin also composed music for subsequent programs is not known.

19. See, e.g., André Wormser's music for *L'Enfant Prodigue: Pantomime en 3 Actes de Michel Carré fils* (Paris: E. Biardot, [1890]), published both in piano score (209 pp.) and in a five-movement suite for orchestra; also, Raoul Pugno's music for *Pour le Drapeau!: Mimodrame en trois actes de Henri Amic* (Paris: Alphonse Leduc, 1895), in piano score (163 pp.). Scores of smaller dimensions include Gabriel Pierné's music for *Pantomime de la Statue*, Scenario de Paul Arène (Paris: Paris-Noël (Supplément), 1889)—a 12-page piano score identified as Op. 24, with the scenario on facing pages but with no cues over the music; and Emile Schwartz's piano music for *Taylor pour Messieurs*, in Paul L'heureux, *Pantomimes* (Paris: J. B. Ferreyol, 1891)—"libretto," pp. 131–59, music, pp. 161–84. (There are nine librettos in this volume, but only the one for *Taylor* includes music.) Also, in Raoul de Najac's *Petit traité de pantomime à l'usage des gens du monde* (Paris: A. Hennuyer, 1887), one of the author's listed credits is a one-act solo pantomime, *Le Retour d'Arlequin*, for which piano music by André Martinet is said to be published "in 4-o"; Najac advises that "le piano ou mieux un petit orchestre doit acompagner le spectacle parce qu'un silence

complet attristerait le public. Si vous avez un compositeur à votre disposition, demandez-lui d'écrire une partition s'adaptant à votre livret" (p. 8).

Wormser and Najac were closely associated with the Cercle Funambulesque: a high-minded organization established in 1888 for the production of pantomimes, led by Felix Larcher, whose stated aims included "a close and constant adaptation of the musical phrase to the situation on stage, to put the utterance of the gesture into the orchestra—that is to say, in the last analysis, to apply quite simply the best theories of Wagner to the pantomime." Archer's statement, translated from an 1892 interview with Paul Hugounet, appears in Robert Storey, *Pierrots on the Stage of Desire: Nineteenth-Century French Literary Artists and the Comic Pantomime* (Princeton: Princeton Univ. Press, 1985), 287. Also see pp. 288–93, for discussion of brief passages from Hugounet, *La Musique et la pantomime* (Paris: Kolb, [1892]), a book of interviews with "composers of the Cercle," including Wormser, and pp. 317–33, for a valuable "Handlist of Pantomime Scenarios."

20. *Unheard Melodies*, 15.

21. The Vitascope premiere at Koster and Bial's took place on 23 April 1896, and was described enthusiastically in the *Times* the next day (Friday); see "Edison's Vitascope Cheered," *NYT*, 24 April 1896, p. 5. (Initially there seems to have been uncertainty as to when the Vitascope's opening night would be: see Koster and Bial's advertisements in the *NYT* on 19, 21, and 23 April, pp. 11, 7, and 7. Advertisements and playbills indicate that Vitascope projections were featured through the week beginning Monday, 17 Aug.: see the Koster and Bial's programs in the Harvard Theater Collection, Pusey Library, in the "Manhattan Theatre" folder. (The theater began as the Manhattan Opera House, but changed to Koster and Bial's in 1893; it closed in 1901.) For numerous additional documents concerning the early history of the Vitascope, see Musser, *The Emergence of Cinema*, chap. 4 ("The Vitascope"), 109–32, and *Before the Nickelodeon*, chap. 4 ("Cinema, a Screen Novelty: 1895–1897"), 57–102.

22. *The Emergence of Cinema*, 122–24.

23. See Hendricks, *Beginnings of the Biograph*, 39–51, and Musser, *The Emergence of Cinema*, 150–57.

24. This theme is eloquently developed in Brooks McNamara, "'Scavengers of the Amusement World': Popular Entertainment and the Birth of the Movies," in *American Pastimes* (exhibition catalog) (Brockton, Mass: Brockton Art Center, Fuller Memorial, 1976), 17–19. McNamara notes that the films in the Vitascope debut at Koster and Bial's "were treated essentially as a vaudeville act and were given the second best position on the bill (just before intermission). . . . Of the six films shown, four—and stretching the point a bit, all six—borrowed their content from the popular entertainment tradition of the day. The skirt [or serpentine] dance, for example, had been popularized at London's Gaiety Theatre, home of burlesque and early musical comedies. The unannounced crowd scene shown that night was abstracted from a play called *The Milk White Flag*. . . .The umbrella dance, performed by a vaudeville team, the Leigh Sisters, was probably borrowed from the blackface minstrel stage, and the burlesque boxing, also presented by a pair of vaudevillians, Walton and Mayon, was an ancient routine seen often in the circus, burlesque, and in the pantomime tradition."

25. See Musser, *The Emergence of Cinema*, 117, and *Before the Nickelodeon*, 63–64 and 84. In the latter, p. 63, he quotes a promotional brochure of Raff and Gammon, *The Vitascope* (New York: n.d., [1896]), which suggests that "a subject can be shown for ten or fifteen minutes if desired, although four or five minutes is better."

26. *Investigation*, 64 and 70. Berg may here be seen to contradict his previous statement, cited earlier (n.8), that in the early days of the motion picture "an accompaniment of any kind was acceptable."

27. "Amusements," *New York Daily News*, 24 April 1896 (clipping in the Raff and Gammon Collection, Baker Library, Harvard Business School), cited in Musser, *Before the Nickelodeon*, 61–62.

28. For example, there is no reference to music in "Edison's Vitascope," *NY Dramatic Mirror*, 2 May 1896, p. 21, nor in the *Times* review cited earlier (n. 21); however, Berg cites the latter for its comment that "when the hall was darkened . . . a buzzing and roaring were heard in the turret," as evidence that such noises were a source of "aural irritation," necessitating the use of music. See his *Investigation*, 15–16: his source is not the original review, but a partial reprint (one paragraph) in Lewis Jacobs, *The Rise of the American Film: A Critical History* (New York: Harcourt, Brace, 1939; 2d ed., New York: Teachers College Press, 1968), 3–4. Both reviews, together with a shorter one from the *NY Clipper*, are given without their titles in Anthony Slide, *Selected Film Criticism, 1896–1911* (Metuchen, N.J., and London: Scarecrow Press, 1982), 33–35.

29. In programs from 1894 through early 1896, various musical groups and directors are named: e.g., "Mr. Gustave Kerker, Conductor, and Mr. Emile Levy, Accompanist" (week beginning Monday, 15 Dec. 1895); "Max Gabriel, Music Director," and intermission music by "Dr. Leo Sommer's Blue Hungarian Band" (24 Feb. 1896). Beginning with the program for 30 March 1896, credits for conductors or music directors are no longer given, though Sommer's band continues to be featured. See, e.g., the first page of Koster and Bial's bill for the week of the Vitascope's debut (20 April 1896), reproduced in Ramsaye, *A Million and One Nights*, facing p. 236: after the Vitascope (no. 8) comes a ten-minute intermission by the Blue Hungarian Band "in the Grand Promenade." (Ramsaye errs by calling the Vitascope the "closing number" on the bill: his illustration contains only the first half of the program.) Moreover, at the start of the program is an overture (Auber's *Masaniello*), and among the other numbers were several that must have required musical accompaniment, including "Cora Caselli, Eccentric Dancer" (no. 3), and "Mons. and Mme. Ducreux-Ceralduc, French Duettists" (no. 6); likewise, the films included an Umbrella Dance and a Serpentine Dance: Berg, *Investigation*, 65, and the passage from McNamara, cited in n. 24.

30. See the plate in Quigley, *Magic Shadows*, facing p. 161. Reductions of the same illustration can be seen both in MacGowan, *Behind the Screen*, 84, and in Musser, *The Emergence of Cinema*, 132, as it appeared on the letterhead of the New York Vitascope Company; and also in Musser on p. 125, within a Vitascope advertisement from the *Milwaukee Sentinel* (26 July 1896). Another drawing—supposed to represent an actual exhibition of the Vitascope at Koster and Bial's—was published in the *New York Herald*, 3 May 1896, rpt. in Ramsaye, *A Million and One Nights*, facing p. 233, and in *Emergence of Cinema*, 117; but in this illustration it is impossible to determine whether musicians are present. (The same is true of the frontispiece to *The Emergence of Cinema:* a film poster, ca. 1900, depicting a screening of "Edison's Moving Pictures" in a darkened theater.)

31. *The Technique of Film Music*, 21. I have not seen an important item listed by Robinson, *Music of the Shadows*, 22: apparently it is a program for the debut of the *cinématographe* at the Grand Café which credits the music to M. Emile Maraval, "pianiste-compositeur," using a Gaveau piano. For examples of English advertisements and playbills mentioning musicians featured in variety shows, though not specifically as accompanists for films, see the following: the program for the Royal Canterbury Theatre of Varieties, London, 14 Aug. 1896, which includes Paul's Theatrograph on the bill, in Barnes, *Beginnings of the Cinema in England*, 105, plate 38; the 1896 or 1897 "Scenimatographe" advertisement reproduced in Ceram, *Archaeology of the Cinema*, plate 225; and later programs of similar content in Low and Manvell, *History of British Film*, figs. 12, 13, and 15.

32. *Histoire comparée du cinéma*, vol. 1, p. 249. Byng is also named as the conductor for

the Empire Theatre in the program dated 11 May 1896, given in Low and Manvell, *History of British Film*, fig. 9.

33. Barnes, *Beginnings of the Cinema in England*, 117.

34. Musser, *The Emergence of Cinema*, 91.

35. For information on Skladanowsky, I have relied mainly upon Manfred Lichtenstein, "I Fratelli Skladanowsky/The Brothers Skladanowsky," in *Prima di Caligari: Cinema tedesco, 1895–1920 / Before Caligari: German Cinema, 1895–1920*, Paolo Cherchi Usai, Lorenzo Codelli, et al., eds. (Pordenone: Edizioni Biblioteca dell'Immagine, 1990), 312–22; Theo Fürstenau, ed., *dif: Filmkundliche Mitteilungen* (untitled special issue, Wiesbaden-Biebrich, Schloss: Deutsches Institut für Filmkunde, 1970); Albert Narath, *Max Skladanowsky*, Schriftenreihe der Deutschen Kinemathek, no. 22 (Berlin: Deutsche Kinemathek, 1970); and Deslandes, *Histoire comparée*, vol. 1, 257–63. I have been unable to consult Friedrich von Zglinicki, *Der Weg des Films: Die Geschichte der Kinematographie und ihrer Vorlaüfer* (Berlin: Rembrandt, 1956), which Deslandes terms the only extended accurate study of Skaladanowksy based on documentary evidence; see, however, the information from Zglinicki cited in n. 37. See also Ceram, *Archaelogy of Cinema*, 146–48, and plates 206–9; Fränkel, *Unsterblicher Film*, 220–23 and 228; and Rune Waldekranz, "La nascita del cinema in Scandinavia," in *Schiave bianco allo specchio: le origini del cinema in Scandinavia*, Catalogo della quinta edizione delle Giornate del cinema muto di Pordenone, 29 settembre–5 ottobre, 1986 (Pordenone: Edizioni Studio-Tesi, 1986), 33.

36. See Prox, "Perspektiven," in Seidler, ed., *Stummfilmmusik gestern und heute*, 11, for a photograph of a bass part, reproduced without comment. The music is for no. 6 (*Kamarinskaja*). My inventory and analysis of the Skladanowsky music is based on what I found in 1978 at the Film- und Fernsehakademie; I thank Gero Gändert for allowing me to make photocopies of all available parts at that time. I also thank Gerrit Thies of the Stiftung Deutsche Kinemathek for enabling me to obtain photographs of four pages from the collection.

37. A humorous example of a performer's signature can be seen in the flute part given in Fig. 1: it appears to read "S. Samehtini, 4 Mei 1896, Amsterdam," with "ninini" appended to the name, perhaps by another player. Other examples include "Hartman Nielsen, Copenhagen, Juli 1896," on the back of the third trombone part for no. 4; and on the top left side of the first horn part for the Introduction, "Amsterdam, Circus Arena, Fritz von Haarlem" with two other names below, labeled first and second horn. The top right side of the same part has penciled in "Grüsse am Herrn Collego."

At the Film- und Fernsehakademie, the music was stored together with a page of Zglinicki's stationery, with the following text (which I have translated from the German): "Unique documents for film history / Very valuable museum pieces! BIOSKOP: A portion of the original score with handwritten annotations by Max Skladanowsky for musical accompaniment of the celebrated exhibition of the Bioskop in the Berlin Wintergarten on 1 November 1895. This was the first 'film'-screening before a paying public in Germany and in Europe." Continuing in this vein, the rest of the text concerns Skladanowsky's historical significance as an inventor of motion pictures—formerly a subject of much disagreement. Zglinicki's text seems to paraphrase the earliest printed reference to this music I have seen, in the reminiscences of Erich Skladanowsky (son to Max), "An der 'Berliner Flora' fing es an," *Deutsche Filmkunst* 3 (1955), 268: "So geschah es dann, dass die erste öffentliche Uraufführung photographisch erzeugter Positivfilme mit Zwischentiteln in Druckschrift und eigensgeschriebener Begleitmusik am 1. November 1895 im Berliner Wintergarten vor 1500 Besuchern stattfand. . . ."

38. For identification of Krüger, see "Daten der Stummfilmzeit," in Fürstenau, *dif*, [15], and Narath, *Max Skladanowsky*, 24—the latter being the source which describes the composer as Skladanowsky's friend.

39. Lichtenstein, "The Brothers Skladanowsky," in *Before Caligari*, 316. Deslandes (*Histoire comparée*, vol. 1, pp. 258–59) states that Skladanowsky made nine films during the summer of 1895, but he gives only eight titles for the premiere (omitting the acrobatic duo); Fürstenau (*dif* [15]), also states that nine films were made, but does not identify them; Ceram (*Archaeology of the Cinema*, 147), lists seven films for the premiere in a different order from both Lichtenstein and Deslandes, omitting the Serpentine Dance (which he says Skladanowsky filmed in 1896) and the Apotheosis, but including a film of "two gymnasts working on the horizontal bar." Ceram's list is identical to one given by Rudolph Oertel in *Filmspiegel: ein Brevier aus der Welt des Films* (Vienna: Wilhelm Frick, 1941), 62, and also by Oertel in *Macht und Magie des Films: Weltgeschichte einer Massensuggestion* (Vienna: Europa, 1959), 46. Oertel cites as his source Hans Traub, *Als man anfing zu filmen* (Berlin: UFA-Lehrschau, 1940).

40. *Loin du bal* was apparently heard regularly during performances by the celebrated Loie Fuller, known in part as the "inventor" of the Serpentine Dance, which she brought to Paris in 1892, after successful appearances in Germany. See John Ernest Crawford Flitch, *Modern Dancing and Dancers* (London: Grant Richards, 1912), chap. 6 ("The Serpentine Dance"), 81–88; and Sally Roberson Summer, "Loie Fuller: From the Theater of Popular Entertainment to the Parisian Avant-Garde" (Ph.D. diss., New York Univ., 1979). A brief entry on Ernst Gillet (1856–1940), Parisian composer and cellist, is in *Baker's Biographical Dictionary of Musicians*, 8th ed., rev. by Nicholas Slonimsky (New York: Schirmer Books, 1991): it notes that *Loin du bal* was "a perennial drawing-room favorite." So it would seem, from the inclusion of the piece in *Masterpieces of Piano Music*, Albert E. Weir, comp. and ed. (New York: Carl Fischer, 1918), 365–67. (Its subtitle in this volume is "Ball-room Echoes.")

According to Ceram, the Serpentine Dance was "one of the most popular numbers on the variety stage of the nineties." See *Archaeology of the Cinema*, caption to plates 210 and 211: the former has a strip from the Skladanowsky film, showing Mlle. Ançion in mid-performance; the latter, a still photograph from Edison's film of the same dance as performed by "Annabelle the Dancer (Annabelle Whitford Moore)."

41. The violin partly plays the melody line of Gillet's waltz, partly accompanimental figures on the second and third beats of each measure.

42. Deslandes, *Histoire comparée*, vol. 1, p. 261; Ronald S. Magliozzi, comp. and ed., *Treasures from the Film Archives: A Catalog of Silent Fiction Films Held by FIAF Archives* (Metuchen, N.J., and London: Scarecrow Press, 1988), 106. The films listed by Magliozzi are *Komische Begegnung im Tiergarten zu Stockholm* (copies in Stiftung Deutsche Kinemathek, Berlin, and Svenska Filminstitutet, Stockholm) and *Eine Lustige Gesellschaft vor dem Tivoli in Kopenhagen* (Deutsche Kinemathek).

43. Lichtenstein, "The Brothers Skladanowsky," *Before Caligari*, 318. The films are *Berlin-Alexanderplatz*, *Alarm bei der Berliner Feuerwehr (depot Lindenstrasse)*, *Ausfahrt nach dem Alarm*, *Unter den Linden / Ecke Friedrichstrasse (Vom Café Bauer aus)*, and *Einfahrt eines Eisenbahnzuges Berlin-Schönholz*—in short, all "actualities."

44. The song is given in Ludwig Erk, comp. and ed., *Deutsches Liederschatz: Eine Auswahl* (Leipzig: C. F. Peters, n.d.), 1: 89. Erk, noting that the song was originally in English—*Long, Long Ago*, words and music by Thomas H. Bayly—attributes the German words to Wilhelm Weidling (1858); an arrangement of Bayly's version is in Margaret Bradford Boni, comp. and ed., *Fireside Book of Love Songs* (New York: Simon and Schuster, 1954), 38 and 40. As can be seen in Appendix part 1, the phrase "Unter den Linden"—the title of the fourth film on the "second program," as given by Lichtenstein—is penciled into a few parts following "Lang, lang ist's her."

45. Since rousing marches were often used to accompany films of military parades,

processions of fire brigades and the like, *Mit Bomben und Granaten* quite probably was played for one or both of the "alarm" films in the second program.

46. See Ceram, *Archaeology of the Cinema*, plate 228.

47. For my overview of the film's historical context I have relied primarily on Sadoul, "Le Film d'Art (France, 1908)"—chap. 31 of his *Histoire générale*, vol. 2, pp. 497–512: still the most comprehensive discussion of the company, and often cited, though Sadoul's evaluation of *L'Assassinat* is no longer fully accepted, in part because he had only an inferior copy to work with. Other useful contextual studies include René Jeanne and Charles Ford, *Histoire encyclopédique de cinéma*, vol. 1: *Le cinéma français, 1895–1929* (Paris: Laffont, 1947), 114–18; James Harding, *Saint-Saëns and His Circle* (London: Chapman & Hall, 1965), 202–4; Jean Mitry, *Histoire du cinéma, art et industrie*, vol. 1: *1895–1914* (Paris: Éditions universitaires, 1967), 252–57; Hans-Christian Schmidt, *Filmmusik*, 21–23; Anthony Slide, "*The Assassination of the Duc de Guise*," in *Magill's Survey of Cinema: Silent Films*, vol. 1, Frank N. Magill, vol. 1, ed. (Englewood Cliffs, N.J.: Salem Press, 1982), 155–57; Michael Stegemann, "Der Mord als schöne Kunst betrachtet: Camille Saint-Saëns und die Anfänge der Filmmusik," *Neue Zeitschrift für Musik* 146, no. 10 (Oct. 1985), 8–14; Stegemann, *Camille Saint-Saëns: mit Selbstzeugnissen und Bilddokumenten*, rowohlts monographien (Reinbek bei Hamburg: Rowohlt Taschenbuch, 1988), 60–73 and 82–90; and Ben Brewster, "Deep Staging in French Films, 1900–1914," in Elsaesser, ed., *Early Cinema*, 45–55. Of these, only Schmidt and the article by Stegemann offer extended discussion of the music, and both have been of great value in the writing of this chapter. (Brief analytical comments can also be found in Wolfgang Thiel, "Pariser Filmmusik-Premiere anno 1908," *Musik und Gesellschaft* 28 [1978], 712–13, likewise in Thiel, *Filmmusik in Geschichte und Gegenwart*, 125–27.)

48. For the original pre-shooting script, see Henri Lavedan, "*L'Assassinat du Duc de Guise*: Scénario en six tableaux," *La Revue du cinéma*, NS, 3, no. 15 (July 1948), 16–32; for a shot analysis ("Réduction découpage après plan à plan à la table du montage"), based on three of the best surving copies of the film, see Pierre Jenn and Michel Nagard, "*L'Assassinat du Duc de Guise* (1908)," *L'Avant-scène cinéma*, no. 334 (Nov. 1984), 57–72. (Comparison of these two versions show considerable differences between the film Lavedan envisaged and the one actually made.)

The French copies of the film analyzed by Jenn and Nygard run about twice as long as one held in MOMA: the latter, the only version which I have thus far seen—and which I have accompanied, using portions of the Saint-Saëns score—was acquired in 1947; it seems to have been the version distributed in America in 1909, as explained in Chapter Three. Brewster notes that many extant prints of the film bear the title *La Mort du Duc de Guise*, which, as Richard Abel informed him, was used for a wartime re-release: see "Deep Staging," 54, n. 7.

49. During the three and a half decades prior to *L'Assassinat* (between 1872 and 1906), he composed music for 12 operas, 4 plays (including Sophocles' *Antigone* and Racine's *Andromaque*), and 1 ballet: see the work list compiled by Daniel Fallon under "Saint-Saëns" (co-authored by James Harding), in *The New Grove Dictionary of Music and Musicians*, 6th ed., vol. 16 (1980), 404.

50. Jean Bonnerot, *Camille Saint-Saëns (1835–1921): Sa vie et son oeuvre*, Nouvelle Édition (Paris: A. Durand et fils, 1922), 187. [Originally published in 1914 as *C. Saint-Saëns.*) This seems to be the only biography of the composer containing any such information. Indeed, most biographers—save Harding and Stegemann, cited earlier—make no mention of *L'Assassinat* at all, and I have found no references in the subsequent volumes of reminiscences by the composer, nor in any editions of his letters.

51. Some sources, including Harding and Fallon, incorrectly give the date of the premiere as November 16. The performance on the 17th was actually a "répétition générale" (literally, a dress rehearsal), before a select invited audience, including members of the

press; the first performance open to the public took place the following evening, a Monday. See the listings under "Théâtres" in *Le Temps*, 17, 18, and 19 Nov. 1908, p. 3 (each day). The column on the 18th announces the event as follows: "À la salle Charras, tentative d'un haut intérêt artistique pour la Société des films d'art. On entendra [*sic!*] des oeuvres 'cinématographiques' de nos meilleurs dramaturges, où apparaissent MM. Le Bargy, A. Lambert fils, Mmes. J. Bartet, Robinne, Bovy. La musique sera représentée par MM. Saint-Saëns, Vidal, le quatuor Battaille et un excellent orchestre dirigé par M. Le Borne."

52. I am grateful to Durand (in particular, to Guy Kaufmann) for allowing me to examine its collection of parts, and for giving me a copy of the published score. In the latter, the title page reads in part "Le Film d'Art / L'ASSASSINAT DU DUC DE GUISE / TABLEAUX D'HISTOIRE / Scénario d'Henri Lavedan / Musique de / C. Saint-Saëns / (Op. 128)" (Paris: A. Durand & Fils, 1908). It is a piano reduction (35 pp.) by Léon Roques, plate no. 7223. The orchestral parts, available for rental from Durand, include flute, oboe, clarinet in A, bassoon, horn in F, piano, harmonium, and the usual strings—all with plate no. 7246. (The wind instruments have often been omitted from descriptions of the score, at least since Manvell and Huntley, *The Technique of Film Music*, 22. Thiel, in *Musik und Geschichte und Gegenwart*, terms the score an "Introduction und fünf Fragmente für Streichorchester, Klavier und Harmonium"; in la Motte-Haber and Emons, *Filmmusik: eine systematische Beschreibung*, 79, it is a "Suite für Streichorchester.") There is also an arrangement of the music by R. Branga for violin, cello, and piano, with bassoon and clarinet parts ad lib. (Paris: Durand & Cie., 1925), registered for copyright in the U.S. on 3 April 1925 (E615766).

An additional valuable source is the recording of the score performed by the USSR Ministry of Culture Symphony Orchestra, conducted by Gennadi Rozhdestvensky, on the album "Music for French Films," Melodiya C10 20459 009 (c1984), side 2, band 1. It lasts more than 18 minutes and includes most of the music found in the piano score. Even better is the recording of the complete score in its original orchestration, performed by the Ensemble Musique Oblique, on a compact disc of music by Saint-Saëns (with his Piano Quintet in A minor, Op. 14, and *Le Carnaval des animaux*): Harmonia Mundi (France) HMC 901472 (1993).

53. See Brisson, "Chronique théâtrale," *Le Temps*, 23 Nov. 1908, p. 1; also the columns cited earlier (n. 51), as well as "Spectacles du Lundi 18 Novembre," 17 Nov., p. 4. Brisson is quoted at length by Sadoul, *Histoire générale*, vol. 2, pp. 505–7, and in many subsequent sources and is given complete in Richard Abel, *French Film Theory and Criticism: A History/Anthology, 1907–1939*, vol. 1 (Princeton: Princeton Univ. Press, 1988), 50–53.

54. See Leborne, *L'Empreinte: Mimodrame en 11 tableaux*, Op. 55, Le Film d'Art (Paris: Mathot, 1908); and Gaston Berardi, *Le Secret de Myrto: Poème musicale*, Édition réduite pour cinéma (Paris: Huegel, 1909). See also Georges Huë, *Le Retour d'Ulysse: Tableaux tirés du poème d'Homère*, Le Film d'Art par Jules LeMaître (Paris: Mathot, 1909). Copies of all three scores are held in LC. *Le Retour d'Ulysse* appears to be the last Film d'Art production for which a score was commissioned.

55. ". . . un poème de M. Rostand, *le Bois sacrée*, illustré d'un ballet ou plutôt d'une vision choréographique"—"Théâtres," *Le Temps*, 19 Nov. 1908, p. 3. In the column for the 17th, one other item is listed for the evening's program: "ballet de *Terpsichore*, réglé par Mme. Mariquita, musique nouvelle de M. Paul Vidal." Vidal is also named, along with the Bataille quartet, in the announcement in the column for the 18th, cited earlier (n. 51); but Brisson makes no mention of them in his review.

56. "Un mot encore: M. Camille Saint-Saëns a écrit pour *L'Assassinat du Duc de Guise* un chef-d'oeuvre de musique symphonique. Il eût été impardonnable de n'en pas proclamer les beautés. Ce fut une des parties les plus goûtées de cette représentation un peu tâtonnante, imparfaite, mais intéressante ainsi que tout ce qui commence et promet."—Brisson, "Chronique théâtrale."

57. *Javotte: Ballet en 1 Acte et 3 Tableaux* de J. L. Croze, Musique de C. Saint-Saëns, Partition pour Piano seul (Paris: A. Durand et Fils, 1896) 14–15 and 21. For information on this work, see the biographies by Bonnerot, Harding, and Stegemann, as well as Otto Neitzel, *Camille Saint-Saëns*, Berühmter Musiker VI (Berlin: "Harmonie" (Verlagsgesellschaft für Literatur und Kunst), 1899), 61–64, and Emile Baumann, *Les Grandes formes de la musiqe: l'oeuvre de Camille Saint-Saëns*, Nouvelle Édition (Paris: Librarie Ollendorff, 1923), 448–53. I am indebted to John Ward for providing me his copy of the music.

58. Beside the indications of the beginning of each Tableau, these are the printed cues in the piano score for *L'Asssassinat*: in the Introduction, "l'annonce" (p. 3); in Tableau 1, "Entrée du Page" (p. 5), "Entrée du Duc" (p. 6), and "Départ du Duc" (p. 9); in Tableau 2, "Quatre heures sonnent" (p. 10); in Tableau 4, "l'Assassinat" (p. 21) and "L'Escalier" (p. 28); in Tableau 5, "On met un croix sur le corps du Duc" (p. 30) and "On place le corps dans la cheminée" (p. 31).

59. See the script by Lavedan and the shot analysis by Jenn and Nagard cited above.

60. Brewster ("Deep Staging in French Films," p. 48), citing Barry Salt, notes the innovative push toward a new type of staging in this sequence: the action moves from one room to the next through doors at the back of each set. Stegemann ("Der Mord als schöne Kunst," p. 10) observes the symmetry of the whole sequence, and correctly sees in it a refutation of Sadoul's description of the film as merely "une succession de tableaux vivants . . . une pièce de théâtre filmée" (*Histoire générale*, vol. 2, p. 509).

61. For discussion of thematic transformation as defined by d'Indy and as found in the works of Saint-Saëns—particularly in the "earliest example," the *Spartacus* Overture (1863)—see the concluding pages of Fallon, "Saint-Saëns and the *Concours de composition musicale* in Bordeaux," *Journal of the American Musicological Society* 31 (1978), 309–25.

62. All musical examples from *L'Assassinat* are based on the piano score, without consideration of orchestration.

63. I am indebted to Schmidt for my analysis of the opening portion of Tableau 1. Stegemann's approach to the score is somewhat dissimilar from mine in its emphasis on motivic analysis without consideration of the overall thematic and harmonic structure; but his examples are most illuminating, and we are in full agreement that throughout *L'Assassinat*, Saint-Saëns achieved "präzises Zusammenspiel von Film und Musik."

64. Not shown in Ex. 8 is an additional intensifying device, imitation: statements of the theme by different instruments overlap throughout this passage, bar by bar. In certain respects, including the use of motives and harmonies based on tritones, the whole passage echoes music from Tableau 2 (mm. 52–71), accompanying a parallel scene in which Henri III shows his guards how they should carry out the murder: thus, for Stegemann, the tritone is the "Leitmotiv des Mordes."

65. A note printed in the score warns that the stairway scene might be cut, and musicians are instructed to watch and be ready to go directly to Tableau 5. (See the note at the bottom of Appendix part 2.) No reason for the cut is given, but it should be noted that in the film this scene actually comes at the beginning of Tableau 6 rather than at the end of Tableau 5. Possibly at the time the score was being composed, the filmmakers were unsure precisely where the scene would be placed, or whether it would be included at all. In any case, if this page of music were to be cut, there would be no return to the opening material and key of Tableau 4, and Tableau 5 would begin with a sudden shift from F major to F minor, rather than from the dominant of F# minor to F minor. Either way, Saint-Saëns skillfully adjusted his music to the requirements of the film, offering two ways of linking the tableaux that are about equal in their levels of tension.

66. See Jenn and Nagard, "*L'Assassinat*," 72.

67. See Gunning, "The Cinema of Attraction: Early Film, Its Spectator and the

Avant-Garde," *Wide Angle* 8, nos. 3/4 (1986), 63–70. In this article, Gunning explains the term "cinema of attraction," which he applies to films made before 1906–1907, as "a conception that sees cinema less as a way of telling stories than as a way of presenting a series of views to the audience." (The term, in its plural form, has rapidly become common parlance among specialists in early cinema.) See also Gunning, "'Primitive' Cinema—A Frame-up? or The Trick's on Us," *CJ* 28, no. 2 (Winter 1989), 3–12. Both articles are reprinted in Elsaesser, ed., *Early Cinema.*

CHAPTER 3. FILM SCORES IN AMERICA, 1910–1914

1. Anthony Slide, "Early Film Magazines: An Overview," in his *Aspects of American Film History prior to 1920*, 98. *MPW* began publication in 1907, as Slide states, and continued until 7 Jan. 1928, when it merged into the *Exhibitors Herald and Moving Picture World*; the only gap in its twenty-year history came between 4 Oct. and 8 Nov. 1919. For the period prior to 1920 he calls it the source of "the most detailed news items, the best reviews and feature articles, particularly by Louis Reeves Harrison, W. Stephen Bush and George Blaisdell, and a vast advertisement section, which can offer the researcher untold treasures." Many of those treasures, including musical ones, were first mined in *The Film Index: A Bibliography*, vol. 1: 74 items are listed and summarized under "Music: Silent Era" (pp. 202–7); it was in perusing those items that I began to discover the periodical's scattered information concerning early special scores.

2. William K. Everson, *American Silent Film* (New York: Oxford Univ. Press, 1978), 60.

3. John F. Barry and Epes Winthrop Sargent, *Building Theatre Patronage: Management and Merchandising* (New York: Chalmers, 1927), 382. The contents of this book were based on essays contributed by both writers to *MPW*, which was also published by Chalmers.

4. *Musical Presentation of Motion Pictures*, 11. I have been unable to find evidence of the Essanay feature or film score to which Beynon refers.

5. Beynon: "Following closely upon the enthusiastic and popular reception of [the *Birth*] score, the writer presented at the Broadway Theatre, New York City, September 16, 1915, a musical score arranged [mostly from Grieg] for the Oliver Morosco picturization of *Peer Gynt*. . . . Paramount saw the possibilities of this new form of music service and by an arrangement entered into with G. Schirmer, Inc., and the writer, presented orchestral scores for one hundred and sixteen [!] pictures"—*Musical Presentation of Motion Pictures*, pp. 11–12. (Schirmer was also the publisher of Beynon's book.) In the late teens Beynon supplied numerous cue sheets to *MPW* and "conducted" the "Music for the Picture" column, from 2 Feb. 1918 to 8 March 1919. The first of Beynon's columns begins with a biographical note that claims "a total of 162" scores written for Pallas, Morosco, Famous Players, and Lasky productions (at the rate of one every three days). Despite these high numbers, copies of only eight Beynon/Schirmer scores are in LC; all were registered for copyright between 5 Oct. 1915 and 7 Jan. 1916. Three are credited as Paramount/Morosco photoplays (*Peer Gynt*, *The Yankee Girl*, and *The Tongues of Men*), three as Paramount's alone (*The Gentleman from Indiana*, *Jane*, and *The Reform Candidate*), and two as Triangle Plays (*The Corner*, *The Missing Link*). The last title links Beynon to both Joseph Carl Breil and D. W. Griffith: the score actually credits Breil as its composer on the outside title page, while Beynon receives credit on the inside, and Triangle was a distribution company set up in mid-1915 by a triumvirate that included Griffith. On the director's part in this troubled company, see Richard Schickel, *D. W. Griffith: An American Life* (New York: Simon and Schuster, 1984), 306–9.

6. See "Latest Films—Pathé Frères," *MPW* 13 Feb. 1909, 184. The film is listed for the last time in 20 March 1909, 348.

7. "Comments on Film Subjects," *MPW* 27 Feb. 1909, 236.

8. J.M.B. "Correspondence: Simpler Subjects Needed," *MPW* 13 March 1909, 308. The author is very likely John M. Bradlet, who became *MPW*'s "Chicago representative," contributing many articles signed variously by initials or by name: see, e.g., the items cited in nn. 16, 17, and 27.

9. Thomas Bedding, "The Modern Way in Moving Picture Making," *MPW* 13 March 1909, 294.

10. See Walter Richard Eaton, "The Canned Drama," *American Magazine* 68 (1909), 493–500; the quoted passage is on p. 500.

11. On the origin of the term "photoplay," see Macgowan, *Behind the Screen*, 185. See also, Ramsaye, *A Million and One Nights*, 681–82. For an explanation of the term "feature" and discussion of early examples, see Bowser, *Transformation of Cinema*, 192–215.

12. See Robert Anderson, "The Motion Picture Patents Company: A Reevaluation," in Balio, ed., *American Film Industry*, 133–52; the quotation is from p. 134. See also the discussion of the Patents Company's significance in Patrick Loughney, "*From the Manger to the Cross*: The First American Film Spectacular," in I. Newsom, ed. *Wonderful Inventions*, 255–56. A penetrating history of the Patents Company is in Bowser, *Transformation of Cinema*, 21–36.

13. Traditionally the nickelodeons have been regarded as lower-class haunts, but scholars now argue persuasively that nickelodeons attracted middle-class audiences. See Russell Merritt, "Nickelodeon Theaters, 1905–1914: Building an Audience for the Movies," in Balio, ed., *American Film Industry*, 83–102. See also Robert C. Allen, "Motion Picture Exhibition in Manhattan, 1906–1912: Beyond the Nickelodeon," in Fell, ed., *Film before Griffith*, 162–75.

14. See Ripley, "Song Slides": he states that song slides were invented during the 1890s as a promotional device to stimulate the sale of sheet music, and that beginning in 1907, "the owners of Nickelodeons almost without exception, adopted song-slides . . . as cheap fillers for their programs of two or three reels of 'flickers'" (p. 150). But long before Ripley, song slides were said to have been originated by Tony Pastor in the 1880s: see Harry S. Marion, "Illustrated Songs," *MPW* Twentieth Anniversary number, 26 March 1927, 331–32.

15. Typical of *MPW*'s reportage concerning song slides are these items in the first issue: "The Buyers' Guide" and "Lantern Slide Review," 9 March 1907, 13 and 14. In addition, there are frequent items of a more general nature, including: Chas. K. Harris, "Illustrating Song Slides," 9 March 1907, 5–6; "Posing for Song Pictures," 22 June 1907, 244–45; "Editorial: Cheap Song Slides—and—," 7 Sept. 1907, 419–20; "The Tremendous Demand for Song Slides," 28 Sept. 1907 467–68; "The Free Music Graft Is Ended," 25 April 1908, 366–67; Dan'l H. Palmer, "Music Publishers as Distributers of Lantern Slides," 23 May 1908 454; H. B. Ingram, "Punishing the Music Publishers," 6 Feb. 1909, 141; "Shaking Down the Song Writers," 17 April 1909, 474–75; "The Value of Lantern Slides as Advertisements for Sheet Music" and De Witt C. Wheeler, "Correspondence: The Reform of the Song Slide," 15 May 1909, 633 and 637–38; H. S. Sanderson, "Correspondence: The History of Song Slides," 29 May 1909, 716–17; and H. F. Hoffman, "The Singer and the Song," 4 June 1910, 935.

16. (1) On *phonographic synchronizing devices*, which were continually being promoted, but never with more than limited success, see: "Editorial: The Perfection of the Phono-Cinematograph," 14 Sept. 1970, 435; "Editorial: Phonographic Song Selections" and "Noted Dramatists to Write Moving Picture Plays," 20 March 1908, 255 and 263; "Talking Machines," 2 May 1908, 390; "Talking Pictures Seem To Be Popular," 8 Aug. 1908, 103; "Editorial: Chronophone Progress," 16 April 1910, 605; and "The Singing and Talking Picture: What Is Its Future?," 7 May 1910, 727–28. (2) For various types of *special instruments* and discussions of their utility, see: "Orchestrion, suitable for high class Moving Picture Theatre" (advertisement), 29 June 1907, 300; "New Musical Wonder" and "Piano Orchestra Attachment" (adv.), 19 Dec. 1908, 498 and 505; "Church Pipe Organs" (adv.), 24 April 1909,

523; "Sound Effects [Devices] for Moving Pictures," 22 May 1909, 675; "The Music Question: The Pian-Orchestra" and "Wurlitzer PianOrchestra" (adv.), 4 Dec. 1909, 804–5 and 817; H. F. Hoffman, "Drums and Traps," 23 July 1910, 184–85; J.M.B., "The Pipe Organ," 3 Sept. 1910, 526–27; Arthur W. Smallwood, "Correspondence: The Music and the Show" (concerning the so-called pian-orchestra), 10 Sept. 1910, 584–85; and (Deagan's) "Musical Electrical Bells" (adv.), idem, 604. See also the page of "Music" advertisements reproduced in Fig. 7. (3) On *lectures*: see "Enterprise Rewarded" (concerning "noted lecturer" W. Stephen Bush's presentation of *The Devil*), 26 Sept. 1908, 233; an advertisement of lectures by Bush for *Ingomar* and *The Devil*, 24 Oct. 1908, 329, and for the *Passion Play*, 14 Nov. 1908, 389; Bush, "The Human Voice as a Factor in the Moving Picture Show," 23 Jan. 1909, 86; James Clancy, idem, 30 Jan. 1909, 115; and "The Lectures" (review), 3 April 1909, 405.

17. See, e.g., "The Nickelodeon," 4 May 1907, 140; "When 'Music' Is a Nuisance," 28 Dec. 1907, 702; Joseph Medill Patterson, "The Nickelodeons" (originally published in the *Saturday Evening Post*), 11 Jan. 1908, 21–22; "The Nickelodeon as a Business Proposition," 25 July 1908, 61–62; Hans Leigh, "How the Vogue of the Motion Picture May Be Preserved," 8 Aug. 1908, 101–2; W. Stephen Bush, "The Coming Ten and Twenty Cent Moving Picture Theater," 29 Aug. 1908, 152–53; Bush, "The Misfit Amusement Parlor," 17 Oct. 1908, 296–97; Bush, "Hints to Exhibitors," 24 Oct. 1908, 316–17; Fred Marriott, "An English View of the American Moving Picture," 24 July 1909, 116; F. H. Richardson, "Vaudeville vs. Moving Pictures," 16 Oct. 1909, 525; J.M.B., "Notes of the Trade: Chicago," 12 Feb. 1910, 218–19; J.M.B., "St. Louis," 5 Nov. 1910, 1053; J.M.B., "Vaudeville—Music—Uniforms," 19 Nov. 1910, 1166; Henry [*sic*], "New England Notes: 'Vaudeville—Music—Uniforms,'" 3 Dec. 1910, 1293, and (a follow-up to J.M.B.'s report from St. Louis), "Letters to the Editors: A St. Louis Exhibitor Who Believes in Good Music," 3 Dec. 1910, 1301.

18. Berg, *Investigation*, 58.

19. "Incidental Music for Edison Pictures," *Edison Kinetogram*, 15 Sept. 1909, 12. This service continued in every issue up to the one dated 1 June 1910, and then ceased (without explanation) until September 1913. (No cue sheets were published in the London edition of the *Kinetogram* from the first issue, of 15 April 1910 through at least 1 Oct. 1912.) That many players needed guidance on how to interpret such lists of cues becomes clear from perusal of Sinn's early *MPW* columns on "Music for the Picture": see, e.g., his discussion of two musical styles, *andante* and *agitato*, in the initial column, 26 Nov. 1910, 1227.

20. Frelinger's *Motion Picture Piano Music* was published by the author in Lafayette, Indiana, in 1909: see the copy deposited in the Music Division, LC.

21. "Musical Accompaniments for Moving Pictures," *MPW* 23 Oct. 1909, 559.

22. See the advertisement for "Descriptive Music to Fit the Pictures," *MPW* 11 Dec. 1909, 845, and "Motion Picture Music: Gregg A. Frelinger Compiler of Valuable New Work," *MPW* 18 Dec. 1909, 879: in this article, Frelinger is described as "one of the best descriptive pianists in America . . . engaged in theatrical work for the past twenty years." At present, it states, "he is devoting himself to motion pictures . . . despite many offers from leading vaudeville houses." *MPW* also published a letter from Frelinger a few months later, in which he both refers to his own collection and praises the periodical's efforts "on behalf of appropriate music for motion picture theaters." See Frelinger, "Correspondence: Music for Moving Picture Houses," 26 Feb. 1910, 303. Both Frelinger and the Edison Company received further commendation in *MPW* from Rothapfel, "Music and Motion Pictures," 16 April 1910, 593.

23. Advertisements for "*The Emerson Moving Picture Music Folio*," 2 July 1910, 36, and for the *Orpheum Collection*, addressed to "Motion Picture Pianists," 1 Oct. 1910, 815. The latter names Clarence E. Sinn as compiler. (He became the "Music for the Picture" columnist for *MPW* a few months after this advertisement appeared.) No copy of either of these collections has been found, though there was published an anthology titled *Emerson's*

Moving Picture Music Folio (Cincinnati: Joseph Krolage, 1913): a copy is in LC. According to the 1909 advertisement the first *Emerson* anthology was also published in Cincinnati, by Groene; and in the 1913 collection several pieces bear copyright dates of 1910 or earlier, with the inscription "copyright transferred 1911 to Krolage Music Co."

24. An untitled paragraph in *MPW* 1 Oct. 1910, 754, reads in part: "Music Program—Good!—The *Vitagraph Bulletin* for [the] first half of October contains several suggestions for appropriate music for individual films. The only fault [is that] it isn't done complete enough. It's a bully good start, though."

25. See chapter 1, note 36. Cue sheet formats varied: at first Sinn incorporated suggestions for music directly into the prose of his columns, as for the film *Auld Robin Gray*, 26 Nov. 1910, and *Mr. Four-Flush* and *Isis* (Pathé), in 10 Dec. 1910, 1345; after that he normally itemized the cues for each film in separate lists, as for *The Lad from Ireland* (Kalem), 17 Dec. 1910, 1405. More than a year prior to Sinn's first column, there had appeared a letter expressing gratitude to the Edison Company for their "big help" to professional pianists and urging *MPW* to "add a music department of this kind with cues for all films of which it gives the synopsis." In reply, the editor confessed that *MPW* was unprepared to act on this suggestion, though the "needs of the exhibitors" were being considered: see Alexander, "Correspondence: Music for Moving Picture Houses," *MPW* 23 Oct 1909, 576; and the same issue contains an editorial (cited in n. 21) praising cue sheets.

26. "Editorial: The Music and the Picture," *MPW* 16 April 1910, 590.

27. "Editorial: Feature Films for Feature Music," *MPW* 16 April 1910, 591. (Another important essay appears in the same issue: Rothapfel, "Music and Motion Pictures.") Two *MPW* staff members took strong interest in music at the Orpheum in this period: Bradlet praised its orchestra (and criticized the musicians in two other Chicago theaters) in "Increase the Beauty of the Pictures," *MPW* 12 Feb. 1910, 217. Sinn referred often to the Orpheum and its music director in his early columns: for example, he described the orchestra's battery of special effects in "Music for the Picture," 10 Dec. 1910, 1345; and he presented King's musical program for *His Last Parade* (Lubin) in 21 Jan. 1911, 135. Cf. the advertisement for the *Orpheum Collection* discussed in n. 23.

28. Though a description of the music for *A Penitent of Florence* was not printed, a synopsis was: see "Licensed Film Stories: Gaumont (George Kleine.)—*A Penitent of Florence*," *MPW* 23 April 1910, 657.

29. Pilar Morin, "Silent Drama Music," *MPW* 30 April 1910, 676.

30. "Editorial: The Music and the Picture, II," *MPW* 14 May 1910, 772.

31. There has been little research on early films of operas and the efforts made to provide them with music. The following examples are mentioned by David L. Parker, "Golden Voices, Silver Screen: Opera Singers as Movie Stars," in I. Newsom, ed., *Wonderful Inventions*, 187: at the Paris Exposition of 1900, Photo-Cinéma-Théâtre presented Victor Manuel in excerpts from *Falstaff* and *Don Giovanni*, as well as Cossira in *Roméo et Juliette*; in 1903, Walter Daw made some 50 synchronized films, including *The Mikado* and *Yeoman of the Guard* "in miniature"; in 1906, Gaumont issued "Chronophone" versions of excerpts from *Lakmé*, *Il Trovatore*, and so on. Three other films mentioned elsewhere in passing include (1) an Edison film of *Parsifal* made in 1904, for which plans to record the music apparently had to be aborted—see Kemp R. Niver, *The First Twenty Years: A Segment of Film History*, Bebe Bergsten, ed. (Los Angeles: Locare Research Group, 1968), 74; (2) a 20-minute version of *Die Fledermaus*, Act II, made by Messter in 1904—see Edmund Nick, "Musik der Stummfilmzeit," in Lindlar and Schubert, eds., *Die drei grossen "F"*, 36, and (3) a 1906 "Chronomegaphone" version of the entire *Faust* [*sic*]—see "Round and About," *Optical Lantern and Cinematograph Journal*, Dec. 1906, 53.

32. Sadoul, *Histoire générale du cinéma*, vol. 3: *Le cinéma devient un art* (1947), 292.

33. Kalem advertisement for "*The Merry Widow*," *MPW* 28 Dec. 1907, 704. Lehar's operetta was first produced in Vienna in 1905. By the end of 1907 it had triumphed in New York and Chicago; a third opening had been announced for Boston; and several more touring companies were in preparation. See "The *Merry Widow* Making a Million," *NYT*, 22 Dec. 1907, pt. 4, p. 8. Kalem's film version was fraudulent, and the owners of the American rights to the operatta succeeded in having it withdrawn: see "Stops Pictures of *Merry Widow*," *MPW* 11 April 1908, 319. (The plaintiff, Henry W. Savage, also sought an injunction at this time to halt a burlesque of the operetta, but in the latter case he was unsuccessful: see "Calls *Merry Widow* an Elderly Dowager," *NYT*, 8 April 1908, p. 7).

34. *Edison Kinetogram* 15 Dec. 1909, 12.

35. "Editorial: The Music and the Picture: A Suggestion," *MPW* 23 April 1910, 637. As had been the case in the previous week's issue of *MPW* (see n. 27), this editorial was supplemented by an essay on similar themes: Paul Evert Denton, "Moving Pictures and Music," 638.

36. Sinn, "Music for the Picture" (henceforth "MfP"), *MPW* 31 Dec. 1910, 1518–19.

37. Sinn, "MfP," *MPW* 14 Jan. 1911, 76.

38. Sinn, "MfP," *MPW* 11 Feb. 1911, 293.

39. Sinn, "MfP," *MPW* 17 June 1911, 1370. According to Sinn, Edison's version of *Faust* was released on 26 June 1911.

40. Buel F. Rissinger, "An Interesting Open Letter to This Department" ["The Movies," Frank Edson, ed.] *Metronome* 32, no. 7 (July 1916), 19. A 1910 *MPW* item might indicate that Rissinger was active in Memphis in 1910, but not that he was "leading" (i.e., conducting) at the time. He (or a relative?) is described as one of the "progressive exhibitors . . . B. B. Risinger [*sic*], the genial manager of the Majestics, of Memphis . . . . Mr. Risinger visited Chicago to engage the best singers he could find and invest in some musical instruments, including the Deagan 'bells.' [He] claims to have the most perfect music arrangement . . . ." See J.M.B., "Vaudeville—Music—Uniforms," 19 Nov. 1910, 1166.

41. Sinn, "MfP," *MPW* 22 July 1911, 116. The composer named by Sinn was possibly Raffaele Caravaglios (b. Castelvetrano, 1860–d.?); see Carlos Schmidl, *Supplemento al dizionario universale dei musicisti* (Milan: Sonzogno, 1938), 159.

42. Robert Grau, *The Stage in the Twentieth Century* ([1912]; rpt. New York: B. Blom, 1969), 139. References to film music can also be found in Grau's other two books from these years: *The Business Man in the Amusement World* (1910; rpt. New York: Jerome S. Ozer, 1971) and *The Theatre of Science: A Volume of Progress and Achievement in the Motion Picture Industry* (1914; rpt. New York: B. Blom, 1969). "Grau knew many of the pioneers, and in all three of his books he has many interesting things to say about the invention of motion pictures, the nickelodeons, the combination of motion picture, vaudeville shows, etc." See "Grau," in the bibliography section of Joseph H. North's *Early Development of the Motion Picture, 1887–1909* [Ph.D. diss., Cornell Univ., 1949], Dissertations on Film Series (New York: Arno, 1973), n.p.

43. Maude Waters Dittmar, "The Language of the Silent Drama," *Motion Picture Classic* 4, no. 5. (July 1917), 52, 64. Dittmar may have misremembered the year in which she saw *Dante's Inferno*: "four years ago" places the film in 1913 rather than 1912, but the film might have taken that long to reach her town. A letter from Dittmar, detailing her choices of music for several films, was posted from Frederick, Md., and printed in Sinn, "MfP," *MPW* 25 May 1912, 717.

44. Bush, "Music and Sound Effects for *Dante's Inferno*," *MPW* 27 Jan. 1912, 283–84. The author recommends the following ensemble: "Whenever possible, an orchestra of six or eight pieces . . . in the absence of such an orchestra, at least two instruments, a piano and a good organ. . . . The organ's place is behind the screen; the piano had best be placed

in the orchestra." For the sound effects, Bush urged restraint. Cf. Bush, "Lectures on Notable Reels: Lecture on *Faust* (Two Reels)," *MPW* 24 June 1911, 1430. Only twice does Bush refer specifically to Gounod's music: in Reel 1, Scene 5, he asks for "The Faust Waltz," and in Reel 2, Scene 4, "strains of the Faust March."

45. Review of "*Mignon*," *MPW* 27 Jan. 1912, 288.

46. Advertisement for *Fra Diavolo* in *MPW* 15 June 1912, 988. Louis Reeves Harrison wrote an enthusiastic review of the film in 22 June 1912, 1114–15, which concluded by calling *Fra Diavolo* a "forerunner of what may some day delight millions who attend the little theaters—really grand photo-opera." A week later appeared a brief announcement that a special score had been arranged for violin and piano: see 29 June 1912, 1204.

47. On the history of the Kalem company, see "The O'Kalems," in Slide, *Aspects of American Film History*, 88–97, and the bibliography for Kalem, 141–43; also the chapter on Kalem in Slide, *Early American Cinema*, International Film Guide Series (New York: A. S. Barnes; London: A. Zwemmer, 1970), 47–64. See, also, Loughney's essay on "*From the Manger to the Cross*," in I. Newsom, ed., *Wonderful Inventions*, 253–67.

48. Sinn, "MfP," *MPW* 25 May 1912, 717.

49. Sinn, "MfP," *MPW* 21 Oct. 1911, 200.

50. Review of "*Arrah-Na-Pogue*," *MPW* 18 Nov. 1911, 536.

51. The first Kalem advertisement to mention music for *Arrah-Na-Pogue* appeared in *MPW* 25 Nov. 1911, 613. Similar announcements were run in every subsequent issue until the end of 1911: for example, "Special music . . . 3 half-tone electros (2 1/2 inches wide)"—*MPW* 2 Dec. 1911, 697. The text of the latter advertisement became characteristic of the entire series, as in the following examples. For *A Spartan Mother*: "Special music . . . specially attractive one, three and six sheet, four-color litho's for this subject" 2 March 1912, 754; *The Bugler of Battery B:* "Special piano music . . . Special one, three and six-sheet, four-color lithographs, reproduced from actual photographs of sensational episodes in this remarkable drama"— 29 June 1912, 1202; *The Siege of Petersburg*: "Special music . . .Special Paper special six sheet posters, depicting The Fight on The Burning Bridge"—6 July 1912, 63; and *The Cheyenne Massacre*: "Special Music . . . Special Plate Pictures: A set of 12 photographs . . . Special one, three, and six sheet poster in four colors, depicting thrilling scenes in the production"—26 April 1913, 409.

52. *Kalem Kalendar*, 22 Dec. 1911: see "News Items of the Kalem Companies," p. 6, and "Special Music for *Arrah-Na-Pogue*," back cover. (A complete set of of the *Kalem Kalendar* is available at the AMPAS Library; the information it contains pertaining to the company's series of special scores is similar to what has been found in *MPW*.)

53. See the advertisement for "*The Colonel's Escape*, *Captured by Bedouins*," (etc.), *MPW* 15 June 1912, 988. In this advertisement and in others, certain films were announced without being billed as features and without special scores, alongside those that were. (In the advertisement cited here, for example, no score is mentioned for *The Pugilist and the Girl*.) Although the basis for Kalem's selection of films to receive music—that is, films designated as "features"—is not completely clear, it seems that the subject of the film was a key factor, but not length.

54. The score for Kalem's *Fighting Dan McCool* was credited to M. Komroff—the only composer beside Simon associated with the Kalem series. Komroff apparently also supplied cue sheets to *MPW* for non-Kalem pictures, and a second Komroff might have done so as well: see Maurice Komroff, "Music for *Madame Roland*," under Sinn, "MfP," *MPW* 6 April 1912, 33; Manuel Komroff, "Suggestions for *The Seventh Son*," in "MfP," 20 April 1912, 211; and M. Komroff, "*The Spanish Cavalier*," "Playing *A Road Agent's Love* (Essanay)," and "Playing *Teaching a Liar a Lesson* (Essanay)"—all three under "MfP," 4 May 1912, 415. Simon also provided *MPW* with a cue sheet at this time: see "Musical Suggestions for *Caprices of Fortune* (Éclair)"—26 Oct. 1912, 356.

55. The *ASCAP Biographical Dictionary of Composers, Authors and Publishers*, 4th ed., Jacques Cattell Press, comp. (New York: R. R. Bowker, 1980), states that Walter Cleveland Simon was born in Lexington, Kentucky, in 1884, and died in New York City in 1958; however, in the 3rd edition (New York: ASCAP, 1966), his birthplace is given as Cincinnati. Both editions state that he played pipe organ in a Bronx film theater in 1912 and "also for all major circuits of theatres, including Pantages, Keith, & Orpheum."

56. [Sinn], "More Help for Picture Pianists" (on the same page as "MfP"), and adv. for "*Progress Course of Music*," *MPW* 21 Oct. 1911, 200 and 223.

57. "Splendid Kalem Feature," *MPW* 2 March 1912, 770–71.

58. "Kalem Egyptian Features," *MPW* 1 June 1912, 826. Previous *MPW* articles reporting on the "Egyptian" features include: "Kalem Sends Company to the Orient," 16 Dec. 1911, 880; "A Voice from the Desert," 2 March 1912, 771; and "Kalem Announces Egyptian Pictures," 20 April 1912, 208. See also the review of "*Tragedy of the Desert*," 22 June 1912, 1112–13.

59. See the synopsis, "Licensed Film Stories—Kalem: *An Arabian Tragedy*," *MPW* 15 June 1912, 1056. For synopses of two other films in the Kalem series—*Captured by Bedouins* and *The Confederate Ironclad*—together with detailed analysis of Simon's music for each of them, see my article "The First American Film Scores," *Harvard Library Bulletin*, NS, 2, no. 4 (Winter 1991): 78–103.

60. Tchaikovsky's "Danse Arabe" is listed under the heading "Exotic Moods," in Lang and West, *Musical Accompaniment of Moving Pictures*, 28; also, under the heading "Arabian Music," in Rapée, *Encyclopedia of Music for Pictures*, 83.

61. Sinn, "MfP," *MPW* 25 May 1912, 717.

62. Sinn, "MfP," *MPW* 13 July 1912, 150. Sinn's musical suggestions for *An Arabian Tragedy* include six titles of music of "Oriental" character (*Mystic Shrine*, *Imam*, *In a Lotus Field*, etc.) and four pieces identified only by mood (Sentimental, Pathetic, Agitato, and Plaintive).

63. Letter from "E.J.L., Brooklyn: An Opinion on Cue Music," to Sinn, "MfP," *MPW* 19 Oct 1912, 235. "E.J.L." may have been Ernst Luz, who apparently became professionally active at this time: Berg (in his *Investigation*, 116–17) cites an article by Luz in *Motion Picture News*, dated 20 Oct. 1911, and he states that Luz began a column on "Picture Music" for the *News* in 1912. Articles by and about Luz from the teens and twenties are cited in Westcott, *Comprehensive Bibliography of Music for Films and Television*; LC has six compiled scores by Luz, all prepared for Metro films of 1922–23.

64. Letter from "R. J. Bessette, Hartford, Conn.," to Sinn, "MfP," *MPW* 7 June 1913, 1020. Following the letter, Sinn notes that he may have gotten the author's name wrong, as it was difficult to read; and when a virtually identical letter concerning the score for *Antony and Cleopatra* was printed by Sinn the following year—see "MfP," 29 Aug. 1914, 1225—the author's name was given as Roy J. Bassett. (According to the second letter the size of the orchestra had grown to ten pieces during the winter.)

65. Two of the Vitagraph films for which scores were advertised were in three reels (Appendix part 3, nos. 56–57), all others were in two. The first Vitagraph advertisement that mentions music appeared in *MPW*, 22 March 1913, 1193. After announcing daily (one-reel) releases for March 17–22 and forthcoming releases for March 24–29, this text appears: "Special release, *The Strength of Men*, in two parts [reels], by James Oliver Curwood, released Wednesday, March 19th. Special release, *The Modern Prodigal*, in two parts, released Friday, March 28th. . . . Special music (piano score) for all specials." Similar announcements appeared in most weekly advertisements through 15 Nov. 1913, 709. After that date there are no further references to music. Vitagraph's promotion of scores lasted for a shorter time than Kalem's, but may have yielded a greater number of scores (though none have been found). Cf. the brief reference to cue sheets in a 1910 *Vitagraph Bulletin*, cited earlier (n. 24).

66. Thanhouser's features, for which scores were advertised, were in four reels. In contrast to the Vitagraph series, references to these scores are found in three *MPW* news items: "Musical Score for *Provence*," 13 Dec. 1913, 1270; "Is Daly Version of *Frou Frou*," idem, 1288; and "Change of Thanhouser *Joseph* Title," 3 Jan. 1914. Thanhouser aggressively promoted the scores—much more so than either Kalem or Vitagraph—beginning with its advertisement in 20 Dec. 1913, 1360: "Come on now, you real showmen, write us for *free* orchestration for *The Legend of Provence*! . . . The orchestration is by the master musicians of the Tams Music Library of New York City, and the THANHOUSER 'BIG' PRODUCTIONS particulars tell how to get these features for *exclusive* first-run use in your locality for a *full year* under an *iron-clad contract*. Just think of getting 4-part productions like *Moths*, *Robin Hood*, *Provence* and *Frou Frou* that way!" (There is some ambiguity as to whether the first two films in this list were provided with scores; the *MPW* news items do not mention either title in connection with music.) The last advertisement which mentions a score—in 24 Jan. 1914, 366—tries just as hard to excite interest: "We want EVERY EXHIBITOR to have, FREE, the bound book of orchestration we are issuing for *LEGEND OF PROVENCE*, but if you've already shown this feature, the score for the following feature, *FROU FROU, is the score you want*. If you wrote us for *Legend of Provence* music, you needn't write us for *Frou Frou* music, for when we listed you for *Legend of Provence* music WE LISTED YOU FOR ALL 'BIG PRODUCTIONS' MUSIC. If you're not on that list, a request for the *Legend of Provence* OR *Frou Frou* piano score will put you there." (Note the discrepancy between references to "orchestration" and piano score.) Thanhouser was apparently the first American film company to tie itself to a leading music publisher—Tams—for provision of its scores. Fragile copies of piano scores for *Legend of Provence* and *Frou Frou*, both of them apparently compilations throughout, have recently been found in the Capitol Theatre Collection, UCLA Music Library.

67. Letter from E.F.B. on "Special Music" to Sinn, "MfP," *MPW* 28 March 1914, 1671.

68. LC has scores by Manuel Klein for the following All-Star Features of 1914: *Soldiers of Fortune* (13 pp.), *Paid in Full* (12 pp.), *America* (61 pp.), *In Mizzoura* (16 pp.), *Pierre of the Plains* (13 pp.), *The Jungle* (11 pp.), and *Dan* (8 pp.). Only the score for *America* comes close to being long enough to accompany a feature lasting an hour or more. The first announcement of a Klein score—"Manuel Klein Writes Music for All-Star," *MPW* 31 Jan. 1914, 556—reads as follows: "Beginning with its latest and current release, the six-part production of Richard Harding Davis' great play and story, *Soldiers of Fortune*, the All-Star Feature Corporation will issue as especially written musical score for this [i.e., each?] production. Manuel Klein, composer and musical director of the New York Hippodrome, whose musical works are known the world over, has been commissioned by the All-Star company and in addition to his present score, will write incidental music to all of that company's releases in the future. The success of the *Soldiers of Fortune* score is well attested to by the eagerness with which both state rights buyers and theater proprietors have accepted it." See also the advertisement for this film in *MPW* 7 Feb. 1914, 642; the advertisement for *Paid in Full* in 28 Feb. 1914, 1109; George Blaisdell, "Hippodrome's *America* in Pictures," 21 March 1914, 1510; and "Manuel Klein Music for *The Nightingale*," 11 Aug. 1914, 975. Despite the last announcement, no score for *The Nightingale* seems to have been published; subsequent *MPW* items concerning the film do not mention music for the film: see the advertisement in 3 Oct. 1914, 20, and the review by Louis Reeves Harrison in 10 Oct. 1914, 192.

69. Walter C. Simon, *Society Dramas: One Reel Special Music for Motion Pictures* (New York: Walter C. Simon, 1915). (A copy is in LC.) The collection contains 11 numbers, one per page, bearing the following titles: 1. Overture; 2. Gavotte; 3. Waltz; 4. Minuette; 5. Romance; 6. Pathos; 7. March; 8. Hurry; 9. [untitled: Andante con moto]; 10. [untitled: Moderato, beginning with a two-measure "Train Imitation"]; 11. Tremelo and Finale.

70. LC has a 39-page score of "Special Piano Music" for *The Black Crook*, "in 5 parts [reels], composed by Walter C. Simon" (New York: Kalem, 1916).

71. "Cinema Opera [*The Echo of Youth*] Given by Composer Walter C. Simons" [*sic*], *MPW* 8 March 1919, 1346. The opening of this report identifies Simon as being "of the Mount Morris Theatre, 116th st. and Fifth Ave, New York City." No references to scores by Simon after *The Echo of Youth* have been found; however, Simon did compose the music for one additional anthology, *Hamilton S. Gordon's Loose Leaf Motion Picture Collection*, 2 vols. (New York: Gordon, 1923), listed on the title page as his "Opus 18." Each volume contains 12 pieces, one per page, as in Simon's 1915 collection described above; these pieces are of greater difficulty, and some specify organ registrations.

72. Loughney estimates the number of features made in America during 1912 and lasting five reels or more to be half a dozen, in his study of *From the Manger to the Cross*. Among these features were *Cleopatra* and *The Life of John Bunyan*; both had special scores: see Appendix part 3, Nos. 36 and 38. For a detailed report on the making of *From the Manger to the Cross* (as a film in progress, not yet given that title), see "Kalem in Palestine," *MPW* 22 June 1912, 1119–20.

73. Ramsaye, *A Million and One Nights*, 372.

74. See the entry under "*La Vie de Jésus*" in the *National Film Archive Catalogue*, 3: *Silent Fiction Films, 1895–1930* (London: British Film Institute, 1966), entry no. F371, p. 47: the length of the archive's longest version of the film is given as 2, 828 feet. See also the entry for a 661-foot version from 1906, under the title "*La Vie et Passion de N.S.J.C.*," in *Cinema 1900/1906*, vol. 2, no. F409, p. 19.

75. The title page of the score for *La Vie de Jésus* reads as follows: "Charles Quef/*Vie de Jésus*/Musique de Scène/composée spécialement pour accompagner la bande cinématographique de la vie de Jésus/Éditée par la Maison Pathé/1re Partie: Naissance de N.-S.-J.-C./2e Partie: Enfance de Jésus/3e Partie: Miracles et Vie publique de N.-S.-J.-C./4e Partie: Passion et Mort de N.-S.-J.-C./Partition Piano seul . . . fr./Parties d'Orchestre (10 parties) . . . fr./Chaque Partie d'Orchestre, en plus . . . fr./[lower l.h. corner:] Propriété de l'auteur/Charels Quef/Rue des Potagers/Bellevue (Seine-et-Oise)." On the top of the page, crossed out: "The property of A. Henderson/Queens Corner [?] Dundee," The final page (56) bears this imprint: "Paris, imp. Chaimbaud, 20 Rue de la Tour d'Auvergne." An offset copy of the score is held by the Scottish Film Council, Glasgow, and a photocopy is contained in the British Film Archive. There are 56 pages of music, six systems per page, with cues, tempo indications, expressive and dynamic markings and penciled comments. It is possible that this score could have been prepared as early as 1907: in that year Pathé exported a version of the film to England whose four-part [reel] structure matches that of the score. See "The Month's New Films," *Optical Magic Lantern Journal* 3, no. 5 (March 1907), 121, 124.

76. MacGowan, *Behind the Screen*, 158. See also Patterson, "The Nickelodeons."

77. "The *Passion Play*" (adv.), *MPW* 14 Nov. 1908, 389. The same advertisement ran for several weeks.

78. W. H. Jackson, review of the "*Life of Christ*" (the film's preliminary title) *MPW* 12 Oct. 1912, 121–24.

79. Epes Winthrop Sargent, "Handling the Kalem Release," *MPW* 19 Oct. 1912, 233.

80. "Exhibition at Wanamaker's Auditorium," *MPW* 26 Oct. 1912, 324.

81. Bush, "*From the Manger to the Cross*," ibid. For further discussion of the picture in the same issue of *MPW*, see "Moving Picture Educator: The Moral and Educational Value of Kalem's *Life of Christ*," 330; see also Bush, "Are Sacred Pictures 'Irreverent'?," *MPW* 30 Nov. 1912, 957.

82. "*From the Manger to the Cross*" (adv.) *MPW* 8 Feb. 1913, 596. The offer was made

by the film's distributor, General Film Co. of New York. There was no advertisement in the next week's issue; in the following issue, an advertisement reappeared, without the offer of a lecture: see 22 Feb., 748.

83. James S. McQuade, "The Belasco of Motion Picture Presentations," *MPW* 9 Dec. 1911, 798. Information on all aspects of Rothapfel's career can be gotten from Hall, *Best Remaining Seats.* Hall states that Rothapfel was rarely known by his full name: at first he preferred "S. L. Rothapfel" in print, but when Germanic names went out of fashion during World War I, he dropped the surname's letter "p"; "Roxy" was the nickname by which he later became known, first as the host of "Roxy's Gang," a 1923 radio program broadcast from Manhattan's Capitol Theatre, later as the impressario of the eponymous Roxy Theatre in Manhattan, the culmination of his career. (In this chapter, because the focus is on Rothapfel's early professional activities, I use the original spelling of his name.) Providing details about Rothapfel's early life, Hall (pp. 26–30) probably errs when he places Rothapfel at the Lyric in Chicago *before* the Alhambra in Milwaukee, and he contradicts McQuade by indicating that the latter theater was not a Shubert house.

84. On each theater managed by Rothapfel, from the Regent through the Roxy, see Hall, *Best Remaining Seats*, 27–69. After the Roxy, Rothapfel went on to one more theater—Radio City Music Hall—and it was his one great failure, as described in ibid., 252–54.

85. McQuade's announcement, dated 4 May 1912 (and cited in Appendix part 6, no. 6), that Rothapfel was preparing a score for Selig's *The Coming of Columbus* came at about the same time as Rothapfel's appointment as manager of the Shubert Circuit. In that position he would have been able to oversee the distribution of the film and score to a chain of theaters. At that time, too, Rothapfel was also manager of the Lyric Theater in Chicago (the same city in which Selig was located); but when Sinn recalled the score for *Columbus*, more than two years later, he attributed it to two musicians who worked in the theater—W. E. Dirks, the orchestra conductor, and Julius K. Johnson, the organist—and not to Rothapfel: see Sinn, "MfP," *MPW* 28 Feb. 1914, 1072.

86. See the note announcing the score for *The Spoilers* in the column by H. S. Field, "Music and the Picture," *Motion Picture News* 13 Feb. 1915, 115. I have not located a similar announcement in *MPW*, nor a copy of the score.

87. See the title pages of the piano conductors, published (with orchestral parts) by G. Schirmer, registered for copyright and held at LC: *The Battle Cry of Peace*, *CCE* E 373407, 12 Nov. 1915; and *Carmen*, E 373892, 24 Nov. 1915. In both of these scores, Rothapfel shared credit with important figures from New York's world of film music: for *The Battle Cry of Peace*, his "editors" were Ivan Rudisill and S. M. Berg; for *Carmen*, Hugo Riesenfeld assisted him with the musical "selections and arrangements."

88. "*Quo Vadis* at Astor," *NYT*, 22 April 1913, p. 11; rpt. *New York Times Film Reviews*, vol. 1 (1976), p. 1.

89. "Facts about *Quo Vadis*" *MPW* 28 June 1913, 1366.

90. Carl Edouarde was a prominent motion-picture conductor in New York throughout the teens and twenties; an early tribute and biographical sketch can be found in Frank Edson's column, "The Movies," *Metronome*, 32, no. 7 (July 1916), 18. See also the passages cited in n. 92.

91. See the Family Theatre (Forest City) playbill reprinted in Hall, *Best Remaining Seats*, 28.

92. When the Regent opened, Bush stated, in "The Theatre of Realization," *MPW* 15 Nov. 1913, 714, that "Mr. Rothapfel did wonders with the music, very ably assisted by Mr. Carl Edouarde and his brilliant orchestra. For the first time in this country I was made

aware of the possibilities of the music." J.A.A., in a review of "*Quo Vadis* at the Regent," 7 Feb. 1914, 680, commented that "the most impressive feature of the entertainment was the awe-inspiring prelude by the capable orchestra under the direction of Carl Edouarde." Also, Bush concluded his report on "Rothapfel Rehearsing," 14 Feb. 1914, 787, by stating that "Carl is at the very top of his profession."

93. *The Legend* was performed with two other one-act American operas—*The Temple Dancers* (John Adam Hugo) and *Shanewis* (Charles Wakefield Cadman)—on 12 and 20 March and 4 April 1919: see Henry Charles Lahee, *Annals of Music in America: A Chronological Record* (Boston: Marshall Jones, 1922), 179; and William H. Seltsam, comp., *Metropolitan Opera Annals: A Chronicle of the Artists and Performances* (New York: H. W. Wilson, 1947), 332–34 (but note that Seltsam gives the date of the second performance incorrectly as 30 March). The libretto (by Jack Byrne), a piano-vocal score, selections for piano solo, and an arrangement for piano and orchestra of the opera's *Intermezzo: Dream Music* were all published in London by Chappell in 1919.

94. Synopses of *The Legend*'s libretto can be found in Leo Melitz, *The Opera-Goer's Complete Guide*, Richard Salinger, trans. rev. by Louise Wallace Hackney (New York: Dodd, Mead, 1921), 532–33, and in Gustav Kobbé, *The Complete Opera Book* (New York: G. P. Putnam's Sons, 1919; rpt. 1929), 840–41. More useful is the entry in Edward Ellsworth Hipsher, *American Opera and Its Composers*, 2d ed. (Philadelphia: Theodore Presser, 1934), 87–90, because it also contains critical comments (quoted from a few reviews) and an accurate biographical sketch. Two useful obituaries are Bruno David Ussher, "Passed Away: Joseph Carl Breil," *Musical America* 30 Jan. 1926, 39; and "Jos. Breil Gone to Rest," *Pacific Coast Musician* 30 Jan. 1926, 4. Briefer references to Breil can found in the following works: Waldo Selden Pratt, ed., *The New Encyclopedia of Music and Musicians*, rev. ed. (New York: Macmillan, 1924); Louis Charles Elson, *The History of American Music* [*to 1925*], rev. by Arthur Elson (New York: Macmillan, 1925), 382; *The New International Yearbook . . . 1926*, Herbert Treadwell Wade, ed. (New York: Dodd, Mead, 1927), 111; Oscar Thompson, ed., *The International Cyclopedia of Music and Musicians* (New York: Dodd, Mead, 1939, and subsequent editions); *Who Was Who in America*, vol. 1: *1877–1942* (Chicago: A. N. Marquis, 1943); *Enciclopedia dello spettacolo*, vol. 2 (1954); *Baker's Biographical Dictionary of Musicians* (1958 and subs. eds.); and John Tasker Howard, *Our American Music: Three Hundred Years of It*, rev. ed. (New York: Thomas Y. Crowell, 1965), 387–88. Many of these sources, though not always the editions cited here, are listed under Breil in the *Bio-Bibliographical Index of Musicians in the United States of America since Colonial Times*, 2d ed. (Washington, D.C.: Music Section, Pan-America Union, 1956.) The most recent biographical sketch, by Katherine K. Preston and myself, appears in *The New Grove Dictionary of American Music*, vol. 1 (1986).

95. Three Breil scrapbooks are part of the collection of Joseph Carl Breil memorabilia at UCLA, in Special Collections, University Research Library. Formerly this collection was included in the holdings of the Hollywood Museum (#62-130). When the museum closed, its collections were acquired by the city of Los Angeles and stored in the (abandoned) Los Angeles Lincoln Heights Jail, where I first examined the Breil materials, in January 1980; in 1983 the collection was transferred to UCLA. I am grateful to Win Sharples, Jr., for informing me of this collection, and to Brigitta Kueppers at UCLA, for allowing me to examine the collection at length.

96. Chloe Arnold, "Joseph Breil Finds That Art Is Long," [*New York*] *Sun Magazine*, 6 Oct. 1918, pp. 10–12. A condensation of this interview was printed by Byron Hagel, in his column "The Bystander: All about Chloe and a Composer," *Musical Courier* 10 Oct. 1918, 23, 32.

97. For additional details about Breil's career as a solo recitalist and composer of art songs, see the column "People and Events," *Music News* (Chicago) 18 March 1910, 12.

98. "Joseph Weber presents *The Climax*, a play in three acts by Edward Locke, with incidental music by Joseph Carl Breil"—according to the title page of a Weber's Theatre playbill, for the week beginning Monday, 19 July 1909 (seen in the Harvard Theatre Collection, Pusey Library, Harvard University). On the second page is listed the play's "Musical Program," consisting of the following numbers: "Overture" to the *The Climax*, by Carl Breil; "Berceuse" from *Jocelyn* by Godard; "Love's Greeting," by Elgar; "Méditation" from *Les Thaïs*, by Massenet; and "Song of the Soul," by Breil. According to *NYT* advertisements, *The Climax* began its run on 12 April 1909, and ended on 18 December. At first it played for lesser matinee performances only, with evenings and Wednesday and Saturday matinees given over to a long-running comedy, *The Girl from Rector's*. Toward the end of its run, *The Climax* became the principal attraction—as indicated by the July playbill cited above—sharing billing with a production called *Travelaughs*, by R. G. Knowles.

99. The review, "*The Climax* Is a Tender Little Play," *NYT*, 13 April 1909, p. 11, describes the main female character as a young woman who dreams of an operatic career, until an amorous doctor treats her with hypnosis and convinces her not to sing. An advertisement for Weber's, *NYT*, 18 April 1909, sec. 6, p. 9, quotes this excerpt form the *Morning Sun*'s review: "an unusual play with music that is effective"; and the following blurb appears in the same paper's column, "Topics of the Stage," 8: "It is a play with music, and Mr. Joseph Carl Briel [*sic*—the misspelling hounded Breil all though his career], who wrote the melodies, is to be commended upon the success with which his part has been accomplished. The 'Song of the Soul' is a haunting little air, and is appropriate to the general theme of the play."

100. The following works connected to *The Climax* were copyrighted by Chappell (London) in 1909: on 15 Feb. (in advance of the opening), *Three Songs from the Incidental Music* (words by Edward Locke); 17 Feb., *Song of the Soul*; 15 April, *The Evensong*; 20 May, *Song of the Soul*, arr. violin solo; 7 June, [Four] *Selections from the Incidental Music*; 2 July, *Song of the Soul*, arr. S. Danks, for orch.; 28 Sept., *Selections from the Incidental Music*, arr. Danks, for piano; 11 Oct., *Song of the Soul*, arr. Danks, for band. On the cover of the 1910 issue of *Music News* containing the "People and Events" column cited in n. 97 is a photograph of Breil with the caption, "Composer, *The Climax* Music"; the column has this statement: "No name has been more in the public print in so far as music papers are concerned . . . through the unprecedented popularity of *The Climax*, for which he wrote the music, all of which is fine and 'The Song of the Soul' being of such immediate appeal and intrinsic worth as to have attained a vogue almost unprecedented." Subsequent copyrighted arrangements of the *Song of the Soul* included a piano roll recording, played by Andrei Kmita (American Piano Co., New York), 20 Jan. 1916. Following Breil's death, Chappell published an arrangement by Clarence Lucas for women's trio, 4 Sept. 1928; a "new harmonization," 16 July 1929; and an arrangement by William Stickles for mixed voices (SATB), 24 Dec. 1929.

101. Three of the stage works that followed *The Climax*—i.e., *Love Laughs at Locksmiths*, *Professor Tattle*, and *The Seventh Chord*—are listed in the reference works cited in Appendix part 7. Two other stage works from the same period were registered for copyright, though these were apparently neither published nor performed. In chronological order, the five known works of 1910–13 are (1) *Love Laughs at Locksmiths*, produced in 1910 by the New York Opera Company—see the Breil scrapbooks (UCLA) for stationery with the letterhead "New York Opera Company, Joseph Carl Breil, Managing Director, New York," and also for clippings concerning various performances; (2) *Madam Alimony*, a "farcical satire in three acts," copyright by O. Selleck and J. C. Briel [*sic*], 4 May 1911; (3) *Blundering Cupid*, a "comic operetta in two acts" copyright by Breil, 25 Nov. 1912; (4) *Professor Tattle*—"a musical farce comedy in two acts by Joseph Carl Breil," copyright by Breil, 4 Feb. 1913, produced the same year in New York (according to the *International*

Who's Who); and (5) *The Seventh Chord*, which ran at the Illinois theater, Chicago, from 31 March through 12 April 1913. Though the last play was not all that well received, and was not presented in New York, five of its songs were separately copyrighted and published by Leo Feist (words by Ashley Miller). For information about the Chicago production, see "News Notes of Plays . . ." in the *Chicago Tribune*, 30 March 1913, pt. 2, p. 1; and Percy Hammond's review in the same paper, 2 April 1913, p. 12. In the first of these items, *The Seventh Chord* is termed "quite a festival of song," and the five published numbers are all mentioned: namely, *Love's Consolation*, *La Coquette*, *Look into My Eyes*, *Follow Me to Arcady*, and *Youth's Rapture*. After 1913, Breil's stage works include: (6) "*The Love Pirate*, a play in 3 acts, book and lyrics by Harlan P. Briggs, music by Joseph Carl Breil," copyright by Briggs (New York), 9 April 1915; (7) *The Sky Pilot*, a play in 3 acts by Frank Mandel and G. H. Brennan, incidental music by Joseph C. Briel [*sic*]—according to a Teck's Theatre playbill (Buffalo, N.Y.), for the week of 17 Sept. 1917 (in the Breil collection, UCLA); (8) *The Legend*, "Lyric Tragedy, book by Jacques Byrne, music by J. C. Breil," copyright by Breil (Los Angeles), 21 May 1917—performed at the Metropolitan, in March and April 1919 (see n. 93); (9) *The Phantom Legion*, "a play in 4 acts," copyright by A. P. Kelly (New York), 2 July 1919—with a song from the play, *Westheart* (words by Kelly, music by Breil), copyright by Chappell, 10 Nov. 1919; and (10) *Asra*, a "miniature opera in one act founded upon the poem" by Heine—performed once, under Breil's direction, at the Gamut Club Theater, Los Angeles, on 24 Nov. 1925 (according to Hipsher, *American Opera and Its Composers*, 90).

102. See the editorial introduction to Breil, "Making the Musical Adaptation," in the anthology *Opportunities in the Motion Picture Industry*, vol. 2 (Los Angeles: Photoplay Research Society, 1922; rpt. New York: Arno Press, 1970), 85–89. It should be noted that the editor makes no distinction between scores that Breil partly or wholly composed, as opposed to scores that he merely conducted, compiled, or arranged. In 1921 Breil had joined the staff of the "Music Score Service Corporation," for which he may well have compiled many dozens, if not "hundreds" of scores. *MPW* provides information on the initial ventures of this firm in "Synchronized Music Score Pleases Audience at *Reputation* Showing," 14 May 1921, 599; "Synchronized Music Scores Ready for All Important May Releases," 21 May 1921, 312; advertisement, "Synchronized Music Scores," 28 May 1921, 447; and "Erno Rappe [*sic*], Conductor at Capitol, Joins Synchronized Music Company," 4 June 1921, 526.

103. For the epithet, see the untitled paragraph on Breil's score for *The Lost Battalion*, in *Musical Courier* 2 Oct. 1919, 20, and also Hipsher, *American Opera and Its Composers*, 88.

104. Breil, "Moving Pictures of the Past and Present and the Music Provided for Same" (under the column "The Movies," Frank Edson, ed.), *Metronome* 32, no. 11 (Nov. 1916), 42.

105. Sources which in Breil's lifetime repeated the claim that *Queen Elizabeth* was the first original film score include "Movie Music and Joseph Carl Breil," *Music News*, 26 Sept. 1919, p. 16; and Hal Crain, "Leaders of Joint Interests United under the Motto Finer Film Music," *Musical America* 29 Jan. 1921, 4; see also the obituaries and Hipsher's biography, cited in n. 94.

106. The American distributor of *Camille* and *Mme. Sans-Gêne* was the French-American Film Co., which seems to have been formed expressly to handle these films. In *MPW* the film was offered to exhibitors between February and June 1912. See these advertisements: 10 Feb. 1912, 498–99; 17 Feb. 1912, 596–97; 24 Feb. 1912, 700–701; 2 March 1912, 799; 16 March 1912, 982–83; 23 March 1912, 1088–89; 30 March 1912, 1214; 6 April 1912, 61; etc., until 22 June, 1912, 1155. Early advertisements are double-page displays; many of the later ones (though not all) are no more than small boxes containing the New York address of the French-American Film Co. In *A Million and One Nights*, 516, Ramsaye writes: "A conspicuous effort at a realization of star values was made with a three-reel version of

Camille, with Sarah Bernhardt in the title role. The picture was loudly proclaimed in advertising by the agents of the amateurish French concern which made it, but it failed utterly of theatre attention." But Sadoul takes the opposite view: according to his *Histoire générale*, vol. 3, pp. 25–26, the film enjoyed such success in America as well as Europe that it brought Bernhardt numerous new film offers. Sadoul gives no direct evidence for this claim, but the reviews of *Camille* and *Madame Sans-Gêne* cited in n. 108, appear to contradict Ramsaye's view that the films "failed utterly of theatre attention"; nor was he correct in calling the Film d'Art company "an amateurish concern."

107. "'Bernhardt and Rejane': World's Greatest Actors in Their Greatest Plays Will Be Shown in Pictures," *MPW* 10 Feb. 1912, 768.

108. See Bush, "Bernhardt and Rejane in Pictures," *MPW* 2 March 1912, 760; and the review in the *NY Dramatic Mirror* 10 April 1912, 26–27, rpt. in George C. Pratt, *Spellbound in Darkness: A History of the Silent Film*, rev. ed. (Greenwich, Conn.: New York Graphic Society, 1973), 115–16. The discrepancy between the dates of these reviews suggests two separate screenings.

109. On *Queen Elizabeth*, the play by Émile Moreau, a valuable source is Ernst Pronier, *Sarah Bernhardt: Une vie au théâtre* (Geneva: Alex. Geneve, n.d.) 133–34 and 345. Scattered through Pronier's bibliography are five Parisian reviews: two in newspapers, by Robert de Flers, for *Le Figaro*, 12 April 1912, and Adolphe Brisson, for *Le Temps*, 15 April; and three in journals, by Henri Bidon, *Journal des Débats*, 19 April, pp. 745–49; Gabriel Trarieux, *La Revue [des Revues]*, 1 May, pp. 113–14; and Louis Schneider, *Le Théâtre*, 1 Aug., pp. 17–22. (The plot synopsis contained in Bidon's review was translated and inserted into "Bernhardt in Motion Pictures," *Literary Digest*, 3 Aug. 1912, 190, where the author's surname is given as "Bridon.") On the making of the film, there are no error-proof sources, but the best are by Sadoul: see his *Histoire générale*, vol. 3, pp. 26–27; also his *Dictionary of Films*, Peter Morris, trans., ed., and rev. (Berkeley: Univ. of California Press, 1972), under the title "Les Amours de la reine Elizabeth." (In his *Histoire*, Sadoul cites a publicity announcement that attributes the play to Eugène Moreau, rather than Émile; the same error appears in the *Dictionary*. *Literary Digest* identifies the playwright as "Amiel" Moreau.) The best recent critical survey of all Bernhardt's films is by Gerda Taranow, *Sarah Bernhardt: The Art within the Legend* (Princeton: Princeton Univ. Press, 1972), 94–96 and 271–73; see also William Emboden, *Sarah Bernhardt* (London: Studio Vista (Cassell, Collier, & Macmillan), 1974), 143–50.

110. Adolph Zukor and Daniel Frohman described the history of Famous Players in these unreliable but entertaining sources: Zukor, "Origins and Growth of the Industry," in Joseph Kennedy, *The Story of the Films as Told by Leaders of the Industry* (Chicago and New York: A. W. Shaw, 1927), 55–76; Frohman, *Daniel Frohman Presents: An Autobiography* (New York: Claude Kendall and Willoughby Sharp, 1935), 275–90; and Zukor, with Dale Kramer, *The Public Is Never Wrong: The Autobiography of Adolph Zukor* (New York: G. P. Putnam's Sons, [1953]), 54–102. These can be compared with Ramsaye, *A Million and One Nights*, 595–602; Sadoul, *Histoire générale*, vol. 3, 273–75, and MacGowan, *Behind the Screen*, 157–59. Macgowan comments that "the story of how Zukor obtained the American rights to *Queen Elizabeth*" demonstrates how difficult it is "getting the facts of film history," and he focuses on disparate claims about the cost of those rights to illustrate the point: Ramsaye put the price at $18,000, while Zukor first said the film cost him $35,000 (in "Origins"), then $40,000 (in *The Public Is Never Wrong*); Sadoul states that $35,000 was the asking price, $18,000 the final figure. One problem with Zukor's account of the film's "Origins" is that he claims it was released in America in March 1912—evidently two months before it was actually made.

111. "Bernhardt in Pictures," *NYT*, 13 July 1912, sec. 7, p. 5.

112. In *MPW*, the initial advertisement for *Queen Elizabeth* appeared in 27 July 1912, 311. See also the advertisements in 3 Aug. 1912, 411, and 14 Sept. 1912, 1036.

113. For a report on the Chicago engagement, see "Sarah Bernhart's *Queen Elizabeth* in Chicago," *MPW* 17 Aug. 1912, 656.

114. See "Moving Picture Men in Session," *Chicago Tribune*, 14 Aug. 1912, pt. 2, p. 5.

115. "Sarah Bernhardt's *Queen Elizabeth* in Chicago."

116. In the *Catalogue of Copyright Entries*, 1912, there is this entry, copyright by Famous Players Film Co., #E 292100, 15 Aug. 1912: "*Queen Elizabeth*, composed by Joseph Carl Breil, musical accompaniment to Sarah Bernhardt's play. 4to."

117. See the advertisement for Powers' theater, *Chicago Tribune*, 18 Aug. 1912, pt. 2. p. 2; the previous week's advertisement (which refers to the film, but not its music) is in pt. 2, p. 11

118. The dispute in Chicago concerned the introduction of "one-man" instruments into the theaters. See the following *Tribune* articles: "Theaters Frame 'One Man' Music," 14 Aug. 1912, p. 8; "Theater Music Worth What?," 15 Aug., p. 2; and "Powers Defies Music Union," 16 Aug., p. 3. When *Queen Elizabeth* opened in New York, at Daly's Theatre in September, reports made no mention of music. See "*Queen Elizabeth* Presentation in New York," *MPW* 7 Sept. 1912, 985; and "Bernhardt in Pictures," *NYT*, 13 Oct. 1912, pt. 7, p. 5, as well as the small advertisement for Daly's on the same page.

119. "Music and 'Movies' Offer New Art Form: Future Wagners Will Develop Dual Appeal to Sense of Sight and Sound," *San Francisco Chronicle*, 12 July 1914, p. 30.

120. See Herbert's remarks, quoted by Edson in the column "The Movies" (subtitled "A Moving Picture Score by Victor Herbert"), *Metronome* 32, no. 6 (June 1916), 16. On the score for *The Fall of a Nation*, see Shirley, "'A Bugle Call to Arms for National Defense,'" in I. Newsom, ed., *Wonderful Inventions*, 173–85.

121. Rissinger, "Interesting Open Letter" (see n. 40).

122. Breil, "Moving Pictures of the Past and Present" (n. 104). Subsequent to this essay, Breil refers to Wagner in the following articles: an interview given at the time of the premiere of *The Legend*, by Dorothy J. Teall, "Mr. Breil's *Legend* Embodies His Theories of Practical Democracy," *Musical America* 28 Sept. 1918, 5; a report on his score for the film *The Lost Battalion*, "Movie Music and Joseph Carl Breil"(n. 105); a manuscript fragment, written ca. 1920, on *The Birth of a Nation* (discussed in Chapter Four); a paper on "The Perfect Motion Picture Music Score" (TS copy in the Breil scrapbooks, UCLA, also discussed in Chapter Four); and the 1922 essay, "Making the Musical Adaptation" (n. 102). Of course, connections between Wagner and the new field of film music were frequently made elsewhere, some well in advance of Breil's published comments: for example, in *MPW* see G. H. Hummel's letter to Sinn, "MfP," 14 Jan. 1911, 76, in which he describes his own use of "the rules laid down by the great R. Wagner"; Sinn's own amplification of Wagner's "thematic principles" in the next column, "MfP," 21 Jan. 1911, 135; Bush's thoughtful essays, "Giving Musical Expression to the Drama" and "Possibilities of Musical Synchronization," in 12 Aug. 1911, 354–55, and 2 Sept. 1911, 607–8; and the consequent reactivation of the discussion by Sinn, in "MfP," 9 Sept. 1911, 787.

123. Directed by Edwin Porter, *The Prisoner of Zenda* ran four reels and featured James K. Hackett, who had long been associated with the play's dual lead roles. For a detailed account of the making of the film, see Zukor, *The Public Is Never Wrong*, 75–89. There he states that Hackett was touring in the play at the time "for Frohman," and that Frohman persuaded Hackett to appear in the film. Despite Zukor's earlier claim that *Zenda* was "the first American photoplay," that is, the first "long picture made in this country" (see Zukor, "Origins and Growth of the Industry," 63–64), Zukor and Frohman apparently filmed James O'Neill in *The Count of Monte Christo* prior to *Zenda*. *Monte Cristo* was the first new Famous Players title to be announced during *Queen Elizabeth*'s run: see e.g., "News of the Theaters," *Chicago Tribune*, 18 Aug. 1912, pt. 2, p. 5, and "*Queen Elizabeth* Presentation in

New York" (n. 118). But when the Selig company rushed out its own version of the story in late 1912, release of the Famous Players version was pushed back to November of the following year. (On the Selig film, see Kalton C. Lahue, *Motion Picture Pioneer: The Selig Polyscope Company* [New York: A. S. Barnes, 1973], 110–17.) The change of plans is evident in the elaborate write-up of Famous Players Film Company, "Daniel Frohman Gets Big Stars To Act for 'Movies,'" *NYT*, 22 Dec. 1912, pt. 5, p. 7: instead of *Monte Cristo*, *Zenda* is announced as the company's next film. See also Ramsaye *A Million and One Nights*, 597–98, and Macgowan, *Behind the Screen*, 159.

124. For references to Breil's score, see "*The Prisoner of Zenda* Is Completed," *MPW* 1 Feb. 1913, 477, and the following *MPW* advertisements for the film: 8 March 1913, 961; 15 March 1913, 1068; 22 March 1913, 1184; 5 April 1913, 10; and 19 April 1913, 245. Three reviews from this period do not mention any score: in *Variety*, 21 Feb. 1913, rpt. *Variety Film Reviews*, vol. 1; "Hackett on the Screen" (signed by "D."), *NY Dramatic Mirror* 26 Feb. 1913, 28, rpt. Pratt, *Spellbound in Darkness*, 99; and Bush, "*The Prisoner of Zenda*," *MPW* 1 March 1913, 871–72.

125. See these advertisements: "*Tess of the D'Urbervilles*," *MPW* 23 Aug. 1913, 854–55, and "*In the Bishop's Carriage*," 20 Sept. 1913, 1246–47; in these, the film's release dates are given as September 1 and 10 respectively.

126. Pratt, *Spellbound in Darkness*, 124.

127. See Paolo Cherchi Usai, "*Cabiria*, an Incomplete Masterpiece," *Film History* 2, no. 2 (June/July 1988), 155–65; he argues that the film is generally known only in its inferior sound version issued (under the supervision of the original director, Pastrone) in 1931, and describes missing footage from the silent version located in various archives. He also states that a copy of the sound version is in the Museo del Cinema, Turin, along with the original score. The film was presented with its score by Peter Randall, conducting the Italian-American Symphony Orchestra, in New York's Town Hall on 8 and 9 May 1982: see Richard Severo, "*Cabiria*, Silent Epic from Italy, on Town Hall Screen, *NYT*, 7 May 1982, sec. C, p.7. In 1990 Kino issued a restored print on video, with a piano adaptation of the score on the soundtrack, arranged and performed by Jacques Gauthier.

128. Advertisement for "D'Annunzio's *Cabiria*," *MPW* 9 Jan. 1915, 271.

129. For coverage of *Cabiria* in *MPW*, see, e.g.: the first advertisement, in 9 May 1914, 772, stating that the film "will shortly be presented in the legitimate theatres of America"; the laudatory review by Bush in 23 May 1914, 1090–91; the announcement in 30 May 1914, 1265, that Werba and Luescher had secured the exhibition rights for the film, with plans for the opening at the Knickerbocker and tours "along the same lines as that of a first-class dramatic production"; and the report on the Knickerbocker premiere, "*Cabiria* Shown on Broadway," 13 June 1914, 1517, with lengthy discussion of the "specially written music." Also these briefer reports: "Knox Gets *Cabiria* for Southeastern States," 1 Aug. 1914, 693; a paragraph on the close of the Broadway engagement, 10 Oct. 1914, 164; a paragraph on the Chicago run in the same issue's "Notes of the Trade," 208; a paragraph on the opening in Los Angeles at the Trinity Auditorium, in "Doings at Los Angeles," 24 Oct. 1914, 479; and an announcement of wider distribution, "*Cabiria* for Picture Theaters," 7 Nov. 1914, 791. A few other important sources from the period are "D'Annunzio as Film Dramatist," *Illustrated London News*, 25 April 1914, pp. 670–71; "D'Annunzio in the Movies," *Literary Digest* 16 May 1914, 1183; the review of the premiere, "Show D'Annunzio's Photoplay *Cabiria*," NYT, 2 June 1914, p. 11; "D'Annunzio's Version of the Second Punic War" (under the column heading "The Moving World"), (New York) *Independent*, 29 June 1914, pp. 560–61; Julian Johnson, "*Cabiria*: A Motion Picture Milestone," *Green Book Magazine* (Chicago) 12 (Sept. 1914), 441–45; and an essay by d'Annunzio, "*Cabiria*," in *Harper's Bazaar* 49, no. 9 (Sept. 1914), 18–21 and 72. The last item contains the author's account of

what inspired him to write the film, a plot synopsis, several photographs from the picture, and, most intriguing, a general discussion of ways in which music relates to drama—though not of any particular music for this film.

130. "*Cabiria* Shown on Broadway."

131. Cherchi Usai, "*Cabiria*, an Incomplete Masterpiece," 156. See also Cherchi Usai, ed., *Giovanni Pastrone: Gli anni d'oro del cinema a torino* (Torino: UTET, 1986), 97–112, for letters of Pizzetti to d'Annunzio. On Mazza there is this entry in Schmidl, *Supplemento al dizionario universale dei musicisti*: "Mazza, Manlio. Pianista, direttore; n. nel 1889; m. il 3 febbraio 1937 a Firenze, ivi insegnante nel R. Conservatorio Cherubini ed alla corale dell'Opera Balilla. Diresse stagioni liriche e alcuni Corpi muscali della Toscana."

132. A copy of the Illinois theater playbill for *Cabiria* is in the Breil collection, UCLA. The front cover reads in part: "**CABIRIA**/Historical Visions of the Third Century, B. C./ by Gabriele D'Annunzio/Musical Accompaniment by Manlio Marza. / Symphonic Orchestra under the direction of Joseph Carl Breil./In Three Acts—Five Episodes."

133. Breil, "Moving Pictures of the Past and Present."

134. Breil, "Original Music in *Cabiria*," letter addressed to "Mr. Metzger" and dated 21 July 1914, printed in *Pacific Coast Musical Review* (undated clipping in the Breil scrapbooks, UCLA). The editorial introduction reads thus: "We take pleasure in publishing the following letter received by us last week from the musical director conducting the orchestra of *Cabiria*, the management pictorial production [*sic*] now exhibited at the Gaiety Theatre." After Breil's letter, there is an editorial postscript explaining that "the expression 'operatic' selections which appeared in our review of the *Cabiria* music was a typographical error. We wrote originally 'oratorio' selections." The postscript continues by noting the film's "unprecedented success. It was originally to be given only two weeks, and the fact that it drew large audiences for three weeks and is now launched upon its fourth and final week speaks highly for its merit." (*Cabiria* did play at the Gaiety Theater for four weeks, from Saturday, 11 July, through Saturday, 8 August, according to advertisements and listings in the *Chronicle*; but the *MPW* advertisement cited in n. 128 states that the film ran 10 weeks in San Francisco. Possibly it moved to another theater or played a return engagement at the Gaiety later that year.)

135. The piano score for *Antony and Cleopatra* (Chicago: George Kleine, 1914) was registered for copyright on 9 Feb. 1914 (#E 334026); a copy is in LC. The composer, George Colburn (b. Colton, N.Y., 1878–d. Chicago, 1925), had received training at the American Conservatory of Music in Chicago, and later taught there, until assuming the position of municipal music director in Winona, Minnesota, in 1915. He is credited with other theatrical works (though no other film scores) as well as one symphonic poem. See the entry for Colburn in *Baker's Biographical Dictionary*, 3d ed. (1919), reprinted more or less intact in each subsequent edition through the 7th (1984). See also Pratt, *New Encyclopedia of Music and Musicians*. On the performance of the score, see McQuade, "Chicago Letter: Chicago Premiere of *Antony and Cleopatra*," *MPW* 24 Jan. 1914, 418; "Photoplay at Christening," *MPW* 16 May 1914, 951; and "The Candler Opens with a Fine Film," *NYT*, 8 May 1914, p. 13. In a letter to Sinn, Roy J. Bassett stated that the piano score for *Antony and Cleopatra* was sent to him but he did not use it, because "we have an orchestra, and it would have taken too long to arrange the music for us." Bassett enclosed a cue sheet for the film, representing his own orchestral compilation. (See Sinn, "MfP," *MPW* 29 Aug. 1914, 1225; and cf. Bassett's earlier letter on *The Cheyenne Massacre*, cited in n. 64.)

136. "Music and 'Movies' Offer New Art Form." (The last clause of the passage I have cited should probably read: "who has attempted no other work than conjoining the music of the classic composers, related by the simplest of modulations.")

137. "New Form of Music Born of the 'Movies': *Cabiria*, at the Gaiety Theater, Suggests a Novel Field for Future Symphony Writers," *San Francisco Chronicle*, 2 Aug. 1914, p. 28.

138. "Marza's Music for *Cabiria*: Why Great Composer and Poet Worked Together," *Los Angeles Times*, 27 Sept. 1914, pt. 3, p. 2. *Cabiria* was the opening attraction for the new Trinity Auditorium, where it played from Monday, 28 Sept. 1914, through Saturday, 17 Oct. (per advertisements in the *L.A. Times*); it was then shown for one week more, beginning on 2 November: see the advertisement in the Sunday *Times*, 1 Nov. 1914, pt. 3, p. 1.

139. "Marza and D'Annunzio: A Partnership That Produced a New Form of Art," *Los Angeles Times*, 30 Sept. 1914, pt. 2, p. 6.

140. Sinn, "MfP," *MPW* 19 Dec. 1914, 1690. Apparently the same elaborate type of accompaniment that was heard originally in New York had by this time traveled to Bridgeport, perhaps one of many cities covered by a touring show.

141. Harlow Hare, "*Birth of a Nation* Music Marvel in Effectiveness," *Boston American*, 18 July 1915, editorial section, p. 6. This article is discussed, along with sources in which it has been reprinted, in Chapter Four.

CHAPTER 4. BREIL'S SCORE FOR THE BIRTH OF A NATION

1. Jean Mitry, "Preface" in John Cuniberti, *"The Birth of a Nation": A Formal Shot-by-Shot Analysis Together with Microfiche*, Cinema Editions on Microfiche (n.p.: Research Publications, 1979), 7. See also Mitry, "Griffith," in *Anthologies du cinéma* 1 (Paris: *L'Avant-scène*, 1966), 65–120, and his "Filmographie de David Wark Griffith," *Cahiers de la Cinémathèque*, no. 17 (Christmas 1975), 119–61.

2. In Mitry's preface to Cuniberti, he considers the semiological implications of Griffith's style: how the spatial and temporal relationships between shots gave them "a *signifying* or *symbolic* value. The denotations lead to a host of diverse connotations, and this movement full of meaning permitted the creation and development of a *language*" (p. 9, Mitry's emphases). Basic studies of the film which consider this aspect of Griffith's achievement, and provide historical contexts, include Lewis Jacobs, "D. W. Griffith: *The Birth of a Nation* and *Intolerance*," chapter 11 of *Rise of the American Film* (1968), 171–210; A. R. Fulton, "Editing in *The Birth of a Nation*," in *The Development of an Art: From Silent Films to the Age of Television* (Norman: Univ. of Oklahoma Press, 1960), 89–101; and Cook, *A History of Narrative Film*, 77–94. The studies by Fulton and Jacobs are reprinted (Fulton in full, Jacobs in part) in Fred Silva, ed., *Focus on "The Birth of a Nation"* (Englewood Cliffs, N.J.: Prentice-Hall, 1971), 144–68. See also Vlada Petric, "Two Lincoln Assassinations by D. W. Griffith," *QRFS* 3, no. 3 (Summer 1978), 345–69. One key publication, which appeared too recently to be of use in the writing of this book, is Robert Lang, ed., *"The Birth of a Nation": D. W. Griffith, Director*, Rutgers Films in Print, vol. 21 (New Brunswick, N.J.: Rutgers Univ. Press, 1994), which contains a continuity script, reprints of sources from 1915 and of current scholarly studies, and new essays, including an introduction to the film's "History, Ideology, [and] Narrative Form," by Lang.

3. The novel was published as *The Clansman: An Historical Romance of the Ku Klux Klan* (New York: Doubleday, Page, 1905); "The Clansman: An American Drama in Four Acts" was never published. See Raymond Allen Cook, *Fire from the Flint: The Amazing Careers of Thomas Dixon* (Winston-Salem, N.C.: John F. Blair, 1968). Russell Merritt traces the relationship between the film and Dixon's writings in "Dixon, Griffith, and the Southern Legend," *CJ* 12, no. 1 (Fall 1972), 26–45; rpt. in *Cinema Examined: Selections from "Cinema Journal,"* Richard Dyer MacCann and Jack C. Ellis, eds. (New York: E. P. Dutton, 1982), 165–84. (*Note*: When citing sources from ca. 1915, I follow their spellings of "Clan" or

"Klan," "Clansmen" or "Klansmen," and so forth—there seems to have been no standard orthography. In my own writing I follow current practice, using "Klan" and its derivatives.)

4. Cuniberti, *Birth*, 142, title following shot 1077.

5. Cuniberti, *Birth*, 168, title following shot 1377b. For more detailed synopses of the plot of the film, see Silva, ed., *Focus on "Birth,"* 169–73; also, Edward Wagenknecht and Anthony Slide, *The Films of D. W. Griffith* (New York: Crown, 1975), 46–48. The synopsis submitted by the film's producers to the U.S. Copyright Office in 1915 can be found in Cuniberti, *Birth*, 180.

6. Much of *Focus on "Birth"* is devoted to the film's anti-Negro bias and the resultant protests and censorship battles: see, especially, Thomas Cripps, "The Reaction of the Negro to the Motion Picture *The Birth of a Nation*," 111–24; and Peter Noble, "The Negro in *The Birth of a Nation*," 125–32. Two of the most valuable recent studies are those by Michael Rogin, "'The Sword Became a Flashing Vision': D. W. Griffith's *The Birth of a Nation*," *Representations*, no. 9 (Winter 1985), 150–95; and Russell Merritt, "D. W. Griffith's *The Birth of a Nation*: Going after Little Sister," in *Close Viewings: An Anthology of New Film Criticism*, Peter Lehman, ed. (Tallahassee: Florida State Univ., 1990), 215–37.

One reporter in New York described the film in part as "a version of Thomas Dixon's novel *The Clansman*, which stirred the hysterical to praise and condemnation in dramatic form some years ago": see "*Birth of a Nation*, $2 Movie, Films Civil War Scenes," *New York Herald Tribune*, 4 March 1915 (a review included in MOMA's collection of files on the film, microfiche 076). Cook surveys reactions to the play in *Fire from the Flint*, 138–49.

7. Early reports of Griffith's battles include "Trouble over *The Clansman*," *Los Angeles Times*, 9 Feb. 1915, pt. 2, p. 6; and "D. W. Griffith Speaks against the Censorship Law Pending at Albany," *New York Clipper*, 13 March 1915, p. 7 (under the heading "Timely Picture Topics"). Reprints of three subsequent newspaper articles in which Griffith responded to criticism are in Silva, ed., *Focus on "Birth"*, 77–99; his 1916 pamphlet, *The Rise and Fall of Free Speech in America*, is in Harry M. Geduld, ed., *Focus on D. W. Griffith* (Englewood Cliffs, N.J.: Prentice-Hall, 1971), 43–45. At the beginning of the film Griffith placed a long title headed "A PLEA FOR THE ART OF THE MOTION PICTURE," in which he demanded "the same liberty [of expression] that is conceded to the art of the written word." (He wrote an almost identical sentence into *The Rise and Fall of Free Speech*: see Geduld, p. 45.) At the beginning of the second half of the film, there appears a title claiming that "this is an historical presentation . . . and is not meant to reflect on any race or people today." Following this come two more title cards containing quotations ascribed to Woodrow Wilson's *History of the American People* (1902). Although Griffith's intention was to demonstrate his film's scholarly authority, the quoted passages were actually an assemblage of short phrases taken more or less out of context: for the first, see Wilson, vol. 5, pp. 46 and 49; for the second, pp. 49–50. (We may wonder if Wilson's reported favorable reaction to the film was influenced by these citations, assuming they were present in the version he saw; see n. 12.)

8. In a build-up of publicity for the film's New York premiere, large advertisements began to appear in the *NYT* on Sunday, 21 Feb., sec. 7, p. 7. The one for the following Sunday, 28 Feb., sec. 7, p. 6, states that "D. W. Griffith's colossal production will startle the world . . . [the film is] the expression of genius in a new realm of art." (A similar advertisement is in Cuniberti, *Birth*, 187.) Hyperbolic praise also appeared in the review by Len, *New York Clipper*, 13 March 1915, p. 8: the film is said to be "the most wonderfully constructed, most artistically photographed, most realistically acted and elaborately produced spectacle that has yet been shown," and Len calls this but "faint commendation." (Laudatory capsule excerpts from 20 other reviews by "New York's Foremost Critics" are quoted in an advertisement from the film in the *NYT*, 7 March 1915, sec. 7, p. 7.)

Estimates of attendance figures for the film have varied widely, but all sources concur in making the film a record-breaker; see the statistical summary in Merritt, "Dixon, Griffith, and the Southern Legend," 27, n. 2. Merritt also compiled figures on lengths of the runs of nine major films of the late teens in seven American cities, and *Birth* comes out far ahead: see his "D. W. Griffith Directs the Great War: The Making of *Hearts of the World*," *QRFS* 6, no. 1 (1981), 64, n. 26. The film's box-office revenues were equally impressive but exact dollar amounts have never been ascertained. Surveys of the estimates are given in Merritt, "The Impact of D. W. Griffith's Motion Pictures from 1908 to 1914" (Ph.D. diss., Harvard Univ., 1970), 247–49 and n. 12; see also "All-Time Film Rental Champs," *Variety*, 5 Jan. 1977, p. 16.

9. The quoted passage is from the review in the *Herald Tribune*, cited above (n. 6). Many other advertisements and reviews emphasized the film's American qualities, and its superiority to previous imported spectacles. For example, an advertisement for the film in *NYT*, 5 March 1915, p. 18, contains this quotation, attributed to the *New York World*: "Makes *Cabiria* seem insignificant by comparison"; and in the next day's advertisement (p. 18), is this line, attributed to the *New York American*: "Beside it *Cabiria* and *Quo Vadis* seem tame." Also, though he had misgivings about the film, Metcalfe, the reviewer for *Life* (18 March 1915, p. 466, under the heading "Drama"), wrote that "some of the imported films have been as impressive in their respective lines, but they were foreign in subject and foreign in treatment. This one deals entirely with American scenes and American characters. . . ."

10. In the film, the phrase "useless sacrifice" comments on the death of the youngest Cameron and Stoneman sons. (See Cuniberti, *Birth*, 63, title following shot 245b.) Compare these subsequent titles: "War's *sad page*," that is, the news of each death being read in the family home (p. 64, following shot 258e); "War's peace," Griffith's oxymoron for the shot of trenches filled with the dead in the midst of battle (p. 75, following shot 367); and "War, the breeder of hate," seen when Flora reacts to the news that a second Cameron brother has been killed and the oldest has been wounded (p. 76, following shot 374e). The allegorical vision which concluded the film (shots 1373–76, pp. 166-67) begins with the mounted God of War swinging his sword over a mass of tangled bodies, while the agonized living extend their arms; the image gives way to others showing harmonious throngs with Christ superimposed, Elsie and Ben together, and the Hall of Peace in the celestial city.

11. From a review by Charles Darnton in the (New York) *Evening World*, as quoted in the advertisement in *NYT*, 7 March 1915, sec. 7, p. 9.

12. Thomas Gregory's review for the *New York American*, 5 March 1915, contains this estimation of the film's historical value: of the "more than five thousand pictures" in the drama, "one and all are faithful to historic fact, so that looking upon them, you may feel that you [are] beholding that which actually happened." (This review was reprinted almost completely in an advertisement in *NYT*, 14 March 1915, sec. 7, p. 10.) After a special White House screening, Woodrow Wilson was supposed to have exclaimed that the film was like "history written in lightning," a statement used in the publicity for the film. See Merritt, "Dixon, Griffith, and the Southern Legend," 28, n. 8; Merritt states that Wilson's famous remark was first quoted in the *New York Post*, 4 March 1915.

13. James Agee, "David Wark Griffith" *The Nation*, 4 Sept. 1948; rpt. in *Agee on Film: Reviews and Comments* (Boston: Beacon Press, 1964), 313–18. The quoted passage appears on p. 314.

14. MOMA's entire collection of music for silent films was transferred to LC, by me, in the spring and summer of 1978, for purposes of microfilming and preservation; subsequently the collection was consigned to LC on permanent loan. In the course of this project, a preliminary catalogue was made of both the MOMA and LC collections, which Gillian Anderson subsequently revised as *Music for Silent Films* (1988).

In addition to *Birth*, the MOMA collection includes a unique set of piano conductors and orchestral parts for 14 subsequent silent films made by Griffith. In alphabetical order: *America* (score by Breil and Adolph Finck), *Broken Blossoms* (Louis F. Gottschalk), *Dream Street* (Louis Silvers), *The Greatest Question* (Albert Pesce), *Hearts of the World* (Carli Elinor), *Intolerance* (Breil), *Isn't Life Wonderful?* (Silvers), *The Love Flower* (Pesce), *The Mother and the Law* (a segment of *Intolerance*, issued separately) (Gottschalk and Breil), *One Exciting Night* (Pesce), *Orphans of the Storm* (Gottschalk and Wm. Frederick Peters), *A Romance of Happy Valley* (Harley Hamilton), *Way Down East* (Silvers and Peters), and *The White Rose* (Breil). Like MOMA's *Birth* materials, most of these scores are in fragile condition; possibly donated directly by Griffith, they were probably acquired through the efforts of Iris Barry, the museum's first curator and author of *D. W. Griffith: American Film Master* (New York: Museum of Modern Art, 1940; rpt., with revisions [by Eileen Bowser], 1965).

15. The Kleiner collection was donated to Minnesota by Mrs. Kleiner in 1981, and consists largely of copies of his own compiled scores; an inventory is given in Anderson, *Music for Silent Films*, 150–53. (Like the *Birth* score, many of Kleiner's compilations were reprinted in offset copies, available to pianists from the museum's film rental library.) Other materials from Kleiner's library are also included in the collection: sheet music, classical piano music, miscellaneous books, cassettes of his performances, and photographs. For further information contact the Special Collections and Rare Books Division of the Wilson Library, University of Minnesota, West Bank Campus, Minneapolis. I am grateful to John R. Jenson and other curators for allowing me to examine the collection.

16. I have seen all of the scores described in this chapter except for the one at Eastman House, which was mentioned in a letter sent in the late 1970s from George Pratt, then curator at Eastman, to Vlada Petric, curator of the Harvard Film Archive. In the letter (shown to me by Petric), Pratt gave a list of Eastman's film music holdings, including sets of orchestral parts for *The Birth of a Nation*, *Orphans of the Storm* (the same music as at MOMA, by Gottschalk and Peters), and *John Needham's Double* (Bluebird Universal Feature, copyright 1916 by Carl Fischer, "music selected and arranged by Max Winkler and F. Rehsen"); in addition, 10 piano scores, for *Ben-Hur*, *The Big Parade*, *Birth*, *La Bohème*, *Dream Street*, *Intolerance*, *The King of Kings*, *Robin Hood*, *The Thief of Bagdad*, *Way Down East*, and *The White Rose*, plus a "Violin Leader" for *The Hunchback of Notre Dame* and a copy of the piano *Selection from Incidental Music to "Intolerance"* (New York: Chappell, 1916) by Breil. Eastman also has an extensive cue-sheet collection, listed as appendix 4 in Anderson, *Music for Silent Films*, 154–63. See also, concerning materials and performances at Eastman, these articles, in *Image* (*Journal of Photography and Motion Pictures of the International Museum of Photography at George Eastman House*) 25, no. 1 (March 1982): John B. Kuiper, "Silent Films for Contemporary Audiences," 1–6; Hunsberger, "Orchestral Accompaniment for Silent Films," 7–16; and Pratt, "Cue Sheets for Silent Films" (also with a list of titles), 17–23.

17. The photocopies at USC are in the Department of Special Collections, shelf number M176.B74B7; they came from the office of the former head of School of Cinema-Television, Bernard Kantor, at an unspecified time, and the whereabouts of the offset copy from which they were made is unknown. I am grateful to Dr. Robert Knutson, librarian, for allowing me to acquire a microfilm of one of these photocopies.

18. All three orchestra sets at LC are contained on one reel of microfilm, along with the piano score, in the MOMA Collection (Music 3236, reel 8, items 5–8). The touring schedule written into the harp part of the "Large Orchestra Set" can be seen inside the front cover, under the heading "Rout. of 1915 & 1916." It began at the Savoy Theater, Asbury Park, N.J., on 23 Aug., and ended at an unspecified theater in Port Davis, N.J., for three

days in April 1916. "*46 weeks*" is written across the list in pencil. There are additional markings at the bottom of the page suggesting that the run might have been extended for one week in Hoboken and two weeks in New York, as well as various numbers adding up to make 283 (days?), changed to 285, and added to 525 to make 810; all of these figures are crossed out.

19. See, e.g., the bassoon part in the "Large Orchestra Set": the inserted page of music is a part for the "*Cocoanut Dance: Piece Characteristic*," by Andrew Hermann, op. 193 (New York: Carl Fischer, n.d.), plate #3082-23. Cuniberti, citing various earlier sources, states that Griffith added a "documentary postscript" to the film concerning two black schools, the Tuskegee Institute and the Hampton Institute; this sequence "made its first appearance" in Boston, 17 April 1915, and was subsequently added to the film in other cities. Cuniberti states that no copy of this footage has survived (*Birth*, 168).

20. The Epoch Producing Corporation was incorporated on 8 Feb. 1915, with Harry Aitken (one of the film's original producers, from Mutual) as president, and Griffith as vice president; see Barry, *D. W. Griffith*, 47.

21. These passing references, all appearing within longer reports, serve as examples: (1) "Carl Biel, well known as the author of *The Climax*, is composing music and adapting certain compositions [for the New York opening]"—Grace Kingsley, "At the Stage Door," *Los Angeles Times*, 8 Feb. 1915, p. 4; (2) "The film is [to be] exhibited to the accompaniment of special music written by Joseph Carl Briel, composer of the music of *The Climax*, and played by a symphony orchestra of forty musicians"—"Written on the Screen," *NYT*, 28 Feb. 1915, sec. 7, p. 7; (3) "A musical score was written for the presentation by Joseph Carl Briel, and this served as supplemental and incidental music to the film. The accompaniment was played by an orchestra of forty pieces"—"Picture Drama of Slavery Presented," *NY Sun*, 4 March 1915 (transcribed from MOMA microfiche 076); and (4) "The music on Wednesday evening, supplied by an orchestra with the occasional singing of popular melodies supplied by a chorus, was well in keeping with the actions of the screen and particularly inspiring in the battle scenes. It was composed by Joseph Carl Briel"—"Griffith Film Scores," *MPW* 13 March 1915, 1587; rpt. in *Focus on "Birth,"* 28–29.

Apart from Breil's authorship, another point established by many sources is that the film was normally accompanied by an orchestra larger than normal in theaters of the day. At the Liberty, the second and third items above specify the number of players as 40. For the engagement at the Brighton Beach Theater in Brooklyn, the manager promised an orchestra of 50. (See the clipping from the *Brooklyn Eagle*, 21 June 1915, Griffith Scrapbook I, on MOMA microfiche 89.) The figure was put at 30 in the review by Charles Bregg, "*Birth of a Nation* Is a Great Spectacle," *Pittsburgh Gazette Times*, 2 Sept. 1915 (clipping, Breil scrapbooks). An advertisement in the *Detroit News Tribune*, 1 Jan. 1916, p. 11, announced the film's opening at the Detroit Opera House with 25 players; on 3 Jan. 1916, p. 8, the number was changed to 30. Sometimes a chorus was also featured: the presence of one at the New York premiere is mentioned in the *NY Sun* review cited above; also at the Boston premiere, according to clippings from two newspapers in Breil's scrapbooks. Just how such choruses were used—whether in prologues to the show, in the Rothapfel manner, or in accompaniment to the film—is not known.

22. Hare, "*Birth of a Nation* Music Marvel in Effectiveness." This article is reprinted in Seymour Stern, "The Film's Score," *Film Culture*, no. 36 (Spring–Summer 1965), 109–12; and in Silva, ed., *Focus on "Birth,"* 36–40. I list the titles of borrowed music mentioned by Hare, all found in the Breil score: *Comin' thro' the Rye*, *Bonnie Blue Flag*, *Light Cavalry Overture*, *Freischütz Overture*, *Dixie*, *Maryland, My Maryland*, *Marching through Georgia*, *Tramp, Tramp, Tramp! the Boys Are Marching*, *Kingdom Coming*, *The Girl I Left Behind Me*, *Home! Sweet Home!*, *Taps*, *The Star-Spangled Banner*, *America*, *In the Hall of the Mountain*

King, *Hail to the Chief*, *Norma Overture*, *Cocoanut Dance*, *1812 Overture*, *Rienzi Overture*, *Zampa Overture*; *The Ride of the Valkyries*, *In the Gloaming*, and a "Gloria" from a "*Mass in C*." (Though the excerpt is in C major, the Mass as a whole is in G; and Hare attributes it to Haydn, though at that time it was commonly attributed to Mozart.) Hare also mentions "Breil's 'Perfect Song,' as an original composition for this play and now published in sheet form." (See n. 25.) The only music he mentions which is not found in Breil's score is "The [Magic] Fire Music" from *Die Walküre*.

It should be noted that although Hare names Breil as the composer of "The Perfect Song," he does not explicitly identify him as the creator or the conductor of the score: "A wonderful art, this the marriage of music and spectacle," he writes, "and one wonderfully achieved by Mr. Griffith and the man who put together the score, a composite of great themes suitable to Griffith's great ideas rather than an original work." In Stern, "The Film's Score," p. 110, on the same page where this passage from Hare appears, he appends a quotation from a report on the film by Frederick Jones, "screen and stage critic," published in the *Boston American* on 18 April 1915. (The film opened in Boston on 9 April, at the Tremont Theatre.) Jones identifies Frederick Arundel, music director of the Tremont, as the conductor of *Birth*, and praises him as "the first director in the country co-operating in the new art of musical spectacle as developed by David W. Griffith."

Breil's scrapbooks contain clippings of several subsequent reports analagous to Hare's, including "Musical Setting of *Birth of a Nation*," *Baltimore Sun* (date illegible, but possibly 2 Jan. 1916); an untitled item apparently from the *Washington Post*, 14 May 1916; and "Old-Time Melodies Add to the Charm of Great War Film," *Atlanta Constitution*, 27 Nov. 1916.

23. *Souvenir: "The Birth of a Nation"* (New York: Epoch Producing Corp, [1915]): credits on the title page include "Music by Joseph Carl Breil." A copy is the NY Public Library (MFL - n.c.610 (misc. vol.)); another is in the USC Cinema Library.

24. *Program for D. W. Griffith's Mighty Spectacle "The Birth of a Nation"* (London: Scala Theatre, [1915]): on. p. 6 are the words "Music by Joseph Breil." Copy in the Breil collection, UCLA.

25. These versions of *The Perfect Song*, all published by Chappell & Co., London, are listed on cards at the Copyright Division of LC, for 1915, in order of date of registration: (1) "*The Perfect Song* from *Birth of a Nation*, by Joseph Carl Breil, of U.S., arr. by S. Deshon; band. 4to" (E365500, 23 Feb. 1915); (2) "*The Perfect Song*, Love Strain from *The Birth of a Nation*, words by Clarence Lucas, music by Joseph Carl Breil, of U.S.; orchestra; arr. by S. Deshon" (E361722, 8 May 1915); (3) [Same title as no. 2, except that the arrangement is called] "Song, no. 3 in F (E361723, 8 May 1915); (4) "*The Perfect Song*, by Joseph Carl Breil, arr. by Clarence Lucas of Great Britain, domiciled at New York, N.Y., piano" (E364082, 27 May 1915); and (5) "*The Perfect Song*, by Joseph Carl Breil, arr. by Otto Langey of Germany; violin and piano, with cello obligato ad lib" (E366701, 2 Aug. 1915). A set of orchestral parts corresponding to the second version listed above is available in the music library of the Paramount Theatre, Oakland, Calif. The final three versions are in the British Library: the song arrangement, shelf number H.1846.h. (15.); the piano solo, h.3284.x. (11.); and the violin arrangement, h.1612.dd. (45.). (See "Breil" in the *Catalogue of the British Library to 1980*, vol. 8 [London: K. G. Sour, 1982].)

The words written for the song by Lucas have nothing specifically to do with the plot of the film. The introduction, or "verse," is in four phrases of four measures each: "The day is grey, and all the way is drear and lonely Though together side by side Through life we go./Without the light of love To shine upon our path We cannot know a friend or foe, Where all is dark/And yet, amid the throngs That pass and mingle, Are hearts that ache For sympathy and love./A look perchance, A word of tender meaning, Lo! two happy hearts are one!" The "Refrain" melody moves more slowly, and, in keeping with its structure, the text is in two parallel phrases: "Perfect song of loving hearts united, Golden dreams of heaven Melting into day!/Perfect love of hearts forever plighted! joy with summer blends and winter ends In perfect love's June day."

26. According to the statement for the half-year ending 30 June 1916 (typed under the letterhead of Chappell & Co., New York), the song sold 5,944 copies in America, 677 in Canada; the piano solo, 390 and 95; the arrangement for violin and piano, 34 and 3. For the next half-year, ending 31 December 1916: 1,726 copies of the song were reported sold in America, 319 in Canada; 200 and 23 copies of the piano solo; and 21 copies in America of the violin arrangement. The figures increased for the half-year ending 30 June 1917, because Australian sales were also counted for the first time; thereafter they show rapid decrease, though even in the half-year ending 31 Dec. 1918 (the last statement included in the collection), 144 copies of the song were sold in America.

27. "*The Perfect Song*, Love Strain from *The Birth of a Nation*, by Joseph Carl Breil, played by Andrei Kmita, of U.S. (Rythmodik record music rolls F13313)," copyright American Piano Co., New York (E387765, 20 Nov. 1915).

28. The following versions of *The Perfect Song* were registered for copyright after 1915, all by Chappell & Co.: (1) "*The Perfect Song*, Musical Theme of the *Pepsodent Hour*... New ed., NY: Chappell-Harms, Inc." (E pub. 10606, 4 Nov. 1929); (2) "*The Perfect Song*, by Joseph Carl Breil, arr. by Chas. N. Grant, orch. pts." (E pub 11097, 30 Nov. 1929)—see the set of parts in the Music Library, Paramount Theatre, Oakland; (3) "*The Perfect Song*, fox trot . . . arr. by Joseph Nussbaum, orch. pts. NY: Chappell-Harms, Inc. 4to" (E pub 13502, 13 Feb. 1930); (4) "*The Perfect Song*, three-part chorus or trio (S.S.A.), Chappell's Vocal Libary of Part Songs, Fifth Series, 3160, Frank B. Cookson, arr." (E pub 74870, 7 Feb. 1939); (5) "*The Perfect Song*, arr. by Stechel [?] for S.A.T.B." (E pub 38186, [card missing, so date not found]); (6) "*The Perfect Song*, arr. for Hammond Organ by William Stickles" (E P 42703, 7 Dec. 1949); and (7) "*The Perfect Song*, Musical Theme for Amos n' Andy, Arr. by J. M. Hanert, in *Chappell's Song Favorites* [for chord organ], p. 17" (E P 75615, 28 Aug. 1953).

The Breil scrapbooks include a page of clippings (with a handwritten comment: "Curator—take note of this page particularly"), discussing the origins of the "Amos 'n' Andy" theme. The longest, an undated item from the *Musical Courier*, comments that "poor Breil never guessed before he passed on, in Los Angeles in 1926, that one of his tunes would be heard by millions," and includes a photograph of the Gallico Ensemble of Chicago, which "plays only one tune, several times nightly in Chicago for 123,000,000 million American listeners alone." The report also notes that for all its performances the tune was then only mildly popular, 15,000 copies being sold annually—"a relatively small number under the circumstances."

29. The *Selection . . . from the Incidental Music to "The Birth of a Nation"* (London: Chappell, 1916) was registered for copyright on 26 Dec. 1916 (E 396419). Copies are held by LC, shelf number M39.B, and the British Library, h. 3284.x.(12.).

30. The keyboard version of *Breil's Original Collection of Dramatic Music* (London: Chappell, 1917) was registered for copyright on 2 March 1917 (E 397795); the version for orchestra, on 16 April 1917 (E 404333). Copies of both versions are in LC, the first under shelf number M176.B, the second under M1357.B. The latter contains parts for flute, oboe, 2 clarinets, bassoon, 2 horns, 2 trumpets, 1 trombone, piano, drums, and strings.

31. See the album, *D. W. Griffith's "The Birth of a Nation": Original Motion Picture Score Composed by Joseph Carl Breil*, New Zealand Symphony Orchestra, conducted by Clyde Allen (Label "X": LXDR 701/2, © 1985); subsequently issued on compact disc (LXCD 701). My reaction to Allen's tempos, etc., is based in part on my own performances of the MOMA score, which I have played as accompaniment to the film on numerous occasions, at the Harvard Film Archive, LC, and elsewhere, over the past decade.

32. In the clarinet part of the "Large Orchestra Set," the first page has "Overture 28" in pencil; at the beginning of number 28 of Act I, "Overture" is also penciled in, and after the first fifteen measures, "Change back to 17"; at number 17 is written "Start." These segments fit together smoothly in harmonic terms, and make a suitable introduction to Act I, with emphasis on the tragic character of its historical events. The first excerpt is the beginning of Bellini's *Norma* Overture, in G minor: it accompanies the final sequence of Act I, Lincoln's assassination; the second is an arrangement of *Marching through Georgia*, which begins in B♭ major and ends by pausing on the dominant of D minor, (the key in which the first number of the score begins): it accompanies a scene of Sherman's troops as they move through open country toward Atlanta, "while women and children weep." For Act II, the instruction is to play number 25 (of the second act) and repeat; this is an equally strong choice: it contains Breil's most striking new music in Act II, representing the Klan. (See Fig. 26.)

Kleiner's instructions for the beginning of the film are as follows: (in pencil) "At *main* title play p. 125 twice for introduction"—that is, the theme for the Klan. (There are other cues penciled in, too, which refer to various titles at the beginning of the film.) Act II, in Kleiner's performances, probably followed the first act without an intermission, and he seems not to have played any music during its introductory titles: he calls for "Silence until T. The Uncrowned King"—at which point the action and first number begins.

33. According to advertisements and reports in the *Los Angeles Times*, exhibitions of *The Clansman* at Clune's Auditorium (Los Angeles) were separated into four segments, as follows: nine weeks, from 8 Feb. to 11 April (each week beginning on Monday and ending on Sunday); three weeks, 26 April to 16 May; four weeks, 24 May to 20 June; and six weeks, 9 Aug. to 19 Sept. Interim engagements were quite varied and generally of musical interest. From 12 to 25 April, Clune's offered *The Sign of the Rose*, first announced during the second week of *The Clansman* screening, and later described as "A Combination of Motion Picture and the Spoken Drama . . . in nine sections / Motion Pictures closing with the Spoken Art . . . A Special Musical and Vocal score accompanied by our Symphony Orchestra" (adv., 11 April, sec. 3, p. 1). From 17 to 23 May, the theater was occupied by the Temple Baptist Church, and two performances of Beethoven's 9th Symphony were given by the L. A. Symphony Orchestra under Adolf Tandler (write-up by Edwin Schallert, 16 May, sec. 3, p. 2). During the summer months, the schedule included *The Island of Regeneration*, a film, 21–27 June; *Fairyland*, an opera judged the winner of a $10,000 competition, music by Horatio Parker, stage direction by Louis F. Gottschalk, 1–3 and 8–9 July (write-up 27 June, sec. 3); and three more films: *The Rosary*, 12–25 July, *Crooky*, 26 July–1 Aug., and *The White Sister*, 2–8 Aug. Each reappearance of *The Clansman* was billed as a "return engagement"; when the last one began, Clune's announced that the film "appears to be without limits as regards its drawing power. So great is the demand for seats that it will be necessary to show the film again next week" (note on theaters, 12 Aug., sec. 2, p. 2)—and, as it turned out, for four more weeks besides. The same announcement mentioned that "special attention has been paid to the musical programme, which sustains the emotional intensity of the film throughout."

34. Stern, "The Film's Score," *Film Culture*, no. 36 (Spring–Summer 1965), 103–32. This essay is part of a monograph of 209 pp. (the entire issue) titled "Griffith I: *The Birth of a Nation*, Part I," published in the year of the film's golden anniversary. (There do not seem to have been published any subsequent "parts.") Two valuable sources which Stern brings to light are the essay by Harlow Hare and a copy of a Clune's theater program, which he says represents the music for the film "before changes to final score."

Of Stern's numerous publications on Griffith, this one contains the most extended discussion of music, though some of the same points can be found, stated more concisely, in

Stern, "*The Birth of a Nation*" (*D. W. Griffith 1915*), published as "Special Issue No. 1" of *Cinemages* (New York: Group for Film Study, 1955). Merritt sums up Stern's work by referring readers to it for "valuable, hitherto inaccessible primary material, buried underneath unreadable prose and extremely shaky scholarship" (see "Dixon, Griffith, and the Southern Legend," 27, n. 3). I know of no other published scholarly work concerned solely with the score, although Charles Berg raised important questions about it in "Music: The Silent Film's Constant Companion," a paper presented at a panel sponsored by the Society for Cinema Studies at the University of Vermont, 1976: see "*The Birth of a Nation* and 1915; Various Historical Perspectives," TS, pp. 18–22 (in the MOMA file on the film). Also, Win Sharples, Jr., collected information on both scores and shared his findings with me. Cuniberti (*Birth*, 40) relies on Stern for his comments about music for the film (repeating the latter's claims about the Capitol score); so, too, does Schickel, in *D. W. Griffith*, 243–44.

35. A "Special Presentation Adapted and Devised by S. L. Rothafel" is promised in the advertisement for the Capitol, *NYT*, 1 May 1921, sec. 10, p. 3. See also the review "*The Birth of a Nation* (Revival)," *NYT*, 2 May 1921, p. 12; rpt. Pratt, *Spellbound in Darkness*, 209–10: the reviewer notes that "the picture has a new musical accompaniment . . . adapted by S. L. Rothafel and arranged by Erno Rapee, William Axt and Hermann Hand, which, though effective now and then, is much too noisy most of the time." In Stern's citation of this sentence (on p. 114 of his monograph), he inserts "[*sic*]" after the adjective "new."

36. James Hart, ed., *The Man Who Invented Hollywood: The Autobiography of D. W. Griffith—A Memoir and Some Notes* (Louisville: Touchstone, 1972), 93. Hart edited the unpublished manuscript that Griffith had written (with Hart's aid) between 1932 and 1940. The anecdote cited here, one of dozens in the autobiography, all told with similar rhetorical flair, is the only part of the book which contains a reference to music for any of Griffith's films. (Written in the late thirties, when the director's fortunes were at low ebb, his narrative is frustratingly incomplete, extending only to 1916.) The same anecdote also appears in these sources: Roy Aitken, with A. P. Nelson, "*The Birth of a Nation" Story* (Middleburg, Va.: Delinger, 1965), 45, where the money put up by Clune is said to be $5,000; Lillian Gish, with Ann Pinchot, *The Movies, Mr. Griffith, and Me* (Englewood Cliffs, N.J.: Prentice-Hall, 1969), 144–45; and Robert M. Henderson, *D. W. Griffith: His Life and Work* (New York: Oxford Univ. Press, 1972), 153. In Allen's liner notes to his recording, he states that "Clune agreed in exchange for a percentage of the profits to book the epic into the Auditorium Theatre Beautiful and to lend Griffith the $15,000 (Clune's grandson later said it was actually $25,000) which the filmmaker needed to complete it."

37. Clarke Irvine, "Doings at Los Angeles," *MPW* 23 May 1914, 1103. When Clune opened his Broadway Theatre in 1911, he claimed it to be "the finest and best equipped moving picture theater in the country," with an orchestra of eight pieces, a $10,000 set of chimes, and two singing booths flanking the stage: see "Clune's Theatre—Los Angeles, Cal.: One of the Handsomest Theatres in the West," *MPW* 11 Feb. 1911, 296–97. Three years later he leased the Auditorium for ten years, according to Irvine, "Doings at Los Angeles," *MPW* 28 March 1914, 1685. Built in 1906, the theater had originally functioned as both a church and a civic hall for opera, music, and drama; Clune exhibited pictures there until 1920, when the Los Angeles Philharmonic moved in and it became the Philharmonic Auditorium. (See Henry Sutherland, "Final Curtain to Fall in Old Auditorium," *Los Angeles Times*, 2 Nov. 1964, pt. 4, pp. 1–4; cited in Neil Erman Wilson, "A History of Opera and Associated Educational Activities in Los Angeles" [Ph.D. diss., Indiana Univ., 1967], 136, n. 51.) After opening the Auditorium with *Home Sweet Home*, Clune continued to prosper with several more films, including Griffith's next feature, *The Escape*. See "*The Seats of the Mighty* in Los Angeles," *MPW* 19 Dec. 1914, 1692: "Under Mr. Clune's management

the Auditorium has been a wonderful success. Features are seen there for indefinite engagements. *The Escape*, for example, played six weeks; *The Spoilers*, three weeks."

38. Grace Kingsley, "Film Flams," *Los Angeles Times*, 26 Sept. 1914, pt. 1, p. 7. (The remainder of this column discusses the Oz pictures then being made and mentions their scores by Louis F. Gottschalk.)

39. The program in Fig. 28 is a copy of the one printed in Stern, "The Film's Score," facing p. 114; dated 24 May 1915, it was issued during the thirteenth week of the engagement of *The Clansman* at Clune's. (Compare the program with the schedule of exhibitions given in n. 33; the heading "fifty-fifth week" at the top of the program refers to the number of weeks the Auditorium has been open under Clune's ownership.) A copy of the program for the eighteenth week, identical in its content to the one found in Stern, is in Cuniberti, *Birth*, 180. A somewhat different program, dating from the second week of the film's engagement ("starting Monday, February 15th") is reproduced within the notes to Allen's recording; it will be considered further later.

40. "From Nickelodeon to Supercolossal: The Evolution of Music-to-Pictures," TS, n.d. (in the Carli D. Elinor collection, USC). On page 3, Elinor writes: "Early in the year 1915, I scored and conducted the world premiere of . . . *The Birth of a Nation* (*The Clansman*) at the Philharmonic Auditorium in Los Angeles, with an orchestra of forty men, solo vocalists and a large chorus—first time to be used with a film. [Elinor errs: the use of a chorus was reported, for example, in reviews of presentations of *Cabiria*.] Those musical interpretations, transposed by unique arrangement, created a sensation throughout the country; some critics named it 'film opera,' best described as the synchronizing of music with dramatic action. A large symphonic orchestra traveled with the film in all key cities."

Elinor's memoir was cited to me in a letter from Clifford McCarty, 10 Jan. 1981, wherein he also quoted a second description by Elinor (who had communicated it to him in a separate letter, in response to a query from McCarty). In the latter account Elinor corrected the impression, created by the passage quoted above, that there was but one score for the film—*his* score—heard "throughout the country," and he acknowledged the existence of Breil's score.

41. Little is known about Nurnberger, except that between October and December 1915, he was given partial credit for six film scores published by the Triangle Film Corporation, a production company which Griffith helped to found. The scores were issued in a series titled "Triangle Plays," and piano and orchestra parts were registered for copyright and are kept at LC. See, in Anderson, *Music for Silent Films*, the scores described under the following film titles: *Between Men* ("Music composed and selected by Joseph. E. Nurnberger, Victor Schertzinger and Wedgewood Nowell"); *D'Artagnan* ("Music composed and arranged" by the same three); *The Edge of the Abyss* ("Music composed" by Schertzinger and Nurnberger); *The Golden Claw* ("Music by" the same three); *Matrimony* ("Music selected by" Nurnberger and Nowell); and *The Winged Idol* ("Music composed and arranged" by the same three). Breil, too, contributed scores for Triangle films at this time, and they also were copyrighted and deposited in LC: see, in Anderson, *Double Trouble* ("Music arranged and adapted by J. C. Breil"); *The Lily and the Rose* ("Music arranged and adapted by" Breil and J. A. Raynes); *The Martyrs of the Alamo*, *The Missing Links*, *Los Penitentes*, and *The Wood Nymph* (all "Music selected and arranged" by Breil). Breil's activities for Triangle (specifically, for the company's Fine Arts productions, over which Griffith presided) were noted by Irvine and G. P. Von Harleman in the column "News of Los Angeles and Vicinity," *MPW* 27 Nov. 1915, 1672. There are also several clippings on Triangle in the Breil scrapbooks, including a review (from the *NY Dramatic Mirror*, 30 Sept. 1915) of the debut program at the Studebaker Theater: praise is given to the "special music" for

all three films on the program—especially for the score for *The Lamb* (starring Douglas Fairbanks), "arranged by J. E. Nurnberger and Joseph Carl Breil," and "interpreted by William Furst [also one of Triangle's staff musicians] and an orchestra of thirty."

42. "A Los Angeles Exhibitor: Blaisdell Discovers Picture Presentation DeLuxe at Clune's Auditorium—Manager Brown a Man of Classic Ideas," *MPW* 1 May 1915, 705–6. Among aspects of the presentations at Clune's, Brown is reported to have devised an elaborate stage prologue to lead into the film, reminiscent of the prologues Rothapfel had created for *Quo Vadis* and *The Eternal City*. (By contrast, no such prologue or stage setting seems to have been prepared for *The Birth of a Nation* when it opened at the Liberty. The stage was described as having only a black blackground, in keeping with Griffith's wish that "attention should not be distracted from the picture." See the *MPW* review, "Griffith Film Scores," given in Silva, ed., *Focus on "Birth,"* 28–29.)

43. John Tibbetts, "Now Hear This: Bernard Brown Talks about the Hollywood Sound Man," (*American*) *Classic Screen* 3, no. 1 (Sept.–Oct. 1978), 36.

44. Correspondence printed in the column of Monroe Lathrop, *Los Angeles Tribune*, 12 Nov. 1915—in the Breil scrapbook, and cited in Allen's notes to his recording. Breil's letter was prompted by the opening at the Auditorium of the same Triangle program that had previously been presented in New York, this time with music by Elinor. "To judge from some of the reviews," he began, "one is led to believe that in Los Angeles a musical score to a photodrama is to be valued by the multiple sources from which it is extracted, irrespective of whether it fits the picture or not." He then mentioned the laudatory *Dramatic Mirror* review (see. n. 41), complained that Clune's had shown the same disregard for his score for *The Clansman*, and ascribed "but two reasons for such a condition. One is puerile jealousy and the other downright incompetency. Which it is I will not say."

45. Breil, "On Motion Picture Music," TS (photocopy of transcription by Win Sharples, Jr.) n.d. This fragment of a memoir, containing about 1,750 words, has disappeared. Both Sharples and Allen examined it within the Breil collection, when the latter was housed in the abandoned Los Angeles County Jail, during the 1970s. By the early 1980s, when I first looked through the collection, it could no longer be found. I am grateful to Sharples for providing me a copy of his transcription. The style of the essay is similar to that of Breil's other writings, published and unpublished.

46. *Adventures with D. W. Griffith*, Kevin Brownlow, ed. (New York: Farrar, Straus and Giroux, 1973), 79. In the course of the premiere, Brown also remembers the "paralyzing electric shock" he felt when hearing "Griffith's voice—not his real voice, of course—but the the brasses imitating his voice as he sang that 'Ha-Haaaah-Yah!' over and over again. Griffith had undoubtedly sung [the Klansmen's theme] for Breil, who wrote it down and orchestrated it for trumpets, trombones and horns, backed by the thunder of hoofs created by the sound-effects men behind the screen" (p. 94).

47. See Tom Patterson, "Riverside Made Movie History with First Showing of Early Classic," (Riverside) *Press Enterprise*, 12 Feb. 1972, sec. B, p. 4 (included in the files of the libraries of AMPAS and MOMA [microfiche 076]). Within the article is a reproduction of a page from the *Riverside Daily Press* for 1 Jan. 1915, containing both an advertisement for the previews of *The Clansman* and also a news item, "*The Clansman* Motion Picture Masterpiece at Loring [Opera House] Tonight." (The advertisement, which promises the seven-piece orchestra, can be seen in Cuniberti, *Birth*, 179.)

48. For reports on his trip, all of them indicating that the circumstances of the film's presentation were still unsettled, see "Griffith Leaves West for New York," *Motion Picture News* 23 Jan. 1915 (dateline 11 Jan.), 30; and "D. W. Griffith in New York," *MPW* 23 Jan. 1915, 491. The former states that "While in New York City Mr. Griffith will also assist in the arrangement of incidental music for this big feature which he has spent eight months

preparing." The latter, a single brief paragraph, contains no mention of music. See also "Griffith in East to See *Clansman* Presented," *Motion Picture News* 30 Jan. 1915, 26: "The number of reels in which *The Clansman* will be presented has not been decided, but it is certain that the picture will be long enough to constitute an evening's entertainment in itself"; and "Early New York Premiere for *Clansman*," *Motion Picture News* 13 Feb. 1915, 34, in which the length of the film is put at "probably in eight reels." (The film was ultimately released in 12 reels.) For the first announcement of the New York premiere in *MPW*, see "Griffith Engages Theater," 20 Feb. 1915, 1121, where is promised a "specially written score . . . by a symphony orchestra of forty pieces."

49. Grace Kingsley, "At the Stage Door," *Los Angeles Times*, 8 Feb. 1915, pt. 3, p. 4. Contrary to this report, the Russian Symphony Orchestra, then under the baton of Modest Altschuler, did not play for the film. See Richard Aldrich, *Concert Life in New York, 1902–1923* (New York: G. P. Putnam's Sons, 1941), for an index of reviews of the RSO's concerts: the dates of these reviews, 14 and 22 Feb., and 1, 7, 8, and 21 March, indicate that the orchestra could not have played for the premiere of *The Birth of a Nation* at the Liberty.

50. There is one intriguing difference in Breil's conceptualization of the two scores, at least as he described them in retrospect. In the music for *Queen Elizabeth*, "each of the *principals* in the cast was given a 'motive,' such as Wagner [used to identify] his mythological characters." (From "Music and 'Movies' Offer New Art Form"; the italics are mine.) In *Birth*, according to the memoir, it was both "principals" and "*contrasting ideas*" that were to be "contra-distinguished."

51. See the Clune's program reproduced in Allen's recording. Grace Kingsley announced the winners of the contest at Clune's—under the heading "Who Got 'Em?"—as part of her column, "At the Stage Door," *Los Angeles Times*, 28 May 1915, pt. 3, p. 4. No one, she reported, had guessed the titles of all the pieces in the score; so the "second prize" place went to a woman who guessed 51 of the 84 selections.

52. Letter to me from Clifford McCarty, 10 Jan. 1981 (see n. 40). According to McCarty, Elinor also wrote that Breil's score was heard "all over the East"; his own was heard "out here, in the West (San Francisco, San Diego, etc.)." However, apart from Elinor's statement, no evidence has been found to show that his score for *The Clansman* was heard anywhere other than at Clune's.

53. "A Los Angeles Exhibitor" (n. 42). Cf. Kingsley's remark that there were 84 selections in the Clune's score: perhaps coincidentally, the same number appears in the Clune's program (Fig. 28), in a different context: "to select and cue scenes it was necessary to run the twelve reels comprising the film eighty-four times."

54. *Adventure with D. W. Griffith*, 87. This passage precedes Brown's account of the premiere, in which he praises Breil's job of conducting the score—"he knew how to make an orchestra talk" (p. 92)—and recalls his "shock" when hearing Breil's orchestration of the Klansmen theme (in the passage already cited, n. 46). Whether Brown is accurate in his assessment of Breil or not, there is a fundamental problem with this whole section of his memoir, because he places the premiere—and Breil, and the Breil score—at Clune's, rather than at the Liberty; he makes no mention of Elinor.

55. *"The Birth of a Nation" Story*, 51. Aitken's account is no less problematic than Brown's, though at least he differentiates between the music at Clune's and at the Liberty. As he remembers the "story," it was his brother and Thomas Dixon who were so impressed by the music they heard at Clune's that they—not Griffith, not Breil—decided to have "theme music" for the New York opening, too. (See pp. 46–47.) He goes on to say that *Birth*'s music consisted of "excerpts from operatic numbers and also folk tunes." However, at least on one point, Griffith's "tireless" work with the musicians in New York, Aitken is supported by an item preserved in the Breil scrapbooks. On a piece of ruled notepaper is

penned "Dear Breil: Mr. G—— wants the rehearsal continued at least till *one* o'clock and as much later as possible. B." (The writer has not been identified, though it was possibly John A. Barry, Griffith's secretary, who was mentioned by Breil in his fragment "On Motion Picture Music.") Above this note, on the scrapbook page, Breil has scrawled in blue crayon, "An order from D W Griffith while rehearsing *The Birth of a Nation* in New York: There were 45 men held at $1.00 per hour on this day from 9 A.M. till 2 the next A.M. with but two intermissions to eat.—All unnecessary but as usual DWG thought 'To hell with expenses.'"

56. *The Movies, Mr. Griffith, and Me*, 152–53. Gish also wrote a brief note about the score for Allen's recording, printed on the front cover.

57. Breil, *Incidental Music to "The Birth of a Nation,"* 6: "The Ku Klux Clansmen's Call."

58. For example, Hare praised the theme as "the biggest thing in the second part of *The Birth of a Nation* and indeed the whole play," and noted its varied impact: "Often the call has a weird effect, as when the thin-voiced oboe plays it alone. Often it comes stridently powerful against entirely different notes." (What he describes is not clearly identifiable in the MOMA score.) Another critic, similarly to Karl Brown, described the theme as "a weird, haunting combination of two notes"; see Stern, "The Film's Score," 108. (The source of this quotation is apparently the *Chicago Examiner*, 18 July 1915, although it needs to be verified; Stern refers the reader to his n. 14, but the citation is actually in n. 13, and the date may be incorrect—it happens to be the same date as for Hare's article in the *Boston American*.) Another laudatory description of the theme appears in the Breil scrapbook, extracted from an undated issue of *Photoplay* (p. 72). Headed "Kukluxklansmenskall," the theme is notated on a single staff (two lines, 7 measures —the form is like that of the "summons" version in Act II, no. 19), and the caption reads: "This is the thrilling 'Call of the Clans,' in the elaborate musical score written for *The Birth of a Nation* by Joseph Carl Briel [*sic*]. It has individuality, and heard in its proper setting, an eerie dramatic power which is as unforgettable as it is stirring. You may not be able to whistle this weird strain, but you'll not forget it once having heard it. This score, notwithstanding its many adaptations of well-known airs, must be known as the fist significant accompaniment written for a photodrama."

59. On Griffith's musical background, see Schickel, *D. W. Griffith*, 24, 27–28, 41–42, and 67. The gist is that he learned to love music at home (his father played country fiddle, his sister the piano), harbored both literary and musical ambitions, had a powerful bass voice, sang in a quartet, and early on wrote a play that "rings with music and dance." Cf. Stern, "The Film's Score," p. 105: "from his early days as a youth in Louisville, he had acquired a music-lover's knowledge of opera and symphony. He carried melodies and tunes in memory for years," and so on.

60. See the list of MOMA scores given in n. 14. Though the Breil collection at UCLA contains no contracts, there is a telegram sent from New York and addressed to "Carl Briel, Eighteen Fourteen Third Ave. Los Angeles," and dated 6 April 1923: "Are You at liberty to come East to write score for new Griffith picture. If so what would you charge for period covering about six weeks please reply immediately and fully. Herbert Sutch, Assistant Director, D W Griffith." Breil attached his signed reply, handwritten and addressed to Sutch: "Am at liberty to go East at once to write score for new Griffith picture. Terms, One hundred dollars per week, plus fifteen hundred dollars to be paid to me at completion and delivery of work. And transportation both ways Los Angeles New York." (Two more lines have been crossed out: "and five hundred and first week's hundred to be advanced before leaving Los Angeles.") The film was surely *The White Rose* (Breil's last collaboration with Griffith), which premiered at the Lyric Theater in New York, 21 May 1923.

61. See Barry/Bowser, *D. W. Griffith*, 48; and also Cuniberti's introduction to *Birth*, 15–27, for details concerning the various versions of the film known to be extant. In his shot

analysis he divides the film into 85 sequences, 42 in the first half, 43 in the second. Despite this balance, individual sequences range from a single shot (e.g., the first sequence), to more than 150 shots (the 28th sequence, the Battle of Petersburg).

62. The "Act I" heading does not appear in the piano scores, nor in most of the orchestral parts in LC; in all sources, the "Act II" heading appears above the final number of the first series (29), rather than above the first number of the second series (which extends from 1 to 30). As can be seen in Appendix part 8, the second series of numbers begins at the start of reel 7. We may surmise that Breil began to put the score together thinking that the film's second part would begin with the sequence at the start of this reel and that Griffith decided to shift the break back into the latter portion of reel 6, at a time when it was too late to renumber the contents of the score. (Sources cited in n. 48 suggest that less than a month before the film opened in New York, Griffith was far from certain how many reels the film would be.)

63. Cuniberti, *Birth*, 40, title preceding shot 23. Throughout the score, the cues are usually preceded by "T," which stands for "Title," or "D," for "Description" of the action.

64. The question of choral performance (raised in n. 21) allows for the possibility that sometimes the words of the songs *were* heard; but this does not seem to have been the norm.

65. Cuniberti, *Birth*, 142, title following shot 1077.

66. According to Wayne Shirley, *Old Folks at Home* and *Auld Lang Syne* were the two tunes most frequently heard in "quote-songs"—his term—during the years 1900 to 1915. See his "Response to 'The First American Film Scores,'" *Harvard Library Bulletin*, NS, 2, no. 4 (Winter 1991), 102–3. Shirley also comments (reacting to my discussion of Simon's use of *Auld Lang Syne* in the score for *The Confederate Ironclad* [1912]), that the tune was not then as strongly associated with New Year's celebrations as it is today. Whether or not he is correct, the situation had changed by 1925: that year, in *The Gold Rush*, Chaplin made use of the song to great emotional effect, for a scene of communal singing on New Year's Eve.

67. Cuniberti, *Birth*, 59, shot 200.

68. Lang and West, *Musical Accompaniment of Moving Pictures*, 29. The passage concerning "standard overtures" continues by noting that many of them "also contain slow movements which will prove useful as love themes, etc."

69. "The Film's Score," 121. Stern cites personal communication with Griffith as his source, and Cuniberti (*Birth*, 65) notes Stern's comments and identifies those shots which contain repeated footage.

70. Lang and West, *Musical Accompaniment of Moving Pictures*, 30. The heading is "Special Characters and Situations."

71. Act I, no. 15. As can be seen in the excerpt from this number given in Ex. 26c, Breil alludes with telling irony to the title phrase of the comic song *Where Did You Get That Hat*, in a manner comparable to his use of *Comin' thro' the Rye*. The phrase had been previously played in Act I, no. 4, for the scene of the young men's first meeting—one of the story's happier moments, with suitably bright music: the rising phrase introduces an extended quick march in comic style, and is played because the words are given on screen and then spoken by Duke Cameron in light mockery of Tod Stoneman. (See Cuniberti, *Birth*, 43–44.) In Act I, no. 15, the phrase functions as a "reminiscence motive": it comes into the fray just as Duke, his bayonet raised, recognizes Tod, lying wounded; it breaks off with a dissonant chord apparently meant to match the moment when Duke is himself shot, and falls to the ground at Tod's side.

72. "The Perfect Motion Picture Score," TS (Breil scrapbooks), 4. Beneath the title is typed "Address delivered by Joseph Carl Breil at the First National Conference of the Motion Picture and Musical Interests under the Auspices of *Motion Picture News*. Jan.

24–26, 1921." (A copy of the program of the Conference is also in the scrapbooks, along with other relevant clippings.) See Hal Crain, "Leaders of Joint Interests United under the Motto 'Finer Film Music,'" *Musical America* 29 Jan. 1921, 1, 3–4; and his follow-up, "Form Permanent Combination in World of Music and the Screen," 5 Feb. 1921, 1–2. In the first article Crain mentions Breil's paper, though he gives the title as "The Complete Musical Score."

73. I take the publication date of *1812 Festival Overture* from the list of works compiled by David Brown, "Tchaikovsky," in the *New Grove Dictionary of Music and Musicians*, vol. 18 (1980); and Grieg's *Peer Gynt* from Roger Fiske's introduction to the Eulenburg edition of the Suites (1970).

74. Two prominent films that make use of Wagner's *Ride* in satirical fashion are Felini's *8 1/2* (1963) and Coppola's *Apocalypse Now* (1977). In the former, the music is first heard as part of a band concert at a health spa, though the seeming realism of the "source music" is undercut by the dreamlike, grotesque shots of the residents, with editing of the footage to match details of the music; it is heard again later, during a fantasy sequence that occurs in the mind of Guido, the protagonist, who uses a whip to quell a revolt in his "harem." In the latter film, the music, supposedly played over loudspeakers placed in helicopters, has become an accessory to the bombing of a Vietnamese village. "I use Wagner," Lt. Colonel Kilgore explains, because it "scares the hell out of the 'slopes.'" (This could be taken as an ironic allusion to the way the music functions in *Birth of a Nation*.) Seeing the helicopters charge to their mission—and seeing that mission filmed in a dazzlingly beautiful style—may inspire the same complex misgivings that we now experience when watching Griffith's film: a combination of esthetic thrills and moral "horror" (Kurz's last word in Coppola's film).

75. Cuniberti, *Birth*, 39, title preceding shot 8.

76. Breil's incomplete essay, "On Motion Picture Music," ends with an account of how he composed this theme. He claims to have found it difficult to coin themes to represent the "primitive barbarism that was so morbidly dominant in the racial exhibits of the film, the brutality and savagery born of ignorance"; so he had recourse to Griffith, after learning that the director "had spend his boyhood days on a Kentucky plantation." After listening to him "hum and chant some of the old croons of (the) mammies and (the) loose jointed young plantation negroes which he still remembered in a vague sort of way," Breil finally composed "the theme which opens the film . . . and which is thereafter ever applied to the description of the primitive instincts of the blacks." (Here Breil transcribes the opening melody on a single staff.) With these words the fragment breaks off, so we may wonder if Breil stopped at this point, owing to uneasiness about the direction the essay was taking.

77. Cuniberti, *Birth*, 109–11.

78. Ibid., 116, title following shot 776b.

79. "The Perfect Motion Picture Score," 2, 3.

80. Cuniberti, *Birth*, 37–38. According to the author's commentary, there is evidence that these two scenes were edited, owing to objections by censors.

81. Ibid., 39, title preceding shot 10.

82. Ibid., 46, title preceding shot 72.

83. Ibid., 47, title preceding shot 90a.

84. Ibid., 49, title preceding shot 106a.

85. Ibid., 50–51.

86. "The Perfect Motion Picture Score," 3.

87. Fore these scenes, see Cuniberti, *Birth*, 102–5. Note that the opening title, written in Griffith's customarily poetic style, literally cues Breil's music: "The love strain is still

heard above the land's miserere." The same phrase, "love strain," was sometimes added as a subtitle to published versions of *The Perfect Song* (see nn. 25 and 27).

88. For these scenes, see Cuniberti, *Birth*, 118–27. On the connection between R12 and Gluck's *Orfeo*, see Appendix part 8, note c. Some listeners may also detect a second operatic reference, to Verdi's *Rigoletto*, in the music that follows the agitato strains: the phrases consisting of parallel thirds, rising and falling chromatically, are reminiscent of Verdi's moaning "wind" theme, sung by a men's choir, wordlessly, during the storm scene—and of course, in both the opera and the film, the central action is the death of a young woman whose innocence has been, or is about to be, destroyed.

89. For the close of the film, see Cuniberti, *Birth*, 165–68.

CHAPTER 5. ERIK SATIE'S SCORE FOR ENTR'ACTE

1. See Gallez, "Satie's *Entr'acte*." Other important studies of the score are to be found in the general works concerning Satie by Gillmor, Shattuck, Templier, and Wehmeyer, cited in n. 2. An earlier version of the present chapter has also been published: see Marks, "The Well-Furnished Film: Satie's Score for *Entr'acte*," *Canadian University Music Review*, no. 4. (1983), 245–77. Portions have been reprinted by permission of the *Review*.

2. Important studies of Satie's life and music include: Alfred Cortot, "Le Cas Satie," *Revue musicale*, no. 183 (1938), 248–72; Alan M. Gillmor, *Erik Satie* (Boston: Twayne, 1988); James Harding, *Erik Satie* (London: Secker & Warburg, 1975); Constant Lambert, "Erik Satie and His *Musique d'Ameublement*," in his *Music, Ho!*, 123–37; Wilfrid Mellers, "Erik Satie and the 'Problem' of Contemporary Music," in his *Studies in Contemporary Music* (London: Denis Dobson, 1947), 16–42, based on an article in *Music and Letters* 23 (1942) 210–27; Rollo H. Myers, *Erik Satie* (London: Denis Dobson, 1948; rpt. New York: Dover, 1968); Anne Rey, *Erik Satie*, Collection Microcosme, Solfèges, no. 35 (Paris: Seuil, 1974); Roger Shattuck, *The Banquet Years: The Origins of the Avant-Garde in France, 1895 to World War I*, rev. ed. (New York: Vintage Books, 1968); Pierre-Daniel Templier, *Erik Satie* (Paris: Rieder, 1932; rpt. Paris: Aujourd'hui, 1978), Elena L. French and David S. French, trans. (Cambridge, Mass.: MIT Press, 1969); Ornella Volta, *L'Ymagier d'Erik Satie* (Paris: Francis Van de Velde, 1979) and *Satie Seen through His Letters*, Michael Bullock, trans. (London and New York: Marion Boyars, 1989); and Grete Wehmeyer, *Erik Satie*, Studien zur Musikgeschichte des 19. Janrhunderts, vol. 36 (Regensburg: Gustav Bosse, 1974). Gillmor's bibliography contains an extensive list of additional secondary sources.

3. On Picabia, the most detailed sources are: William Camfield, *Francis Picabia: His Art, Life and Times* (Princeton: Princeton Univ. Press, 1979); Picabia, *Écrits*, vol. 1: *1913–1920*; and vol. 2: *1921-1953 et posthumes*, Olivier Revault d'Allonnes and Dominique Bouissou, eds., Les Batisseurs du xxe Siècle (Paris: Pierre Belfond, 1975 and 1978); Michel Sanouillet, ed., *"391": Revue publiée de 1917 à 1924 par Francis Picabia* (1) (Paris: Le Terrain Vague, 1960), and Sanouillet's companion volume, containing biographical data and critical notes, *Francis Picabia et "391"* (2) (Paris: Eric Losfeld, 1966). See also Sanouillet, *Dada à Paris* (Paris: J.-J. Pauvert, 1965).

4. Works presented by the Ballets Suédois prior to *Relâche* include *Skating Rink* in 1922 (scenario by Canudo, music by Honegger, decor by Léger), and *La Création du monde* in 1923 (Cendrars, Milhaud, and Léger); both works were offered again in 1924, on the program with *Relâche*. On the Ballets Suédois, the principal sources are *Les Ballets Suédois dans l'art contemporain* (Paris: Trianon, 1931), and Cyril W. Beaumont, "Jean Börlin," in *Complete Book of Ballets: A Guide to the Principal Ballets of the Nineteenth and Twentieth Centuries* (New York: Grossett & Dunlap, 1938), 667–84. Also, for an exhibition at the Moderna Museet, Stockholm, from 27 Feb. to 7 April 1969, a valuable catalogue was published: see

Svenska Balletten—Les Ballets Suédois, 1920–1925: Ur Dansmuseets samlingar, Bengt Häger, ed. (Stockholm: Moderna Museet, 1969); this catalogue was translated and published for subsequent exhibitions in other European cities: a much abbreviated version was issued as *Modern Swedish Ballet: Exhibition Catalogue* (London: Victoria and Albert Museum, 1970); a full, revised edition was issued as *Cinquantenaire des Ballets Suédois, 1920–1925: Collection du musée de la danse au Stockholm*, Karin Berqvist-Lundgren, ed. (Malmö: Skanetryck, 1970). The latter version accompanied exhibitions at the Musée d'art moderne de la Ville de Paris (3 Nov. 1970–17 Jan. 1971) and at the Théâtre National du Belgique, Centre Rogier, Brussels (17 Feb.–3 April 1971).

5. In a letter to Picabia dated 22 Jan. 1924, Pierre de Massot included the following paragraph:

> Je suis chargé par ERIK SATIE de demander votre collaboration à un ballet pour les Suédois: *votre entière liberté* vous est laissée—*on attend tout de vous*. Hébertot et de Maré seront ravis. Pour la première fois, le Théâtre des Champs-Elysées verra peut-être une révolution véritable qui n'aura rien de commun avec les manifestations des Mariés [i.e., *Les Mariés de la Tour Eiffel*, a work first presented by the Ballets Suédois in 1921, with music by five of "Les Six"]. Peut-être un nouveau DADA. Réfléchissez et dites-moi oui.

This letter is held in the *Bibliothèque Littéraire Jacques Doucet* (Paris), in the *Dossiers Picabia* 10, p. 331; it is partially quoted in Sanouillet, *Picabia et "391,"* 168, and fully translated in Volta, *Satie Seen through His Letters*, 190.

6. In his letter to Milhaud, dated 27 Sept. 1924, Satie commented on a real tornado, and of his progress on the ballet, before writing metaphorically of his hopes for *Relâche*:

> Cher Grand Ami. Vous en avez eu une tornade! Comment cela a-t-il pu avoir lieu? C'est incroyable! . . . Votre "clos" n'a pas été touché, au moins? . . .
> . . . J'ai orchestré la moitié de *Relâche*. Je continue . . . La première est fixée au 17 novembre, à 9 heures du soir [later rescheduled for 27 Nov.] . . . La saison suédoise sera assez mouvementée. On redonne la *Création du Monde*. Content, suis . . . Le soir de la première de *Relâche*, il y aura une assez jolie "tornade," dans la salle! . . . Je commence à connaître . . . .

The letter is quoted in Roland Bélicha, "Chronologie Satiste ou photocopie d'un original," *Revue musicale*, no. 312 (June 1978), 49. In two subsequent letters, Satie expressed himself in similar terms. To Paul Collaer, on 18 Oct. 1924, he wrote as follows:

> Dans deux jours, l'orchestration de *Relâche* sera terminée. Quel Ballet! . . . La "première" sera mouvementée, je vous prie de le croire. Le forces ennemies, cette fois, rencontreront les nôtres. Nous mobilisons.

Satie alludes here to a previous encounter with "enemy forces," on the occasion of the premiere of his ballet *Mercure*, in June 1924: see Collaer, "La Fin des Six et de Satie," *Revue générale*, no. 6/7 (June/July 1974), 21 (and also n. 7). In a letter to Marcel Raval, dated 21 Oct. 1924, Satie wrote:

> C'est de *Relâche* que sera donné le signal du "départ." Nous commençons, de *Relâche*, une nouvelle periode. Je le dis immodestement, mais je le dis . . . Picabia crève l'oeuf, & nous partons en "avant," laissant derrière nous les Cocteau & autre "bridés." . . . Oui . . .

This text appears in Volta, *L'Ymagier d'Erik Satie*, 82.

7. Picabia's final issue of *391* (Oct. 1924) appears in Sanouillet, *"391,"* 157–160; on the last page of the issue, he advertised *Relâche* as follows:

> Les Ballets Suédois donneront le 27 novembre au Théâtre des Champs-Elysées *Relâche*, ballet instantanéiste, en deux actes, un entr'acte cinématographique et la queue du chien . . . Apportez des lunettes noires et de quoi vous boucher les oreilles. Retenez vos places. Messieurs les ex-Dadas sont priés de venir manifester et surtout de crier: "A BAS SATIE! A BAS PICABIA! VIVE *LA NOUVELLE REVUE FRANÇAISE*!"

Picabia here alludes to the performance of *Mercure*, in June 1924, at which Aragon had provoked a riot by leaping on stage and crying "Long live Picasso! Down with Satie!" Picabia responded with the polemic "Erik Satie," *Paris-Journal*, 27 June 1924, p. 1 (rpt. Picabia, *Écrits*, vol. 2, pp. 145–47): in this essay, he proudly announced his collaboration on *Relâche*, concluding "Je crie: Vive Erik Satie!"

8. Accounts of the false and true premieres of *Relâche* are included in the discussion of the ballet by Camfield, *Francis Picabia*, 208–14; Harding, *Erik Satie*, 222–33; and Wehmeyer, *Erik Satie*, 258–92. See also Picabia, "Pourquoi *Relâche* a fait relâche," *Comoedia*, 4 Dec. 1924, p. 1; rpt. *Écrits*, vol. 2, pp. 169–70 (where the essay's original date of publication is given incorrectly as 2 Dec.): "Devant les portes fermées [du Théâtre Champs-Elysées]," Picabia writes in this essay, "on m'accusa d'avoir eu peur! D'autres bruits fantaisistes circulèrent . . . La verité était bien plus tragique. Jean Börlin, écrasé par l'effort donné depuis plusieurs semaines, n'avait qu'une idée: se lever de son lit, courir au théâtre, danser *Relâche*; mais ses forces le trahissaient, il ne pouvait pas même aller à la porte de sa chambre!"

9. Between 4 and 31 Dec. 1924, *Relâche* was performed by the Ballets Suédois 13 times at the Théâtre des Champs-Elysées, according to Sanouillet, *Francis Picabia et "391*," 170; however, listing in two daily newspapers, *L'Éclair* and *Le Figaro*, indicate that there may have been a few more performances. On the night of the final performance, a special live "Ciné-sketch" was added to the program, in which Picabia, Satie, and Clair all took part: see "Figaro-Théâtre," *Le Figaro*, 28 Dec. 1924, p. 5, and Paul Achard, "Les Adieux aux Ballets Suédois," *L'Éclair*, 31 Dec. 1924, p. 4. De Maré announced his decision to disband the company on 17 March 1925, "après une morne soirée donnée à Épernay": see de Maré, "Naissance et évolution des Ballets Suédois," in *Les Ballets Suédois dans l'art contemporain*, 33. After the Ballets Suédois disbanded, *Relâche* was apparently not performed again until 1970; since that date it has been presented at least four times: see Philip Holland, "*Relâche* Revisited," *Ballet News* 2, no. 5 (1980), 26–30. Holland's essay was written on the occasion of the first presentation of *Relâche*—together with *Entr'acte*—in the United States; it was revived by the Joffrey Ballet in New York, with an attempt to recreate the original sets and choreography, under the direction of Moses Pendleton.

10. Shot analyses of *Entr'acte* have been published in three languages: Glauco Viazzi, ed., *Entr'acte*, Biblioteca cinematografica, seconda serie: sceneggiatura (Milan: Polignono Società, 1945); Clair, "*Entr'acte*, [et] *À Nous la liberté*," in *L'Avant-Scène du cinéma*, no. 86 (1968); and Clair, *"À Nous la liberté" and "Entr'acte*," Richard Jacques and Nicola Hayden, trans. (from the French version), Classic Film Scripts (New York: Simon & Schuster, 1970). All three of these editions include useful supplementary materials (documents and essays). Also, I have found the following three studies of Clair and the film very helpful: Jean Mitry, *René Clair*, Classiques du cinéma (Paris: Universitaires, 1960); R. C. Dale, "René Clair's *Entr'acte*, or Motion Victorious," *Wide Angle* 2, no. 2 (1978), 38–43; and Paul Sandro, "Parodic Narrative in *Entr'acte*," *Film Criticism*, 4, no. 1 (Fall 1979), 44–55. See also Dale, *The Films of René Clair*, 2 vols. (Metuchen, N. J.: Scarecrow Press, 1986).

11. I have seen prints of *Entr'acte* held by MOMA, the MIT Film Study Center, and the Harvard Film Archive. They differ in details, as do the analytical scripts described above: for example, Viazzi's version is divided into 281 shots, the French version leaves

shots unnumbered, and the English version contains 346 shots. Henceforth I refer to the latter version, which is the most complete; however, it should be noted that, like some prints now in circulation, this version begins with a "prologue" (shots 1–27), which was originally projected at the beginning of Act I of *Relâche*, and for which Satie wrote separate music. (In this sequence, filmed on the roof of the Champs-Elysées, Satie and Picabia are seen to descend into the frame in slow motion and load a cannon; the cannon fires a shell in our faces after Satie and Picabia have exited in fast motion.) I have not yet seen the synchronized-sound version of the film that was made in France in 1968, with Satie's music conducted by Henri Sauget.

12. "*Entr'acte* est un véritable entr'acte, un entr'acte à l'ennui de la vie monotone et des conventions pleines de respect hypocrite et ridicule." From Picabia, "À propos d'*Entr'acte*" *Films*, no. 28 (supplement to *Comoedia*), 1 Nov. 1924, [3]; rpt., with revisions in the text, in the "program" for *Relâche*—i.e., in the special issue of *La Danse* devoted to the Ballets Suédois (Nov.–Dec. 1924), on the "Page René Clair"; also rpt. in Picabia, *Écrits*, vol. 2, p. 167. The quotation given above is from the revised version; a facsimile of Picabia's handwritten draft of the essay in its original form can be seen in *L'Avant-Scène du Cinéma*, no. 86, p. [2].

13. "*Entr'acte* ne croit pas à grand-chose, au plaisir de la vie, peut-être: il croit au plaisir d'inventer, il ne respecte rien si ce n'est le désir *d'éclater de rire*. . . ." (Picabia, "À propos d'*Entr'acte*.")

14. Apollinaire termed the cinema one of the most important "new means of artistic expression" in a 1917 lecture (published the following year) on "The New Spirit and the Poets": see *Selected Writings of Guillaume Apollinaire*, Roger Shattuck, trans. (London: Harvill, 1950), 237. By an interesting coincidence, it was also Apollinaire who had termed Satie's ballet *Parade* "the starting point . . . of that New Spirit," in a statement for the ballet's program: see Harding, *Erik Satie*, 158–59.

15. "Voici *Entr'acte* qui prétend donner une nouvelle valeur à l'image"—quoted from Clair's essay, "Avant-l'*Entr'acte*," in *Films*, no. 28, [3]; rpt. in *La Danse* (Nov.–Dec. 1924), "Page René Clair": in both sources, Clair's essay appears alongside Picabia's, cited in n. 12. See also the essays written by Clair in 1925, "Rhythm" and "Pure Cinema and Commercial Cinema," translated in Abel, *French Film Theory and Criticism* (vol. 1, pp. 369–71), as well as Abel's introductory essay to this part of his anthology, "1925–1929: The Great Debates" (320–48)—especially the segment headed "Mainstream Narrative Cinema Versus Pure Cinema" (329–32).

16. The importance of *Entr'acte* as an example of furniture music has been affirmed in almost all of the major Satie studies. Compare these references (listed in chronological order, by date of original publication): Templier, *Erik Satie* (1932), 45–46; Mellers, "Erik Satie and the 'Problem' of Contemporary Music" (1942), 223–26; Myers, *Erik Satie* (1948), 60–61; Shattuck, *The Banquet Years* (1968), 170–72; Wehmeyer, *Erik Satie* (1974), 227–29; Gallez, "Satie's *Entr'acte*" (1976), passim; and Gillmor, *Erik Satie* (1988), 255–56.

17. References to *musique d'ameublement* are widely scattered among Satie's letters, notebooks, and manuscript jottings, as well as in reminiscences of his contemporaries. For a sampling, see Satie, *Écrits*, Ornella Volta, comp. (Paris: Champ Libre, 1979), 190, as well as Cortot, "Le Cas Erik Satie," 269–71; Lambert, *Music, Ho!*, 132–37; Volta, *L'Ymagier d'Erik Satie*, 73, and *Satie Seen through His Letters*, 173–78. See also the sources cited in n. 16.

18. "Nous, nous voulons établir une musique faite pour satisfaire les bésoins 'utiles.' L'Art n'entre pas dans ces bésoins. La 'Musique d'Ameublement' crée de la vibration; elle n'a pas d'autre but; elle remplit le même rôle que la lumière, la chaleur—& *le confort* sous toutes ses formes." Satie's comments are from an undated letter to Cocteau; the excerpt quoted in English is Shattuck's translation, given in *The Banquet Years*, 169. A facsimile of

the original letter, headed "Pour le vieux Jean," is given in *Les Empreintes*, no. 7 (1950), a special issue devoted to Cocteau, on p. 98. The French text is also given in Satie, *Écrits* (loc. cit.), and on p. 308 Volta notes that in 1918 Cocteau wrote to Poulenc, asking for *musique d'ameublement* for an "entr'acte." Leger recalled similar comments by Satie (again without a precise date) in "Satie inconnu," *Revue musicale*, no. 214 (June 1952), 137–38. Cortot, in "Le Cas Erik Satie," notes a connection between Satie's "prospectus" for furniture music and these remarks of Matisse: "Ce que je rêve, c'est un art—sans sujet inquiétant ou préoccupant, qui soit . . . quelque chose d'analogue à un bon fauteuil." See Matisse, "Notes d'un Peintre," *La Grande Revue*, 25 Dec. 1908; cited in Jean Selz, *Matisse* (Paris: Flammarion, [1964]), 92.

19. Stravinsky, in an interview with Ingolf Dahl, was asked "What is the function of music in moving pictures?" and responded in part as follows: "I realize that music is an indispensable adjunct to the sound film. It has got to bridge holes; it has got to fill the emptiness of the screen and supply the loudspeakers with more or less pleasant sounds. The film could not get along without it, just as I myself could not get along without having the empty spaces of my living room walls covered with wall paper. But you would not ask me, would you, to regard my wall paper as I would regard painting, or apply aesthetic standards to it?" See "Igor Stravinsky on Film Music, as told to Ingolf Dahl," *Musical Digest*, Sept. 1946, pp. 4–5 and 35–36. This interview was translated into French, and published under the title "Le Musique du film? Du papier peint," *L'Écran français*, no. 125 (1947), [3]. (Stravinsky's remarks recall these comments of Debussy, critical of Saint-Saëns: "How is it possible to go so completely wrong? . . . Why this itch to write operas and to descend from Louis Gallet to Victorien Sardou, spreading the detestable error that it is necessary to 'write for the stage'? A thing never compatible with 'writing music.'" See Debussy, "A Talk about the Prix de Rome and Saint-Saëns," in *Monsieur Croche: The Dilettante Hater*, B. N. Langdon Davies, trans. [1928; rpt. Freeport, N.Y: Books for Libraries Press, 1972], 72.) In the *Musical Digest*, two Hollywood composers and one music critic carried on a debate, in response to Stravinsky: see Dimitri Tiomkin, "A Film Composer's View of Film Music: Opposing Stravinsky's Ideas," June 1947, pp. 18 and 39; and in the same issue, Harold Schonberg, "A Music Critic's View of *Duel in the Sun*: Opposing Tiomkin's Ideas," pp. 19 and 39. See also, Schonberg, "Music or Sound Effects?" Nov. 1947, pp. 8–9 and 14; and David Raksin, "Hollywood Strikes Back: Film Composer Attacks Stravinsky's 'Cult of Inexpressiveness,'" *Musical Digest*, Jan. 1948, pp. 5–7.

20. The details of the presentation of *musique d'ameublement* at the Galerie Barbazanges are in doubt. The two earliest sources are Templier, *Erik Satie*, 45–46, and Lambert, *Music, Ho!*, 132. Templier lists the instruments used as a piano, three clarinets, and a trombone "scattered in the corners of the hall"; Lambert states the music was for "piano duet, bass trombone and a small clarinet." Subsequently Milhaud described the instrumentation as being written for a piano in one corner of the hall, a clarinet in each of the other three, and a trombone in the loggia above; he explains that the wind instruments were used because they were already on hand, being required for Jacob's play. However, Milhaud names a different play from the one given in most other sources. See Milhaud, *Notes sans musique* (Paris: René Julliard, 1949), 137–39. Pierre Bertin, who organized the affair, alludes to it without giving any details in "Erik Satie et le groupe de six," *Les Annales Conferencia* 58, NS, no. 4 (Feb. 1951), 58. See also, Satie, *Écrits*, pp. 307–8.

21. Sets of the orchestral parts and copies of the conducting score of *Entr'acte* are available from Salabert on a rental basis; those copies I have seen all contain conductors' markings in more than one hand. No score of *Entr'acte* was published when Satie was still alive, but Milhaud describes his friend going over proofs from Rouart-Lerolle shortly

before his death on 1 July 1925: see Milhaud, *Notes sans musique*, 195. One other source which I have found useful is the recording of *Entr'acte* performed by the Ensemble Reihe under the direction of Friedrich Cerha (Candide Records, no. 31018, n.d.). This recording makes one vividly aware of the problems which arise when performing the score. For example: on the recording, nearly every musical unit is repeated at least once, and often there are changes of tempo not indicated in the score. Such adjustments are unavoidable, as I have discovered when using the score to accompany the film in performances (including one at the Harvard Film Archive in the fall of 1978, with an orchestra conducted by John Green); but many details of the Cerha recording do not work in accompaniment to the film. There are no notes on the album to explain the circumstances behind the recording. However, if it originated in an actual performance of film and music, the tempos and repetitions indicate that the film was run at or near a speed of sixteen frames per second, which is too slow. Gillmor, in his discography, p. 362, lists another recording of the score, by the Ensemble Ars Nova under Marius Constant (Erato STI 71336; Musical Heritage Society MHS-4700), which I have not heard.

22. There are four pages containing Satie's handwritten cues and other jottings for *Entr'acte*: pages "A" and "B" are back to back on one sheet, "C" and "D" on another. The first sheet is held by the Houghton Library, Harvard University; the second, by the Bibliothèque Nationale, Paris, catalogued under Satie, "Dispositions/*Relâche*," #9678. Facsimilies of "A" can be found in Templier, *Erik Satie*, plate 83; Rey, *Erik Satie*, 148, and Volta, *L'Ymagier d'Erik Satie*, 87. Gallez terms these pages "Satie's working notes" and transcribes some portion in "Satie's *Entr'acte*," 76–80; however, some aspects of his transcription are open to question. One may question, too, the assumption that these pages represent Satie's pre-compositional jottings; Satie may have drafted them later, as a shorthand guide—for himself, possibly, as he proofread, or for Rouart-Lerolle, or for Milhaud to use in making his reduction—so that the cues would be printed in their proper places.

23. All the musical examples found in the text of this chapter are based primarily on the two-piano reduction published by Salabert in 1972. In a few examples, percussion parts have been added in order to convey the complete rhythmic structure of a unit.

24. The description of the opening of *Entr'acte* is based on the English shot analysis cited in n. 10: see Clair, *"À Nous la liberté" and "Entr'acte,"* 121.

25. "Le cinéma ne doit pas êntre une imitation mais une invitation évocatrice aussi rapide que la pensée de notre cerveau. . . ." This statement is taken from one of Picabia's pre-*Relâche* promotional essays, "L'Instantanéisme," *Comoedia*, 21 Nov. 1924, p. 4; rpt. in Picabia, *Écrits*, vol. 2, pp. 159–60. Passages from this essay are cited in English by Camfield, in *Francis Picabia*, 212; on 208, Camfield notes that "Instantanéisme" was a "one-man movement," Picabia's "antidote to Surrealism." (Picabia advertised *Relâche* as a "ballet instantanéiste": see n. 7.)

26. Clair writes: "Il appartenait à Francis Picabia, qui a tant fait pour la libération du mot, de libérer l'image. Dans *Entr'acte*, l'image 'détournée de son devoir de signifier' naît 'à une existence concrète.'" These sentences, from "Avant l'*Entr'acte*," follow the one cited in n. 15. (Clair takes the quoted phrases from an essay by André Breton, "Les Mots sans rides," *Littérature*, NS, no. 7 [Dec. 1922], 12–14; rpt. in Breton, *Les Pas Perdus* [Paris: Gallimard, 1924], 167–71.) Though the director gives Picabia the credit for the "liberation" of the film's images, Picabia, in his parallel essay, gives Clair the lion's share of credit for the film: "J'ai donné à René Clair un tout petit scénario de rien du tout; il en a fait un chef-d'oeuvre."

Picabia's original idea for the film was indeed close to "nothing at all," though evidently he was the first to conceive such an innovative event and imagine its overall design. When sketching a scenario for the ballet (tentatively titled *Après-Dîner*, before Satie and

Clair had joined the project), what he imagined for the beginning was thirty seconds of film "à déterminer," accompanied by music; and, between the two acts, "no *entr'acte*, properly speaking," but five minutes of music "avec projections cinématographiques des auteurs assis face à face, échangeant une conversation dont le texte s'inscrira à l'écran durant dix minutes. Pas de musique pendant la projection écrite." The scenario is cited (from the *Dossiers F.P.*, 10, p. 289) by Sanouillet, *Francis Picabia et "391,"* 256–57; rpt. in Picabia, *Écrits*, vol. 2, pp. 155–56 (and see the editors' comments, p. 371, n. 137).

27. The sequence begins with shot 64: "Medium shot of the columned façade of a building, blocked in behind."

28. For the ballerina sequence, see shots 93–109.

29. Gallez, in "Satie's *Entr'acte*," 47, notes the transitional rhythmic effect of unit 19. This effect becomes clear when the unit is performed, as in Cerha's recording, with a ritard.

30. The simile is from Mitry, *René Clair*, 20.

31. Shot 121: "Dissolve to the sheet of water seen previously. Various images fade into superimposition. First, what appears to be the eyes of an owl [or monkey?] which come and go with the following images. The a close-up of a pair of eyes, upside down, together with the ballerina's tutu, moving to and fro. The movement of the tutu remains throughout the rest of the shot. The eyes slowly fade out as a face [from a sculpture?] appears upside down in profile. The same [?] face is superimposed in reverse and melts into the first; together they make up a strange double profile. The water ripples behind them."

32. The instruction to repeat unit 27 ad lib appears only in the 1926 edition of the orchestral score. Gallez (in "Satie's *Entr'acte*," 41) attributes the idea to Roger Désormières, conductor of the premiere. In the Cerha recording the unit is repeated five times, with a very broad ritard that anticipates the tempo of the next section.

33. As early as 1892, Satie had jotted down a fragment called "Vexations," marked to be played 840 times. See Wehmeyer, *Erik Satie*, 46 and 229, and Gillmor, *Erik Satie*, 102–3.

34. Gallez, "Satie's *Entr'acte*," 43, describes the form of the music as "an unorthodox rondo, but not a classical one"; Wehmeyer, *Erik Satie*, 288, asserts that the score's rondo form matches no analogous structure in the film.

35. Chopin's "Marche funèbre," movement 3 of the Piano Sonata no. 2 in B-flat minor, Op. 35 (composed 1837), is printed or recommended for death and funeral scenes in many sources from the silent period. See, e.g., *The Witmark Moving Picture Album* (1913), 42–43, which includes all of the movement's principal themes, much simplified and transposed down a half-step (as in *Entr'acte*); the *Remick Folio of Moving Picture Music*, J. Bodewalt Lampe, comp. and ed. (1914), p. 36, which has a 12-bar excerpt from the beginning of the movement; likewise in Rapée, *Motion Picture Moods* (1924), 160, though this excerpt runs 30 bars. See also True, *How and What to Play for Pictures* (1914), 11, which lists "Grand Marches" of various types; Lang and West, *Musical Accompaniment of Moving Pictures* (1920), 30, where Chopin's music is listed under "Special Characters and Situations: *Death*"; Rapée, *Encyclopedia of Music for Pictures* (1925), 302, "March—Funeral," and so forth.

36. The metrical ambiguity in units 39–41 is noted by Gallez ("Satie's *Entr'acte*," 47), though he offers no explanation for it.

37. Instructions in the 1926 orchestral score call for unit 51 to be played ten times; in Cerha's recording it is played nine times, *accelerando*. According to Gallez ("Satie's *Entr'acte*," 41), an instruction for ad lib repetition appears once more, at the end of Section IX (unit 54); I have not seen this in the copies of the score available to me.

38. Picabia's comments about the music of *Entr'acte* appear in two of his essays, one written to help publicize the work, the other on the occasion of a presentation of the film, whether with or without its score is unclear, at a theater in Cannes, in the winter of

1926–27: (1) "Je trouve parfaite la musique de *Relâche*, la partie qui accompagne l'acte cinématographique est un chef-d'oeuvre, je ne pouvais rien désirer qui s'adaptât mieux à ma pensée"; (2) "La musique de Satie me semble inséparable d'*Entr'acte*." See (1) Picabia, "Pourquoi j'ai écrit *Relâche*," *Le Siècle*, 27 Nov. 1924, p. 4; (2) "*Entr'acte*: Un peu de Picabia au Star," *Journal des hivernants*, Jan. 1927, p. 29. Both essays are reprinted in Picabia, *Écrits*, vol. 2, pp. 162–63 and 181, with n. 160, on p. 373, explaining the context of the second essay.

39. René Clair: "Il s'agit d'un rêve avec toute l'incohérence des rêves véritables." The sentence is quoted in Sanouillet, *Francis Picabia et "391*," 169; Sanouillet cites the *Dossiers F. P.* 10, p. 253, and gives the date of the source as 20 Nov. 1924, but he does not identify it further.

40. Satie's three comments about the music of *Relâche*, and the sources for each are as follows: (1) In a letter to Milhaud dated 10 Aug. 1924, Satie indicated that he was working on the ballet ("Je travaille fortement. Ça 'marche.'"); he enclosed a sketch ("*petit truc*") for the "Rentrée de la Femme," in Act II; at the end of the sketch he wrote "'RELÂCHE' (Ballet obcène)." See Wehmeyer, *Erik Satie*, 284–85, for facsimiles of letter and sketch, and also Volta, *L'Ymagier d'Erik Satie*, 85 and 116, as well as *Satie Seen through His Letters*, 195. (2) "Deux parties de ballet séparées par dix minutes de cinéma. Un film de Picabia, mis en scène par René Clair. Pendant l'ouverture musicale [of *Relâche*], les deux auteurs apparaissent sur l'écran. La partition? J'ai voulu la faire chaude, chatoyante. Pour ces 'bons types' [i.e., Picabia and himself?], il me fallait une musique amusante, pornographique (*sic*)." See W. Mayr, "Entretien avec Erik Satie," *Le Journal Littéraire*, no. 24 (4 Oct. 1924), 11. (3) "La musique de *Relâche*? . . . Je ne voudrais pas faire rougir un homard, ni un oeuf." See the "Page Erik Satie" of the program for *Relâche* printed in *La Danse* (cited in n. 12). Facsimiles are in Wehmeyer, *Erik Satie*, 276, and in Camfield, *Francis Picabia*, plate 253.

41. Picabia: "Quand se déshabituera-t-on de l'habitude de tout expliquer?" From the frontispiece of *Relâche*, piano reduction (Paris: Rouart-Lerolle, 1926). The frontispiece is not found in reprints of the score; facsimiles are given in Myers, *Erik Satie*, 106, and in Volta, *L'Ymagier d'Erik Satie*, 82.

42. In October 1924, Breton published his first *Manifeste du Surréalisme: Poisson soluble* (Paris: Sagittaire); Picabia responded antagonistically with his own manifesto, the last issue of *391* (Oct. 1924), called the *Journal de l'Instantanéisme*. The latter has been interpreted as his attempt to resuscitate Dada, just in time for the premiere of *Relâche*: see Sanouillet, *Francis Picabia et "391*," 166, and nn. 7 and 25.

Index

Numbers in italic refer to figure, musical example, or table numbers.